RACE IN NORTH AMERICA

FOURTH EDITION

Race in North America

Origin and Evolution of a Worldview

AUDREY SMEDLEY, PH.D.
Emerita, Virginia Commonwealth University, Fellow AAAS

BRIAN SMEDLEY, PH.D.
Vice President and Director, Health Policy Institute of the Joint Center for Political and Economic Studies

A Member of the Perseus Books Group

Westview Press was founded in 1975 in Boulder, Colorado, by notable publisher and intellectual Fred Praeger. Westview Press continues to publish scholarly titles and high-quality undergraduate- and graduate-level textbooks in core social science disciplines. With books developed, written, and edited with the needs of serious nonfiction readers, professors, and students in mind, Westview Press honors its long history of publishing books that matter.

Published by Westview Press,
A Member of the Perseus Books Group

Find us on the World Wide Web at www.westviewpress.com.

Library of Congress Cataloging-in-Publication Data
Smedley, Audrey.
Race in North America : origin and evolution of a worldview / Audrey Smedley and Brian Smedley.—4th ed.
p. cm.
Includes bibliographical references and index.
ISBN 978-0-8133-4554-3 (pbk.)—ISBN 978-0-8133-4555-0 (e-book) 1. Race. 2. Racism—History. 3. Racism—North America—History. 4. Black race. 5. Slavery—History. I. Smedley, Brian D. II. Title.

GN269.S63 2011
305.8—dc22

2011014052

10 9 8 7 6 5 4 3 2 1

CONTENTS

PREFACE TO THE FOURTH EDITION

In the last several decades there has been an explosion of materials on *race* published by a wide variety of scholars and general writers. Numerous studies of racial inequalities have appeared, including a massive study by the Institute of Medicine of the National Academy of Sciences (2003) that documents an array of ways by which people in the medical establishment have discriminated against blacks and other low-status races and continue to do so. Dozens of new publications on racism and the law have demonstrated how thoroughly our legal institutions have been impacted by the racial worldview. The result is that many Americans have been encouraged, or perhaps compelled, to confront race as never before. A number of events and circumstances have fueled these developments.

There are first of all demographic changes. People identified as Latinos or Hispanics have become the largest minority population, surpassing African Americans, who until recently held that status. Although identified in the U.S. Census as an ethnic group, Hispanics comprise multiple ethnicities. Biogenetically they are the results of the historical intermixture of European (mostly Spanish), Native American, and African ancestries. Even though some Americans think of them as a racially differentiated population with distinct physical features, they are phenotypically highly varied, some showing more or less Indian or African features along with their Spanish or Portuguese ancestry. They also vary ethnically, although they speak dialects of the same Spanish language. Their presence in North America brings a new dynamic to the social system, and their identities are often contingent. They are descendants of populations whose origins span vast territories in the New World, from islands such as Puerto Rico, to the southern tip of South America, to the western coasts of Mexico.

Second, immigrants from new regions of the world have graced our society—people such as the Dinka and Nuer peoples of east Africa—some of whom have been settled in areas (such as Minnesota) where few Africans or African-descended peoples are found. Other East Africans are widely scattered, particularly in the eastern coast cities, where such ethnic phenomena as Ethiopian restaurants now abound. These peoples can often be physically distinguished from one another. Moreover, they do not share common languages or common cultures. They add to the mixture of other African-derived populations of recent immigrant status, such as West Indians or Caribbeans, both Hispanic speakers and non-Hispanics. Many scholars are curious about how these peoples will be integrated into an already divided, racialized society.

Third, events of September 11, 2001, and the wars in the Middle East have generated a high level of fear and even panic among many Americans, who now respond negatively to anyone who appears to have an "Arab" phenotype. As a consequence, many black and Hispanic American men have found themselves being viewed suspiciously because of their physical resemblance to Middle Eastern men. Some have been harassed or attacked on the assumption that they are "Arabs." British police in London recently killed a Brazilian man because they mistook him for an Arab Muslim. Some Americans are beginning to learn for the first time that physical features are not a good clue to a person's identity. Indeed, with the immigration of many new peoples from around the world and increasing intermarriage, physical features are becoming more and more ambiguous as markers of "racial" identity. Many of these people do not fit very well into our American categories of race. Very dark-skinned Asian Indians were once unfamiliar in most American cities and towns. Nowadays Asian Indians of a wide range of skin colors are seen in cities, in businesses, on television, and in universities all over the nation. So Americans are often finding themselves in situations where they are uncertain of the "racial" identity of their coworkers and other people they may meet.

Fourth, increasing intermarriage and admixtures of peoples have blurred those physical features that traditionally were cues to one's racial identity. When individuals have grandparents from four different corners of the world, geography ceases to be of much help in establishing a "racial identity." In the 2010 U.S. census, more than fourteen million people identified themselves as having multiple racial ancestries in California alone. But history shows that such admixtures have occurred in North America since at least 1620, and the resulting genetic configurations hardly represent the total reality of our complex biology. Yet race is still the most salient element in our identities, and Americans still rely on a person's physical appearance to ascertain his or her racial status. The U.S. government officials still agonize over the race categories in the census, and Americans still believe that everyone has a single racial identity.

Fifth, as if to further confuse us, an enormous scientific development occurred early in the twenty-first century, whose ramifications will be far reaching and are at the moment unpredictable. Two groups of scientists in 2001 finally sequenced the genetic material in human chromosomes; that is, they have revealed the patterns of DNA in the human genome. This is one of the great revolutionary breakthroughs in science. The most valuable aspect of this discovery is what it can tell us about the genetic correlates or determinants of diseases.

At the same time, the sequencing of the DNA has led some race scientists to focus on the ways DNA refracts human differences, not only in disease patterns, but especially those that relate to human physical variations, such as skin color, hair texture, body size, and facial features. The salient question becomes: Do the differences found in the genetic patterns of human groups over geographic space constitute *race*? Most scientists are now declaring that race has no basis in the biological sciences; more and more are concurring that it should be seen as a social invention. Thus, a major debate has surfaced over this issue. A discussion with some perspectives on this debate appears later in this book.

More subtle and perhaps less visible to the public is the transformation in the ways historians are writing history, which has major implications for our attitudes toward race. Some historians have argued that certain aspects of American history, such as racial slavery, have never been fully explored or confronted, that we have often skimmed over the ignoble and shameful episodes of history or sanitized the realities of slavery and racism. These historians are pressuring scholars to reexamine our history and fully confront these painful realities. We shall see in chapter 5 how this relates to the development of the ideology of race.

Numerous other forces are at play in our society, some of which appear to be chipping away at our perceptions of one another as racial beings. The recent development of studies on "whiteness" reflects the social conditions, debates, and legal maneuvering that have characterized the creation of white identities. The strange, often contradictory, ways in which U.S. courts have historically assigned, or not assigned, white identities to various immigrants is indicative of the arbitrariness of racial categorization and the hierarchical social nature of *race*. "Whiteness" has positive meanings in our culture; any change in the valorization of whiteness would clearly signify a change in the meaning of race.

I have argued that biological variations among peoples have no social meanings except what we humans give them. This is what is meant when we claim that races were culturally constructed. We must investigate the social meanings imposed on the varying human populations to understand race. This study shows that the elements of the ideology of race have been utilized since the eighteenth century as a mechanism to stratify society and accord privileges, benefits, and rights to some and not to others, with the justification that the groups called "races" are innately unequal and that their differences cannot be transcended. Race ideology is essentially a boundary-making and barrier-inducing force that is meant to be divisive and restricting.

Arguments about hereditary differences and their immutability have been critical to constructing and preserving race ideology from the beginning. When these beliefs have been linked to such natural features as skin color and other physical differences, race assumes the status of an unassailable truth. That is why the conditioning to the belief in the reality of race has been so powerful and so difficult to eliminate. We think we see "race" when we encounter certain physical differences among people such as skin color, eye shape, and hair texture. What we actually "see" (or more accurately "perceive") are the learned social meanings, the stereotypes, that have been linked to those physical features by the ideology of race and the historical legacy it has left us. As this history shows, physical features were institutionalized as markers of lower or higher race status. They carry those meanings that were created and associated with the different status groups, and it is these meanings that we have been socially conditioned to respond to.

The best way to comprehend all of these phenomena is to examine how they came about; in other words, to know their histories. That is what this book is all about. I started looking at the history of the idea of race in the 1970s as part of a course on the history of anthropology. After living and traveling throughout Europe and parts of Africa, I had long concluded that *race* was a way of looking at the world's populations that was peculiar to certain societies. By 1978 I had developed a course on the origin and evolution of the idea of race, to which most students responded very positively. The first edition of this book, published in 1993, was an effort to create a textbook that not only would provide answers to some of the queries that we all had, but would supplement traditional histories and bring together new information not easily accessible in a single volume.

This fourth edition adds further information about how racial slavery came about and why the early colonial planters had a preference for Africans, a topic not well dealt with in traditional histories. The research has led me to the hypothesis that in the early decades of colonial America, this society had a brief opportunity to become a multicolored society, but not a "multiracial" one (see chapter 5). That it did not take that path may be the subject of interesting speculation for scholars in the future.

Some sections of this volume have been shortened or eliminated altogether in order to add discussions of some of the topics mentioned above. In the chapters on science, I have reorganized the materials and shortened the detailed histories. However, every American should know something about the history of the sciences dealing with human variation, the nature of heredity, and our DNA, and what this means in terms of human group differences. Thus far the information provided largely by the media has not represented the new science very well, in part because authors fail to deal with the broader contexts and do not report fully what is known and not known about the science of DNA—what it can tell us and what it cannot tell us at the present time. There are opposing perspectives on how to interpret the evidence provided by molecular biologists and geneticists. We will look at some of the controversies regarding the differentiation of races. What this book does not do is to examine those moral and ethnical issues raised by the new technologies that have given us access to bountiful knowledge, but perhaps not much wisdom.

Finally, an extraordinary event has happened in American lives. In 2008 Americans elected as president Barack Obama, an African American, which has caused many to query what this means for "race relations." Has American society transcended race? Is it OK now to be black in America? And especially, does this mean we are now living in a post-racial society? This election has opened up a wide range of opportunities for reflection on the meaning of race and the future of our racial ideology. Although this volume cannot address all of these questions, I briefly comment on some of the implications for the history and meaning of race (see chapter 14).

It is my hope that this book, in its many incarnations, will help Americans to realize this fundamental truth: that our cultural selves (our real identities) are independent of whatever physical characteristics we may possess.

There are many people whose presence in my life has made this book possible. I have thanked most of them in previous editions. For this edition I acknowledge with thanks the information and scientific knowledge offered by Dr. S. O. Y. Keita. He provided numerous references and helpful interpretations in those fields, such as genetics, where I have had limited training. My son Dr. Brian Smedley was also a good source of information, especially about the works of those psychologists who have dealt with race. While a project director at the Institute of Medicine of the National Academy of Sciences, he learned much about the effects of the racial worldview, but thankfully has not become jaded by what he knows. I have asked him to provide a chapter for this edition on his area of expertise, the health consequences of the racial worldview. My son David Smedley, also a university professor, has been helpful in so many, many ways, and I am eternally grateful to him for always being available.

At Westview Press, Karl Yambert served initially as editor for this edition. He solicited comments from professors who have used this book as a text and was very helpful with advice regarding the structure of this edition. Evan Carver graciously replaced Karl, and Sandra Beris did an excellent job as project director. I warmly thank them all. Finally, at least a half-dozen mostly anonymous readers took the time to write comments and suggestions for this edition. Although I could not incorporate all of their suggestions, I am extremely grateful for their advice.

Introduction

There are few topics in Western intellectual and social history that have been subjected to as much investigation, speculation, analysis, and theoretical scrutiny as the phenomenon of race. Whether one accepts race as a God-given denouement of the complexity of an imperfect world or as a misguided conception of group relationships, race is a pervasive element in the cognitive patterning of Western thought and experience. It has been so fundamental, so intrinsic to our perceptual and explanatory framework that we almost never question its meaning or its reality. In nations like the United States and South Africa, where race is the important calculus of social identity, our interactions with other individuals are influenced, whether we admit it or not, by a racial identity that we attribute to others and to ourselves. We perceive this identity as reflected in tangible and easily recognized physical characteristics. Indeed, the very existence of physical differences among populations is accepted as concrete evidence of race. Thus we have been conditioned to respond automatically to the presence of certain varying physical features as indicators of race and the differences it connotes.

More important, as I document in the following chapters, race is seen by most people as a part of the natural order of things, and the existence of races is believed to have been confirmed as part of nature by science and scientists. Yet the scientific record has shown enormous ambiguity on the matter of race, much confusion, and little common agreement among the experts on its meaning.

Since 1970 there has been a progressive decline in the use of the term *race* in anthropology textbooks published in the United States. This decline occurred most precipitously during the late 1970s, when either the term was no longer mentioned in the texts or the authors argued that races do not exist or are not "real." There has also been less emphasis on racial typologies and classifications than on descriptions and explanations of biophysical variation. Documentation of the lack of support for the retention of the term *race* as a scientific concept is seen as dramatic evidence of the development of a "no-race" position in the science of humankind (Littlefield, Lieberman, and Reynolds 1982). Experts in fields such as evolutionary biology and genetics have also concluded that there is no biological basis for the term *race* in science.

As we move beyond the turn of the twenty-first century, debates have increased between those who continue to maintain that biological races and race differences exist and those in increasingly larger numbers who oppose them. When we recall that the first textbook in anthropology defined that field as the study of "man and the races of man" (Tylor 1946) and that the "races of man" were at the heart of the development of anthropology in the United States, as elsewhere, it appears that either anthropology is defining itself out of an identity, or some other more crucial metamorphosis in the wider world of knowledge has taken place. How are we to interpret this change? If the field that had the most to do with the identification and definition of human races is relinquishing its activities and related conceptual apparatuses in this area, what does this mean for other sciences that have focused on racial differences? What does this convey to us about the nature of anthropology or science in general? Are scientific discoveries or conclusions so ephemeral or arbitrary that such a crucial concept can be so easily discarded?

More important, what possible meanings or implications might there be for society at large? How can a scientific discipline overtly contradict a reality that so many of us daily experience? If scientists are no longer accepting the existence of biological races, does this mean that societies like the United States and South Africa will ultimately give up their preoccupation with race? What is the proper approach to the study of "race relations," "race consciousness," or discrimination in the light of such a confusing trend?

This transformation in the sciences stimulates numerous questions about the relationship between science and social thought, beliefs, and values. There are intricate and complex relationships between the scientific community and the processes that take place within it, on the one hand, and the larger cultural-historical setting in which science functions, on the other. The history of science shows that events and processes occurring in one arena inevitably have consequences for the other, often unanticipated and/or unintended. For the most part, scientists cannot operate outside of the knowledge systems of their cultures and the potentials inherent in them. The state of that knowledge, both technological and social, as well as perceived cultural values and needs, will determine, in general, the directions along which science develops. The very queries posed by science, the premises and assumptions implicit in them, the methods of investigation, and the configurations by which science objectifies reality, emerge out of often specific cultural contexts. Feedback between the realms of science and contemporary trends in popular belief and knowledge may enhance one particular trajectory and diminish others. Thus scientific advances, experimentation, and theorizing have generally reflected not only the prevailing state of technological knowledge but also economic, social, ideological, ethical, and/or political trends (Greene 1981).

But some scientific discoveries or advances may also propel knowledge beyond the boundaries of hitherto socially accepted wisdom or visions of the world. Since the nineteenth century, rapidly cumulating technological and scientific knowledge has emerged as a major stimulant to social and historical changes, most of which have been unpredictable. Few will doubt that techniques of birth control, rapidly expanding television viewing, the microchip and computers, the Web and cyberspace, and the digital world have all brought unanticipated changes in social behavior, values, and habits.

The trend away from race as a scientifically useful means of classifying human beings has to be comprehended in much the same way. What modern scientists are saying is that *race as a biological concept cannot be supported by the facts that we have learned about human biophysical variations and their genetic basis*. The frames of reference and database of science have changed dramatically. Most scientists work with definitions and conceptions of human variation specific to their disciplines—that are confined to physical, genetic, biochemical, and molecular factors. These fields have had the benefit of tremendous advances due to highly sophisticated instrumentation for observation, identification, measurement, and analysis. New methods and techniques have enabled scientists to identify variability in perhaps thousands of hereditary traits from analyses of DNA, the genetic materials that determine our biophysical characteristics. The discovery of the range and complexity of genetic variation has prompted scientists to rethink the ways by which we classify populations and to question the extent of real differences between so-called races (see chapter 13).

The twentieth century brought unprecedented freedom for scientific experimentation and speculation, so that growth in the sheer numbers of researchers, together with their ideas and products in all areas, has given science itself a dominant role in everyday life. It has also provided science with a powerful voice in social policy formulation and political decision making. Thus a combination of liberal social values of the 1960s and 1970s; scientific advances in the study of hereditary traits brought about by new technology; a more educated public; and an ethos of change, growth, and progress may all be responsible for the "no-race" trend in science. Until the latter part of the twentieth century, science had been central to the legitimization of folk ideas about human differences expressed in the idiom of race. With the "no-races" perspective, modern science appears to be abandoning its support of popular ideas about race.

Scientists who today reject the idea of race as a useful biological concept argue that it is a myth or an abstraction that does not correspond with the reality and complexities of human biological variation. This has been confusing to those who grapple with the social reality of race and the concomitant experience of the same phenotypic variation that is assumed to be the basis for racial classifications. The major reason for the confusion is that we seem incapable of making a necessary distinction between the natural biological variations in the human species that are products of largely evolutionary forces and the social meanings that were imposed on peoples with these varying features during the construction of the ideology of race. This is because we lack knowledge of the origins and social history of this remarkable idea about human differences. This history, it seems to me, is crucial to understanding the apparent divergence today between popular views of race and the advancing thrust in science. We need to know much more about its origin—specifically what the term *race* meant in those societies where it first became a critical parameter of social identity. We also want to know more about the historical forces that influenced both its origin and its meaning as it changed over time.

Despite referential discrepancies, the social categories of race are still very real. We understand this best when we distinguish and separate analytically the range of actual physical diversity in our heterogeneous population from the meanings, beliefs, and attitudes about these differences that evolved in the past and that we inherited as part of our social legacy. The position of this study is that *race does indeed exist* and should be viewed not as something biologically tangible and existing in the outside world that has to be discovered, described, and defined, but rather as a cultural creation, a product of human invention very much like fairies, leprechauns, banshees, ghosts, and werewolves.

The history reveals that *race* has never been an objective scientific classification of human group variation. From the beginning of its use in the English language, the term reflected a particular folk way of looking at and interpreting human differences, both physical and cultural. It was intricately linked with certain presuppositions and beliefs developed by English colonists from the seventeenth to the eighteenth centuries. During that period the word was transformed in the English language from a mere classificatory term to a folk idea that expressed certain attitudes toward human differences and prejudgments about the nature and social value of these differences.

It is essential that we comprehend race as a sociocultural phenomenon conceptually separated from human biological variations. This is the genesis and major premise of this book. It is not enough to argue that race is a myth because it fails to accord with any measurable discontinuity of biophysical realities. We have known for a long time that being a member of a certain "racial" category does not amount to having all or any of the physical attributes associated with that category. The first black Miss Americas in the mid-1980s were physically little differentiated from their white colleagues/competitors. In the United States, people who identify as African Americans are perhaps the most heterogeneous biophysical population with a group identity in the world. They range from fair-skinned, blond-haired, and blue-eyed individuals to those with dark brown skins and wooly hair, and every possible combination in between. And those who identify as Native Americans often share more phenotypic features with their European ancestors than with their Indian ones. Analysis of the historical construction of the idea of race will help us to comprehend these apparent anomalies.

In this work I emphasize a way of defining race that is consonant with this historical development and continues to reflect contemporary social realities. Scholars as diverse as Alexander Alland Jr., Michael Banton, Jacques Barzun, Pierre Van den Berghe, George Fredrickson, Ashley Montagu, Stephen Steinberg, Ronald Takaki, and many others have taken similar approaches, insisting that race should be treated as a sociological or sociopolitical phenomenon. As an alternative way of looking at the concept, this view renders much of the disputations, controversies, and uncertainties over biological definitions of race irrelevant. Race was and is just one of several ways of perceiving, interpreting, and dealing with human differences. It is a particular worldview perpetuated as much by the continued use of the term in our daily lives and in the media as it is by the stereotypes to which so many of us have been, often unconsciously, conditioned.

Those Europeans who came to dominate the colonial world of eighteenth-century America created a world in which the status of "whiteness" achieved supremacy, while inferior or lower-status identities were imposed on those populations encountered and exploited in the New World (also in Asia and later Africa). *Race* conveyed a model of the world as being divided into exclusive groups that were naturally unequal and had to be ranked vis-à-vis one another. That it brought in its wake horrendous human misery and intractable social, economic, political, and moral problems no doubt could never have been predicted five centuries ago.

This book is not designed to be a comprehensive study of the concept of race or a survey of all the literature on the topic and related ones, such as slavery and colonialism. The universe of materials is so large that it would have been virtually impossible to incorporate everything. I chose instead to delineate what seemed to be a little-explored perspective on race and to present some new insights and interpretations on U.S. history, while utilizing only sufficient data to illustrate or illuminate the major points. Much of the historical material used here is already well known through the publications of many brilliant scholars, so an interested reader would not find it difficult to search out more detailed coverage of any particular topic.

For scholars and advanced students, one of my aims is to raise new questions and suggest new areas of research not hitherto covered by existing studies on race. It is vital that scholars rethink the prevailing epistemological categories and approaches to their subjects from time to time. With this book, I hope to provide an analytic framework for the study of race as a sociocultural phenomenon.

The people most instrumental in the development of the idea of race as experienced in North America were the English colonists who began settlements in the seventeenth century. The book thus focuses on English beliefs, values, and social practices, brought with them to the colonies, that set the stage for a racial worldview in America. Under the influence of English customs and beliefs, Europeans in the United States developed and institutionalized the concept to a more extreme degree than any other society outside of twentieth-century South Africa. The book therefore concentrates on the American experience and some of many influences that led to the formulation of the racial worldview most familiar to Americans.

Each race-based society (where race is central to the social structure) developed its own unique patterns and practices, although the ideological components of the racial worldview, when clearly analyzed, have been essentially similar (see chapter 1). All have race classifications identified in law; all structure and institutionalize racial classifications hierarchically; all associate stereotyped behavior with each race category; and all hold, in an abstract sense, that racial characteristics (both physical and behavioral) are innate and unalterable. As I will show, these are the essential and fundamental features of American race ideology. They appear in varying degrees in other societies.

Scholars have just recently begun to describe and analyze the idea of race as it has been manifest in other societies. The first international conference that attempted to take a comparative look at race and race ideology in other parts of the world took place in 2002 in Japan. Some of the findings of researchers at this conference have been included in this book. The evidence suggests that elements of the Western ideology of race have spread around the world through the influence of missionaries, businesspeople, the military, and other institutions. It seems to have appeared in different intensities and forms, with modifications to accommodate different social and political realities.

The race system that evolved in the United States is distinctive in several ways. First, the dichotomous race categories of black and white are set and inflexible. Unlike in South Africa or Latin America, there is no legal or social recognition of a racial category in between black and white ("mixed-race" or "colored"), and one cannot belong to more than one race. Second, the category "black" or "African American" is defined by any known descent from a black ancestor, thus conflating and socially homogenizing individuals with a wide range of phenotypes and ancestries into one racial category. Third, one cannot transcend or transform one's race status; no legal or social mechanism exists for changing one's race.

Under the system of apartheid in South Africa, a government board existed that reassigned hundreds of people every year to different racial categories. In much of Latin America, exclusive racial categories do not exist, although descriptive terms are used to reflect the perception of individuals with varying degrees of admixture of Indian, African, and Spanish (or Portuguese) ancestry. In many areas, individuals may shift between Indian and mestizo ethnic identities with ease, although their physical traits do not change. And lower-status people of more negroid physiognomies may be transformed to higher social status ("whitened") by virtue of education, wealth, or professional accomplishments. In the United States, neither social class, education, wealth, nor professional, governmental, or business achievements evoke a change in race identity. *Race* is more highly institutionalized in America's collective consciousness, and the boundaries are more rigidly drawn. A major objective of this book is to explain this reality, the uniqueness of the race concept and ideology in the United States. The use of limited comparative materials and data from other societies aims only to refine and accentuate the parameters of the race concept in American culture.

This book will not satisfy everyone, for it touches only lightly on some topics and ignores others that scholars in particular fields might judge important. My hope is that people of all backgrounds will find in this work useful information and enlightening interpretations of history and social realities. Most important, I hope that it will introduce the reader to a more critical way of looking at the phenomenon of race and stimulate new thinking and research about the issues and problems created by this concept.

The book follows both a chronological and thematic format. But the chronology is not rigidly bounded by precise dates, nor is it inclusive and comprehensive. What one should understand are developmental stages in the growth of the ideas that became specific components of the racial worldview and the events and circumstances that pinpoint the hardening and softening of ideas and beliefs. Chapter 1 introduces certain concepts, definitions, and theoretical perspectives that guide the arguments to follow. Chapters 2 and 3 re-create the antecedent historical conditions out of which elements of American racial thought were generated. Some of the seeds of the ideology of race were planted in English culture before colonization.

Chapter 4 describes the early colonization of North America and the development of English attitudes in their interaction with Native Americans. Chapter 5 details the coming of Africans and the conditions under which racial slavery was established. Chapter 6 examines the nature of slavery in a more global and historical context and highlights the distinctiveness of North American slavery. Chapters 7 and 8 take a closer look at developments in the eighteenth century and explore themes that relate to the racialization of African slaves.

Because the sciences have been so critical to American beliefs about race, I next introduce the emergence of those fields of science, anthropology, biology, and psychology that initially functioned to confirm popular beliefs about human differences. Chapters 9, 10, and 11 explore the rise of science and how its techniques and conclusions harmonized with popular thought in both America and Europe. Science continued its dominant role in the twentieth century, as I show in chapter 12. But as I reveal in chapters 13 and 14, some scientists began to have doubts about the meanings and classifications of race. Many attempted to extract the subject matter of physical variations from the broader social and cultural context adhering to the term *race*. Ultimately, with increasing knowledge of human variations and the discovery of DNA, the units of heredity, scientists began to deny that races exist.

Controversy ensued, and continues today, between those who deny any scientific basis for race and those who would continue to believe that races are real. Among the latter are those who have attempted to medicalize race; that is, they hold to the idea that different races have innate differences in disease manifestation and responses to medication. This is a major thrust of race scientists and some drug manufacturers today, and I present some of their arguments.

The sequencing of the human genome has been a major impetus to research into human history and the identification of genetic correlates to many human diseases. It has also shown not only how similar we are genetically, but how complex and minuscule are our differences. Modern race scientists, however, exaggerate minute elements of DNA, speculating that they have greater significance for the diversity and identification of races. These scientists insist that there are meaningful hereditary differences among the races, which accounts for their inequality in society.

Over the past century there has been massive research, primarily by sociologists, psychologists, and social psychologists, into all aspects of our American social system. Tens of thousands of volumes document the conditions and causes of our behavior. Dr. Brian Smedley, an expert on inequalities in health care prepared chapter 15, which provides some of the alternative answers to those who continue to believe in hereditarian determinants of behavior.

CHAPTER 1

Some Theoretical Considerations

This work presents an anthropological perspective on history, one that seeks the interconnections among cultural features and events over time and the ideologies that humans use to embrace their cultural developments, to explain present-day realities. It is an analytic study and should not be read as conventional history.

The theoretical premises and assumptions of this volume are outlined in this chapter. I hold that there is indeed a meaning to the term *race*, but it is not to be found in the physical features of differing human populations, and it does not rest in the lists of taxa of biological scientists. Rather than looking inward for some esoteric genesis, we must peel away the intricate layers of Western cultural history and look at the material conditions, cultural and naturalistic knowledge, motivations and objectives, and levels of consciousness and comprehension of those who first imposed the classifications of race on the human community. It is important that we understand race as its meaning unfolded in the cognitive world of its creators and first formulators, in part because subsequent formulations have been so ambiguous and elusive. A major goal of this book is to help eliminate some of the existing confusion about the concept and to analytically examine its constituent elements.

In this chapter I first offer a historical perspective that is now held by many scholars, who see race as a sociocultural phenomenon that appeared only within the past several hundred years. Next I explain the theoretical context in which it is useful to conceptualize, define, and analyze the components of race. Race is treated as a reality whose ingredients can be ascertained through historical and social analysis. It is not a unitary phenomenon, but rather a synthesis of a number of identifiable elements that, bound together, constitute a particular way of viewing human differences. I then briefly describe the social reality of race in North American culture, emphasizing what I think are often unacknowledged realities, and show how one derives the analytic components of race ideology from the social behavior of different categories or groups of people in the United States.

Because the vast majority of people equate visible physical variations with race, I next address this relationship. To comprehend the real meaning and nature of race in American society, it is necessary and essential to distinguish naturally occurring physical diversity in the human species from culturally based perceptions and interpretations of this diversity; that is, we must separate in our minds variations in skin color, hair texture, body size and shape, eye formation, and so forth from prevailing cultural attitudes and beliefs about people with these different physical features. The cognitive leap that this requires is not easy, but I have found that as students learn accurate information about both of these realities, most experience an epiphany, a jolt of sudden awakening and understanding that surprises them.

The position taken here is not without its detractors, and a stream of scholars in the biological and social sciences have argued that the human perception of phenotypic differences as *race* is universal. I therefore present the arguments and a brief critique of the "primordialists," those who would preserve the term *race* for what we might call psychosocial reasons, not necessarily related to the evidence and arguments of contemporary biologists. The next section offers the theoretical perspective of this book, defining race as a worldview and specifying its minimal basic components. Undergraduate students sometimes find this material a bit daunting. However, as they read into the history, ideas that at first seem abstract and incomprehensible often become very real, and many find it clarifying to re-read this first chapter.

Finally, I differentiate *race* from *ethnicity*, a concept that has too often served to complicate the more general and profound issues of accounting for variability in both biology and behavior. Throughout history, ethnocentric portrayals of other peoples in the written literature have often denigrated the "alien others." If the alien others were physically different, this sometimes led to negative and derogatory statements about those physical features. But negative comments, pejorative descriptions, and even associations of such people with animals are not the same as the phenomenon that we call *race* in American society. Negative aesthetic judgments of both negroid-looking and pale-skinned people can be found in some ancient literature, and our immediate reaction is to consider them racist. But the institutionalized foundations for racism require much more than that.

The approach of this book has been inspired in part by studies in the sociology of knowledge and the history of ideas. Concepts such as *race* can appropriately be conceived as a composite of elements, each of which may have had certain distinct functions or cultural meanings in earlier times. These elements, such as the idea of human inequality, had their origins in historical circumstances and do not alone constitute the meaning of race. When the beliefs and attitudes were conjoined and gave rise to a new perspective on human beings, which I call the *racial worldview,* the term *race* became a shorthand method of expressing this new synthesis.

Many other concepts are open to the same sort of exploration, whereby one can separate out specific components. Concepts such as *democracy, fundamentalism, evolutionism,* and *socialism* represent widespread and diffuse ideas that have become integrated into a systematic body of knowledge and thought, ways of looking at things, and understandings that constitute part of our cultural repertoire. Such terms thus become shorthand methods of expressing a particular worldview. *Race* is a shorthand term for, as well as a symbol of, a "knowledge system," a way of knowing, perceiving, and interpreting the world, and of rationalizing its contents (in this case, other human beings) in terms that are derived from previous cultural-historical experience and reflect contemporary social values, relationships, and conditions. Every culture has its own ways of perceiving the world; race is the kaleidoscope through which Americans have been conditioned to view other human beings. But the concept itself and its substantive meanings are clearly not confined to Americans.

RACE AS A MODERN IDEA

It is significant that many contemporary scholars have concluded that race is a relatively recent concept in human history. The cultural structuring of a racial worldview coincides with the colonial expansion of certain western European nations during the past five centuries, their encountering of populations very different from themselves, and the creation of a unique form of slavery.[1] Expansion, conquest, exploitation, and enslavement have characterized much of human history over the past five thousand years or so, but before the modern era, none of these events resulted in the development of ideologies or social systems based on race. Dante Puzzo put it explicitly: "Racism . . . is a modern conception, for prior to the XVIth century there was virtually nothing in the life and thought of the West that can be described as racist" (1964, 579). Though referring only to the West, this view unambiguously challenges the claim that race classifications and ideologies were or are universal or have deep historical roots.

In one of the most recent publications on the history of the idea of race, Ivan Hannaford states: "In the sixteenth century dynastic ambitions and religious issues were of such great consequence that there was little room for the growth of a conscious idea of race as we understand it today" (1996, 182). He identifies the first stage in the development of race as taking place between 1684 and 1815, with two other stages occurring during the nineteenth and early twentieth centuries (187). Although he derives most of his data from the works of a wide range of philosophers and early scientists, his time frame coincides with that of Theodore Allen (1994, 1997) and other writers who examine material, economic, political, and social conditions for their explanations of the emergence of race. This is the context in which I also have investigated the causal factors for the rise of such an extraordinary view of humankind.

During the age of exploration and European expansion, rising competitiveness among the European nations and consciousness of their power to dominate others affected the way Europeans perceived indigenous peoples; these elements were factored early into their methods of dealing with all aliens. *Race* as a mode of describing and categorizing human beings appeared in the languages of the Spanish, Portuguese, Italians, French, Germans, Dutch, and English as these groups established colonial empires in the New World and Asia and set about dealing with their heterogeneous populations. However, conceptions of and references to race varied greatly among the colonizing powers. The English in North America developed the most rigid and exclusionist form of race ideology, and it is on this racial worldview that this book focuses.

Reviewing this history helps to make us aware of certain facts that, for the most part, have often escaped analysis. The peoples of the conquered areas of the New World, and the other "colored" peoples of what is now called the Third World, did not participate in the invention of race or in the compilation of racial classifications imposed upon them and others. To the extent that these peoples utilize the idiom today and operate within its strictures, they have inherited and acquiesced in the system of racial divisions created for them by the dominant Europeans (Banton 1977). As a paradigm for portraying the social reality of inequality, the racial worldview has spread around the globe, and its use often exacerbates already existing interethnic animosities (Barzun 1965). Some of this development is discussed in later chapters.

Accepting the fact that race is a cultural construct invented by human beings, it is easy to understand that it emerged out of a set of definable historical circumstances and is thus amenable to analysis, as are other elements of culture. No amount of comparative definition and synchronic exploration of modern race relations will lead us to more refined definitions and understandings of race. On the contrary, race is a complex of elements whose significance and meanings lie in the historical settings in which attitudes and values were first formed. We should be able to isolate the central components, investigate their probable genesis, and comprehend how they evolved over time.

This approach is different from that of scholars who have written about the history of the idea of race in the past. Louis Snyder, Earl Count, Thomas Gossett, and others have documented the various definitions of races and the numerous classifications that early taxonomists invented. Historians such as Gossett, John Hope Franklin, John Haller, Gary Nash, Winthrop Jordan, David Brion Davis, C. Vann Woodward, Carter G. Woodson, Eugene Genovese, Robert Berkhofer, Roy Pearce, and George Fredrickson, as well as many other experts on slavery and race in the New World, have explored the attitudes of Europeans in the Americas toward peoples whom they identified as racially different from themselves. My concern in this volume is not to repeat these well-known studies, but to specify and analyze the ideological ingredients of which the idea of race itself was composed and identify the cultural contexts that nourished those ingredients.

IDEAS, IDEOLOGIES, AND WORLDVIEWS

By exploring the probable origin and history of the idea of race, dissecting it into its component elements, and attempting to relate these to their sociohistorical contexts, I am not reifying the concept or elevating ideas into a realm of absolute autonomy. Ideas should not be viewed as prime movers of the cultural process, nor should they be considered mere secondary phenomena of cultural developments in other arenas. Ideas are critical, necessary aspects of culture that may vary in strength and form of expression over time and space, but they invariably meet some cultural need or advance the interests of those who hold them. From this perspective, ideas cannot even be interpreted or analyzed apart from their cultural matrices. They arise out of specific material and social circumstances and are constituted of individual and group perceptions, understandings, and decisions made by human beings who inevitably have an imperfect comprehension of the complexity of the situations that confront them. The human animal has the capacity to come to conclusions and make decisions out of self-interest, devotion to some abstract principle, or his or her perception of the larger interests of the group, however defined. Multiple individual decisions may well accumulate and become entrenched as cultural orientations that persist through time and space.

As such decisions become incremental parts of the cultural order, they reflect specific understandings of the world and its environmental and social realities. They provide explanations for, and often a means of controlling, social and natural forces. As their usefulness is realized, they become established as givens, as worldviews or ideologies; thus institutionalized, they feed back into human thought and actions. By *worldview* I mean a culturally structured, systematic way of looking at, perceiving, and interpreting various world realities, a society's *weltanschauung*, to use a term made popular in sociological studies. Once established and conventionalized, worldviews become enthroned in individuals as mind-sets. They may even achieve the state of involuntary cognitive processes, actively if not consciously molding the behavior of their bearers.

I define race as such a worldview. In the United States, Australia, South Africa, and many other areas of the world, race is a cosmological ordering system that divides the world's peoples into what are thought to be biologically discrete and exclusive groups. The racial worldview holds that these groups are by nature unequal and can be ranked along a gradient of superiority–inferiority. My use of the term *worldview* depicts the deep-seated nature of this essentially folk vision of the human species and the often unconscious processes of perception or imagery that it generates. *Worldview* also contains and reflects a variety of folk beliefs about human differences that in the United States we see as stereotypes of various populations. Because these are cultural beliefs to which we Americans are all more or less conditioned, their truth or falsity is rarely questioned. In this volume I call them *ideologies*.

Race as a worldview can be understood as composed of specific ideological components. By *ideologies* I mean sets of beliefs, values, and assumptions, held on faith alone and generally unrelated to empirical facts, that act as guidelines or prescriptions for individual and group behavior. Substantive beliefs about human differences tend to vary in time and space, depending on the values, histories, and experiences of the colonizing powers. We can use the terms *worldview* and *ideology* interchangeably, with the recognition that there is a high level of correspondence between them. I tend to think of a worldview as a more systematic and comprehensive set of ideological beliefs that have an integral relationship to one another. When I speak of the concept of race, I am referring to the fundamental worldview, including its basic ideological components and all of the adhesions that each culture may add to it. The ideological elements in this worldview can be confirmed by empirical research. Where necessary, varying ideologies within societies can be compared for their similarities and differences, as some historians do, for example, for North and South America or for the United States and South Africa.

Some worldviews are highly flexible and generalizable, capable of being diffused to and adopted by other societies. Their adaptability and usefulness must be perceived by other culture bearers, who may modify the components to fit their own group's needs, fears, beliefs, biases, ambitions, and goals. The ideological components of race have been eminently adaptable to a wide variety of sociopolitical situations, as this history reveals.

THE SOCIAL REALITY OF RACE IN AMERICA

There is a kind of intellectual or cognitive paradox posed by some contemporary scientists' abandoning use of the term *race*, while in most Western cultures, South Africa, and much of the rest of the world, it is taken for granted as part of folk belief that everyone belongs to a race. If modern science has not been able to produce studies that can confirm the reality of race; if indeed some scientists are increasingly arguing that races do not exist, then it can be legitimately asked: How can public attitudes and understandings retain the notion of their verity and the belief that science has proved their reality?

I think the facts will show that among the general public, the fundamental belief that races exist is unaffected by contradictions or inconsistencies. We do not discard the basic patterns of thought or question the need for racial classifications when we are faced with great variation and complexity in physical traits and ambiguous realities and uncertainties about the racial identity of an individual or group. There are important reasons for the deeply ingrained sense of racial reality that we inherit as part of our cultural baggage. As I show in the following chapters, race is the major mode of social differentiation in American society; it cuts across and takes priority over social class, education, occupation, gender, age, religion, culture (ethnicity), and other differences. It is essential, then, to understand race as a sociocultural reality independent of the history and uses of the concept in science and distinct from whether or not scientists can agree on a common biological definition. In this sense, race is a social principle by which society allocates desired rewards and status. It belongs, as Joel Kovel has argued, to "the regulative aspects of our culture" (1970, 26) and is intricately involved in all relations of power.

For some scientists to deny the existence or reality of biophysical races seems to challenge, perhaps inadvertently, one of the most powerful, deeply entrenched canons of Western thought and belief. The "no-races" position calls into question fundamental truisms that have been accepted for more than two centuries. For most people, race is a given, a biological reality that does not require great leaps of consciousness or intellect to comprehend. They see it (or so they believe) in the phenotypic variability experienced in interactions with heterogeneous populations like those in the New World. Moreover, even those scientists who have taken the no-races position are very much aware of the social reality of race in Western societies. Even as they deny its existence, they cannot avoid it.

There is, then, a great disjunction between the no-races position of modern scientists on the matter of biological races and the social parameters of race by which we conduct our lives and structure our institutions. Experts in many fields who have grappled with the sociology of race and race relations are not apt to find answers to the weighty problems of interracial conflict in the laboratories of modern physical anthropologists, human biologists, or geneticists. Scholars of social behavior and modern scientists investigating problems of human biogenetic variability are really not talking about the same thing. Biogenetic variations in the human species are not the same phenomena as the social clusters we call *races*; it is crucial to understand this, even though the use of a common term confuses the issue.

Reflecting this disjunction are some curious features about the semantics of race and its related terms. If, for the general educated community, *race* refers to biophysical variations between populations, it should be regarded as a neutral classificatory term. On the other hand, such derivatives as *racism*, *racist*, and *racialism* convey an agreed-upon sense of insalubrity—prejudice, ignorance, hatred, narrow-mindedness, malice, and other noxious defects. Virtually no one wants to be accused of being a bigot or of practicing racism. Even members of the White Knights and the Ku Klux Klan will deny that they are *racists*, which in American culture is an invidious appellation. There seems to be a strange inconsistency here; we attempt to use one term in an objective, impartial, scientific way, but its related and derivative terms are so infused with negative and judgmental elements that they cannot be functionally neutral.

We may not always be conscious of the dilemma reflected by these subtle contradictions. But it unmasks for us a paradox that is critical to any attempt to examine the whole phenomenon of race. The paradox has to do with the attitudes toward and treatment of race in some of the scholarly, journalistic, and social science literature since the beginning of World War II and the social realities of race that we daily experience. Stressing the concept of "sociological" or "social" race as distinct from biological race does not obviate the dilemma. Any descriptor is likely to lead to more confusion than clarity, in part because it cannot deal with the complexities of the various popular and scientific versions of race and because it adds no greater clarity or comprehension to the problem of the perception and interpretation of human variation.

The fact is that, at the level of public consciousness, the presentation of the no-race position by scientists constitutes a challenge to our cultural worldview, to what we perceive as commonsense knowledge, and to the kinds of relationships that large numbers of people experience. The challenge, were it to become widespread, would in a real sense negate the very structure of American society. For there is a reality to the idea of race that is grounded in America's historical consciousness and all of its political, economic, religious, recreational, and social institutions.

Race is about status and inequality of rank in a society where competition for wealth and power is played out at the individual level. Any social scientist objectively observing American culture for the first time would readily recognize patterns of behavior that reflect the important social dimensions of racial status in America. From Americans' behavior alone, the social scientist would conclude that different races rank unequally along several dimensions, and that there are specific mechanisms for maintaining separateness and inequality among them.

A fact denied by none of the experts is that race in the American mind was and is tantamount to a statement about profound and unbridgeable differences. In whatever context race comes to play, it conveys the meaning of social distance that cannot be transcended. This sense of difference is conditioned into most individuals early in their lives and becomes bonded to emotions nurtured in childhood. In the United States it is expressed in all kinds of situations and encounters between peoples. It is structured into the social system through residential separation; differential education, training, and income; and informal restrictions against socializing, intermarriage, and common membership in various organizations, including, most visibly, the church. It is reflected in virtually all media representations of American society and institutional aspects of culture such as music, the arts, scientific research and educational institutions, politics and political forums, businesses, the theater, television, the music and film industries, and recreational activities.

Not only are there separate churches, social organizations, and residential areas for blacks and whites, but there are also separate magazines, journals, and newspapers. Music is defined as black or white (although most of it shares the same musical roots), even though some of America's most outstanding musicians perform in both black and white arenas. There is "black" literature, poetry, and art, thought to be distinct from white versions of these cultural genres. There is black entertainment, presumed to be different from white entertainment, and even some of the literature on health is targeted at a separate black or white audience. The media constantly portray and support the racial divide. Advertisements and politicians design their communications for a specific racial constituency. This is true for blacks and whites, and increasingly for Latinos (Hispanics), who are being racialized to some degree in the contemporary world.

Race provides the unspoken guidelines for daily interaction between persons defined as being of different races, especially black and white. It often sets the standards and rules for conduct, even though individuals may not always be conscious of this fact. All of this suggests that Americans believe unarticulated differences between the races to be profound and ineradicable. Although the reasons given are often incoherent or desultory, the underlying belief is that the differences cannot be overcome under any circumstances. This belief is unfortunately often held by some who have been the victims of racism as well as those who have not. The important point is that this sense of difference reflects the cultural construction of the reality of the racial worldview in those societies where such differences evolved and became useful.

The reality of race rests in the uniqueness of the attitudes toward human diversity that it expresses. Race is a way of looking at the kaleidoscope of humanity, of dividing it into presumed exclusive units and imposing upon them attributes and features that conform to a ranking system within the cultures that are defining the races. This is a way of saying that specific cultures have been responsible for racializing human groups, for formulating ideas of race and the social values encompassing racial differences. Race as a cultural construct is only one way of looking at human differences.

ON THE RELATIONSHIP BETWEEN BIOLOGY AND RACE

Stressing the cultural nature of race requires excising the empirical reality of biophysical variation from our cognitive perspective. In other words, it is useful to ignore actual phenotypic or biological differences if we want to understand how the ideology of race functions in American society. Yet clearly physical variations had something to do with the origin and persistence of race categorization. Perhaps the best way of expressing this connection is to state that race originated as the imposition of an arbitrary value system on the facts of biological (phenotypic) variations in the human species. It was the cultural invention of arbitrary meanings applied to what appeared to be natural divisions. The meanings had social value, but no intrinsic relationship to the biological diversity itself. Race was a reality created in the human mind, not a reflection of objective truths. It was fabricated as an existential reality out of a combination of recognizable physical differences and some incontrovertible social facts: the conquest of indigenous peoples, their domination and exploitation, and the importation of a vulnerable and controllable population from Africa to service the insatiable greed of European entrepreneurs. The physical differences were a major tool by which the dominant whites constructed and maintained social barriers and economic inequalities; that is, they consciously sought to create social stratification based on these visible differences (cf. Banton 1967, 1977, 1988). Theodore Allen's study (1997) of the invention of the "white" race provides indisputable evidence of the deliberate way in which colonial plantation leaders manipulated the social system in this manner (see chapter 5).

Today, the complex patterns and combinations of genetic intermixture have transformed, indeed have increased, the biogenetic diversity that results from blended gene pools. Yet the sociocultural reality of race persists; it no longer depends on the preservation of discrete biological boundaries, or for that matter on any form of phenotypic markers. We comprehend this best when we realize that western Europeans since the mid-nineteenth century have constructed their own notion of race, not out of overt phenotypic differences within their populations, but out of what were class and ethnic parameters. The ideology of race imputes a permanence and heritability to differences fashioned out of cultural meanings. Phenotypic diversity still obviously exists in many societies, but the conflict between the English and the Irish, as well as twentieth-century German Nazi beliefs, demonstrates that it is not a prerequisite for the creation of race ideology.

THE PRIMORDIALISTS' ARGUMENT

Certain deeply held attitudes tend to confuse and inhibit attempts to understand, with the necessary detachment, race as a cultural phenomenon. Collectively, I call these attitudes "primordialist," because their proponents rely on the naive belief that it is basic human nature to be fearful of those who are different from ourselves. Many writers have assumed that there is a universal human tendency to interpret physical differences between populations as socially meaningful. Following this premise, Thomas Gossett argued that race prejudice has an ancient lineage—that it was present among the ancient Aryans of India, the Chinese of the third-century Han dynasty, as well as among the ancient Egyptians, Hebrews, and Greeks (1965, chap. 1). In fact, he appeared to accept any historical reference to color and other physical characteristics of populations as a reference to race. Bernard Lewis has interpreted race and racism in the attitudes and behavior of medieval Arabs toward sub-Saharan Africans.[2] Pierre Van den Berghe (1967) defined race and racism as broad enough to encompass historical conflicts between the Tutsi and Hutu of the lake region of East Africa and the Fulani and Hausa in West Africa.

There appears to be a common tendency among many historians and social scientists to regard biophysical variations as the basis for, and equivalent to, races and to presume that racial classifications are the norm for any society in which such variations occur. Some authors even attempt to explicate social conflict as a natural concomitant of such biophysical diversity. Thus, Edward Shils (1968) argued for the ubiquity of a connection between color and race, explaining that self-identification by color stems from a primordial need for connectedness to others like ourselves. In the same volume, Kenneth Gergen (1968) speculated that skin color differences may in fact be responsible for conflict between peoples. Operating from a Freudian perspective, he argued that self-love tends to eventuate in the love of others who are like ourselves. The obverse, dislike and suspicion of those who differ from us, leads to the drawing of battle lines between physically different groups. Thus race and racism, these authors concluded, may be natural components of the human psyche. And where certain colors are associated with negative symbols—such as black representing evil, dread, mourning, or filth—and where there are also great differences in skin color within a population, there will be "a pronounced tendency toward strife between the light and the dark" (Gergen 1968, 122).[3]

The arguments made by some of the primordialists sound more like self-serving and self-deceiving rationalizations that stem from culturally conditioned personal bias (compare, for example, the arguments expressed by proponents of slavery during the pre–Civil War era) than like objective examinations of social facts. There are so many exceptions in history and contemporary circumstances that we are inclined to question such generalizations. We do know with certainty that when people are conditioned from childhood to have negative feelings about dark skin color, they may indeed respond to it with fear, hatred, and loathing.

This raises to the level of irony the fact that most of the world's greatest violence and the strongest and most hate-filled passions have been expressed among peoples who are physically (and often culturally) similar, as manifested in the two world wars of the twentieth century among various European populations and hundreds of other wars in previous centuries. A prime example of centuries-old hate found in the Western world today is the conflict between the Irish and the English. Most of the world's great wars during the last half millennium have had as protagonists Europeans who were culturally similar and physically undifferentiated. The same is true of Asia and the Middle East, where neighbors who are physically similar have fought numerous wars. Moreover, in some instances peoples with extensive biophysical, as well as cultural, differences have come into contact and intermingled with little or no conflict. There has always been some degree of commingling, and often amalgamation, even when the circumstances entailed devastating conquest (as in the example of some Europeans and Native Americans). We are told that in the ancient world the Persians had "respect for the customs and languages of others" (Rowe 1974, 63). Alexander the Great exhorted his soldiers to mingle and intermarry with the peoples they conquered. Neither the Aryan conquests and movements into India nor the Muslim conquests in Africa, southern Europe, and throughout the Near and Far East resulted in racially structured societies. So we are not convinced by such Freudian-based arguments.

In any case, we cannot explain the phenomenon of race by reference to psychological processes that may be taking place within individuals. The structure of individual personalities comes about only within the context of cultures and ongoing social systems, and within the meanings, values, and proscriptions that are impressed upon individuals as they are socialized within a given cultural matrix. As the song from the musical *Bali Hai* (*South Pacific*) claims, "you've got to be taught to hate." The idea of race is complex; it cannot be understood or analyzed outside of its cultural integument. Nor is it a simple question of the juxtaposition of dissimilar human groups and resulting conflict between them. Race and racism do not simply or necessarily follow from the mere propinquity and interaction of two peoples who happen to be physically different. As Van den Berghe has also pointed out, "It is not the presence of objective physical differences between groups that creates races, but the social recognition of such differences as socially significant or relevant" (1967, 11).

I argue that race is even more than the imputation of social significance to physical differences. For example, skin color variations in many regions of the world and in many societies have been imbued with some degree of social value or significance, but color prejudice or preference does not of itself amount to a fully evolved racial worldview.[4] There are and have been many societies in which the range of skin color variation is quite large, but they have not all imposed on themselves worldviews with the specific ideological components of race that have been experienced in North America and South Africa.[5]

It is nevertheless historically accurate to recognize that physical differences were (and still are) an important and perhaps necessary ingredient in the development of the idea of race in North America. Their existence, however, became much less critical even before the elaboration of the worldview and ideology of race that appeared in the mid-nineteenth century, when Europeans began to extend its components to one another. Today actual color and other phenotypic differences are not crucial to the functioning of race ideology in our society, although color and physiognomy remain in the public mind as symbols of race differences. It is enough to know that a person identifies as a member of a particular *race*, regardless of physical features.

RACE AS A WORLDVIEW: A THEORETICAL PERSPECTIVE

The primary thesis of this book—and what the research has shown—is that *race* was from its inception a folk classification, a product of popular beliefs about human differences that evolved from the sixteenth through the nineteenth centuries. As a worldview, it was a cosmological ordering system structured out of the political, economic, and social experiences of peoples who had emerged as expansionist, conquering, dominating nations on a worldwide quest for wealth and power. By a folk classification, I refer to the ideologies, distinctions, and selective perceptions that constitute a society's popular imagery and interpretations of the world. People in all societies comprehend the world through prisms that their cultures and experiences proffer to them. They impose meanings on new discoveries and experiences that emanate from their own cultural conditioning and interpret these realities in terms with which they are familiar. One of the first examples of this described in this book is the way the English fabricated an image of savagery from their experiences with the Irish and then imposed this image on Native Americans and later Africans.

Like all elements of culture, the racial worldview is dynamic, subject to oscillations in its expression and interpretation, from time to time intensified or contracted, sometimes modified and/or reinvented in response to changing circumstances. It also manifests contradictions and inconsistencies as life experiences, various social forces, and new knowledge provoke subtle modifications in attitudes about human differences. In the United States, the racial worldview has waxed and waned largely in response to economic forces that alter the conditions of labor competition and political realities that from time to time have incorporated or advanced the interests of the low-status races.

Race, then, originated not as a product of scientific investigation but as a folk concept; it initially had no basis, no point of origin, in science or naturalistic studies. The folk idea was subsequently embraced, beginning in the mid- to late eighteenth century, by naturalists and other learned people and given credence and legitimacy as a supposed product of scientific investigation. The scientists themselves undertook efforts to document the existence of the differences that the European cultural worldview demanded and had already created. In their efforts to promote a valid basis for the idea of race, scientists not only reflected the biases, beliefs, and conditioning of their times, but, as in the cases of Louis Agassiz in the nineteenth century and Sir Cyril Burt in the twentieth, they often expressed their own personal fears, prejudices, and aesthetic evaluations of peoples whom they saw as alien. That their judgments and scientific conclusions mirrored popular beliefs should come as no surprise. As John Greene (1981) has shown, science is inevitably shaped by existing knowledge, values, beliefs, and presuppositions.

From its first continuous application to human populations during the eighteenth century, *race* was a way of categorizing what were already conceived of as inherently unequal human populations. Indeed, had all human beings been considered at least potentially equal by European explorers and exploiters, there would have been no need for the concept of race at all. People could have continued to be identified in the ways that had been employed ever since the first distinct groups came into contact with one another—that is, by their own names for themselves (their ethnic names); by the categorizing terms such as *people*, *group*, *society*, and *nation*; or by labels taken from the geographic region or locales they inhabited. Separateness and inequality are central to the idea of race.

By the early decades of the nineteenth century, the race concept in North America contained at least five ascertainable ideological ingredients, which, when taken together, may be considered diagnostic of race in the United States. Some were reflections of presuppositions deeply embedded in English culture and history; others were relatively new ideas that appeared with the colonial and slavery experiences but were compatible with the values, beliefs, and interests of the leaders of, especially, the southern colonies. When combined, these formed a singular paradigm constituting the racial worldview.

The first and most basic element was a universal classification of human groups as exclusive and discrete biological entities. The classifications were not based on objective variations in language or culture, but rather eclipsed these attributes and included superficial assessments and value judgments of phenotypic and behavioral variations. The categories were arbitrary and subjective and often concocted from the impressions, sometimes fanciful, of remote observers. A second element, emphasized above, was the imposition of an inegalitarian ethos that required the ranking of these groups vis-à-vis one another. Ranking was an intrinsic, and explicit, aspect of the classifying process, derived from the ancient model of the Great Chain of Being (a hierarchical structure of all living things; see chapter 7), which had been adapted to eighteenth-century realities.

A third element of North American race ideology was the belief that the outer physical characteristics of human populations were but surface manifestations of inner realities, for example, the cognitive linking of physical features with behavioral, intellectual, temperamental, moral, and other qualities. Thus, what today most scholars recognize as cultural (learned) behavior was seen as an innate concomitant of biophysical form. A fourth element was the notion that all of these qualities were inheritable—the biophysical characteristics, the cultural or behavioral features and capabilities, and the social rank allocated to each group by the belief system itself. Finally, perhaps the most critical element of all was the belief that each exclusive group (race) was created unique and distinct by nature or God, so that the imputed differences, believed to be fixed and unalterable, could never be bridged or transcended.

The synthesis of these elements constituted the folk concept and worldview of race in America, when this term began to replace other classificatory terms and to be widely used in the English language during the eighteenth century. The ideology enveloped in the concept was universal, comprehensive, and infinitely expandable. By the nineteenth century, all human groups of varying degrees of biological and/or cultural diversity could be subsumed arbitrarily into some racial category, depending on the objectives or goals of those establishing the classifications.

Once structured on a hierarchy of inequality, different races became socially meaningful wherever the term was used and to whatever groups it could be extended. Attitudes, beliefs, myths, and assumptions about the world's peoples, developed during the period of greatest European expansion and exploitation of non-European lands and peoples, were embroidered into systematic ideologies about their differing capacities for civilization and progress. All colonial peoples were seen as distinct races, all had to be ranked somewhere below whites, and even some Europeans had to be divided into racial groups and ranked.

As it evolved in the nineteenth century, the concept of race posed a new dimension of social differentiation that superseded "class." Race offered a new mechanism for structuring society based on a conception of naturally fixed, heritable, and immutable status categories linked to visible physical markers. The idea of "natural" inequality was a central component of race from its inception, but few recognized this as a mere analogue of social position transformed into myth. Devout Christians saw it as God-ordained, and the irreligious rationalized the inequality as a fundamental part of "natural laws." In the same century, racial groups began to be confirmed in their inequalities by science, which cast their imagery to reflect the unquestioned verities of the dominant society's beliefs. Finally, the legal apparatus of the United States and various state governments conspired with science to legitimize this structural inequality by sanctioning it in law. Thus, the racial worldview was institutionalized and made a systemic and dominant component of American social structure.

This cultural construction of race as social reality reached full development in the latter half of the nineteenth century. After the Civil War it was utilized as a social device to transform the freed black population of the North American continent into a subordinate, subhuman caste. It was further used to degrade and brutalize the Native American peoples and establish specific social parameters for other, newer immigrants, including the Irish, who had first experienced some of the elementary features of the racial worldview (see chapter 3).

In the nineteenth and early twentieth centuries, the idea of race differences was seized upon to divide, separate, and rank European populations and justify the dominance of certain class groups or ethnic elements. This led inexorably to the mass terror, incalculable atrocities, and genocide of Nazi race ideology and practices. These events had a major impact on American social consciousness and generated growing antiracist sentiments among a populace prepared by its own ideals to combat Nazism. Also in the twentieth century, the state of South Africa came much closer to realizing and operationalizing the mandates of this worldview under its system of apartheid.

The legacy of the historical development of the idea of race has been the retention into the twenty-first century of the folk sense of fundamental differences and inequality between peoples classified as separate races. It persists as an unarticulated reality despite recent developments in the biological sciences, which, as we shall see, have failed to confirm the existence of differences between groups greater in magnitude than those found between individuals. The idea of race continues in large part because of its value as a mechanism for identifying who should have access to wealth, privilege, loyalty, respect, and power, and who should not. And of course, for some individuals in the high-status race, it is a powerful psychological force, providing scapegoat functions as well as a facile external means of establishing and measuring one's self-worth. Race became, and still is, the fulcrum and symbol of a worldview and ideology that promotes an easy and simple explanation for human history and progress, or the lack thereof. Most important, it declares a kind of ordered structure to society that appears to be grounded in the very diversity created by nature.

This is the story that this book tells, but it is not an easy one to learn.

RACE AND ETHNICITY: BIOLOGY AND CULTURE

As we have seen, a fundamental dichotomy made by modern anthropologists and other scholars is that between culture and biology. We emphasize that culture is learned behavior that varies independently of the physical characteristics of the people who carry it. People who live and interact together in a common community develop lifestyles, value orientations, language styles, customs, beliefs, and habits that differ from those of their neighbors. Over large geographic areas, variations in language and cultural traits may become quite noticeable, so that populations may differ radically from one another even within the same political community. People who share cultural characteristics such as religion, a common cultural history, a group name and identity, and language traits see themselves as distinct from other populations. A modern way of expressing the common interests of people who are perceived by others and themselves as having the same culture is to speak of them as an *ethnic group*. When ethnic groups evolve values that project their own lifestyles as superior to the cultures of others, we identify such attitudes as *ethnocentric* (or chauvinistic).

It is important at the outset to have a clear understanding of the difference between race and racism on the one hand, and ethnicity and ethnocentrism on the other. These terms reflect conceptually, and realistically, quite different kinds of phenomena, and their use should be so restricted in the interest of accurate communication. It is unfortunate that the languages of the sciences, particularly the social sciences, have sometimes tended to proliferate and obfuscate meanings rather than provide precision and clarity. *Ethnicity* is one of those relatively modern terms that has sometimes been hailed as a suitable substitute for *race*, but that has also itself taken on a confusing plethora of meanings and nuances. Just one of the meanings listed in *Webster's New International Dictionary* shows how imprecise and impracticable the term can be; *ethnicity* is defined as "racial, linguistic and cultural ties with a specific group." Ethnicity is a quality of ethnic groups, and *ethnic* itself seems to be almost anything and everything. The automatic linkage of biology and behavior (culture) in our collective consciousness obviously precipitated the inclusion of "racial ties" (here seen as physical traits) and the confusion of these very different domains.

Somewhat more sanguine about how we deal with physical, psychological, linguistic, and cultural phenomena, anthropologists have been cautious to relate the terms *ethnic* and *ethnicity* to real, as well as perceived, cultural differences between peoples. Nowadays, "culture" is defined, following E. B. Tylor's inclusive and unsurpassed rendering, as "that complex whole which includes knowledge, belief, art, morals, law, custom, and any other capabilities and habits acquired by man as a member of society" ([1871] 1958, 1).[6] In our time, we would substitute *human beings* for *man* and emphasize the term *acquired*. The point is very simple: Culture is learned, not inborn, behavior; it refers to ways of behaving and thinking that we learn as we grow up in any society. It also refers to the things we learn when we adapt to or assimilate features of a different culture. *Ethnic* and *ethnicity* are best used to refer to all those traditions, customs, activities, beliefs, and practices that pertain to a particular group of people who see themselves and are seen by others as having distinct cultural features, a separate history, and a specific sociocultural identity. It is important to note that members of an ethnic group need not have common physical traits.

On occasion we have all used certain physical attributes of individuals as clues to their nationality or geographic origins, such as, for example, in the identification of East Indians or Asians. But physical characteristics do not automatically proclaim the *cultural* background or behavior of any individual or group. There are many people who look East Indian but have no such ancestry or cultural background. Some Middle Easterners have been mistaken for Puerto Ricans and vice versa. Some Arabs have been mistaken for black Americans, and so have many peoples from the tropical islands of the South Pacific. Biophysical traits should never be used as part of the definition of ethnicity. Every American should understand this explicitly, since there are millions of physically varying people, all sharing "American culture" (ethnicity), who know little or nothing about the cultural features of their ancestors, who may have arrived here from almost anywhere.

One of the tragedies of the racial worldview is that certain differences in physical appearance (especially among blacks and whites), the insignia of *race*, are so powerful as social dividers and status markers among Americans that they cannot perceive the cultural similarities that mark them all as Americans to outsiders. Europeans and Asians, however, not only tend to recognize these similarities but to treat such persons as part of a single ethnic American category. Michael Banton (1988) noted that in studies of children of nursery school age in Sweden, children were classified according to their home languages. This resulted in some African children being classified and referred to as Swedish, a much more realistic cognition of identity than skin color. Speaking the Swedish language reflects their participation in and acquaintance with Swedish culture, a fact that distinguishes them from foreigners who do not know the language or culture. Fourth- or fifth-generation Chinese and Japanese Americans who do not speak an Asian language or maintain elements of an Asian culture resent being mistaken for recent immigrants who have little experience and knowledge of American culture. One would think that Americans, of all people, would understand the power of enculturation and the rapidity with which ethnic characteristics and consciousness can change. But the force of the racial worldview prevents the cognitive acceptance of their implications.

Ethnic differences, interests, and identity are probably nearly as old as the human species, and so is ethnocentrism. Except for systems of supernatural belief and prohibitions against incest, few things are as universal in human societies as the penchant for dichotomizing their worlds into "we" and "they." That *our* customs, *our* laws, *our* food, *our* traditions, *our* music, *our* religion, *our* beliefs and values, and so forth are superior to or somehow better than those of other societies has been a widespread, and perhaps useful, construct for many groups. Ethnocentrism has varying manifestations, intensities, and consequences; although it may often convey an element of rivalry, it need not be accompanied by hostility. But nations and segments of modern nation-states reveal the greatest ethnocentric behavior when they are rivals for territory, resources, political hegemony, markets, souls, and so forth. Such rivalry may erupt into physical hostilities, or it may be expressed in some other, nonlethal form. It may appear abruptly and diminish just as rapidly, or it may smolder for decades, generations, or even centuries, influencing the long-range interactions of both peoples. The important point about all cases of ethnocentrism is that it is grounded in the empirical reality and perceptions of sociocultural differences and the separateness of interests and goals that this may entail. There could be no ethnocentrism without cultural differences, no matter how trivial or insignificant these may appear to an outsider. (Consider the Walloons and Flemish, the Ibos and Yorubas, the Protestants and Catholics in Ireland, the Irish and English, the Basques and Spanish, the English and Germans, the Turks and Armenians, the Serbs and Croats, and dozens of other historical conflicts.)

Many situations reveal the most significant aspects of ethnocentrism, that is, its fluidity or flexibility and its potential transience. In the 1940s most Americans had hostile feelings toward the Germans and the Japanese. This attitude and the feelings it engendered changed in less than a generation. The transformation had nothing to do with alterations in our genetic structure. Values, attitudes, and beliefs are cultural traits and are nongenetic; they are extrasomatic, learned and transmitted through enculturation processes. Individuals and groups can and do change their ethnic or cultural identities and interests through such processes as migration, conversion, and assimilation, or through exposure to other modifying influences.

Racism, on the other hand, does not require the presence of empirically determinable cultural differences. It substitutes, as it were, a fiction and a mystique about human behavior for the objective realization of true similarities and differences of language, religion, and other aspects of culture. This mystique is bound up with biological heredity and a belief in its ineradicable bonding to moral, spiritual, intellectual, and other mental and behavioral qualities. The mystique itself is the presumption of cultural-behavioral differences that phenotypic or physical differences are thought to signify. It is a belief in the biological determinants of cultural behavior—a critical ideological component of the concept of race.

But because phenotypic differences in a heterogeneous society can become muddled and confused (human mating habits not being thoroughly subject to coercion), and because the realities of true cultural similarities and differences sometimes penetrate its consciousness, a society predicated on race categories has to construct another fiction. This is the phenomenon of "racial essence," which is seen as the ultimate determinant of racial character and identity. The belief that an African American, for example, who appears phenotypically "white" (think ex-congressman Harold Ford or TV newscaster Soledad O'Brian) carries the racial essence of his or her black ancestors maintains the illusion of difference, distinctiveness, and innateness even without visible physical signs.

Race signifies rigidity and permanence of position and status within a ranking order that is based on what is believed to be the unalterable reality of innate biological differences. Ethnicity is conditional, temporal, even volitional, and not amenable to biology or biological processes. That some biophysical and ethnic (cultural) differences have coincided in the past (and still do) for largely geographical, ecological (adaptive), and historical reasons should not be permitted to confuse us. Nor should the fact that extreme ethnocentrism and race hatred often manifest some of the same symptoms. They can, and often do, accompany and complement each other, along with stereotypes that appear unabashedly racist. But ethnic stereotypes and ethnic boundaries can and do change, and much more rapidly than racial ones; ethnicity is based on behavior that most people understand can be learned.

Where race is the more powerful divider, it does not matter what one's sociocultural background may be or how similar ethnically two so-called racial groups are. In fact, the reality of ethnic, or social class, similarities and differences is irrelevant in situations where race is the prime and irreducible factor for social differentiation. The best example of this is blacks and whites in America, whose cultural similarities are so obvious to outsiders but internally are obfuscated by the racial worldview.

When the racial worldview is operant, an individual's or group's status can never alter, as both status and behavior are presumed to be biologically fixed. Stephen Steinberg captured this reality clearly in his discussion of ethnic (European) immigrants and racial minorities. "Immigrants," he observes, "were disparaged for their cultural peculiarities, and the implied message was, 'You will become like us whether you want to or not.' When it came to racial minorities, however, the unspoken dictum was, 'No matter how much like us you are, you will remain apart'" (1989, 42). The ideology of exclusion and low-status ranking for blacks in America precludes recognition of how culturally similar whites and blacks are. This is particularly true in the southern states where, class differences aside, they have shared a common culture for centuries.

Where ethnocentrism governs, a people's biophysical characteristics, no matter how similar or divergent, are immaterial to the sociocultural realities. What obtained in most of human history, and certainly throughout the ancient world, was an unarticulated understanding of these principles. This explains why so little was mentioned in ancient texts about the physical features of various groups. The ancients knew that differences of language and custom were far more significant than mere physical traits. They also knew, despite many statements that appear to us as "racist" (in some of the works of Tacitus and Herodotus, for example), that a German tribesman, or any other "barbarian" on the outskirts of civilization, could learn the language and culture of Romans and become a citizen—in other words, that the ethnicity of a person or group was not something inborn and irredeemable; it could be transformed.

But the modern world, after the great migrations of Europeans and the intermixtures among them and with non-Europeans, experienced disorder and confusion of class and ethnicity that crumbled old patterns of social identity and division. It was in large part the uncertainties of this situation that made the idea of race acceptable and useful. Indeed, it can be argued that, beginning in the nineteenth century, many differences that were once essentially ethnic in nature and origin have become transformed and expressed in a racial idiom. Race, because its characteristics are thought to be innate, exaggerates whatever differences do exist and renders them even more profound and permanent. Thus, race structures a social order that is perceived as unalterable.

Although the 1960s and 1970s brought a resurgence of ethnic consciousness and the application of the term "ethnic group" to blacks and other groups, Ronald Takaki has shown that Americans have historically treated ethnic and racial groups very differently. He concludes from a study of the political status of different groups that "what actually developed . . . in American society was a pattern of citizenship and suffrage which drew a very sharp distinction between 'ethnicity' and 'race'" (1987, 29). He argues that it is erroneous to treat subordinate racial groups in American society as if they were merely ethnic. Race is a qualitatively different mode of structuring society.

Race represents a systematic worldview that has proved useful to some people in situations of conflict and competition. It provides its own rationalization for the instigation and perpetuation of intergroup animosities and reduces or eliminates any potential for recognizing commonalities or reach-

ing compromise. It evolved in the Judeo-Christian world as a justification for perpetrating inhumanities on others. Perhaps this is why so many people are made uncomfortable by its persistence. We can achieve a greater level of understanding of this phenomenon by examining how it was molded as an idea and an ideology throughout history.

NOTES

1. Compare Banton 1977; Harris 1968; Montagu 1969; Stanton 1960; Van den Berghe 1967; and Williams [1944] 1966.

2. See Lewis 1971, 1990; Brown 1968; Davis 1984; and Hunwick 1978 for different perspectives on this topic.

3. See also Degler's strange argument regarding Brazilian "racial" feelings, especially where he assumes that negative attitudes toward darker-skinned (negroid) peoples who form much of the lower classes is due to a "universality of prejudice where there are visible differences among peoples" (1971, 287). Some writers who look at ancient documents immediately assume a racial element wherever they see negative descriptions or derogatory comments about the physical characteristics of an alien people. Were we to accept such a wide view of race, virtually all relationships among human groups would involve some form of racial belief, and we would not be able to refine this definition so that comparative studies could be made.

4. St. Clair Drake made a similar distinction between color prejudice and racism (1987, 8–10). Many cultures place social meanings on differences in skin color that have nothing to do with race. In Japanese history, women with pale skins were aesthetically highly valued, in part because this skin tone signaled that their fathers (or husbands) were wealthy and the women therefore did not need to work outside in the fields (Wagatsuma 1968). In contrast, white Americans often acquire deep tans to convey an aura of affluence, high status, and leisure. Drake also believed that, among other factors, negative aesthetic evaluations of negroid physiognomy affected attitudes toward Africans in many societies quite apart from mere skin color preferences or prejudices. But aesthetic values are subjective and highly personal. One would be hard-pressed to identify the kind of evidence needed to prove this.

5. See Frank Snowden's description of blacks in ancient Greek and Roman societies ([1970] 1983).

6. This definition is frequently quoted in introductory textbooks in anthropology. See, for example, Harris 1995, 7; Swartz and Jordan 1976, 4; and Keesing and Keesing 1971, 20, among many others.

CHAPTER 2

The Etymology of the Term *Race* in the English Language

In the fifteenth century, western and northern Europeans ventured out from their geographic and historical isolation and discovered the rest of the world. During the next five hundred years, European exploration, expansion, colonial settlement, and exploitation changed the course of human history and generated complex new relationships among the peoples of the world.

In the process of exploration and penetration into what was terra incognita, European adventurers encountered previously unknown peoples. The sometimes awesome and exotic groups had material, religious, and social lifeways alien to and unexpected by the peoples of Europe. The strangeness of these peoples and their habitats challenged the European imagination, prompting a rash of speculation about and novel interpretations of the discoveries. To grapple both intellectually and practically with these alien societies, Europeans imposed upon them meanings and identities that fit within their own historical understandings, experiences, and preconceptions of what the world was all about. Somewhere in the process they began to use the term *race* to characterize differences among human groups. They left little record of the source of the term and give us only a hint of the specific meaning(s) attached to it.

The term *race* is found in all the languages of European settlers in the Americas, where it generally denoted populations of differing origins in the heterogeneous mix of peoples. However, the substantive meanings in different European languages have varied. In English, the term has had nearly a dozen distinct meanings dating from medieval times. But as a semantic form referring to human groups, the English term has a curious history. Its etymology appears obscure, although most dictionary descriptions suggest that the term probably stems from the Italian, thus assuming a Latin origin. Some British experts have debated this. H. W. Fowler claimed in 1926 that there is no Latin term from which it is known to have descended ([1926] 1962). Noted zoologist Cedric Dover argued that it came from the Arabic term *ras*, meaning "chief head, origin or beginning" (1951). From there, he speculated, it diffused into Spanish in the form of *raza*, meaning a kinship group or follower of a headman. Subsequently it spread to the other Latin-based languages and eventually to English. In a brief reply to Dover, J. C. Trevor, a Cambridge anthropologist, restated his argument (1951) that *race* derived from the Latin *ratio* in an accusative form that had similar meaning to other classificatory terms such as *species*, *kind*, and *nature*. It came into Italian as *razza* and from there went into other related languages.

Trevor added a significant piece of information, noting that the earliest use of the word *race* in English known to him occurs in William Dunbar's poem, "The Dance of the Sevin Deidly Synnis," written in the sixteenth century, in which the author refers to "backbyttaris of sindry racis." Etymologist Leo Spitzer concurs with Trevor in his belief that the transformation of *ratio* to Italian *razza* and into modern languages was most likely the true direction of development, and he mentions in a footnote its "characteristic connection with animals" (1948, 160). The *Oxford English Dictionary of Historical Principles* (1933) shows no earlier date than that of the Dunbar poems. Other rare instances of its use are shown during the late sixteenth century in two ways: "A group of persons, animals, or plants, connected by common descent or origin" and "A group or class of persons, animals, or things, having some common feature or features" (87).

Only occasionally during the rest of the sixteenth century do we find the term used for humans. Edmund Campion did not employ the term in his descriptions of the Irish people in one of the earliest histories of Ireland, compiled in 1571, although some of his contemporaries as well as later writers sometimes spoke of the "Irish race" (Myers 1983). The term was only infrequently used to refer to aliens less familiar to the English.

In fact, *race* did not appear in the English language as a technical term with reference to human groups until the seventeenth century, when it was apparently employed in several ways. One referred to the characteristics or common qualities of certain types of persons. Thus, for example, John Bunyan in *Pilgrim's Progress* referred to a race of "saints." Shakespeare, along with other writers, seemed to associate the term with the idea of the inherited disposition or temperament of individuals. Other writers conveyed the sense of a class or type of person when they spoke of a "race of bishops" or "the race of womankind." The second usage was more incipiently technical in that various learned men, in attempting to describe and classify different human groups, occasionally used the term interchangeably with *species* as a general mode of categorizing peoples. William Petty and a few other writers connected *races* with *generations*, which perhaps was an apt reflection of its source (Slotkin 1965, 89).

The earliest Spanish dictionary, the *Tesoro de la Lengua Castellana o Española* of Covarrubias Horozco ([1611] 1943), specifically identifies *raza* as referring to the "caste or quality of authentic horses," which are branded with an iron so as to be recognized. But two other meanings are given. One pertains to threads in the weave of a cloth; the other refers to humankind. Here, *raza* is taken in a negative sense to connote the existence of Moorish or Jewish ancestors in one's lineage (56, 57). During the period of the Inquisition in Spain, the term was sometimes applied to families suspected of heresy and to New Christians to distinguish them from the older peasant Christian community. By 1737, a *Diccionario de la Lengua Castellana* gives as the first and primary meaning, "the caste or quality of origin or lineage," when describing "los hombres," noting only later in that same passage its earlier usage for animals and cloths.

Although the information is thus slim, it seems that the most direct evidence of the origins and early meanings of *race* derives from the Middle Ages. The word may have been a folk concept in the Romance languages (Spanish, Italian, French, Portuguese), which evidently emerged from customs of breeding domestic animals. Its original meaning seems to have related to a breeding line of animals, a "stock" or group of animals that was the product of a line bred for certain purposes. As such, the term probably has a long history in the folk cultures of the Latin world, for human cognizance of breeding animals dates well back into early agrarian communities. In the sixteenth century, Spanish writers employed the term as one of several ways of referring to new populations discovered in their travels.

During the fifteenth and sixteenth centuries, Spanish hegemony in Europe was extensive, and the country's contacts with the English increased significantly.[1] It is quite likely that the English adopted the term *race* from the Spanish, applying it also to New World indigenes. At that time, the Spanish pronunciation *reazza* could have been easily transformed into the English *race* in a manner consistent with other known linguistic transformations.

From the sixteenth to the eighteenth centuries, *race* developed as a classificatory term in English similar to, and interchangeable with, *people*, *nation*, *kind*, *type*, *variety*, *stock*, and so forth. By the latter half of the eighteenth century, when scholars became more actively engaged in investigations, classifications, and definitions of human populations, *race* was elevated as the one major symbol and mode of human group differentiation applied extensively to non-European groups and even to those groups in Europe who varied from the subjective norm. Of all the terms commonly employed to categorize human beings, *race* became, as we shall see, the most useful one for conveying the qualities and degrees of human differences that had become increasingly consonant with the English view of the world's peoples.

The identification of race with a breeding line or stock of animals carries with it certain implications for how Europeans came to view human groups. One is that the question of species differentiation is essentially left moot. The line or stock is perceived as a variation of a larger entity or group within which all individuals can interbreed. The fact of a perceived capacity for members of one line to interbreed with another, or others, is in itself a recognition of the sameness, the oneness, of the category, and reflects adherence to biblical authority. Second, among farmers and herders, who were perhaps the first to invent and utilize this term, it is well known that certain behavioral propensities are inheritable in highly inbred lines of animals. This is cognitively associated with the unmistakable observation of the heritability of biophysical features.

Following from this, a third and related implication is that value judgments are critical to the identification of the breeding line, for it is specifically for some culturally valued quality, or qualities, that deliberate intervention in the reproductive process has occurred. That is, qualities that the human controller has deemed desirable are obtained by the deliberate breeding of certain animals within the same population. Thus, inherent within the term *race* is a potential, and real, ranking and evaluation of both physical and behavioral traits. To those using the term, such ranking and judgment are real because of the known centuries of human experimentation with and breeding of domestic animals. They become potential wherever the *race* can be or is applied to other biological forms, including humans.

Finally, unlike other terms for classifying people (e.g., *nation*, *people*, *variety*, *kind*, and so on), *race* places emphasis on innateness, on the inbred nature of whatever is being judged. And whatever is inheritable is also permanent and unalterable (except through calculated breeding in future generations), whether it be body size, horn length, fur length, or color; aggressiveness, fearsomeness, docility, dullness, or intelligence; or any other states of being that humans attribute to domesticated animals. The term *race* made possible an easy analogy of inheritable and unchangeable features from breeding animals to human beings.

Race, then, was not just a reasonably felicitous term applied arbitrarily and sporadically to indigenous peoples of other lands. This analysis shows that useful and important substantive aspects of its referential meaning were already present when Europeans began to utilize the term as the prime mechanism for conveying human group differences. It was an eminently appropriate term for the worldview about all human differences that the English and other Europeans were beginning to evolve.

However, the English in North America were to develop and elaborate the implications of the term *race* to a much higher degree than the Spanish, the Portuguese, or the French. The Spanish and Portuguese who settled Latin America evolved a very different perspective on human differences, which did not result in the construction of rigidly exclusive racial groups, as occurred in North America and South Africa. Although this book cannot fully examine all of these situations, a few comparative references are made to underscore the uniqueness of the Anglo-American ideas of race. What does seem clear is that some factors in the experiences and circumstances of contact encountered by the English predisposed them to think of indigenous peoples in ways that varied from earlier levels and forms of ethnocentrism found throughout the world. New dimensions of difference were added to previous beliefs and attitudes, and new ways of relating to variant human groups were instituted. We must turn to the history of the English to investigate this phenomenon. To understand the English situation, we must examine briefly the wider context of developments in Europe during the age of expansion.

NOTES

1. Commercial contacts had increased rapidly, and there was much travel back and forth, especially on the part of London merchant adventurers and their representatives. In addition, some Bristol merchants and seamen settled a small colony at the major Spanish port of Seville. Intermarriages between English and Spanish royalty even led to the Spanish King Philip II ruling England for several years conjointly with his wife, Mary, daughter of Henry VIII and heir to the English throne.

CHAPTER 3

Antecedents of the Racial Worldview

Among the English, some of the seeds of a racial worldview were in place long before they encountered peoples who were dramatically different from themselves in the New World and Africa. In this chapter, after discussing general characteristics of this period, I look at several specific events and circumstances of English life and sociopolitical experiences that affected their views of other peoples. And because the English drew some of their cultural cues in the New World from the Spanish, I also briefly consider aspects of Spanish culture that influenced English attitudes toward non-Europeans in the New World.

THE AGE OF EUROPEAN EXPLORATION

In the fifteenth century, northern Europeans and the peoples of the British Islands in particular had very limited direct knowledge of the world. Few had traveled even to the southernmost regions of the Eurasian continent, although political and commercial intercourse had increased since the Crusades. Although many influences had percolated into southern Europe from the East and especially from North Africa, virtually everything that European savants knew about these regions was encompassed within the stock of scripturally based knowledge, draped in fairy tales and myths, or bits and pieces of theories derived from newly discovered writings of the ancients. As Margaret Hodgen has emphasized, "The Renaissance and Reformation were only in part periods of dazzling enlightenment. They were streaked and furrowed with inherited ignorance, confusion, and traditionalism" (1964, 359).

During the Crusades, roughly the eleventh through the thirteenth centuries, thousands of Europeans, mostly men, had converged on the islands of the eastern Mediterranean and attacked towns in the Near East. Those who survived the many battles and returned home brought back new tastes and knowledge of Eastern cultures. Their experiences contributed to the profound social and economic changes that were already beginning to take place in Europe. Beyond the crusaders, there were very few individuals—men like the Polos (Marco and his father and uncle), Daniel of Kiev, Benjamin of Tudela, John de Plano Carpini, and Lancelot Mallocello—who for trading purposes ventured far beyond the then known boundaries of Europe.

The details of the adventures and travels of such men did not become widely known. With the generally low level of literacy, communication among intellectuals, religious and political leaders, commercial travelers, geographers, merchants, and adventurers was quite random and slow, especially before the invention and widespread use of the printing press. Still, many Europeans, especially in the cities and port towns, heard through rumors and hearsay about bizarre and extraordinary peoples and customs. The often exaggerated tales revealed news about the "heathen Mohammedans" and "Turks," and even stories of a fabled black Christian king of some strange land beyond the Mediterranean named Prester John, who some historians later thought might have been the king of Ethiopia.

Southern Europeans, however, were less isolated and more sophisticated about the diversity of peoples and cultures of the Old World. The Mediterranean world had from time immemorial seen an intermingling of peoples from Europe, Asia, and Africa. In what are now Spain and Portugal, congeries of Islamic peoples (Arabs, Egyptians, Berbers, Carthaginians, Libyans, and others) had invaded from North Africa and settled as early as the beginning of the eighth century. The various waves of invaders, immigrants, soldiers, sailors, merchants, slaves, scholars, and religious leaders helped to keep viable a huge intercommunication zone. Complex networks of trade and travel not only existed among peoples of the lands bordering the Mediterranean, but also connected some of the peoples of western Africa and the Sudan zone, the eastern Mediterranean, the Arabian peninsula, East African trading cities, the Iranian plateau, and parts of India and China. Indeed, although northern Europeans tended to languish in relative isolation during these Middle Ages, this was a period of advanced development for many of the peoples of the Islamic world.

Throughout the Middle Ages Spaniards, particularly in the urban centers, interacted with Africans and Middle Easterners of many ethnic backgrounds. Among their conquerors, the Moors (a term taken from the Almoravid invasion of the eleventh century) consisted of many peoples from North and West Africa, where the religiously inspired movement had congealed. From as far south as the Senegal River, the leaders of the Islamic jihads, or holy wars, had conscripted followers who were eager to spread the words of Muhammad. Swarthy sailors of Arab dhows, from the coastal areas of southern Arabia and East Africa, were seen as far north as the western coasts of France.

Famous Muslim travelers of this period covered even more territory than did their European counterparts. Al-Masudi traveled in India, Sri Lanka, China, Russia, Persia, and Egypt as early as the tenth century. Al-Idrisi, a geographer and cartographer of great repute, traversed North Africa and Asia Minor. In the process he compiled a description of the known world and created a map that was still in use in eighteenth-century Europe. He was the first of the great geographers to show that the world was round, and this in the early twelfth century. Al-Idrisi's renown was such that he was commissioned by the Norman king of Sicily to prepare a comprehensive geography of the world.

Perhaps the best known of the Islamic travelers was Ibn Battuta, a fourteenth-century Moroccan who traveled from West Africa to what is now Sumatra and the Indonesian islands, leaving excellent descriptions of great states from the empire of Mali in West Africa to India and China. What he had to say about the world was vital to some Europeans, both scholars and commercial travelers. Yet his works lapsed into obscurity with the growing focus on Atlantic exploration. Interest in Ibn Battuta's works did not revive until the mid-twentieth century, when scholars experienced a reinvigorated concern for Africa and the precolonial history of its peoples. Ibn Battuta's understanding and tolerance of other cultures, as well as his relatively objective approach to the reconstruction of human history, lay in abeyance until the era of modern anthropological and historical inquiry.

Some Europeans nevertheless benefited from the knowledge that Islamic scholars had gathered about the world, from the translations that made Greek and Roman scholarship again available as well as from the numerous technological developments that originated in or were transmitted by the Islamic world. The great scholar Ptolemy's *Geography*, with its principles of calculation by latitude and longitude, was rediscovered and translated early in the fourteenth century, generating great excitement in some circles. Even so, for the vast majority of educated people, knowledge of peoples and cultures outside western Europe was acquired second- and thirdhand and always filtered through the prism of European religious beliefs, myths, legends, and social values.[1]

It is important to emphasize that those Europeans with the most direct knowledge of the cultural and physical diversity of humankind—the peoples of Spain, Portugal, southern Italy, and the islands of the Mediterranean—had experienced a heterogeneity of peoples and cultures long before the age of discovery. During Greek and Roman times, military conquests and commercial travel took large numbers of people into remote areas of the Old World. Alexander the Great conquered peoples all the way to the Indus Valley of India, and Greek sailors traded with peoples along the East African coast. The northern coastal regions of Africa, including the Nile delta of Egypt, have been invaded periodically and ruled by outsiders for most of the last three thousand years. Mongols, Turks, Assyrians, Persians, Phoenicians, Greeks, Egyptians, Ethiopians, Babylonians, Romans, Carthaginians, Hittites, Libyans, Berbers, and numerous other peoples have interacted for thousands of years. Although not as widely known, for reasons that have to do with the rise of racial ideologies in recent centuries, both Greeks and Romans used mercenaries from inner Africa (variously called Nubians, Ethiopians, Kushites, and so on) in their many conflicts, including the Persian and Peloponnesian Wars.[2] Frank Snowden (1970, 1983), among many other contemporary historians, has shown that "black" Africans were present in many other roles in the ancient world. They were depicted in numerous artistic media, along with other peoples of varying physical characteristics.

As discussed in chapter 6, the long familiarity of southern Europeans with people with dark skin, varying textured hair, and a wide range of other physical features was a critical factor in their interaction with peoples of the New World and Africa.

Columbus's epic voyage to the New World was part of an ongoing European push westward for new routes to the East. Although historians have identified his voyages as among the first and most famous, numerous others took advantage of new sailing techniques to venture into unknown regions. In 1494 the pope, Alexander VI, divided all of the newly discovered (yet unexplored) "heathen" lands of the world between Spain and Portugal, which provided great impetus to Spanish and Portuguese adventurers as well as those of other nationalities. Pedro Álvares Cabral claimed what is now Brazil for Portugal in 1500. For Spain, Amerigo Vespucci explored much of Central America and Mexico beginning in 1497, and Alonso de Ojeda established a Spanish settlement in Panama in 1508. Ponce de León, Vasco Núñez de Balboa, Estevan Gomes, Ferdinand Magellan, Hernando Cortés, Hernando de Soto, and Francisco Pizarro are merely the more well known of what was to become a vast army of "conquistadors" who explored the New World and gathered much of its riches during the first half of the sixteenth century.

Within the first century after the discoveries, Europeans had established themselves permanently in new colonies. Each group brought their different experiences with strangers and different perceptions of, and beliefs about, the nature of humanity. The Roman Catholic Church, with its focus on the papacy, its heritage from ancient Rome, and its stress on the salvation of souls, dominated the Spanish and Portuguese settlements. But northern Europeans, especially the English, brought unique historical experiences and quite different cognitive values that governed their views of the native peoples they encountered.

THE RISE OF CAPITALISM AND THE TRANSFORMATION OF ENGLISH SOCIETY

English society in the sixteenth and seventeenth centuries experienced much turmoil connected with massive social, economic, religious, and political changes. The Protestant Revolution and subsequent political developments of the sixteenth century enhanced the power of the monarchy and created divisions and conflict among the nobles, gentry, and aristocracy. In the seventeenth century, two major revolutions transformed the monarchy and led to the concentration of power at the highest levels in the hands of Parliament, representing the triumph of republican ideology over the values of divine kings and absolute monarchy.

The greatest changes were economic. Historians have widely held that the sixteenth century marked the gradual demise of feudal society and the rise of early capitalism, which evolved as a new economic system both in England and western Europe, particularly in the Netherlands. It was complex, often drastic, and multifaceted in that it had implications for all aspects of culture and society. Dramatic and irreversible changes in social organization and values, politics, and attitudes toward wealth and property took place. According to many scholars, the major elements of this process were the rise of free wage labor, the separation of this labor from the land and from the means and instruments of economic production, and the transformation of both labor and land into commodities that could be exchanged in a widening world market.[3]

The emergence of a bourgeois class whose increasing wealth was based on commerce, trade, and finance was to leave the greatest legacy. A largely urban middle class composed of merchants in the expanding overseas trade, financiers, bankers, shopkeepers, artisans, manufacturers, and industrialists took form, eventually creating a lifestyle of vast material consumption and challenging the gentry and nobility for influence in government. Some wealthy merchants obtained large estates, purchased royal titles (such as knighthoods and baronetcies), and even married some of their offspring into the aristocratic class. An entrepreneurial spirit characterized town life, and even the younger sons of the gentry, prevented by the rule of primogeniture from inheriting their fathers' estates, often turned to commerce and trade and helped to provide a veneer of polish and refinement to the rough-and-tumble competitiveness of town life.

Merchant capitalism fostered other values: individualism, absolute private property, and the unrestrained accumulation of wealth. It was a concomitant, and a cause, of the breakdown of kinship and community ties, a process that had begun toward the end of the feudal period. Feudalism had tended to associate men with particular areas of land, the fiefs granted by the king or a noble lord to a wealthy individual for his services. Lords, villeins, tenants, and serfs were bound to landed estates and to one another through personal ties; they had obligations to the land and one another. In this way generations of kinspeople remained settled together, with tenants and serfs working the same lands.

Profound changes in the nature of kinship ties began early in England. Marc Bloch (1961) noted that from the thirteenth century on, there was a contraction in the social recognition of kinship. Kindreds that had existed under feudalism began to atrophy and were slowly replaced by much smaller family groupings and eventually nuclear families. Because of the growing frequency of voluntary refusal or withdrawal from the obligations of kinship, the cluster of kinspeople bound by obligations of vengeance, for example, had diminished to include only first or second cousins.[4]

The growth of trade and the development of free wage labor in the wake of the decline of feudal estates and serfdom were major factors in the attenuation of kinship ties, as individual men were forced to become mobile in order to sell their labor. Also, increasingly protection from wealthy and politically powerful men became more important than the support of a circle of kinspeople. As the towns and cities grew, and as warfare dislocated people, some men found that their only option for making a living was to leave their native village and family and seek work in the towns or port cities. Another option was to join a militia, where they then had opportunities to engage in adventures abroad (on the continent, or in Ireland) in the many wars taking place at that time in England and on the continent. The unlucky ones drifted into poverty and homelessness. A few men acquired the skills to participate in industry or commerce and devoted their lives to the private accumulation of wealth. The desire for personal enrichment as a major consequence of, and motivation for, free market ideology became a dominant cultural value. During the reign of Edward III (1327–1377), in the midst of the Hundred Years' War, English soldiers returned from France with massive amounts of plunder, injecting a new sense of acquired personal wealth into English culture and inspiring the desire for more.

Another development strengthened the importance of private property. Beginning in the fifteenth century, the "enclosure movement" had resulted in the transformation of what were once communal lands, forests, and meadows in English villages to private property, enclosed by hedges and fences and held in absolute possession by landowners whose objectives were the production of commodities for growing towns and greater profits. When the English turned to fencing in parcels of land and the use of titles became widespread, the sense of exclusive private use of natural resources expanded and matured. Some men became very wealthy as the value of these lands increased, while others, those dispersed or dislocated by the privatization of land, were reduced to abject poverty (see below).

Also of great significance was the development of the use of money "in the relations of life to such an extent that it was possible to buy for money goods of any kind and to secure any variety of services" (Dietz 1932, 119). Money became the measure of all things, functioning not only as a means of exchange but as a mode of payment and a standard of value. The accumulation of money, its use and investment, became a fundamental goal of all ambitious men. Although the English Church denounced the sins of usury, hoarding, and profiteering, F. C. Dietz tells us: "Worldly pursuits acquired an importance of their own, and the unity of all activity envisaged in the Christian view of life was broken, never to be achieved again" (1932, 122). Gold and silver, which could buy virtually anything, totally transformed English life.

Not only did opportunities for acquiring wealth become greater from the beginning of the sixteenth century, but new forms of social inequality based on acquired wealth came into play, particularly in urban areas. Many historians distinguish this newly created property, linked with the rise of the middle class and the values associated with it, as "bourgeois property," referring to those forms of wealth privately held to the exclusion of all others. The accumulation of private wealth became a dominant cultural value, which was underscored by the increasingly atomistic nature of society and linked individuals to a new sense of social identity. As Eugene Genovese and Elizabeth Fox-Genovese observed, "Material possessions . . . became the sine qua non of respectable and responsible selfhood" (1983, 275).

The power of the church to establish and maintain ethical and moral standards had already atrophied and begun to decline before the rise of capitalism as a way of life. Thus the pursuit of wealth by individuals was unencumbered by the demands of either kinship or any other moral order.

Over the course of several centuries, merchant capitalists involved in trading and financial institutions developed a collective power based on their wealth and investments in overseas enterprises. The constellation of cultural features that emerged with and surrounded the lifestyles of the merchant capitalists provided some of the ideological ingredients of the continuing bourgeois revolution that brought about industrial capitalism. But some Marxists, such as Genovese and Fox-Genovese, have argued persuasively that merchant capital hindered rather than advanced economic development toward industrial capitalism. They insist that it was a conservative force that "played handmaiden to feudalism in the early overseas expansion," led to the reinstitution of serfdom in parts of Europe, and was responsible for colonial conquests in the New World and the subsequent exploitation of slave labor (1983, 6–8). Merchant capital was transformed during the political and economic crises of the seventeenth century when the feudal system was finally abolished.

C. B. MacPherson characterized the unifying political thought of English society in the early seventeenth century as based on a central assumption that he calls "possessive individualism." He says: "The basic assumptions of possessive individualism—that man is free and human by virtue of his sole proprietorship of his own person, and that human society is essentially a series of market relations—were deeply embedded in the seventeenth-century foundations" (1962, 270). It was more than just a political theme. Its features impacted economic, religious, and social institutions; values, laws, customs, and beliefs about individual, natural, and civil rights; and the whole range of cultural phenomena. It was intricately linked to the English conception of property, to a sense of proprietorship that extended beyond mere material matter, and was connected to English concepts of individual personhood, autonomy, and freedom.

Looking at some of the century's dominant political philosophers and theorists who reflected and articulated the values of merchant capitalists and industrialists, MacPherson demonstrates that freedom was equated with rights in property, with "property" defined in an unusual way. The basic right of every man was the right to property in his own person—his body, labor, and capacities. A man can only alienate his labor property by "selling" it to another man, a clear indicator of the market or contractual nature of the relationships among men. Exercising proprietary rights in his own selfhood, independently of the will of others, gives a man freedom, and such freedom makes him fully human (1962, 264).

MacPherson argues that, among other implications of the theory of possessive individualism, it justified the appropriation and accumulation of property in land and other resources and goods. A man is fully free when he can accumulate and retain the property of his own labor, holding it exclusively against the demands of others. MacPherson notes that John Locke's philosophy sanctioned the right to the unlimited acquisition of property, which Locke defined as "Life, Liberty and Estate" (MacPherson 1962, 198). Government exists to protect men in the exercise of their property rights. Thus Locke made a positive value out of the unequal appropriation of most of society's wealth, in the form of capital, by a few individuals, reasoning that such accumulation was a "natural right" (MacPherson 1962, 208–221). These ideas and ideals, as well as Locke's general vision of civil rights and human liberties, were transported to the American colonies in varying forms and modifications and ultimately became part of the economic worldview, and rhetoric, of most Americans.

Capitalist ideology, then, had taken shape before some Englishmen turned fully to African slavery as a way of producing commodities for a world market and generating wealth for themselves. Many historians tend to agree that English culture, as manifested in its early development of a capitalist ethos, differed from most of the cultures of western Europe, which lagged behind in their development toward industrial capitalism. Most emphatic about the uniqueness of the English economy and culture is the work of Alan Macfarlane (1978). In arguing that England had ceased to be a rural peasant society by as early as the thirteenth century, Macfarlane points to the atomistic quality of life already expressed in that century, as demonstrated by its individualism, the felt sense of independence from others, and the privatization of wealth. Wage labor, land commoditization, absolute and exclusive ownership of property, extensive geographic and social mobility, the decline in kinship ties and arranged marriages—all predate the sixteenth century. Primogeniture, which signifies private property in real estate, was "apparently firmly established in England by the thirteenth century" and was widespread even "among those at the lower levels of society" (Macfarlane 1978, 87–88).

Macfarlane quotes from a number of medieval sources written by foreign travelers in England that described the extreme individualism of the English (sometimes seen as arrogance), their preoccupation with their own private interests, their overbearing pride, and their suspiciousness not only of strangers but also of one another. "Combined with their self-confidence and arrogance went a mutual suspiciousness: each individual was out for himself and trusted no one else," Macfarlane paraphrases (1978, 174). Foreign observers often spoke of English wealth, abundance of food, fine clothes, love of freedom and independence, pursuit of money and trade, and lack of affection for their children.[5] "All these writers," Macfarlane notes, "clearly felt that there was something different not only about the economy, but also the personality of the English" (173).

Thus, Macfarlane argues, a market mentality, the prevalence of social interactions based on contract rather than status, and the value of all transactions governed by the laws of supply and demand had already characterized the English socioeconomic system even before the Protestant Revolution and the emergence of capitalism. If the English were perceived as culturally distinct by their European contemporaries long before the age of exploration and conquest, surely these cultural traits uniquely influenced the nature and quality of their colonial experiences. English ideologies about individualism and accumulating property guided their assault on foreign lands and their treatment of the indigenous peoples of the New World. These ideologies also helped to determine the kind of slavery that evolved in North America. Possessive individualism and the near sacredness of property and property rights in seventeenth-century English culture facilitated the transformation of Africans into slave property and their concomitant demotion to nonhuman forms of being (see chapter 6).

SOCIAL ORGANIZATION AND VALUES OF EARLY CAPITALISM

At the apex of the hierarchical English social order was the monarch and his or her relatives, the royalty, a genealogical reticulum of births and marriages that cut across polities. Aristocrats and nobles were in the next tier, and these families provided the ruling class. Below this ruling elite were the gentry—large landowners, farmers, merchants, commercial agents, wealthy craftsmen, artisans, and financiers in the towns and ports. Next came the yeomen landowners, the proper and respectable farmers. The working class constituted the bulk of the people, and they were mostly small farmers, regular laborers, small craftsmen, or petty traders. Near the bottom were the working poor; the unemployed or irregularly employed unskilled laborers; and finally the vagabonds, the paupers, and the masterless, homeless men, women, and children who tended to cluster in the poorhouses and byways of towns and villages.

Although the hierarchical system appeared rigid, there was some flexibility and movement both vertically and horizontally across social barriers. This was particularly true of the bourgeoisie in the urban centers. Wealthy merchants, for example, flourished with the expansion of overseas trade. Their political power increased along with their wealth as they competed for the attentions of royalty. They educated their offspring well and sometimes married them to royalty. But Macfarlane has also found considerable geographic and social mobility in some rural parishes, with a "growing cleavage between rich and poor" that often split entire families (1978, 70). Individuals left their natal homes in their teens to make their fortunes and often never returned to their hometowns or villages.

Business, government, and the church had imposed on the English public the values of hard work and sobriety; free labor, it was assumed, would work toward these goals. Such labor had been attracted to the towns and cities by the burgeoning commercial, banking, manufacturing, and shipping enterprises. In the sixteenth and seventeenth centuries, England experienced even larger population movements, exacerbated by the migrations of peasants displaced as a result of the enclosure movement. There were not enough jobs for the poor. Now, through no fault of their own, they were without work. These conditions produced a large class of idle, rootless men and women who roamed the streets scratching, stealing, and begging for food.

The English propertied classes saw these people, often called "vagabonds," as a threat to proper social order. Their communities had long been structured in hierarchies of what many preferred to see as clear and seemingly unambiguous statuses. Men of substance and civility were those who owned property and thus were also those who had power, or at least could wield some influence in the governance of society. A man without property was essentially a social nonentity, unable to undertake civic responsibilities or exercise civil rights. Laboring men worked for those who owned property, and they were bound together by civil laws, contracts, and statutes. Thus the identity of a man in terms of his lands, stock, money, or other resources, or his attachment as a subordinate to a man with property, was a fixed part of the hierarchical system. New forms of contractual relationships appeared between laborers and those who needed labor but could not afford, or desired not to pay, living wages. This "indentured labor" system was to develop most fully in the plantation economies of the New World in the seventeenth century. Indentured servitude became one of the principal ways of linking an impoverished person to a master in order that the former might work for a few years, acquire sufficient funds to establish himself, or seek his fortune elsewhere.

We have already seen associated with the concept of property certain ideas about personal freedom. For a man to acquire property during these times of vigorous change, he had to be free to sell his labor, acquire some semblance of education or training, and make his fortune as best he could without social constraints. A man lacking such ambitions was suspect or considered part of the rabble that constituted the underclasses. Most men saw personal freedom as the normal status for Englishmen, an ideology that had deep roots among the middle classes in medieval cities, as Henri Pirenne tells us ([1925] 1952, 193).

The greatest concern that Englishmen had was with those "masterless" men who went about robbing, raping, and looting. To the proper English, this group lacked the fundamental qualities of Protestantism: self-control, responsibility, ambition, and thrift. Bourgeois English rigidity about personal behavior, the containment of the emotions, a sense of dignity and good taste, and submission to the rules of social propriety no doubt has a much longer history. But suffice it to say that with the development of the Protestant ethic, the autonomy of the individual was greatly elevated, and certain ideals and standards of personal behavior came to be established. Conformity to the formal rules of one's social-class position was heavily monitored by one's peers (or would-be peers) and one's betters. This contrasted sharply with the behavior of the vagabonds, looters, and "mischievous" men, some of whom were swept up off the streets of cities like London and Liverpool and shipped off to the New World to work as bonded laborers.

Thus it was that English values about the ownership of property and its linkage to a proper social and civil identity became firmly established. English beliefs about and obsessions with property became so transfigured that ultimately they were conjoined with religious values. Success in the acquisition of material goods was equated with, and in an important sense confused with, rewards for the pious. The aggrandizement of material wealth seemed to confer moral virtues on individuals. It was these values that Anglican, Puritan, and other Englishmen brought with them to the New World, values that would have a long-term effect on the ways in which they viewed and dealt with non-English and non-European groups. In the New World, they elevated individual property rights to a position sanctioned by divine authority and considered superior to all other rights, including the human rights of indigenous peoples, bonded laborers, and those whom they bought as slaves.

ENGLISH ETHNOCENTRISM AND THE IDEA OF THE SAVAGE

Leonard Liggio, in exploring the race idea and raising a more general question about the differences between the English colonization practices and those of other Europeans, asks: "How is it possible to explain the fact that the English developed the most racist attitudes toward the natives wherever they expanded or established overseas colonies?" He proposes a hypothesis that is now becoming a more general part of our understanding of history: that the English experience with the Irish "was the root of English racial attitudes" (1976, 1). Perhaps because of the intractable and seemingly irreconcilable contemporary conflict between these two peoples, other historians have turned their attention to this long-standing belligerence for insights into the general English attitudes toward indigenous peoples and the nature of their colonial and imperial policies.[6]

Throughout the sixteenth and seventeenth centuries, and especially during the reign of Elizabeth I, the English focused their attention, and a great deal of hostility, on Ireland and the Irish people. The era was punctuated by periodic attempts to finally conquer the Irish, on the one hand, and by several major Irish rebellions on the other. The last of the sixteenth-century rebellions, in 1597, which brought forth the wrath of Elizabeth and the triumph of her forces over the Irish chieftain Hugh O'Neill, was the climax of four centuries of repeated invasions, implacable Irish resistance, and failed attempts to consolidate English power over the western island. A brief review of this history is very instructive.

The first English invasion and attempt to settle Ireland occurred under Henry II, in 1169 and 1171, as part of the expansion of Anglo-Norman civilization following the Norman invasion of England. By the end of the century most of Ireland had fallen under some semblance of English control in the form of Anglo-Norman barons who had been given titles to Irish lands, which they ruled as personal fiefdoms. But the scattered Irish clans, lacking a centralized government, proved impossible to vanquish and control. Within a short time they had regained much of their lands and embarked on the first of several great revivals of Gaelic culture, which flourished from time to time from the thirteenth through the fifteenth centuries.

One development, however, was particularly upsetting and threatening to the nominal rulers of Ireland. Those Englishmen who had settled in Irish lands (called the "Old English"), especially in remote areas away from the Pale, intermingled with the Irish and increasingly "went native"; that is, they assimilated to Irish culture and language. To halt what the English saw as an erosion of civilized culture and the degeneracy of Englishmen in Ireland, the English Crown established legal restrictions forbidding Englishmen to wear Irish dress or hairstyles, speak the Irish language, or intermarry or trade with the Irish. These restrictions, the Statutes of Kilkenny (1367), also outlawed Irish games, poetry, and music, apparently under the assumption that these cultural features were too seductive for young Englishmen to resist. These prohibitions and others stayed in effect until the seventeenth century. But they had little consequence for the preservation of English culture, even though increasingly greater numbers of Englishmen were encouraged to settle in Ireland throughout this period and to promote English culture.

The English were frustrated by their inability to establish complete suzerainty over Irish lands (some of which were in the control of Irish brigands) or to transform the natives and absorb them into English culture. Throughout the period of English attempts to subdue these lands and peoples, one ostensible objective was to spread English civilization. But the underlying reality and primary aim was the confiscation of Irish lands, the establishment of an agrarian economy, and the exploitation of native labor.

The English attitude toward the Irish, almost from the beginning of penetration into the western island, was contempt for Irish culture and lifestyles. This was matched by intense Irish hatred of all that was English. Thus extreme ethnocentrism ensued between these two peoples early in the contact period, a common result in situations in which one group of people attempts to conquer another. But the conflict was not only based on the ethnic chauvinism of two peoples competing for political supremacy, as was the case in many other confrontations among the emerging nation-states of Europe. The hostility between the Irish and English ran much deeper. It exemplified an age-old struggle, symbolized in biblical times by the conflict between Cain and Abel, that has recurred repeatedly in many places throughout history: the clash between nomadic or seminomadic pastoralists and peoples who had settled on the land as farmers and cultivated a sedentary way of life. This was a fundamental conflict between two very different lifestyles, two different views of the world, two different value systems, two different sets of problems and solutions for them.

We should understand how the incompatibility between these basic subsistence patterns has led to conflict and interethnic hatred in many areas of the world. After the establishment of farming, pastoralism developed as an alternative economic strategy, primarily in marginal lands. An economy based on the herding of animals, pastoralism has proved highly adaptive in a wide variety of environments. The basic needs of pastoral societies are herds of domestic or semidomestic animals that are amenable to human manipulation and control, sufficient grazing land to maintain the herds and provide for increases in their numbers, accessible water and salt, and strategies for protecting this highly mobile form of wealth and the requisite resources. This lifestyle requires the human community to adjust itself to the needs of the herds. This means that their culture is oriented around, and circumscribed by, territorial mobility, the placement of highest value on the animal herds, and intensive interaction with those herds.

In recent millennia, pastoralism has been sustained as a specialized way of life in areas marginal to agriculture. Yet in many places, pastoralists seeking to expand grazing land for their herds and farmers attempting to increase their crop production have come into conflict over land, a situation not unlike that of the farmers and cattle ranchers of the American West.

Although many recent studies have shown that there is a great deal of variation in the cultures of nomadic pastoral people, so that it is impossible to speak of a "typical" nomadic way of life, certain features have appeared both in history and in the comparative ethnographic literature that reflect common themes in such cultures.[7] Herding peoples do not recognize land or territory as having specific boundaries, nor have they evolved the concept of property associated with demarcated plots of land. The territory over which they roam belongs to all in the community. Because of their need for mobility, and often rapid movements, pastoralists usually have very little of what sedentary peoples would identify as private property. Most material goods must be portable and often disposable. Their dwellings are generally not permanent, nor do they seem to be very solid to those people who value proper houses and all the accoutrements that accompany them. Tents or other types of dwellings that can be taken apart and packed for moving are the common living quarters, but depending on the environment, most activities take place outside. Some groups who live in relatively harsh environments and engage in seasonal migrations, like the Kazakhs of central Asia, may construct more permanent houses of sod and/or logs for their winter dwellings.

Among many pastoralists, human dependence on animal herds is virtually complete. The basic diet of milk and substances like butter and yogurt processed from milk, meat from older animals or surplus bulls, and blood extracted from adult animals generally suffices, but may be supplemented with occasional vegetables. Skins of animals are used to make a wide variety of utensils, clothing, storage containers, bedding, and other items. Even animal hoofs, horns, bones, tails, and entrails have their uses, so that little is wasted. This contrasts sharply with the diet and materials utilized or exploited by farmers.

Camping units, or some other kinship-based units in which face-to-face contact is possible from time to time, are usually autonomous both politically and economically, operating well beyond the sphere of control of centralized authorities. When quarrels arise between such communities, one resolution is for one group to simply move away. More typical, however, is the institutionalization of feuding relationships—continuous and insistent conflicts that separate herding units. But constant preparedness for fighting, even wholesale combat, means that nomadic herders are perceived by sedentary peoples as militaristic and aggressive. It has been argued that this type of behavior is necessary, and children are so conditioned to it, because of the need to protect a form of wealth that is volatile and easily stolen (Goldschmidt 1965). It is indeed a characteristic of many nomadic pastoralists that they engage in a high level of feuding with others and that the raiding of the animals of other groups, usually to replenish their own losses, is commonplace (Sweet 1965).

Because of their militarism and aggression and their facility for rapid mobility, some nomadic herders have from time to time throughout history come to dominate their sedentary neighbors. In some cases, vast movements of large pastoral groups have led to conquests and the consolidation of large new empires, such as the migrations of Turkish peoples in Russia, the Middle East, northern India, and Persia; the Fulani in West Africa; and the Mongols in Asia.

One of the more striking cultural themes among virtually all nomadic pastoralists is their love for their animals, a theme that is often accorded priority in their ideologies over love of kinspeople or wives. Some of the best-known and most cherished poetry among the Arabs honors or praises their animals or a particular animal. Among East African pastoralists, songs are composed to cattle, and women and cattle are referred to in proverbs and legends literally as substitutes for one another in men's hearts. Cattle or camels are a singular and unique form of wealth and are the major property used in bridewealth transactions and other exchanges between large patrilineal kin groups. Concomitant with this lifestyle is the pastoralists' extraordinary love of freedom of movement and disdain for farmers, who are bound to the land and scratch in the earth for a living.

The Gaelic peoples of Ireland shared many of the habits and customs of nomadic peoples in the Old World. As a herding people, their greatest form of wealth and most strategic resource was their cattle. But techniques of growing crops were not unknown, and many Irish families grew some barley and oats, primarily to feed their animals during the long winter months. Farming, however, was not considered fitting for a man's major occupation. It was generally left to women. A man's herd was the source of his prestige and pride, and families spent their lifetimes trying to increase the size of their herds. Like all pastoralists, the Irish believed that their way of life was superior to the wretched lives of farmers, valuing above all the freedom that it gave them.

English culture, by contrast, was ordered, structured, and controlled. As we have already seen, men were bound in permanent relationships of stratified ranks to one another and to property in land, houses, and commercial enterprises. The centralized governance of a strong civil state was mirrored in the hierarchical structure of the church, the parish, and the town. It was a system that provided for the preeminent values of order, stability, and security. Until the Reformation, it also imposed restraints on the freedom of individuals. What most distinguished English culture from Irish was the advanced elaboration of the jural concept of rights in property in land and the social identity and status that derived therefrom.

From the standpoint of English cultural values, Irish utilization of the land was a monstrous waste; the rich soil that their animals trampled could be put to better use cultivating grains, vegetables, and other goods to be marketed abroad and in expanding urban centers. Moreover, the younger sons of English gentlemen, who had no hopes of inheriting paternal lands, could earn their fortunes from great estates that would be established in Ireland with the aid of Irish labor. Yet all attempts to force Irishmen to settle on the land were rebuffed. When the English met their intransigence by confiscating and destroying their cattle, the Irish fled into the forests and let it be known that they preferred starvation to life as forced laborers on English farms.

Each people thus expressed the different orientations of its culture; different values, interests, and beliefs; and differing ways of viewing the world. The extreme ethnic chauvinism bred of such contrasting understandings of different worlds was exacerbated by the lasting conflicts fundamentally over land. Neither side displayed the moderating force of Christian benevolence, although both groups claimed to be on the side of God.

The contempt and hatred that the English had for Irish culture was expressed by Giraldus Cambrensis as early as 1187. "They are a wild and inhospitable people," he claimed. "They live on beasts only, and live like beasts. . . . This people despises agriculture, has little use for the money-making of towns."[8] He described their uncleanliness, their flowing hair and beards infested with lice, their barbarous dress, and their laziness. "They think that the greatest pleasure is not to work and the greatest wealth is to enjoy liberty." James Myers (1983) asserts that it was this inordinate love of liberty to which Giraldus and his successors objected, and this critique of the Irish continued throughout succeeding centuries.

At the time that Columbus was exploring the New World, the English under Henry VII in 1494 began a new policy designed to settle the Irish problem once and for all through forced colonization. Henry VIII was more benign in his approach, preferring to provide mechanisms by which the Irish would voluntarily submit to his rule. But it was he who built defensive forts and established the first standing army in Ireland, with the intention of ridding the fertile areas of all those who refused to submit to English rule. The colonization policy was continued by Henry VIII's successors.

Irish resistance throughout the sixteenth century enraged many Englishmen, who persisted in viewing the Irish as "rude, beastly, ignorant, cruel and unruly infidels" (Liggio 1976, 8). According to William Thomas, writing in 1552, the "wild Irish" were unreasonable beasts who knew neither God nor good manners and lived with their wives and children in filth along with their animals (Liggio 1976, 8). Some Englishmen argued what was to become a familiar strain in European attitudes toward Native Americans and Africans in the New World during the coming centuries: that the Irish were better off becoming slaves of the English than retaining the brutish customs of their traditional culture. When confiscating Irish lands, many English military leaders, some of whom were later to be involved in the colonization of New England and Virginia, regularly killed women and children, which has prompted some historians to accuse the English of genocide.[9] Humphrey Gilbert, whom David B. Quinn called a "blood-thirsty sadist," justified this barbaric treatment by arguing that the men who fought the war could not be maintained without the women who milked the cattle and provided them with food "and other necessaries" (1966, 127). During the final years of the Nine Years' War, many Irishmen were driven off to western Ireland, and their primary form of wealth, their cattle, was destroyed. Lands were taken over by the younger sons of English gentry, who subsequently set about creating an agricultural and commercial society. The Irish who remained were reduced to involuntary laborers. Under English law they were not allowed to own land, hold office, be apprenticed to any skill or craft, or serve on juries. Their principal identity was that of cheap labor.

Toward the middle of the seventeenth century another, more widespread, rebellion by Irishmen and some of the Old English took place. This was followed by extremely repressive measures on the part of the English under Oliver Cromwell. According to Liggio:

> Cromwell's army in Ireland, often New England Puritan led or inspired, carried out the most complete devastation that Ireland experienced until that time. Extermination became a policy. Massacres were carried out. Prisoners of war were transported to servitude in the new English colonies in the West Indies. Ireland like New England was taken with the Bible in one hand, the sword in the other. Lord Clarendon observed that the Cromwellian policy was to act without "any humanity to the Irish nation, and more especially to those of the old native extraction, the whole race whereof they had upon the matter sworn an utter extirpation. (1976, 28)

The significance of this brutal treatment, and the transport of large numbers of captive peoples of both sexes to the sugar plantations in the West Indies, rested upon the growing image of the Irish as something less than human, as a people whose capacity for civilization was stunted. This view took form slowly, but was perhaps common among the English elite by the early seventeenth century.

Unremitting disdain for the customs and habits of the "wild Irish" is found throughout the literature of the sixteenth and seventeenth centuries. Edmund Campion, himself a Catholic, excoriated the Irish for their supposed cannibalism, their lewd marriage customs (they had trial marriages and sometimes engaged in polygamy and free sexual behavior), and their "whores" and "strumpets . . . too vile and abominable to write of" (Myers 1983, 26–30). And Barnabe Rich, in his 1610 description of the Irish people, their manners, and their customs, claimed that the Irish were educated in "treason, in rebellion, in theft, in robbery, in superstition, in idolatry" (Myers 1983, 130). In their resistance to British civilization, Rich noted, "The Irish had rather still retain themselves in their sluttishness, in their uncleanliness, in their rudeness, and in their inhuman loathsomeness, than they would take any example from the English, either of civility, humanity, or any manner of decency" (Myers 1983, 131).

The habits and customs of the Irish reminded some learned men of the descriptions of primitive peoples found in the recently recovered literature of the ancient Greeks and Romans. Doubts about the capacity of such barbaric people to accommodate themselves to civilized behavior hardened. Many people came to believe the notion, first expressed in the early fourteenth century, that it was "no more a sin to kill an Irishman than a dog or any other brute." Thus, in the English mind there crystallized out of this long saga of tension and hostility a very real image of "barbarism" that had concrete referents in the Irish but could be abstracted to apply to others.

Perhaps worst of all was the heathenism of the Irish. Despite the fact that the Irish were nominally Catholic, the English could see nothing in Irish behavior that was suggestive of morality or virtue. In fact many, like Campion, tended to blame Irish heathenism on their adherence to the papal religion, though this was a tenuous linkage. Their alleged wildness, lack of self-control, and tendencies toward drunkenness and violence were all evidence of the insufficiency of Catholicism to uplift people.

This antagonism to Catholicism had its origins in the tumultuous breakaway of diverse groups from the older Roman Catholic establishment that began during the early part of the sixteenth century. Though we know of this historical transformation as the Protestant Revolution, it was not a single episode in European history, but rather multiple defections from the Roman Church for various reasons. Henry VIII was a critical figure in this revolt, and his support of hostilities against the Irish had as much to do with his anger against Pope Clement VII for the latter's failure to sanction his divorce as with hatred for the Irish. Still, the antagonism against the Irish was compounded by an intensity of opposition to the powers of the Roman Church and by growing competition with the Spanish, another Catholic country, some of whose leaders sided with fellow churchmen in Ireland.

At the same time, the English were beginning to receive reports about the indigenous peoples encountered by the Portuguese and the Spanish in their

New World ventures. Interaction between the Spanish and English was intensified during this century. For a while there were close diplomatic, commercial, and political contacts between the two countries, punctuated by the marriage of Henry VIII to a Spanish princess, Catherine of Aragon, and the brief ascendancy of Philip II of Spain to the joint possession of the English Crown by virtue of his marriage to Henry's daughter, Mary I, from 1553 to 1558. English merchants and sea captains visited Spain frequently, and English politicians and adventurers studied closely the developing colonial policies of the Spanish. Quinn points out that for the first time, Englishmen began to regard their problems with the Irish as similar to those presented by the natives of the New World to the Spanish. They found that some of the same barbarous and uncivilized qualities that they ascribed to the Irish were attributed to the New World natives by the Spanish. Moreover, Spanish settlers were demanding laws enforcing perpetual servitude on the indigenous peoples of the Spanish colonies, a situation the English found most congenial with their own goals.

Following the successful and brutal squashing of the Desmond rebellion in Munster (1579–1583), the English attempted to establish plantations in that region deliberately based on Spanish models and the principles that they perceived to be operant in both Spanish colonial settings and Italian Mediterranean island plantations. After the victory over Hugh O'Neill in 1603, which "marked the passing of Gaelic civilization and the beginning of England's first meticulously planned effort to effect the cultural subjugation of an alien people" (Myers 1983, 8), England planned to create a colonial outpost along plantation lines. At the heart of the plantation model was the coercive exploitation of Irish labor with the objective of "maintaining the labor force in a permanent state of inferiority to and dependence on the English settlers" (Quinn 1958, 27).

It is not surprising that the English view of the Irish had solidified by the seventeenth century into an image summed up by the term *savage*. It was the invention in the English mind of the Irish "savage" that made possible the development of policies and practices that could be perpetuated for gain, unencumbered by ethical or moral considerations. The savage was first of all a "heathen," a godless and immoral creature, "wicked, barbarous and uncivil." He was lazy, filthy, evil, and superstitious; he worshipped idols and was given to lying, stealing, murdering, double-dealing, and committing treachery. His nomadic tendencies and presumed lack of social order and laws were the antithesis of the habits of civilized men, who were sedentary and bound not only to the land but to other men by laws. The savage was a cannibal whose lust and licentiousness never yielded to the strictures of self-control, of which he was totally lacking.[10] Even as some of the Irish were being transformed into what late seventeenth-century England considered "civilized" men, this goal, an early rationalization for settlement in Ireland, became more and more remote. What did increase in English theories and images of the Irish was the belief that the "wild" Irish, those who most vigorously resisted English hegemony, would remain untamed, and that the only way to bring them under some form of civilized control was to enslave them.

After major battles throughout the early and especially the mid-seventeenth century, the English decided to transfer Irish captives to work as slaves on the New World English plantations in the Caribbean, especially Barbados and Jamaica. Under Cromwell, particularly during the wars of 1649–1655, the most widespread devastation of Irish lands took place. Tens of thousands of men, women, and children were killed, and upwards of fifty thousand people were shipped to the Caribbean Islands, especially Barbados and Trinidad, and some to the mainland. Indeed, Irish people formed the bulk of the slaves who were eventually transferred to the New World English plantations during the seventeenth century.[11]

To document and confirm the spreading beliefs about the unsuitability of the Irish for civilization, many of the English pointed to the experiences of the Spanish with peoples in the New World. They cited Spanish practices of exterminating Indians not only as justification for policies of killing Irish men, women, and children, but also as an appropriate solution for dealing with those who refused to be enslaved.

In the English collective consciousness, "the savage" was thus a kind of composite of these streams of negative ideas and images that flourished during a period of great social disorder, change, and unrest. The savage came to embody all of those repulsive characteristics that were contrary to English beliefs, habits, laws, and values. The imagery induced hatred for all things Irish, which persists among some English people right up to the present. But it also had a feedback effect: it was an enormous convenience for those who hoped to profit from the plantations created in Irish lands. Due in large part to Irish resistance, the few English plantations that were established there were often failures. It was the disappointment of the English in their Irish ventures that prompted even greater interest in the New World, where the Spanish had profited greatly from the slave labor of the native population and imported Africans.

The English were not unique in their attitudes. As Margaret Hodgen has pointed out, European opinion during this period of ethnological reflection was generally "anti-savage, and strongly so" (1964, 362), an attitude that was not challenged until well into the Enlightenment period, which began toward the end of the seventeenth century. But such attitudes were more strongly felt by the English and were instrumental in molding English cognitive perceptions of other conquered peoples in the New World, as well as later in the Middle East, India, Burma, Southeast Asia, and Africa. They became important subthemes of the ideology of race and in the characterization of race differences.

ENGLISH NATIONALISM AND SOCIAL VALUES IN THE SIXTEENTH AND SEVENTEENTH CENTURIES

The consolidation of an image of the savage was a major factor in the evolution of English attitudes toward aliens. It fed into an expanding cultural chauvinism as the English began to view themselves as not only distinct from others, but superior to them. Events seemed to propel them toward increasing nationalism and an arrogant pride in being English, a trend that had been nourished during the Hundred Years' War. The break with the Roman Catholic Church in the sixteenth century was both a political and religious underscoring of the separateness of the English polity from those of the rest of Europe. Consciousness of being English, and uniquely Protestant, not yet perceived in biological terms, flowered during Elizabethan times (1559–1603). A sense of growing competition with other Europeans, particularly the Spanish, made the English turn inward, where for some a sense of unity and purpose was found by harkening back to a mythical time of greatness and glory.

Reginald Horsman (1976, 1981) points out that the myth of Anglo-Saxonism originated during this period. Depicted as a branch of a heroic and freedom-loving Germanic people, Anglo-Saxons were described not only as great lovers of liberty, but as originators of civilization's free institutions and equitable laws. It is worth noting, as Horsman specifically points out, that this early form of Anglo-Saxonism was not racial. It was a cultural feature rooted in the attempt to rationalize the existence of a pure pre-Norman church and thus to justify Henry VIII's break with the Roman Catholic Church. It was also consonant with developing ethnocentrism in other emerging states of Europe. The focus on biologically inherited "racial" features as a way of explaining Anglo-Saxon cultural institutions did not take place until the middle of the eighteenth century, a timing that, as we will see in chapter 8, was not fortuitous.

The unexpected English defeat of the Spanish Armada in 1588 was a major event in the eclipse of Spanish domination of the seas. It spelled the rise of this once isolated island culture, which eventually not only assumed supremacy of the seas but became the most vigorous and successful of the competing, empire-building states of Europe. The English citizenry became increasingly united around a peculiar sense of their own identity, and indeed superiority, which ultimately precluded the acceptance of others as equals.

A basic element in that identity was religion. The English were above all else Christians and, even though they were becoming highly secular and materialistic in their cultural orientation, they were conditioned to that sense of religiosity that pervaded much of Europe during this time. Most important, from the time of Henry VIII on they were predominantly Protestant, and their consciousness of an identity dramatically wrenched from the stale traditionalism of what they saw as an archaic Catholicism was at its peak. Among Protestants themselves, various sects (Anglicans, Puritans, Presbyterians, and such splinter groups as the Dissenters and Arminians) vied with one another in and out of Parliament for ascendancy in political, economic, and religious matters.

The priority given to religion as a major diacritic of a person's or a people's identity in Europe is explicable in the wider framework of European history and culture. All of Europe was undergoing tremendous social and political turmoil. One factor, as we have seen, was the decline of feudalism. These older forms of labor bound to landed estates gradually gave way to a very different contract laborer, who was for hire and, most important, was mobile, a fact that promoted social instability. Social dislocations also resulted from periodic pestilence and disease, going back at least to the Black Death of 1348–1350, which disrupted lives and institutions across the continent. In the absence of a scientific understanding of epidemic diseases and methods to combat them, such crises called forth supernatural explanations and supernatural supplications. No institution was more suitable to deal with this than the church.

Then there was the sudden discovery of a whole new world, drawing men not only into contact with an unanticipated paganism, but also to the lure of great wealth, apparently there for the taking by anyone with sufficient ambition, motivation, and greed. In this context, precedents for how diverse peoples were to relate to one another were absent or elusive. The possibility of adventure and profit attracted men and women away from familiar forms of social control, away from family, kinspeople, employers, patrons, friends, and clients, into interactions with alien merchants, adventurers, pirates, sailors, and other strangers. The frequent anonymity of these new interactions underscored the need for a familiar identity to which others could relate. With growing competition and proto-nationalistic conflicts among the various nations of Europe, the English, like other Europeans, often found it critical to establish political and/or commercial alliances predicated on religious affiliation. Thus, whether one was Catholic, Protestant, or some variant thereof was usually the key not only to the identity of others but also to how they were to be treated.

Another factor underscoring the importance of religious attachment was the existence of an atmosphere thick with the belief in and fear of witchcraft. Anthropologists have long observed that in times of tumultuous social, political, and economic disorder; devastating warfare; or massive and inexplicable natural disasters, human beings often turn to some form of witchcraft to help explain the turmoil, restore some sense of order and stability, and regain control of their lives and natural phenomena.

From about the twelfth century on, Europeans began paying much closer attention to, and showing greater concern with, witches and their activities. This trend reached a crescendo in the fifteenth century as various sects began to break from the Roman Church and devised their own theologies and measures of the faith. Although all of the Protestant groups were opposed to the alleged oppressive nature of the Roman Church, and especially to the Inquisition, they retained much of the underlying theological, historical, and scriptural beliefs. One of these beliefs concerned the nature of the devil and how he manifests himself.

Christian tradition has it that the devil is the Antichrist, the incarnation of all evil, who was in mortal combat with the forces of good to win men's souls. The devil has the ability to enter men's and women's bodies and make compacts with individuals to carry out malevolent aims. Thus one knew the existence of this evil force by the behavior and actions of those individuals in league with the devil. If Christianity created the devil, it also prescribed means of reckoning with this evil—through obedience and living an exemplary life, prayer and the intervention of the Holy Mother, and more directly, the sign of the cross or the use of holy water. A good Christian theoretically could not be harmed by the courtship of the devil.

One's reputation as a good Christian was a major protection against being accused of witchcraft. Those who were not Christians often became identified with the devil, with evil and sinfulness. This sense of identity was solidified in most of Europe, and it helps to explain why relationships between Europeans and the indigenous peoples whom they colonized often became so harsh and cruel. As we shall see later, when heathens were perceived to be as wicked as, or agents of, the devil, then there need be no moral restraints against brutalizing or killing them.

Coinciding with the rise of witchcraft, and a factor in the drastic social changes occurring, was the breakup of the Muslim empire in Spain and the subsequent expulsion of the Jews and Moors. While the Moors made their way back to North Africa and other parts of the Mediterranean world, the Jews began a series of migrations that led some of them to other parts of Europe and to England (and some to America). The growing presence of these Jews came to be perceived as a threat in some parts of Europe, making Christians even more conscious and protective of their own religious identities.

Thus, in the context of a multiplicity of forces that swirled around them and often threatened their sense of security, Christians in Europe magnified the importance of religion not only as a criterion of identity, but as a source of protection, security, and comfort. For many Europeans who traveled abroad, in whatever direction, a strong religious faith was of greater force even than allegiance to king, patron, or community.

HEREDITARY SOCIAL IDENTITY: THE LESSON OF CATHOLIC SPAIN

Because of the mutual influences that the Spanish and English had on one another during the early centuries of exploration and colonization, it is useful to consider those features of Spanish life and thought that may have influenced English ideologies about human differences. As already suggested, the Spanish experience with human diversity was very different from that of the English. Since the eighth century, the Iberian peninsula had been dominated by a civilization that was at that time among the world's most tolerant. Under Muslim hegemony, Spain had experienced the formation of a heterogeneous, multicultural society whose population exhibited a broad range of physical features, from the fair skin and blond hair of older Germanic inhabitants to the dark skin and crinkly hair of West Africans. Religious tolerance and acceptance was the rule. For a while, Muslims, Christians, and Jews led culturally productive lives together and on the whole had remarkably benign relationships, even intermarrying with some frequency (Castro 1971, 499 ff.).

However, with the rise to political power of some of the Christian kingdoms and the thrust to regain Spanish territory for the Catholic Church ("the Reconquest"), beginning as early as the ninth century, Jews and Muslims came under pressure to convert. Conflict ensued, and the entire social system gradually became rigidified into three ethnic-religious "castes," whose relationships in the fifteenth and sixteenth centuries were often characterized by fear, mistrust, envy, and hatred.

Some three hundred thousand Jews became Christian by the end of the fifteenth century, when the marriage of Ferdinand and Isabella had become the political fulcrum symbolizing the rise of modern Catholic Spain. Known as *conversos*, many of these former Jewish families were wealthy and urban; they also constituted the largest proportion of the educated population. With the fall of Granada in 1492, those Jews who had not converted were expelled. The Moors, who tended to be concentrated in the southern regions of Spain, in Valencia, Granada, and Castile, underwent forced baptisms early in the sixteenth century, but their customs, traditions, and language (Arabic) continued intact for a while. Many Moors came to constitute an underclass of laboring people who remained somewhat culturally distinct from the Spanish. Eventually the state expelled all of the Moriscos, as they were called; some two hundred seventy-five thousand were shipped to North Africa between 1609 and 1614.

Jealous of the wealth, power, and influence of the Jewish families who had converted, many of whom were using their new Christian identity to advance themselves in the civil or church hierarchies, some Christian leaders began to question the theological probity of some *conversos*. Many Christians in the countryside of peasant background emerged as antagonists, not only to the declining Muslim influence but to what they believed to be the Jewish domination of trade, banking, scholarship, and the arts. In a social drama characterized by intrigues, petty jealousies, and political machinations, opponents began to charge that some of the *conversos* and their descendants (the New Christians) were secretly practicing Judaism. An Inquisition directed at heretics was established in 1478, sanctioned by the Catholic kings and the church. It was designed to weed out recalcitrant converts, or "secret" Jews, by investigating personal behavior and genealogies for evidence of Jewishness. Some of the seminal ideas that later became basic ingredients of a racial worldview were set into motion during this period of rising Christian intolerance and rampant persecution of Jews and Moors.

A major contribution to Western thought was the belief in the hereditary nature of social status, engendered by the Inquisition; this theme was often interpreted in the most extreme manner. Family ties were closely scrutinized to discover the "hidden Jew," and a social stigma was attached to anyone or any family that had even a remote association with someone prosecuted by the Inquisition. Although lineal descent seemed to be the avenue of heritability of social standing (vis-à-vis the church), this was not consistently observed. The result was that many Spaniards, including some non-Jews, sought a certificate of "purity," which, for a fee, would be issued by the church. It constituted a guarantee of one's genealogical purity from "any admixture of Jew or Moor" or from connections with anyone condemned by the Holy Office (Roth 1964, 197–207). These "certificates of Limpieza de Sangre" (literally, "purity of blood") were not only a major source of revenue for the church but were vital requirements for social mobility, because certain occupations and activities were closed by law to the families of converts.

The idea that social standing is inheritable is an ancient notion associated with many societies characterized by class divisions, occupational specializations, and private or lineage property. Spanish folk ideology and the practices of the Spanish church and state seemed to define Jewishness and Moorishness as almost biological traits, using the idiom of "blood" ties. Elaborate tests for finding social genealogical connections were mechanisms for establishing social placement. And the Spanish use of the term *race*, along with *castas*, for both Jews and Moors, bespeaks a potentially new kind of image of what were essentially ethnic (religious) differences. Ronald Sanders, however, makes an important point about the Spanish attitude toward the treatment of Jews: "In the notion that a certain group within society is unclean and should be quarantined we can perceive an incipient racism—still only incipient, however, since the idea remains that the uncleanness resides in doctrine, not in blood" (1978, 25).

Americo Castro agrees that what was occurring in Spain under the Inquisition was a hardening of ethnic differences rather than an appeal to some biogenetic reality. He says: "From the fifteenth century on, 'purity of blood' has meant consciousness of caste" (1971, 68). It had nothing to do with physical traits or "racial physical type." Yet to equate sections of the society with breeding lines of animals, even symbolically, is to suggest a kind of permanence and immutability to their social qualities that is found only in biological transmission. This attests to the great degree to which Catholic political powers, both papal and secular, were anxious and willing to separate out these Jewish and Moorish populations and eliminate their cultural influences in Spain. In this way, the Catholic leaders of Spain could extend and consolidate their power over a population that was essentially homogeneous in religion and culture and uniformly responsive to imposed laws and sanctions.

But any idea of biologically hereditary social positions was contradicted by the more massive uses of conversion, essentially baptism, to eliminate the presence of Jews and Moors in Spanish society. The vast majority of those converted remained Christian, and the acceptance of these ex-Jews and ex-Muslims and their descendants as legitimate members of the Catholic community and the state is in opposition to the tenets of modern race ideology, which precludes forever the possibility of such a transformation. The apparent contradiction between the reality of the alteration of social identity, under pressure, and the notion that social identity is a concomitant of unique biological features that are exclusive and unalterable was never resolved and probably never even recognized by the thinkers and philosophers of the Inquisition.

One of the reasons for this may be that, though some of the attitudes and beliefs about the Moors and Jews were expressed in a seemingly biological idiom, at the deepest layer of reality was the more archaic sense of interconnectedness between generations that stems from a peasant context. In anthropological studies, some scholars have argued that kinship is a cultural creation, unrelated to actual biological realities. Human populations take the basic facts of our animal biology, sex differences, and bisexual mode of reproduction and configure genealogical connections in a variety of patterns. They then imbue certain of these connections with moral and jural qualities. The result is what anthropologists study as kinship. The fact that kinship patterns, processes, obligations, and connections differ from one population to another is the clearest indication of their arbitrary and culturally created nature. Thus anthropologists have come to recognize that kinship relationships are best analyzed as social, sometimes sociopolitical, constructions.

Throughout most of human history and in all human societies, an emphasis on a true biological connection was absent or irrelevant, in large part because the male role in parturition was little understood. Nor could the biological father (genitor) of a child be precisely known. It was not until the advent of modern technology, beginning with the invention of the microscope and progressing to the discovery of genetic material and the development of powerful electron microscopes in the twentieth century, that one could ascertain with certainty the biological father of any given child. Yet every human society has created the role of the *pater*, or social father, and surrounded it with certain moral and jural prescriptions. In many societies the *pater* is the husband of the mother, regardless of the genitor's identity; it is irrelevant whether the two are not the same. In some societies, a man whose wife does not become pregnant within a reasonable time may, in fact, call upon another man to beget children for him. His (legal) fatherhood of those children, however, is never questioned.

The adoption and purchase of children to create kinspeople in the next generation have been widespread practices throughout human history. Thus, genealogical descent is a jural concept that links men and women together across generations. It is only in the modern world that we have confused biological and social fatherhood, assuming the necessity that both be the same.

This sense of kinship as an elemental social device for structuring human relations has been perpetuated especially among peasant and poor people who have little or no property to transmit but maintain customs of mutual obligations and responsibilities that are deemed essential for the preservation of society. That human beings structure their kinship systems on biological models stemming from the facts of bisexual reproduction should not obscure the fundamental socially invented nature of kinship. That we culturally create such relationships and imbue them with biological parallels in symbols, terms, and expressions conveys a need to make them natural and indissoluble.

Although I have not seen a study of the Spanish Inquisition that expresses this idea, I suspect that any statute under which, for example, a man would have to prove that his grandmother was not a Jew was more a reflection of the real fact that social behavior, identity, and wealth are transmitted within the genealogical context of families than a belief that Jewishness actually resides in the blood. It reflected the jural dimensions of structured kinship rather than the fact of biological connection, the significance of the *pater* rather than the genitor. The cognitive connection linking biology with social status did not appear until the crystallization of the idea of race in the eighteenth century.

A clearly related aspect of the Spanish experience is the restructuring of the Spanish state as a Catholic society. The thrust toward homogeneity in society by religion, certainly not by "bloodline," was one of the many ramifications of nation-state building in Europe in general.[12] Obviously such homogeneity is best facilitated by eliminating those sects that vary from the desired theology, belief, and ritual. The easiest way to make Spain exclusively Catholic was to convert non-Catholics, a process totally unrelated to biology, and this is what was done.

Exclusiveness, however, is fundamental to the ideology of race, and it can only be maintained by the erection of sociocultural boundaries between populations that (1) become broad barriers against interaction between "races," (2) preclude any possibility of egalitarian relationships, and (3) do not recognize or provide for intermediate realities. Such boundaries are most effective when they can be transmuted into a biological axiom. The Spanish experience is suggestive in that it came very close to infusing a "racial" element into the criteria of social identity, but more important was its elevation of religious-cultural homogeneity to a high social value.

The Spanish brought with them to the New World many of the cultural values and features of the Inquisition era and grafted them onto the societies created in the colonial setting. Among these were the idea of *castas*, the belief that the "purity" of one's Hispanic genealogy entitled one to higher social status; the fear of mixed or tainted lineage; the judicial codes, customs and proceedings of the Inquisition; religious fervor and intolerance; and most of all the customs, practices, and traditions of medieval slavery. In the context of a colonial society that included peoples from different areas of the world with extensive physical variations among them, the Spanish came very close to equating social identity with physical variation. But as we will see in chapter

6, the ranking system was never as carefully structured and rigidified as in the English colonies. Some of the Spanish customs and habits of thought were no doubt picked up by the English.

Thus some of the major ingredients for the ideology and worldview of "race" were present in the thought and practice of both the Spanish and English peoples during the critical period when European colonial settlements in the New World were established. All of the European conquerors and colonizers turned to the use of the term *race (raza, race, reazza)*. They all shared a common belief that those whom they conquered were in some sense "savages," despite the recognized diversity among the indigenous cultures and the different conceptions of savagery among the Europeans. And all of the Europeans engaged in the practice of slavery, both with Indians and imported Africans. Yet the degree to which they conceptualized and institutionalized the perceived differences varied, as we shall see later, for reasons that relate to their own cultural histories, experiences, and demographic realities. The English took the term *race* and molded it into a phenomenon unlike that of their competitors, structuring closed and exclusive groups out of the mélange of peoples of the Americas. It is to the history of the English in America that we now turn to examine those facets of culture and experience that led them to this point.

NOTES

1. See Boies Penrose 1955 for a description of early travels by Europeans and the fables, myths, and tales concocted by them about peoples and places that were still unknown.

2. In his histories of the Persian Wars, Herodotus lists upward of two dozen states and ethnic groups that were involved in the wars. They came from far-ranging regions around the eastern Mediterranean, the Middle East, North Africa, and East Africa. He distinguishes them not only by their ethnic names and sometimes a former name, but most particularly by their military dress and types of arms. The only time he mentions physical variations among these very diverse peoples is a note, almost in passing, that there are two nations of Ethiopians, who differ only in their language, and that eastern Ethiopians have straight hair "while they of Libya are more wooly-haired than any other people in the world" (Godolphin 1942).

3. Karl Marx and Max Weber were major nineteenth-century writers who provided theoretical paradigms for the transition from peasant feudal society to industrial capitalism. For more than a century, many historians of England have documented, interpreted, and reinterpreted the development of modern capitalism and its attendant features. The theory simplified here is fairly conventional. See, for example, Bober [1927] 1965; Genovese and Fox-Genovese 1983; and Macfarlane 1978.

4. Most of Europe had developed a dual or bilateral system of kinship in which connections on both sides, maternal and paternal, were given almost equal recognition. A corollary and perhaps consequence of this was the absence of corporate kinship groups with stable,

permanent, and exclusive membership. Instead, each generation of siblings had a circle of relatives unique to it, known as a kindred, radiating outward on both sides. Obligations of kinspeople were based loosely on genealogical closeness, with the greatest sense of solidarity between brothers, then first cousins, second cousins, and so forth. In some cases, this could be extended to sixth or seventh cousins, but at that distance (which may have corresponded to geographic distance) the sense of responsibility often became muted.

5. See especially Macfarlane 1978, chap. 7, in which he observes that some of these traits of the English, described by a writer of the late fifteenth century, most certainly evolved long before that time.

6. Canny 1973; Quinn 1966; and Jones 1964 are some of the historians who have looked at this phenomenon. But the most detailed exploration of this theme in recent years has been that of Theodore Allen (1994, 1997).

7. See the section on pastoralism in Cohen 1974 and the papers in Goldschmidt 1965. Although I concur with the perspective that views cultures as open, dynamic systems, it is also true that there are persisting themes manifest over broad ranges of time in many areas of the world. My concern here is the frequent examples of seemingly irreconcilable differences and overt hostilities that have recurred between mobile herding societies and sedentary cultivators.

8. Quoted in Myers 1983, 15.

9. See brief descriptions of the Munster and Ulster uprisings and the brutal reprisals and eventual conquests by the British forces in Liggio 1976 and Quinn 1966. Theodore Allen's more recent two-volume study (1994, 1997) goes into greater detail in describing the attitudes and practices of the English in Ireland. He observes clear analogies between the English treatment of the Irish and their later interactions with Native Americans and Africans in the New World.

10. After some of their military campaigns in Ireland, the English pursued a scorched-earth policy, destroying livestock and vegetation so that the Irish would be reduced to famine. It was reported that some Irish resorted to eating human flesh, thus confirming the imagery of cannibalism (Quinn 1966, 132).

11. The first recorded incident of Irish slaves taken to the Caribbean occurred in 1612. They continued to be transported at various times during the first half of the century. No one knows how many Irish slaves were sent to the New World. Some estimates are as high as three hundred thousand, although the English apparently did not keep good records of these transactions. For numerous references, Google "Irish Slaves in the Caribbean."

12. Robert Berkhofer Jr. has recognized the political significance of such homogeneity. "One king, one faith, one law," he notes, protect the political stability of new regimes in a time of religious (and secular) conflicts. Robert Berkhofer Jr., personal communication, 1993.

CHAPTER 4

The Growth of the English Ideology About Human Differences in America

In the North American colonies, the ideological components of race grew and flourished; the sense of exclusiveness and discreteness of group membership, the ranking of groups according to English cultural standards of Christianity and civilization, and the explanation of behavior and ranking in terms of the innate and distinct nature of biophysically defined groups evolved together. The elements may have appeared at different stages, but they were ultimately synthesized into a systematic set of coherent beliefs that clearly served the needs and desires of their creators. One can identify some of the stages in this process in certain specific circumstances, decisions, and events. The step-by-step process by which the idea of *race* and *races* was manufactured can be seen in the events and especially in laws that formalized and institutionalized the differences among the early populations. These processes are explored in this and the next chapter.

EARLIEST CONTACTS

The first colonization attempts on the part of the English took place in the late sixteenth century. Like other Europeans, the English had acquired a taste for sugar, spices, and other goods that were imported from the East. They also had been the consumer beneficiaries of thriving sugar plantations, on Cyprus and other Mediterranean islands, which were worked by a mixture of free and slave labor. This was a pattern of exploitation that the Spanish and Portuguese had already transmitted to the New World.

The English were keenly aware of the large colonial enterprises and the great wealth that the Spanish and Portuguese were deriving from them. As early as 1497, John Cabot had tried to establish for England a claim to Labrador and Newfoundland. Throughout the sixteenth century, English contacts with Spanish merchants, both peaceable and belligerent, increased. Some Englishmen, like Sebastian Cabot, hired themselves into the service of the Spanish.[1] An English ship under the leadership of John Rut reached Santo Domingo in 1527 to trade in wool and linen. Englishmen entered the slave trade with John Hawkins's trips in the 1560s to the west coast of Africa, during which he plundered villages and kidnapped hundreds of people. The queen herself, Elizabeth I, invested in some of his slaving enterprises in 1567. Hawkins involved his cousin, Francis Drake, in some of his trips, and the latter subsequently amassed a fortune through piracy of Spanish ships in the Caribbean and plunder of the indigenous peoples.

In Panama, Drake made alliances with a group of slaves known as Cimarrons, who had escaped from their Spanish masters and formed communities deep in the interior. They periodically raided the Spanish settlements and helped Drake and his men hijack caravans of Spanish goods crossing the isthmus to Atlantic ports. Edmund Morgan (1975) emphasized the significance of such an alliance. He noted that even though Drake and other English adventurers had engaged in slaving from time to time, they were not averse to forming unions with black Africans against the Spanish. They indeed "had cast themselves as liberators and had allied with blacks against whites. . . . The alliance seems to have been untroubled by racial prejudice" (13). Drake frequently freed Indian and African slaves from the Spanish; in 1586 he arrived on Roanoke Island (see below) with a shipload of Indians and Negroes, whom he left there (41–42).

By the latter part of the sixteenth century, Englishmen like Humphrey Gilbert, John Davis, Ralph Lane, and Walter Raleigh were heavily involved in explorations of the coasts of North America as organizers or active explorers, from Newfoundland to Florida and the Caribbean. Some found it profitable to plunder Indian villages or seize vulnerable Spanish and French ships.

In the 1580s, Walter Raleigh was given a patent to establish a colony that would carry the name Virginia (after the virgin queen, Elizabeth). He sent out ships in 1584 to scout the area and find a suitable location. His emissaries returned with positive descriptions of Roanoke Island and its indigenous inhabitants. Their glowing account was designed to promote the colonial enterprise (Kupperman 1984). In 1585, Richard Grenville arrived on Roanoke with six hundred men. A plunderer and pirate of aristocratic background, as were many of the other explorers, Grenville came into conflict with the Indians, which he resolved by burning an Indian village and adjacent cornfields. When he departed for home he left behind a party of one hundred men to explore the area around Roanoke. When Francis Drake arrived in the following year, all of the surviving men chose to return with him to England, thus abandoning the project.

In 1587 a new group of potential settlers, this time including women and children, arrived on Roanoke. John White, selected as governor, returned to England for supplies after a few weeks. According to Carl Sauer, he left a colony of "would-be settlers who knew nothing of the country. . . . The innocents were left on Roanoke Island; their governor who had experience of the country sailed home for supplies and left them to face an indefinite time in ignorance and inevitable need" (1971, 264). By the time White attempted to reestablish contact with the infant colony in 1590, there was no sign of the "innocents." The little settlement was lost, presumably exterminated by Indians, although there remains the probability that some simply merged into existing Indian populations (Sauer 1971, 253, 301; see also Kupperman 1984).

The history of these earliest contacts between English adventurers and the native populations of the coastal regions of the Americas is of interest because of the nature of the relationships, however tenuous, that were established. Historians point out that in the first Roanoke Island expedition, the inhabitants not only approached the newcomers without any overt manifestation of fear or doubt, but actually welcomed them with open arms. The native peoples were described as "very handsome and goodly people, and in their behavior as mannerly and civil as any of Europe" (quoted in Sauer 1971, 252). Throughout the six weeks of that first stay, the Indians were hospitable; their guests were entertained with "all love and kindness." Most revealing was the report that "we found the people most gentle, loving and faithful, void of all guile and treason, and such as lived after the manner of the golden rule" (252). The Indians brought food daily to the visitors. If there ever was a universal primordial reaction of fear toward strangers, the indigenous peoples of the Americas had never heard of it.

On the second Roanoke expedition, the Indians again came to the aid of the English. But when some of the English colonists began to help themselves to food in the fields and storage areas, to cross into Indian lands that were not open to them, and to generally ignore Indian rights and customs, the latter began to withdraw support. Many even decided to flee from the strange ingrates who made such arrogant demands of them.

Ronald Sanders suggests that a division between two types of colonists was discernible on that expedition: "those, on the one hand, who were inclined to resort to force as soon as possible in the resolution of all problems with the Indians, and those, on the other, who clung to the ideals of gentleness and carefully cultivated friendship that had been advocated by humanists back in England" (1978, 233). Ralph Lane, whom Raleigh had appointed governor of the colony, was a leader of the pro-force-and-violence contingent; it is not surprising that he, like Raleigh, had dealt with "savages" while doing military service in Ireland.

The earliest settlers at Jamestown, which became the first permanent English settlement in 1607, also found the Indians unexpectedly generous, kind, and curious, willing to enter into amiable trading relationships, teach the colonists what they needed to know to survive, and learn from them. According to Gary Nash, the Indians provided much-needed food for the colony in its early years, even though much of it was stolen by the settlers (1992, 53–59). The English were not the only ones to experience the initial warm hospitality of Indians. The Dutch, who settled a fur-trading station in Albany in 1614, and the French, who had established relations with the Indians of Quebec and in the St. Lawrence River area, had all engaged in amicable relationships with the Indians and peacefully promoted trade.[2] Thus all the settlers had reason to form positive views of the Indians.

Yet the English consistently distrusted the Indians, interpreting their generosity and friendliness as, potentially at least, trickery and deception. This distrust seemed to reflect ambivalent feelings that were never resolved during the first years of colonization. Europeans simultaneously maintained two contradictory views of the Indians, which had been formed even before they sailed to the New World (Berkhofer 1978; Bidney 1954; Hoover 1976; Kupperman 1984; Nash 1986, 1992; Pearce 1953). On the one hand, there was a relatively benign and positive attitude inspired by the writings of Spanish travelers like Columbus and Giovanni da Verrazzano, which depicted the Indians as civil, honest, uncorrupted, generous, and noble.[3] This view was buttressed by the missionary zeal of some Puritans, whose stated objective was the eventual conversion of the natives and their assimilation into Christian society. Such conversions were indeed the genuine and sincere goal of many of the settlers, as Alden Vaughan has emphasized (1965). It was also the view of those whose main purpose was trade or exploration to find a northwest passage to China.

This benevolent view later came to be symbolized in the stereotypic phrase "the noble savage," an image that became more pronounced in the literature of philosophers and other intellectuals in Europe, particularly during the eighteenth century, than in the thoughts of the colonists. It had its roots in some of the descriptions of, and attitudes toward, Indians held by many early missionaries beginning in the sixteenth century, particularly the Dominicans and Jesuits. It was a charitable, and perhaps gratuitous, apprehension of barbarous folk as being potentially moral beings, innocent and trustworthy and hungering for the word of the true god. Their conversion would provide a magnificent expansion of the Christian religion. The theological underpinnings of this perception of the indigenes was the unity of man under the fatherhood of a single god.

On the other hand, the image of Indians as fearsome, brutish, and depraved also persisted in many English minds. These images too were based in part on the many reports of the early Portuguese and Spanish explorers that were unfavorable to the native populations. During the latter part of the sixteenth century, many pamphlets were published that "were filled with portraits of the Indians as crafty, brutal, loathsome half-men [with] cannibalistic instincts" (Nash 1992, 37). Bizarre and unexplainable customs, heinous practices, nakedness, lascivious behavior, uncleanliness, and bestiality also were said to characterize the Indians.

Gary Nash, Howard Mumford Jones, and Nicholas Canny show few doubts about another source of the strong impulse on the part of English settlers to accept the more negative image of the Indians, despite personal experiences of kindness and hospitality and pragmatic reasons for establishing friendships. Nash makes a telling point. He notes that when trade with the Indians was uppermost in English minds and their services were needed in the search for a northwest passage or for mineral wealth, the Indians were portrayed as "primitive but winsome, as ignorant but receptive individuals. If treated kindly, they could be wooed and won to the advantages of trade and cooperation." But "when permanent settlement became the primary English concern . . . and land the object of desire, the image of the Indian as a hostile savage became ascendant in the English mind" (1972, 132–133; see also Berkhofer 1978; Nash 1992).

Karen Kupperman explains the hostility that the English exhibited at Roanoke toward the Indians in terms of the English theory of human nature. The English felt that if they showed weakness or vulnerability, this would invite contempt from the Indians. "People of this period seem to have felt that those who were vulnerable were responsible for whatever happened to them; blame attached to them as much as to anyone who attacked or cheated them. . . . When one was vulnerable, the assumption was that someone would inevitably take advantage of that fact" (1984, 69). The use of force was thus justified, with violence as the harbinger of English strength and invulnerability.

THE ENSUING CONFLICTS

The contacts between the English and the natives in the Americas soon devolved into open conflicts and intrigues. In 1608 Captain John Smith burned Indian canoes and corn in order to extort food from and frighten the Indians (Hoover 1976, 18; Morgan 1975, chap. 4). Intimidation and acts of aggression against the Indians became frequent on an individual level and a regular policy for obtaining food and other goods. According to Morgan, the early Virginia settlers, an unusually large number of whom were nobles and gentry, had not come to the colony prepared to grow food for themselves, an enterprise that many thought beneath them. They preferred to beg, bribe, and steal from the Indians (1975, chaps. 3, 4). Moreover, it is clear that the English expected resistance, even violent resistance, to their takeover of Indian lands and resources. Some of the descriptions of the brutal and humiliating behavior of individuals toward Indians prompt the conclusion that the English were, perhaps unconsciously, trying to provoke the Indians into a violent confrontation (Lauber [1913] 1970).

The inevitable happened. After some colonists murdered a well-known Indian leader in 1622, the Indians attacked Chesapeake Colony, killing 347 of 1,240 persons, over a quarter of the colony's inhabitants (Morgan 1975, 101). This had the effect that perhaps most Englishmen unconsciously wanted and could now even verbalize. It swept aside whatever benign attitudes they had developed toward the Indians, eliminating any inhibitions about attacking and destroying Indian villages. The Reverend Samuel Purchas, a chronicler of this history from the settlers' point of view, expressed his relief that now the English "have the right to do virtually as they please—or rather, virtually as God would be pleased to have them do" (Pearce 1953, 7).

The colonizers' retaliation was brutal. Some tribes were completely destroyed; others were subdued and their members forced into slavery. Dwight Hoover notes that from 1622 to 1629, settlers attacked and burned the crops of all the remaining Indian villages every summer (1976, 19). Despite intrigues and pacts with Indian leaders like Powhatan, agitation against the Indians swept through the settlements and even reached overseas. A tract was published in London encouraging not only the instigation of hostilities toward the Indians but also their enslavement (Lauber [1913] 1970, 118).

Further Indian attacks led to even more brutal reprisals on the part of the English, including large-scale campaigns in 1644 and 1676. The inexorable expansion of the colony and the superior European weaponry brought about the rapid decimation of the Indians. Through treachery and deceit, such as William Tucker's poisoning of two hundred Indians invited ostensibly to celebrate a peace treaty, Virginians acted out their hostility toward the Indians. Many Indians died of disease and malnutrition, often induced by deliberate destruction of their fields and stores. Others fled farther inland, only to find themselves eventually threatened by the incursions of new settlers. Those who remained in the vicinity of the colonial settlements were reduced to the status of impoverished laborers and slaves, occupying the most degraded and subservient positions on the outskirts of an increasingly heterogeneous society.

In the Massachusetts Bay Colony and other New England settlements, overt hostilities were a bit later in arriving, but they were equally fierce. Puritan colonists who took seriously their mission to proselytize among the Indians were able to realize some success. Christian converts, however, were forced to form their own congregations and to live within the confines of their own towns, on which numerous restrictions were placed. No attempt was made to assimilate them within the social arena of the colony itself. These "Praying Indians" endeavored to acquire the accoutrements of "civilization" while meeting all the demands that the Puritans imposed on them. Yet as G. E. Thomas tells us, they found that despite their loyalty and proven commitment, "white racism and local white land hunger made their color alone an insurmountable barrier" (1975, 20 n). What Thomas reveals here is extreme English contempt for the native population. Their color and physiognomy made them visibly different, a fact that undoubtedly facilitated the discrimination they experienced at the hands of the English. But physical features alone were insignificant as causal factors in the propagation of English scorn and abuse. They had already learned patterns of inhumanity and contempt for others from their experiences with the Irish, a people physically similar to themselves.

When the violence did come, it was the logical outcome of the policies and practices of the Puritans. Thomas claims that "continued encroachment of their land became the Indians' main grievance and the prime cause of violence between Indians and whites" (1975, 11). A series of brutal confrontations between individuals had a lasting effect on relationships between Indians and whites. Nash speaks of petty acts of violence and plunder by the white settlers (1992, chaps. 2, 3, 6). Sometimes such acts became provocations to additional violence, as in the case of Thomas Weston at Wessagusset in 1621. Weston settled in the area with a group of other Europeans who were by all accounts ruffians and scoundrels. When they ran out of food, they began to rob the Indians. When the Indians complained to the Plymouth officials, the latter simply interpreted their complaints as a threat to the colony. Miles Standish was sent to deal with the situation. In March 1623, he and his men attacked, chased down, and murdered some of the complaining Indians without warning. This, says Thomas, became the standard response of the Puritans to any Indian resistance or complaint. "No Indian dared raise his hand or even his voice against a white, even in defense of his life, family or property" (1975, 12).

One of the major historical confrontations was the Pequot War of 1637, the first of a series of wars that devastated the Indian populations and left the survivors in shambles. Again, the fighting was triggered by the actions of certain Europeans with reputations among the colonists as renegades and exiles. After Captain John Stone, himself a violent man, kidnapped two Indians on the Thames River in 1634, he was killed by Pequot Indians. In 1636 another renegade white man was killed for reasons that the Puritans refused to allow the Indians to explain. Instead, John Endecott was commissioned to lead a Puritan force to avenge this death and punish the Indians. He burned down the Block Island Indian village and fields and then, in violation of existing treaties, invaded the mainland Pequot territory. In May 1637, John Mason launched a major attack on the Pequot village at Mystic Fort, burning the village and murdering five or six hundred Indians, including women and children. The few survivors were reduced to slavery, and many of these were sold to plantation owners in the Caribbean. An even more insidious reason for the attack on Mystic Fort was revealed in Mason's report: "Thus the Lord was pleased to smite our enemies in the hinder parts and to give us their land afor and inheritance" (quoted in Thomas 1975, 15).

Perhaps the most vicious and brutal of all the battles was King Philip's War (Matacom's War) of 1675. As in the other conflicts, the basic issue was that of the land rights of the Indians, in this case the Wampanoag and their Sachem King Philip (Matacom). The Indians' complaints about white incursions led to meetings with the Plymouth leaders, as a consequence of which the Indians were forced to give up some of their arms. After three Wampanoag Indians were sentenced to death on trumped-up charges and a white youth killed another Indian, some of Matacom's people attacked the village of Swansea.

When the war started, it involved Indians on both sides, in part because of traditional enmity between certain tribes. But what was particularly tragic, aside from the extensive involvement of so many different Indian groups, was the fact that the war led the colonists to turn against the Christian tribes who had started as their allies. Christian Indians were trusted no more than were the heathens. The uniformity with which all Indians were perceived reflected the growing dichotomy in English attitudes. Ignoring the diversity among Indian peoples, Europeans had begun to homogenize all Indians into an inferior category, not only because of their conquests but because of the exaggerated differences between indigenous peoples and themselves. Eventually most of the Native Americans in the area were forced onto restricted reservations, the first to be established for North America's indigenous peoples.

Even after cessation of the major battles of King Philip's War, the violence continued. Considerable raping and kidnapping of Indians continued, and hundreds of captured natives were sold to places as far away as the West Indies (Lauber [1913] 1970; Nash 1992). Remnants of some tribes fled north to the French territories, where they received better treatment at the hands of a very different European ethnic group. The rest scattered throughout the northeast, never again to reestablish their traditional culture and social lifeways. Friendly Indians were confined to reservations, while bounties were offered for the scalps of "hostiles," a practice that continued throughout the first half of the eighteenth century.

Many American historians have emphasized that some of the early Puritan settlers made a genuine and sincere effort to convert and civilize the Indians, and that their motivations and actions were essentially magnanimous. They stress the role of such men as Roger Williams, who held quite liberal views about the potential for creating a heterogeneous, multicultural society in the New World. But Berkhofer, Morgan, Nash, Pearce, and Thomas provide overwhelming evidence of an essentially self-serving, brutal, and aggressive colonizing people who devised all manner of strategies for justifying their inhumanity toward the Indians and seemed to have few ethical or moral compunctions about their actions.

In summing up this era and the complex realities of the earliest American settlements, any reviewer of the literature is impressed by two factors. One is the degree to which religion and God were used as justifications for both the colonization of North America and the barbaric maltreatment of the Indians. The second is the intriguing similarities between the conquest and colonization of Ireland and the attitudes engendered during this process and the subsequent colonization of the New World, with its associated prejudices toward the Indians. Both factors require further exploration, since they figure so prominently in the creation of racial ideology.

THE BACKING OF GOD AND OTHER JUSTIFICATIONS FOR CONQUEST

From the very beginnings of English overseas exploration and trade, the rationale most frequently expressed was that such ventures were sanctioned by God. John Hawkins, the earliest and most successful of the English slave traders, once led an expedition of slave ships with names such as *Jesus of Lubeck* and *John the Baptist* (Wright 1965, 9). Not only were ships commonly given names with biblical references, but virtually all had clerics aboard to bless the expedition. Leaders of expeditions invariably referred to the Lord's blessings and special care for them, his children, in their ship's logs.

Without question, the military dominance of the English and their success in ultimately destroying the Indians and their cultures were seen as God's will, no matter how brutal and insensitive their actions and how innocent the Indian victims. A high degree of self-righteousness and arrogance characterized the religious beliefs particularly of the Puritans. Products of the Protestant Reformation, the Puritans had evolved a sharply focused sense of the nature of salvation and what was needed to achieve it. Their theology relinquished the vast majority of souls on Earth to be damned forever. Only the select few would ultimately enter the glorious kingdom of God. These were individuals who adhered strictly to Puritan ideals of proper behavior and laid claims to personal salvation through faith. Knowledge of Christ, including a personal relationship with him, was a prerequisite. In their strict division of the world into the saved and the damned, there was no explicit, or intrinsic, requirement for tolerance and understanding of others. And there was no commitment to humanistic values that might have inhibited or curtailed the excessive cruelty dispensed to the damned. Instead, the Puritans developed the very convenient belief that all sinners, witches, and savages who opposed the word of God deserved the atrocities inflicted upon them. These were a fitting retribution for their opposition to the civilizing efforts of Christianity.

In the New England area, many settlers rejoiced at the extraordinary decline of the Indian population due to epidemic diseases. John Winthrop, who led the Massachusetts Bay Colony in the 1630s and 1640s, wrote that the smallpox epidemic of 1617 was God's way of "thinning out" the Indian population to make room for the Puritans. Later he recorded that the Indians "are neere all dead of the small Poxe, so the Lord hathe cleared our title to what we possess" (quoted in Nash 1972, 136).

According to Louis Wright, it was the preachers of England who "induced in public consciousness a sense of mission, a feeling often not put into words but nonetheless strong, that Englishmen had a destiny overseas" (1965, 151). These preachers, both Anglican and Puritan, had a powerful influence on the colonization process. From their pulpits and in their publications, they exhorted the public to become involved in the colonization of the New World, a region seen as a new Canaan. The commercial companies and promoters of colonization encouraged the clergy to advertise their schemes.

The English clergy themselves were motivated by a number of considerations, all of which were highly publicized at the time. Chief among these was their desire to thwart the further spread of Catholicism. The success of Spanish proselytizing in the New World was well known, and nothing irked the Protestants so much as the idea of Spain winning the battle for new souls. Economic and political competition with the Spanish intensified these feelings of religious antagonism. The defeat of the Spanish Armada had made the planting of English colonies all the more pressing.

Another important reason for ministerial preachments was the increasingly large numbers of the poor and unemployed who roamed the streets and byways of English cities. Several lines of reasoning led clergymen to advocate the exportation of these "vagabonds" to the new colonies. As educated men, they concluded that England was facing a problem of overpopulation, and there was a need to do something about this demographic situation. Moreover, unemployment was acute in many areas, and existing charitable institutions were hard pressed to provide sufficient services to an expanding impoverished class. The clergy saw colonization as a way of siphoning off an excess of able-bodied workers and putting them to useful labor in the plantations overseas.

Exhortations to send the poor and unemployed off to the colonies should be understood within a wider framework of English, and specifically Puritan, beliefs. Seventeenth-century preachers, we are told, "looked upon idleness and consequent poverty as moral iniquities" (Wright 1965, 152). Those virtues most valued in the Puritan lifestyle were work, sobriety, thrift, diligence, and honesty. An idle or lazy person would be lacking in all of these traits. Thus poverty, immorality, and sloth were bound together in the Puritan mind as evils that had to be overcome, if necessary by forced labor. Hoover claims that the Puritans created a new class of evil people, the poor, who were seen as "being wicked and outside the bonds of society" (1976, 31). Colonization would not only relieve poverty at home but, by putting sinful, idle men and women to work, it would also restore them to the true and proper values of religion and improve their characters.

Finally, Wright argues that many English clergymen, who "were almost unanimous in supporting colonization in America" (1965, 86), were motivated by a sincere desire to save the souls of the heathens of America. They were convinced, and they convinced others, that God had commanded them to go forth and preach the gospel. There was no better setting in which to do this than among the indigenes of newly discovered lands. However, this missionary zeal peaked in the early stages of settlement, as we have seen. The Puritans and their church leaders soon concluded that if the savage could not be saved from himself, his extermination would be a worthy enterprise in the sight of the Lord. This notion of a God-given right to mistreat others, especially for private gain, runs through much of Western culture, and after the emergence of capitalism it became especially acute in North America.

When they were not invoking God's blessings or permission for their exploitation of the Indians, the colonizers provided other rational and pragmatic arguments for co-opting Indian lands. One was that the Indians did not make proper use of the land "and thus could be justly deprived of it by the more enterprising English" (Canny 1973, 596). Such an argument, as we have seen, had been invoked to force the Irish off their lands. A more pervasive argument was the ancient one of the right of conquest. This was often linked to a religious position; God had chosen the English to find these new shores, so he must have wanted them to possess such bountiful land. Conquest was thus God's ordained plan; it was he who had led them thence. The Puritans, as God's "chosen people," were responsible merely for carrying out his will.

Although God's supposed will should have been sufficient, an even more secular and philosophical argument was also put forth, which derived from some knowledge of ancient codes of laws. John Winthrop expressed this in his rationalization of English rights to land in North America. There are, he declared, two types of rights that God has given mankind: natural rights and civil rights. Natural rights were held by all men, including those who live in a state of nature; under a system of natural rights, land and resources are held in common. But when some men began to enclose parcels of land and hold them separate from others, to have a settled habitation on it, and to use domesticated cattle to improve the land, then they acquired civil rights to the land. Because the Indians had not done these things, they gained no civil rights, retaining only the natural ones. And because the English clearly had developed superior modes of utilizing land, they enjoyed lawful civil rights that inevitably took precedence over natural rights. Under this argument, superior, "civilized" people had legitimate cause to seize land, as long as they left sufficient areas for the "uncivilized" to exercise their natural rights (Thomas 1975).

Partly because of the myths of origin that Americans created for themselves, too few Americans have sufficiently noted the cruel and barbaric treatment that the English imposed on the Indians, although the evidence, largely from the pens of the colonists themselves, is overwhelming. The incidents described above—in no way exceptional—attest to extreme and callous brutality and a policy of treachery and deceit that seems hardly consonant with the English history of concern for the rights of mankind and even less with England's image of itself as the most "civilized" of the European nations.

Some historians have labored hard to explain this seeming paradox. Although we might accept Nash's psychologically oriented argument that the dehumanization of the Indian was "one means of justifying one's own inhumanity" (1972, 137), this is a somewhat circular or teleological explication that does not reveal much about underlying causes. Nicholas Canny's explanation (1973) follows in a similar vein to that of Winthrop Jordan (1968). Both refer to the insecurities and uncertainties of the English and their need to know who they were in a rapidly changing society and in a setting in which they constantly felt threatened. More evident than such psychological needs, however, were the drives to achieve power and control, to establish and maintain political, economic, and social dominance, all of which arose from an English sense of moral and cultural superiority. The Indians, said Morgan, "presented a challenge . . . to their image of themselves, to their self-esteem, to their conviction of their own superiority over foreigners, and especially over barbarous foreigners like the Irish and the Indians" (1975, 89).

Christian values regarding humane behavior—the Sermon on the Mount, the Golden Rule, and the Ten Commandments—had little impact on the minds, morals, and consciences of the settlers. Jordan gives a brief analysis of the kind of Christianity that developed among the English after the Protestant Reformation. He argues that it was "altered in the direction of Biblicism, personal piety, individual judgment, and more intense self-scrutiny and internalized control" (1968, 40). Englishmen came to evaluate and judge themselves according to their own individual interpretations of the scriptures. The older institutional and external constraints of Catholicism were replaced with a less certain and more nebulous sense of personal responsibility and control.

Such inner controls, however, were virtually antithetical to the spirit of adventurism and greed that characterized the English in the seventeenth century and later. English colonists were caught up in a dilemma that might have evoked massive ambivalence, leading to a catatonic inability to take action. Instead, or perhaps because of this, too many of them in the New World opted for the path of moral and ethical duplicity, hypocrisy, and the priority of aggrandizing wealth no matter the cost. A self-serving moral order had replaced the constraints once exercised by the institutions of family, kinship, class, community, and church. It was not merely self-control that the new settlers sought; it was control over others and over potentially advantageous situations and resources. Jordan's discussion of an age driven by the twin spirits of adventure and control euphemistically glosses over this reality. But Morgan's description of the ruthless, coldhearted, and avaricious men who led or participated in the Virginia colony leaves us little room for doubt (1975).

THE NEW SAVAGES

The seemingly gratuitous violence and brutality of the English settlers are incomprehensible without reference to a second factor, which reaches beyond religion. This is the wider historical context of five hundred years of conflict with the Irish and the patterns of violent interaction that it had generated. David Quinn, Nicholas Canny, Leonard Liggio, Gary Nash, Theodore Allen, and other historians have emphasized the significant parallels between the English attempt to conquer and colonize Ireland and their subsequent exploration, conquest, and colonization of North America and the Caribbean. What appears obvious is that the motivations, objectives, and rationalizations of individuals, many of whom were involved in both Irish and American colonial enterprises, were essentially the same. The one generated interest in the other, as Quinn suggests: "Ireland in a real sense turned English minds toward America" (1966, 106). Ireland also provided the standard of comparison by which other foreign societies and cultures would be judged.

The identity of a large number of individuals involved in both the Irish conquests and the colonization of the New World would suggest similarities of purpose and methods, even if there were no written records of such. As Liggio notes, "many with experiences in Ireland had been active in the plans for the colonies in America and their experience with the natives of Ireland was an important part of the heritage which they transferred to the treatment of the natives of America." He adds that "more than forty members of the Virginia Company had an interest in Irish conquests and the colonization of Englishmen in Ireland" (1976, 28). Among the names most familiar to Americans are Sir Walter Raleigh, Lord De La Warre, John Cabot, Humphrey Gilbert, Sir Richard Grenville, Lord George Carew, and Sir Francis Drake.[4]

Patrick O'Farrell tells us that the English early established a habit of violence in the attempted settlement of Irish affairs (1971, 6). Moreover, the sense of a religious mission, the rightness of their cause as justification for their violence, was also a part of the ideology driving the Irish conquest. English takeovers of land from the Irish and the Indians followed much the same methodologies and strategies and had the same consequences. The forced removal of those who resisted and the justification of such removals in the name of conquest, the presumed "legal" rights of cultivators over nomads, and religious motivations characterized English encounters with both peoples. Jones points out that "the doctrine that the only good Indian is a dead Indian first took shape in the belief that the only good Irishman is a dead Irishman" (1942, 454). Lord Essex's slaughter of the entire population of Rathlin Island in 1574, about six hundred people, had its parallels in the New World—for example, in the killing of the inhabitants of Mystic Fort in 1637. The rationales for such brutality were virtually the same. Canny quotes a letter from Barkley about Essex's final solution, "how godly a dede it is to overthrowe so wicked a race the world may judge: for my part I thinke there canot be a greater sacryfice to God" (1973, 581). Finally, the belief that the Indians were incapable of civilization and therefore merited no attempt at redemption, which rapidly took root after the hostilities at Chesapeake Bay in 1622, stemmed directly from the Irish experience, especially the ruthless developments of the late sixteenth and early seventeenth centuries.

Many factors thus influenced English perceptions of and reactions to the Indians. English interaction with the Irish, guided by their desire for expansion; greed for land; and ethnocentric view of the superiority of their own English laws, customs, and religion, had generated in their cultural perspectives a clearly focused view of savagery. By the end of the sixteenth century, O'Farrell tells us, "the English image of the Irishman was that of a savage" (1971, 25). And the Indians of the Americas, particularly as their very presence became an impediment to similar English aspirations, could be perceived as being very much like the "wild Irish." Such a transference of symbolic references was probably inevitable, in part because, at least to the English, there were some deeply disturbing similarities.

Both the Irish and the Indians seemed to lack shame, in that they went about naked with little care about the visibility of even their "most private parts." Both were polygamous, and the combination of nudity and plural marriage was interpreted as stemming from sexual immorality. The way of life of both groups was viewed as disorderly, without government or laws, and most important of all, with no concept of private property. They were both perceived as nomadic peoples who did not appear to make use of the bountiful land that God had given them. In addition, they both resisted, often ferociously, attempts on the part of the English to "civilize" them. What were thought to be their obsessive love of freedom, carefree lifestyles, and brutish customs and habits were galling to civilized Englishmen and equated with licentiousness. Perhaps the worst blemish of all was their refusal to accept the civilizing blessings of Protestant Christianity, preferring instead to worship idols, spirits, and devils. Such inability to grasp the saving grace of the only true religion was inexplicable to the English mind.

One feature shared by both the Irish and the Indians perhaps generated the greatest frustration for the settlers. For some strange and powerful reason, English people who were captured by the Indians, like those who in early years had been seduced into the ways of the wild Irish, tended to find the lifestyles of these savages irresistibly attractive. Captured whites, given the opportunity to escape, time and time again opted to stay with their Indian hosts and families rather than return to "civilization." After Queen Anne's War of the early eighteenth century, in which six hundred white women and children were captured, less than 30 percent ever returned to the white community. Most refused to be repatriated, either staying with the Indians or going over to the French (Hoover 1976, 42).

The curious attraction of Indian life raised a question, still posed later in the eighteenth century: "Why, given the choice, did the converted Indian always revert to savage ways, while the converted white, given the taste of savagery, so seldom wanted to return to civilized society?" (quoted in Hoover 1976, 43).[5] For many, there was an answer that stirred fear in their hearts: The Indians, like the Irish, were in league with Satan in the quest for human souls (Pearce 1953). Thus it was that a negative and fearful image of the savage in North America emerged and solidified among the English very soon after the first settlements.

Robert Berkhofer (1978) has argued very skillfully that "the Indian" is an invention of white men. In literature, art, science, and philosophy, every variation of "the Indian," whether ignoble, noble, or degraded, was contrived in the minds of European settlers and continues to influence the way we think about Native Americans. I have supplemented this analysis by showing that what facilitated this homogenization of such diverse peoples into a negative construct in white minds was the preexistence of a powerful cultural image of the "savage." English culture may have been more relentless in the preservation and perpetuation of this image than were the cultures of other European colonizers, for reasons that have to do in large part with England's prior experiences attempting to conquer Ireland.

Many strands of English life and thought converged in the seventeenth century. English attitudes and beliefs about the nature of savagery provide us with our earliest glimpse of the elementary features of a worldview soon to be structured around the term *race*. The conclusion that some populations were too savage to ever undergo redemption or conversion would become the prevailing attitude. The ready relegation of both Irish and Indians to the lowest status of humanity underscores the many parallels. It most pointedly reveals the impact of an inegalitarian philosophy that had survived the Middle Ages and the Renaissance before reemerging as a major ingredient in the elaboration of the ideology of race.

Given the circumstances, one has to wonder about the English consciousness of who they were and about the substantiveness of their design for the future of the American colonies. The English could not tolerate the diversity manifested in Irish culture on their own side of the Atlantic. The growing intolerance in the Puritan movement—with its base in Calvinist doctrines that allocated privilege, profits, and saintly status only to the pious few and condemned to damnation the vast majority of virtually all other human groups—did not augur well for the plural society that some had envisioned for the

Americas. Surely there was no reason in the colonies to assume that conversion of the Indians, another "savage" people, would or could result in their happy assimilation into English life and society. Whether Anglican, Puritan, or Catholic, the English kept themselves apart for the promotion and protection of what they perceived as their own ethnic interests and superiority.

The Puritans were more proselytizing than most other Christian groups. Their missionary activities, however, never led them to assimilate converted natives into their own communities. One can perhaps explain the introspective and defensive Puritan reactions in part as a result of the tensions of their lives both in England and the New World. They were a people beleaguered, perhaps not only by their own self-doubt, but also by external factors already generating tremendous social change over which they had little control.

This was a period when, as we have seen, the old social order was giving way to new social forms: an era of growing trade and urbanization, the disintegration of older institutions, the decline of the church and its influence especially in the frontier areas, and, most particularly, the breakdown of older class structures. Many of the "vagabonds" and "masterless men" of England came (or were brought involuntarily) to the Americas in search of adventure and fortune, and the Puritans had a difficult task in keeping these men, who tended to wander to the frontiers, within the bounds of civil society. For many, Puritanism provided a new moral universe and a social doctrine that would help to reestablish an orderly world in which the religious community would monitor and discipline the extremes of individual behavior. Through hard work, piety, self-restraint, service, and obedience, people could achieve salvation as well as worldly success.

As they tried to reestablish self-restraint and discipline, the Puritans recoiled from the overwhelming temptations of their external world. But the turning inward; the control; the dogmatic assertions of righteousness; and the attendant intolerance, bigotry, and fear of the unknown, which led to the witchcraft trials of the 1690s and other excesses, were somehow incompatible with the simultaneous thrust for individualism, adventure, and independence of action that seemed to be called for in the colonial situation. Moderation and uncurtailed greed are fundamentally opposite qualities of temperament and training. The older, more pristine Puritan values died rapidly as the colonists began to justify their overweening avarice under the guise of furthering the scheme and purposes of a God who favored only them.

Early colonial society in Virginia lacked the self-imposed moral and religious controls of the Puritans. Its members were a motley crew made up of too many men who were unwilling to work and who lived by begging, stealing, and extorting food from the Indians. The colonists had to enact harsh laws merely to force settlers to contribute to their own survival (Morgan 1975). They were a brawling, rough, aggressive lot, given to strong drink, gambling, and fighting among themselves. They were vicious, brutal, and often sadistic to one another, and especially to their servants. But they were also Englishmen who cherished their freedom; they learned to profit from the cultivation of tobacco and soon found themselves in even greater need of labor.

Some of the rudimentary elements in the synthesis of the idea of race thus appeared early in the American experience. They were transferred to the New World in the minds and hearts of the English and were further strengthened, fertilized, and given vastly expanded meaning in the context of English interaction with the native peoples of North America. It was no longer a question of just the one group of savages, the "wild Irish"; now there was emerging in English minds a generic, ever more monolithic category of savages made up of many groups. Not only did the existence of this category buttress the Englishman's sense of his own identity as a member of a superior nation, but its contrasting features provided him with a measure of his own worth. It further led him to construct social attitudes and policies that would become institutionalized as part of a broader worldview.

It was into this evolving context that the first Africans were introduced a little over a decade after the settlement of Jamestown. Fifty years later, the Africans and their descendants were being submerged into a form of servitude that had hitherto not existed in the Old World. The slavery that the English colonists instituted in North America was very different in certain basic features from that which the Spanish and Portuguese had inherited and transmitted to those areas of the New World that came under their control. English slavery was intimately connected with their preexisting conceptions of human differences and property rights and with many other aspects of English culture and history that we have just examined. Having already formulated an image of "savagery" that helped to justify uninhibited brutality toward the native population, it was but a small step for the English to transform colonial society into one based on chattel slavery. The institution of slavery provided the foundation for the further magnification of human differences, which the English came to express as "race." It is to this story of the coming of the Africans and their enslavement that we next turn.

NOTES

1. John Cabot (Giovanni Caboto), an Italian adventurer, navigator, and explorer, was originally employed by Venetian merchants but moved his family to London about 1484. After Columbus's success, Cabot was employed by the English King Henry VII to explore

new territories and took possession of what is believed to have been Newfoundland in 1497. His son Sebastian was a cartographer to Henry VIII and later received several commissions in the Spanish navy, subsequently making a number of voyages of exploration for Spain. He thought of himself as an Englishman, however, and upon returning to England accepted a naval post under Edward VI. He spent the rest of his life in England as governor of the Merchant Adventurers, during which time he helped to establish trade between England and Russia.

2. According to Olive Dickason, all American Indians shared a common reaction to Europeans. They welcomed them and sought by means of diplomacy to make accommodations with them (1979, 182).

3. Columbus often wrote quite positively about the Indians, although on his first landing he captured a number of Indians by force and speculated on their value as slaves.

4. The common class interests of these men and others are illuminated by the kinship links among them. Gilbert was a half brother of Walter Raleigh. Both were cousins of the Carews and the Grenvilles. Some of them and their immediate ancestors had contacts, and investments, with Italian merchants, and in the sugar plantations of the eastern Mediterranean. They all shared the vision of overseas colonies with large plantations on cheap land, worked by cheap native labor. Liggio notes that when they were frustrated in their attempts to colonize Ireland, they turned their attention to America (1976, 13). Gilbert, Raleigh, and Grenville took part in the suppression of the Munster rebellion of 1579–1583, and Gilbert particularly, who was noted for his use of massacre as a military stratagem, was among the first to articulate the policy of extermination of native peoples in both Ireland and America.

5. Hector St. Jean Crevecoeur, a Frenchman who lived for many years in the colonies, offered an interesting and insightful answer to this query. "There must be in their [Indian] social bond, something singularly captivating, and far superior to anything to be boasted of among us; for thousands of Europeans are Indians, and we have no examples of even one of those Aborigines having from choice become Europeans" (quoted in Nash 1992, 285). We can better understand the choices that some Europeans made when we learn from Morgan (1975) and Allen (1997) how harsh and difficult were the lives of poor whites, especially indentured servants, in the early colonies. Facing imminent starvation, cruel punishment from their owners or masters, and a death rate of over 50 percent, life with the Indians might well have seemed a better choice. For an interesting study of the ways by which Native Americans incorporated outsiders into their societies, see Theda Perdue (2003).

CHAPTER 5

The Arrival of Africans and Descent into Slavery

There were Africans and men of mixed European and African ancestry on the ships that came with Columbus and on many of the ships of later conquistadors, merchants, pirates, and immigrants. Many were descendants of the Africans brought back to Portugal and Spain after trading forays along the west coast of Africa in the mid-fifteenth century. Others descended from the Almoravid invaders of the eleventh century and later immigrants. Most had been baptized, had assimilated to Iberian cultures, and were accepted as part of the Christian community. There may have been a few who were African born, men with sailing expertise who were taken aboard ship when Columbus stopped to rest and refuel at Ceuta on the coast of West Africa. It is said that Pedro Alonzo Niño, the pilot of one of Columbus's ships, was a Negro. According to John Hope Franklin and Alfred A. Moss:

> Thirty Negroes, including Nuflo de Olano, were with Balboa when he discovered the Pacific Ocean. Cortes carried blacks with him into Mexico, and one of them planted and harvested the first wheat crop in the New World. Two accompanied Velas in 1520. When Alvarado went to Quito, he carried two hundred with him. They were with Pizarro on his Peruvian expedition and carried him to the Cathedral after he was murdered. The Africans in the expeditions of Almagro and Valdivia saved their Spanish masters from the Indians in 1525.
>
> . . . They were with Alarcón and Coronada in the Conquest of New Mexico. They accompanied Narváez on his expedition of 1527 and were with Cabeza de Vaca in the exploration of the southwestern part of the present

> United States. One of the outstanding Negro explorers was Estevanico, who opened up New Mexico and Arizona . . . and prepared the way for the conquest of the Southwest by the Spaniards.
>
> Africans were with the French in their explorations of the New World. . . . When the conquest of the Mississippi Valley was undertaken by the French in the seventeenth century, Negroes constituted a substantial portion of the pioneers who settled in the region. Around 1790, Jean Baptiste Point du Sable, a French-speaking black, erected the first building in a place that came to be known as Chicago. (1988, 30–31)[1]

The documentation of the number of people of African ancestry who participated in the exploration of New World territories represents a major departure from the usual image of "the discoverers" of the Americas conveyed in the media and by traditional educational institutions. But this should be understood and explicated in light of Franklin and Moss's next sentence: "Negroes did not accompany the English on their explorations in the New World" (1988, 31).

This is a point of critical significance, particularly when we look at the manner in which history has been written by English-speaking peoples. It is also at the heart of major historical debates over the origins of American slavery and differences in the "racial" attitudes and behaviors between the Europeans who settled in North America and those of Latin America. Of the major European colonizing nations, only the English had not had substantial experience with dark-skinned peoples prior to settlement in the New World. Although the English public had heard about Africans, very few had had encounters with black persons before the mid-seventeenth century.[2] Whereas the Portuguese had established trading relationships with West Africans as early as the 1440s, and Africans had been in Spain and Portugal since ancient times, the English did not begin to interact directly with Africans until well over a hundred years later.[3]

Like other Europeans, the English went to Africa primarily as traders and engaged in business transactions with native leaders or their representatives. During the reign of Elizabeth I (1558–1603), when Englishmen increasingly turned their attention to overseas enterprises, a few men became involved in the slave trade, long before the institution of slavery was actually established in North America. John Hawkins organized three raids into Africa for slaves. On one occasion alone he captured more than three hundred Africans. Like John Cabot and Sir Francis Drake, Hawkins also pirated Spanish ships carrying slaves. Before the English established their own trading connections, this was a favored source of slave merchandise. Such slaving activities must have encouraged a callous indifference to the slaves as human beings and increased the perception of the Africans as mere cargo, like cattle, horses, and pigs. The attitudes toward Africans and treatment of them by slave traders were probably shared among all nationalities, mirroring the hard-hearted nature of the slavery enterprise. Slave traders throughout history have been unique in their indifference to the humanity of their cargo.

Francis Drake met Africans in a somewhat different context, as we have seen, when he allied with the Cimarrons against their former Spanish masters. Throughout Central and South America, escaped slaves earned a reputation as fierce fighters, and in the competition among the various European states for colonial possessions, these men and women would lend their support to any group that promised them their freedom. Drake was thus in a position to have a positive image of some Africans as allies and potential confederates in settling the New World. For several years, Drake maintained alliances with the Cimarrons, during which time they attacked Spanish settlements, wagon trains, and ships and looted a fortune in gold, silver, and precious jewels. According to Edmund Morgan and other historians, the friendship between the English and the Cimarrons "suggest[s] a camaraderie that went beyond the mutual benefits of the alliance." The Spanish feared that the English, in collusion with the Cimarrons, might make themselves "masters of the Pacific" (1975, 13).

Aside from these experiences, knowledge of which filtered into communities both in Europe and the Americas, English people had other, quite vague, impressions of Africans. Some early seventeenth-century writers made comparisons between the Africans and the Irish (Quinn 1966, 26–27). Among a few commentators there was a general sense that the Irish, the Africans, and the Indians were all more or less savages. But this was not a uniform or homogeneous view. It reflected more than anything the ethnic chauvinism of many English people. As was to be expected, there was unmistakable ethnocentric bias against what were presumed to be the habits, dress (or lack thereof), customs, and supernatural beliefs of the Africans.

Winthrop Jordan made the point that when Englishmen did begin to interact with Africans in overseas trade, it was not within a context "which prejudged the Negro as a slave" (1968, 4). They were just another type of humankind, albeit black and with curious languages, religious beliefs, and other cultural features. Some reports show that they were initially judged to be both civil and hospitable; the earliest records do not suggest the more virulent image of savagery that was to come much later.

Those advocates of colonization who held a utopian view of the potential New World colonies, where different kinds of men lived together in peace and harmony, must undoubtedly have had a benign attitude toward the Africans and the Indians without much prejudgment about their potential for civilized behavior. Under the colonization schemes of Walter Raleigh and Humphrey Gilbert, for example, the first English colony in North America, Roanoke Island, was to be populated with Indians and Africans freed from the Spanish. These first English traders, like their Latin predecessors, evinced unmistakable cognizance that they were dealing with people from well-organized sociopolitical systems, people who were sophisticated and intelligent.

In the broader historical context of over a hundred years of enslavement of Indians and Africans by the Portuguese and Spanish, it was reasonable to expect that the English would show little reluctance to ultimately accept Africans as slaves. Other Europeans had successfully used Africans in such a manner, and they were known to be productive workers. When the English did enter the slave trade, not only did their North American and Caribbean colonies become major importers of Africans, but English traders eventually dominated the slave trade until it was outlawed in 1807.

THE FIRST AFRICANS

Africans were first introduced into the English colony at Jamestown in 1619. They were part of a "cargo" of people sold from a Dutch ship that had been trading along the Virginia coast. The little Jamestown colony thus found itself the beneficiary of a new group of laborers for which its settlers had had no previous preparation or experience. In the New England colonies, a few African servants were introduced as early as 1633; they were in Connecticut by 1639 and in New Haven by 1644. In none of these areas were their numbers initially very large.

For the rest of that century, a steady stream of Africans was brought to the mainland colonies, particularly after the development of the tobacco industry. In 1670, Virginia still relied for most of its laborers and servants on imports from England. Sugar plantations requiring massive labor had developed in the West Indian islands after about 1640, and the number of Africans imported there increased rapidly from mid-century on. The French, the Spanish, the Dutch, and the English were busily establishing plantations in the Caribbean islands, while competing and fighting among themselves. Those who were successful came increasingly to rely on African slave labor.

A key issue that has prompted much debate and speculation among contemporary historians has been the precise status of these Africans in North America before the institutionalization of laws creating permanent slavery.

Some historians have suggested that the Africans were slotted into already existing roles as servants, working for the normal period of debenture, from four to seven years. The term *slave* was rarely applied to these Africans during the first decades of their presence in North America. At the same time, historians have noted that varying degrees of servitude were recognized by the English, although the distinctions between them were not very precise.[4]

On this point David Brion Davis observes: "Not only did slavery and serfdom coexist and overlap, but medieval jurists tended to confuse the two conditions" (1966, 48). Jordan claims that there was a measure of precision in the English concept of "slave," but that it has not been well analyzed. He argues that for most Englishmen, slavery denoted a complete loss of freedom, akin to the loss of one's humanity, and to treat a man as a slave was to treat him as a beast (1968, 54). That some ordinary European servants were sometimes called slaves may reflect not only the confusion of the two categories, but most likely the subjective feelings of those who held positions as owners and masters.

Perhaps the best exploration of this issue is the work of Theodore Allen. With meticulous detail, he has examined the primary sources, from the earliest records of the Virginia colony through the seventeenth and early eighteenth centuries. He has concluded that the status of the first Africans was "indeterminate because it was being fought out" (1997, 178) (see below).

What is indisputably clear is that beginning in the latter part of the seventeenth century, major social and economic transformations began to take place that eventually obliterated the uncertain status of Africans and their descendants. Through the passage of various laws, "Negroes" were separated out from other servants and gradually reduced to the status of permanent hereditary slavery. A date frequently noted by historians to mark the first official recognition of permanent slave status in law is 1661, when the Virginia assembly passed an act making a servant who ran away with a Negro responsible for serving the time of the Negro slave (Morgan 1975, 311). However, North American slavery was not the result of a single law or a single court decision, but of numerous individual acts, decisions, and practices that over time became codified into the legal framework of colonial society.

These changes continued into the early eighteenth century, and in the process produced a system of bondage that was unique in human history. Its primary distinctiveness rested on the fact that such slavery was reserved exclusively for black Africans and their descendants. This was a critical step in the evolution of the social construction of race. The next section examines this process more intensively.

THE DESCENT INTO PERMANENT SLAVERY

There is a tradition in American history that rightly connects race and racism with slavery and thus focuses on the relationship between the two peoples who were most entangled in that institution, Africans and Europeans. The inerrancy of a historical linkage between slavery and racism in North America has to be recognized, although, as we shall see later, there is no intrinsic relationship between the two institutions. Nevertheless, much of the historiography of the twentieth century has centered on the issue of which came first, racism or slavery.

One school of thought has argued that it was the slave condition itself, especially the debased status of the slave, combined with the physical differences in the populations of masters and slaves, that generated the negative attitudes of racism and subsequent social discrimination. Alexis de Tocqueville, one of the earliest external chroniclers of the American experience, observed in the 1830s that slavery had given birth to what he saw as "immovable" prejudice against the Negro (1945, 359).[5] He was followed in this view by most historians of the slave period.[6] The implication of this position, not always apparent to scholars, was that without slavery, race and racism might not have occurred.

Another school of thought holds that a kind of racial antagonism was present from the beginning of English contact with Africans. And the institutionalization of racial discrimination, including the separation of blacks and whites both spatially and socially, preceded the establishment of slavery. The arguments on both sides are compelling and can be illustrated by the works of several scholars.

In the late 1950s, Carl Degler raised the question of causal priorities again and proceeded to suggest evidence that, in all of the English colonies, "discrimination against the Negro preceded the evolution of a slave status and by that fact helped to shape the form that institution would assume" (1959–1960, 62). The institution of slavery, he argued, came to mirror the discrimination that had occurred from the first contact with Africans on American soil, and "in so doing, perpetuated it" (66). Likewise, Arnold Sio argued that "discrimination against the Negro occurred before the slave status was fully defined and before Negro labor became pivotal to the economic system" (1964–1965, 304).

Somewhat later, Winthrop Jordan offered an expanded version of this view. He attempted to explain or rationalize English attitudes and behavior toward Africans by suggesting that the very blackness of Negroes was, on first contact, sufficiently traumatic to ensure the development of bias toward them (1968, 4–20). Their skin color apparently rarely went unnoticed, and he feels that the frequent comments on this characteristic were a measure of the impression that it made on the English. On this feature alone, Africans contrasted strikingly with the English, who were among the lightest-skinned peoples of Europe. He speculated that the "powerful impact which the Negro's color made upon Englishmen must have been partly owing to suddenness of contact." He added that the English experience with Africans was "markedly different from that of the Spanish and Portuguese who for centuries had been in close contact with North Africa and had actually been invaded and subjected by people both darker and more highly civilized than themselves" (1968, 6).

Jordan saw as the basis of English hostility the fact that the concept of blackness in the English language conveyed predominantly negative images. In this respect, the English language and culture helped to predispose its carriers toward prejudice against Africans. On the one hand, black meant filthy, evil, vile, sinister, ugly, fearful, and deadly. It was the color of mourning, "an emotionally partisan color, the handmaid and symbol of baseness and evil, a sign of danger and repulsion" (1968, 7). White, on the other hand, was the color of beauty, virtue, purity, goodness, wonder, and perfection. These contrasting elements in the meaning of these color terms insinuated their way, perhaps subliminally, into English thought and may have become incipient molders of the English attitude toward and evaluation of the Africans.

Degler agreed with Jordan that the English had a cultural predisposition, derived from values associated with the color black, toward a negative view of African people. He argued: "From the 1630s up until slavery clearly appeared in the statutes in the 1660s, the Negroes were being set apart and discriminated against as compared with the treatment accorded Englishmen, whether servants or free" (1959–1960, 53). Even though the term *slave* was rarely used, the actual practice, according a distinct and lower status to Negroes, was already in place. For some Negroes, Degler continued, the reality of their servitude already amounted to slavery in that they served for life.

These authors cited examples of white men who were whipped or otherwise penalized in some other way for consorting with Negroes or for "lying with a negro," or they received different sentences for the same crimes. They noted that Virginia and Maryland after the mid-seventeenth century passed laws prohibiting Negroes from bearing arms, imposing separate punishments for Negro and white servants, requiring Negro and Indian women to work in the fields, and taxing Negroes separately. There is evidence that lifetime servitude had been imposed on at least some Negroes and their offspring in practice even before the existence of laws permitting it. And these authors consider the frequent incidences of higher prices paid for Negroes over white servants as evidence of the practice of keeping blacks in servitude for life. Thus it was not the economic need for slaves alone that explains the inferior social status accorded to Negroes even before slavery was instituted.

Other historians have argued that the experiences of the first Africans in North America was never so clear; their position was in fact somewhat ambiguous. Many feel that there is insufficient evidence in the available sources to declare for certain that all Africans were from the beginning kept separate and apart from the white population. Mary Handlin and Oscar Handlin, among prominent historians, have presented considerable evidence and logical arguments for the position that the first Africans were not slaves. "Slavery," they claim, "had no meaning in law; at most it was a popular description of a low form of service" (1972, 26). They point out that Africans were brought into a society where large numbers of people were unfree to some degree, so that the lack of freedom for Africans was not at all unusual.

We have already seen that among the many indentured servants in the New World, some of whom were the "wild Irish," were other kinds of bonded laborers, including some who were permanent. Indian slavery had commenced within a few years of the early settlements and the first conflicts with the Pilgrims, and many of these Indians were held for life. Although their numbers were not large, Indian slaves were found throughout the early colonies. That they were heathens and had been conquered in a just war was the reason put forth as justification for such treatment. Because of variations in the condition of bonded servants of European background and in the treatment of Indians, there were many degrees of servitude in the colonies. Not only immigrant servants, bound to a stated number of years of service, but convicts, vagabonds, orphans, illegitimate children of all "races," and debtors were frequently bought and sold and even occasionally referred to as "slaves."[7]

As to the laws passed that appeared to discriminate against Negroes, Thomas Breene and Keith Innes (1980) point out that some of the statutes passed in Virginia and other colonies, such as the 1640 law prohibiting blacks from holding firearms, did not really translate into social practices as some historians have interpreted. In fact, historians have made too much of these laws, because Negroes continued to carry firearms up to and during Bacon's Rebellion (1676) and beyond. Also, it was common practice among the peoples of the colonies not to obey laws, which accounts for the fact that certain laws had to be enacted many times over decades later.

Jordan's own final analysis obviates the question of causal primacy. "Rather than slavery causing 'prejudice,' or vice versa," he avers, "they seem rather to have generated each other. Both were . . . twin aspects of a general debasement of the Negro. Slavery and 'prejudice' may have been equally cause and effect, continuously reacting upon each other, dynamically joining hands to hustle the Negro down the road to complete degradation" (1968, 80). There is probably unerring accuracy in this portrayal, but it does not adequately answer the query about the ultimate causes of either black slavery or racism.

The imposition of permanent slavery on Negroes was not the result of a single, abrupt decision, as virtually all historians now note. Slavery as an institution only gradually developed. In Virginia, over the critical years between 1660 and 1705, dozens of statutes and regulations were passed restricting some of the rights of blacks, establishing servitude for life, limiting their rights to bear arms and to hold certain property, and providing penalties for interracial marriage or fornication. Both Virginia and Maryland systematically and step by step enclosed blacks, both bonded servants and free Negroes, in a tightening vise of legal restrictions, the most telling of which were the prohibitions against private manumissions during the 1690s. North and South Carolina followed suit in the early decades of the eighteenth century. By 1723, the right to vote was ultimately denied to all Negroes in the southern colonies, free as well as slave.

Little is known about the legal treatment and social position of blacks in New England during the early decades of their presence there. Although both bonded servants (slaves) and free blacks could be found in New England during this time, there were few documented laws or statutes that differentially affected them. Their skin color had seemingly little effect on opportunities to obtain training and employment, rights to police protection, access to justice and the court system, and some level of participation in the political system.

Yet in the 1650s, the New England colonies enacted laws prohibiting Indians and Negroes from serving in the militias. This was the earliest of a number of legal restrictions affecting blacks and Indians alike. In the 1680s, more regulations of a confining nature applying to Indians, Negroes, mulattoes, servants, and apprentices were enacted. These acts seem to reflect a perception of a common identity among these categories of people and a clear intent to exclude them from the privileges and responsibilities enjoyed by Europeans.

The major restrictions on Negroes in all of the colonies had been fully implemented by the first decades of the eighteenth century, when manumission was made more difficult or even impossible, curfews were imposed, and property and marriage regulations were established to separate Negro slaves from free persons and other servants. Although there were far fewer slaves in New England than in the South, and the economic value and need for slavery in this region has been questioned, every colony passed laws defining "the Negro" as a subordinate and differentiating blacks from other residents.

Nash encapsulated the process of transforming Africans into chattel slaves in a powerfully succinct manner:

> In rapid succession Afro-Americans lost their right to testify before a court; to engage in any kind of commercial activity, either as buyer or seller; to hold property; to participate in the political process; to congregate in public places with more than two or three of their fellows; to travel without permission; and to engage in legal marriage or parenthood. In some colonies legislatures even prohibited the right to education and religion, for they thought these might encourage the germ of freedom in slaves. . . . Gradually they reduced the slave, in the eyes of society and the law, from a human being to a piece of chattel property. (1992, 159)

WAS THERE *RACE* BEFORE SLAVERY?

George Fredrickson ([1971] 1987, 1981) believes that Jordan's argument on the psychological reaction of the English to the blackness of the Africans is too speculative and lacking strong evidence.[8] He finds little to suggest that before the 1680s Africans were treated any differently from other servants. All were subjected to the same discipline and general living conditions. The fact that some blacks gained their freedom, acquired property, and seemingly suffered little or no discrimination is indicative that they were not set apart from all others in their station until the 1690s. Heathenism and captivity, Fredrickson claims, made people enslavable, not the pigment of their skin (1981, 73).

Historians Edmund Morgan (1975), Anthony S. Parent Jr. (2003), and Philip D. Morgan (1998) agree that the initial status of blacks was not permanently fixed at the lowest social level. They seemed to suffer no greater debilities than white servants or freed white men. After their terms of service, many blacks gained their freedom and apparently had no difficulty in acquiring property or even voting. Some became landowners or entrepreneurs and commanded the respect of others because of their success. Wealthy black men who owned hundreds of acres of land were called *planters*, a term reserved for men with large estates. Such black men of substance even acquired slaves and servants of their own. They engaged in trading and other commercial activities and had business dealings on an equal footing with whites. They were able to experience the same degree of civil rights, with access to the courts and police protection, as Europeans (Morgan 1975, 154–157; see also Morgan 1998).

Early references to blacks reveal little clear evidence of a uniform or widespread social antipathy on account of their color. Records show a fairly high incidence of cooperation among black and white servants and unified resistance to harsh masters. Blacks and whites sometimes escaped from bondage together or collaborated in insurrections, especially in the English Caribbean islands. Running away together implies a high level of trust and close cooperation, and this does not square with a society where racism and discrimination exist.

Both Liggio (1976) and Morgan (1975) suggest that in the 1660s and 1670s, the ruling classes in the island plantations were more afraid of a general uprising of the servile classes and landless poor than of any threat presented by the Negroes per se. "There is more than a little evidence," writes Morgan, "that Virginians during these years were ready to think of Negroes as members or potential members of the community on the same terms as other men and to demand of them the same standards of behavior. Black men and white serving the same master worked, ate, and slept together, and together shared in escapades, escapes, and punishments" (1975, 155).

Intermarriage among black and white servants was not unusual and was apparently accepted. A number of episodes in court records are suggestive that racial attitudes familiar to us in the late nineteenth and twentieth centuries were absent in the seventeenth century. On this point alone, the social behavior shows striking differences with that of whites and blacks after slavery, when the latter were again free. Many black men married white women servants; records from one county in the 1660s show that one-fourth of all children born to white servant girls in several counties were mulatto. Five out of ten free black men on the Eastern Shore were married to white women (Parent 2003). One servant girl declared to her master that she would rather marry a Negro slave from a neighboring plantation than him with all his property, and she did. This was at a time when there were five or six times as many men as women; doubtless she could have had her choice of any man. There seemed to be no stigma associated with these marriages. Widows were always remarried and brought their property with them. One white widow of a black farmer had no problem remarrying to a white farmer. She later accused her second husband in a court suit of squandering the property that she had accumulated with her first husband. In one interesting case, a black woman servant successfully sued for her freedom and then married the white lawyer who represented her in court. Lawyers were among the few literate members of colonial society, and their abilities gave them elite status. Yet such a marriage did not seem to threaten that status or cause him to lose his position.[9] Some of the early laws enacted against intermarriages, especially with Indians, may have had other motivations than antipathy toward physical differences (Fredrickson 1981; Nash 1992).

Like their European counterparts, free black property owners were often contemptuous of government, arrogant and insulting toward those considered their inferiors, assertive of their rights, and prone to fighting. They thumbed their noses at governmental orders, as when one farmer, told by a messenger from the court that he should come in and serve on a jury, flogged the young man and sent him back with the reply that he would come in when he pleased, after he had got his harvest in. In fact, numerous court records provide clear evidence that blacks did not act differently from whites of the same class, nor did the courts make distinctions on the basis of color.

The bits and pieces of ethnographic information that historians have gleaned from scarce records about the status of blacks in the seventeenth century have always seemed anomalous to scholars who have tried to interpret them. The interpretations appear contradictory, tentative, and uncertain, as the discussion above demonstrates. Much of the problem has to do with historians projecting back into history the racial values, beliefs, and understandings of contemporary times. How could a white woman, even of the servant class, prefer to marry a Negro slave? How can any black man be so dismissive of a government order? Africans were perceived as better workers, not only because of their knowledge, but for their ability to work hard in an environment for which they were already adapted, and they lived longer than European men. According to Parent, "Most Africans arrived with extensive knowledge of hoe agriculture, mound cultivation, replanting techniques, fallow or rotational planting, crop processing, and tobacco culture" (2003, 61). This may have prompted some European women to prefer African men.

When we connect together these ethnographic data with other facts, we come to the conclusion that the hardening of "racial" identities and boundaries had not yet occurred in the mid-seventeenth century. We've already seen that the collaboration between Sir Francis Drake and the Cimarrons was unaffected by a sense of racial differences. Another source of information about English perceptions of Africans relates to the presence of Africans in Europe during the Middle Ages and later. Historian Peter Fryer (1984) notes that there were blacks in Britain before the English came; they were brought to England as mercenaries with the Roman Conquests in the third century AD. Records show that there were blacks born in England in the sixteenth century. They served in the court of James IV and in many later courts. Some are described as entertainers, musicians, drummers, dancers, and singers, but there were also men of skilled crafts. In the late sixteenth century it was a status symbol among the high-class families to have a black servant or two among the household servants. During the sixteenth through the eighteenth centuries, black slaves brought to English ports were helped in escaping slavery by the English working class. It was the English working class that later formed a large segment of the antislavery movement, as we shall see in chapter 8.

All of this evidence suggests that the ideology of race had not yet developed. Moreover, the theory that English people had a "natural" antipathy to black skins is hardly supported by this evidence. It also suggests that until toward the end of the seventeenth century, the English colonies in North America probably had a window of opportunity to create a society that was "multicolored" but not "multiracial."

WHY THE PREFERENCE FOR AFRICANS?

The question has been legitimately raised of why, after forty or fifty years of relatively indifferent or indecisive social treatment, the leaders of the English colonies found it necessary to impose permanent bondage on Africans and their descendants. The enslavement of Indians was comprehensible in the context of the conquest situation, where historical precedent reinforces the tendency of conquerors to reduce victims to forced labor. Both the Indians and the Irish were people whose lands the English had coveted and confiscated. But the Negro did not fit into this classic mold, and this may help us to understand the early ambiguity of the Africans' relationships to the European community.

Overtly the English really had little reason to compare the Africans with the Indians, except in their powerlessness. The African was neither native to the Americas nor an enemy captured in war and thus the target of the enmity or belligerence of his conquerors. Moreover, by their own criteria of the requisites for civilized behavior, Africans met at least the basic ones. They were all farmers, and some were artisans and craftsmen, adept in a range of skilled activities from blacksmithing and goldsmithing to bricklaying, carpentry, weaving, and leatherworking. Some were known for their knowledge of cattle-keeping and breeding and leather-working (see Skinner 1964 for an excellent summary of economies and technologies of West Africans at the time of European contact). Some undoubtedly came from areas of highly organized state societies and were accustomed to social hierarchies and obedience to positions of legitimate power. Englishmen consequently had no reason to see in the Africans the same image of the "savage," whom they had interpreted in earlier contexts as an impediment to progress.

The answer to the question "why Africans?" is complex and perhaps best understood in the broadest historical context, encompassing economic and material explanations along with those cultural and historical variables that are so important in human lives but, under recent trends in scholarship, are much too often ignored. What seems absent from the calculations of many recent historians of this phenomenon is the recognition and inclusion in their analysis of the historical penchant that the English had long displayed toward extreme ethnic chauvinism, independently of any contact with Africans and Indians. Certain conditions presaging a negative evaluation of Africans were present even before Englishmen arrived on the coasts of North America.

By the sixteenth century, the English had developed belligerent or competitive relationships with virtually all other groups with whom they had had any contact. Their animosity and willingness to treat others inhumanely has already been documented in the descriptions of the relationships they established with the Irish and the Indians. Even before they established settlements in the New World, the English had developed a view of the world composed of unequal groups, at the bottom of which were the "savages." This pattern of inhumane treatment of non-English peoples encompassed not only their long-standing conflicts with other Europeans but a culturally induced belief in their own superiority that reflected extreme ethnocentrism and shortly would be nourished by a newfound and at times fanatical Anglo-Saxonism.

What seems strange is that most Englishmen did not immediately identify the Africans as wild men or savages. It was not until the eighteenth century, at least in the written record, that widespread English attitudes toward Africans mirrored popular evaluations and stereotypes of Irishmen and Indians. The same negative language and antiprimitivistic characterizations of savagery that had been used to refer to the Irish and Indians were then widely applied to Africans and greatly amplified in the next century.

This then is the broader context in which we must look for answers explaining English attitudes toward the Africans and their offspring. But there are also some very specific circumstances that are far more revealing about why English colonizers, long imbued with notions of liberty and righteousness, turned to a system of black slavery.

THE PROBLEM OF LABOR

Consider the circumstances of English expansion. Faced with an abundance of rich lands, what was lacking for their successful exploitation was the labor to fully cultivate or explore them for minerals or other forms of wealth. Following earlier precedents, English settlers throughout North America attempted to coerce the native populations into the kind of controlled labor that they perceived would be most profitable. When the Indian population proved to be insufficient and ineffective (see below) as slaves, the English turned to importing impoverished men, women, and children from the streets of Liverpool and Bristol, or to rounding up peasant Irishmen and Scotsmen conquered in warfare, and shipping them off to provide labor for the early settlements, especially the sugar plantations in the West Indies. In fact, the wholesale shipment of Irishmen into servitude in the New World became an acceptable option for "disposing" of them. The English knew that slavery was not illegal under international laws, so it did not matter who the slaves were so long as they were not proper Englishmen, Protestant, and "civilized."

Englishmen were involved in the Irish "slave trade" to the West Indies beginning in the late 1620s, long before they became the major carriers in the transatlantic trade in African slaves. The largest numbers of Irish were brought in during midcentury, when Oliver Cromwell had instigated his scorched-earth policy against the Irish; the choice as he saw it was to exterminate or expel them.[10]

Throughout this period there was no reason to predict that the African–Atlantic trade would ultimately supplant the white "vagabonds," "destitutes," and convicts with an unlimited supply of black labor. Moreover, it did not matter that the English had no immediate experience, or recognition, of slavery in British law. As a human institution, slavery was widely accepted as legal and appropriate for some people. For the English plantation owner, what was needed was a docile workforce over whom he had absolute authority, who could be put to work for no more than minimal keep, and who could be treated as property such as livestock. The English attempted to put this kind of system into practice with European labor even before the Africans figured significantly in the equation. By the second decade of the seventeenth century, the colonists had already established a plantation system with separate, substandard, and miserable servant housing; poor food; whippings and maiming for punishment; and forced gang labor.

In the 1620s, claims Theodore Allen, some colonists already acquiring wealth from tobacco had transformed the immigrant European labor force from "tenants and wage laborers to chattel bond-servitude in Virginia" (1997, 178). Opportunities for such profit-generating activity were realized after the 1622 attack by Indians on Jamestown that killed off nearly a third of the small colony's population. The survivors from outlying areas fled to the better-protected town, abandoning their fields and forestlands. During the chaos of the next few years, numerous unoccupied and unclaimed lands were taken over by members of the small elite, and they began to use coercive tactics to force laborers and servants to work these lands. The unexpected drop in the price of tobacco during the 1620s exacerbated the situation, compelling tobacco producers to constantly seek reductions in the cost of labor; their preference was for bonded laborers who did not have to be paid wages.

For the most part, the institution of bonded or indentured servitude, though not unknown in Europe, was an aberration from traditional English laws and customs. Whereas English servants contracted to serve for a year and were paid wages, indentured bondsmen were obliged to serve a stated number of years (usually four to seven) without pay to work off their debt. Moreover, they could be, and frequently were, bought and sold, maltreated, abused, and even brutalized with impunity. Morgan, in his detailed study of the Virginia colony, gives convincing evidence that servants in Virginia were generally degraded and treated as objects: "Virginians dealt in servants the way Englishmen dealt in land or chattels" (1975, 128). White servitude, he claims, came closer to slavery in the tobacco fields of Virginia than anything hitherto known by Englishmen (296). Such degradation, Fredrickson notes, was tolerated by the English and colonial governments because of their own "conviction that the poor deserved no better" (1981, 60).

Because the death rate was so high, most of these usually young servants never lived out their debenture to acquire freedom. So lifetime servitude had already become a reality for many. For those who survived, there was little or no land available, primarily because wealthy colonists, in their desire to increase tobacco profits, had already laid claim to all lands not under Indian control. The demand for indentured laborers, not only for the production of tobacco and corn (the principle food) but for defense of the settlement, the crafting and maintenance of tools and equipment, and other laboring chores, increased. England, with a surplus of labor during the first half of the seventeenth century, was anxious to siphon off the excess poor, convicts, vagabonds, captured Irish, and homeless Scots and English to the colonies.[11]

One of Allen's major theses is that this turning to heavy usage of bond labor, which he calls the "chatelization" of English plantation labor, "constituted an essential precondition of the emergence of the subsequent lifetime chattel bond-servitude imposed upon African-American laborers" (1997, 300 ff.). He provides supporting quotations from a number of other historians, among them Eric Williams and Lerone Bennett, who claimed that the major features of black slavery were first tried out and perfected on white men and women, providing a "proving ground" for the institution that was to come (Bennett 1975, 40–41).

Thousands of people were conscripted or forced into this labor system. But by midcentury, more and more were living longer and becoming freed men and women, and this soon became a problem. Freed men demanded land and other perquisites of their free status. This was just one of the circumstances that compelled English colonists to try to develop a more permanent, and cheaper, labor force.

Morgan's analysis of the early Virginia colony provides the kind of cultural-historical context out of which we can better grasp the process of transformation to a slave society in the Chesapeake region. Unlike the New England colonizers, Englishmen in this rough and disorderly world set out to exploit other people, including one another, with few scruples about it. The colony contained an increasingly large number of rebellious and unruly young men, predominantly unmarried, freed after serving their years of indenture, and on the make. But Morgan claims that in fact there were fewer opportunities for them to make their fortunes than history has portrayed, and they formed an unhappy cadre of idle, restless drifters who caused more than a little trouble and embarrassment to colony leaders. Eager for action, frustrated by those who tried to control and exploit them, these drifters were more than willing to rebel against the colony's elite. The tragedy was that they took out their frustrations on a population relatively easy to hate with impunity, the Indians, who became the scapegoat for their ire. Not only did they often physically attack Indians, but they demanded of the colonial government the right to move neighboring Indians off more and more land and to confiscate it for their own private use.

Bacon's Rebellion of 1676 prompted wealthy planters to realize clearly the dangers posed by the dissatisfied laborers, according to Allen (1997) and Parent (2003). This rebellion was one of a number of acts of opposition that threatened the colonial government. Although originating in anti-Indian agitation during the winter of 1675–1676, part of the significance of the rebellion lay in Nathaniel Bacon's leadership of certain county planters in opposition to the policies of the governor, William Berkeley. With hundreds of volunteer militia attacking Indians and internal disputes within the wealthy planter and ruling classes, by May 1676 there was a complete breakdown of law and order. The rebels turned their grievances against the government because of perceived corruption, abuses of power, and the imposition of unfair taxes. Various factions demanded more equitable distribution of land, less focus on the monoculture of tobacco, greater land and resources for cattle ranges, an end to the patronage system that dominated the fur trade, and a host of other measures. Among the strongest demands was freedom from the kind of chattel servitude that oppressed the servant class. In 1676, bond laborers began to join the rebellion in masses. In September they burned Jamestown to the ground.

What most frightened planters was that the rebellion brought together several thousand poor, working class men and women, the majority of the colony's population, including both white and black servants. It was this threat to the system of bond servitude that engaged the planters and their supporters in responding to the rebellion. Production in the tobacco industry required a servile and disciplined labor force, and now this labor force virtually ceased to exist. With bond laborers deserting and joining the rebel forces, all social order broke down. When the British sent an expedition to put down the rebellion, its leader, Captain Thomas Grantham, had to promise freedom to the bond laborers, "about foure hundred English and Negroes," who constituted the rebel army (Allen 1997, 214). The significance of this, says Allen, is that "128 years before William Lloyd Garrison was born, laboring class African-Americans and European-Americans fought side by side for the abolition of slavery. In so doing they provided the supreme proof that the white race did not then exist" (215).

The rebellion dissipated; some say it was put down, having been weakened by the death of Bacon. But the royal commissioners sent out by the British government noted that the population at large was sullen and obstinate and that the vast majority had supported the rebellion. Social stability had not yet been achieved. As late as 1698, the governor of Maryland reported that nearly four hundred bond laborers, mostly from Africa, had arrived, as well as "600 or 700 bond-laborers" from Europe, "chiefly Irish" (Allen 1997, 218). He feared that if that trend were to continue, the two groups might join forces in both Virginia and Maryland and make "great disturbances, if not a rebellion." Such fear was expressed on other occasions, and Allen believes that it lay at the heart of the conscious decision to develop a stratagem for social control that would also ensure the presence of sufficient bond laborers to promote the production of tobacco and other goods in increasing quantities.

At the end of the rebellion, the planters were greatly strengthened, especially when armed ships from England arrived. Now the colony's leaders could restore the masses of rebellious workers, who were continuing to plunder and loot, to their proper places. The answer to many of the problems came increasingly to be seen as permanent black slavery. The defeat of Bacon's Rebellion, says Allen, "cleared the way for the establishment of the system of lifetime hereditary chattel bond-servitude" (1997, 239).

But this was not the sole cause of the changes that were to come. Several developments, perhaps unanticipated, led to the growing preference for Africans as laborers and indeed to the fashioning of the institution of slavery for Africans only. In the West Indies as well as on the mainland, quite early in the contact period, Europeans began to realize that the native populations were a poor source of potential labor. For one thing, the Indians had little or no immunity to the Old World diseases that Europeans brought with them. Ordinary children's diseases and respiratory infections from the common cold to tuberculosis had a fatal impact on the indigenous populations, many of whom succumbed rapidly or became weakened to the point of incapacity. In fact, between disease and warfare, the Indian population was drastically reduced and in some cases, particularly on the Caribbean islands, eliminated entirely. Moreover, the surviving Indians, after capture, were still on their own territory, and often individuals or groups would escape and disappear into the hinterlands. In most cases, these runaways would never be recaptured, and this posed a major problem for plantation owners. Enslaved Indians had communities of support among their own people, and the threat of Indian attacks to recapture their own tribespeople was constant. Besides, Indians were dealt with as whole societies, not as disconnected individuals who had no social identity other than that provided by their owners. Trading and other agreements, though often breached by Europeans, also acted as a bar to the wholesale enslavement of Indians.

Added to this was the fact that, except in some of the southeastern regions, none of the Indian groups represented large populations. The native peoples of the eastern coastal areas of North America were thinly scattered, so that even when conquered they did not supply sufficient labor to meet the demand. Indians were also needed as trappers to satisfy the growing demand in Europe for furs. Most of the natives of the regions settled by the English were food collectors or simple horticulturists. Although the eastern woodlands and southern Indians grew some food crops, their techniques and customs did not allow for substantial or continuous surplus production. When some southeastern tribes, such as the Creeks, Cherokees, and Choctaws, did take up settled farming lifestyles, they were able to establish treaties with the whites that prevented efforts to enslave them. On the tropical islands, where Europeans had established plantations early on, food cultivation was little known among the native populations, who quickly succumbed to the ravages of disease and warfare.

English willingness to use fellow Europeans as forced labor in the West Indies was not an insignificant precursor of their massive involvement with African slaves. As we have seen, European servants came under the same restrictions as all servants and slaves, and they were often treated worse than others.[12] The Irish particularly were a rebellious lot. Their comparatively high linguistic and cultural homogeneity allowed them to plot mutinies and insurrections, in several of which they were successful. Often they went over to the side of the French or the Spanish in their battles with the English, alliances also experienced in Europe and based on their common Catholic faith. Support from these coreligionists was often critical to the success of some Irish rebellions. That they were threatening to the English planters is evidenced by the report that "English officials armed their black slaves rather than trust the Irish" (Liggio 1976, 29). But adding to the angst of the plantation managers and owners was the fact that the Irish, who as we have already seen had been primarily pastoralists, knew nothing about intensive agriculture, the tropical environment, or techniques for the cultivation of tropical plants. "Not unlike the Indians to which they were so frequently compared, the Irish, as the English had constantly said, would not submit to the kind of agricultural work which feudalism had demanded. The Indian tended to escape or die; the Irish either resisted work discipline, tending toward idleness, or they rebelled" (Liggio 1976, 30).

There were other factors about the Irish that diminished their value as a controllable and powerless labor force. Individual Irishmen could escape and blend in with the free white population in the ports and other towns, especially on the mainland. Plantation owners soon determined that the expense and difficulties of retrieving these runaways were not worth the bother. Planters also thought of the Irish as having a dangerous nature. Irish servants frequently engaged in drunken brawls and thus quickly gained a reputation for aggressiveness and violence. Predictably, they often turned on their masters. Liggio has concluded that Irish servitude became either impractical or burdensome to the planters. "The Gaelic insurrections caused the English to seek to replace this source of servile labor entirely with another source, African slaves" (1976, 29).

White indentured servitude was never certain or predictable. For upward of seventy years it had been the dominant source of labor, but it was self-limiting. The treatment of European servants was subject to criticism abroad, and economic and social developments in Britain soon diminished the supply. White servants were products of European cultural values, and many knew that certain laws protected them in their servitude, even if they happened to be convicts. In the latter part of the seventeenth century the numbers of newly arriving indentured servants began to diminish, in part because of a general population decline in England and the opening of new job opportunities in the homeland. They were never again significant as a labor pool in the exploitation of the colonies, either in the West Indies or on mainland North America.

The advantages of African labor over that of either the Indians or the Irish were very obvious to English plantation owners by the mid-seventeenth century, as they had been earlier to the Spanish and Portuguese. The supply of African slaves increased to meet a growing demand for labor, and the cost to the planters of purchasing a slave for life soon fell below the cost of a European servant. Perhaps more striking, as revealed in the records of the early West Indian planters themselves, was that the Africans initially were considered a civilized and relatively docile population whose members had knowledge of and experience with tropical cultivation and were accustomed to discipline, one of the hallmarks of civilized behavior, as well as to working cooperatively in groups. Their knowledge of tropical agriculture alone made them desirable as workers. Africans had had experience of growing tobacco, corn, sugar cane, and cotton in their native lands (Blackburn 1997). These crops were unknown in Europe, and the colonists soon realized that without Africans and the skills that they brought, their enterprises would fail.

A factor of equal importance was that Africans had natural immunities to Old World diseases, an ecologically adaptive feature they shared with their masters. Africans in North America were also in a strange land, with no place to hide and no powerful European friends or allies to support them in their cause. They were essentially alone and without external political support.[13] Accordingly, individual planters began to hold some Africans in servitude indefinitely, conscious that they were encountering no moral or legal resistance to the practice. It was the clearly recognized vulnerability of Africans, along with the positive features, that led colonial leaders to prefer Africans and demote them to the status of permanent slaves.

A FOCUS ON PHYSICAL DIFFERENCES AND THE INVENTION OF SOCIAL MEANINGS

There should be no doubt that the Africans' physical differences facilitated their reduction to the kind of servitude that the English planters had long wanted and that agricultural circumstances demanded. The visibility of Africans made it possible to structure the demarcation point of permanent slavery solely on the basis of color. Captured Africans, removed from any possible source of aid and comfort and thrown together with others who did not share their language, culture, or religion, were the most vulnerable of all the subordinate populations, even without the vast difference represented by the physical badge of color. Yet it is interesting that the justification for their reduction to slavery did not hinge initially on this physical difference. In fact, English arguments for embarking on the enslavement of Africans rested on the same issues of religion and "savagery" that they had applied to the Irish and the Indians. The colonists convinced themselves, and others, that the Africans deserved the status of slavery because they were heathens and had lived in sin and savagery in Africa. Indeed, many colonists of the seventeenth century believed, or vindicated their actions with the belief, that enslavement was a major step toward saving the souls of the Africans.

Nevertheless, consciousness of the physical distinctiveness of dark-skinned Africans and of their political and social vulnerability became a core component of English thinking about their own social and economic predicament during the late seventeenth century, especially in Virginia and Maryland, when sources of European servants began declining. English traders entered the slaving business, lowering the costs of importing Africans, whose numbers increased rapidly. The singular identification of dark skin with slave status progressed just as rapidly. Jordan believes that "by the end of the seventeenth century dark complexion had become an independent rationale for enslavement" (1968, 96).

However, it is important to emphasize that complexion alone was not put forth as a primary justification for slavery. The growing imagery of human differences was much more complicated. Dark skin color would soon become a symbol of savagery and heathenism and all the other negative characteristics that these terms connoted in the English worldview. The image evolving in the English collective consciousness, not yet fully articulated, was that the Africans were different in a way that transcended all other modes of ethnic differentiation. As the eighteenth century wore on, their savagery became intrinsic and terminal.

It must be emphasized that permanent lifelong slavery, passed on from parent to child and relegated solely to Africans and their descendants, was not a single political decision made in a moment's time. It was a series of decisions building upon one another, made by wealthy colonial leaders who were conscientiously creating a new institution. Jordan portrayed the process as an "unthinking decision" growing out of the desperate need for labor, the increasing availability of Africans from numerous traders, and the already existing subtle association of blacks with slavery in Latin America (1968, chap. 2). But other historians have concluded that such a decision was hardly "unthinking." Anthony Parent (2003) argues that a powerful planter class, acting to further their own economic interests, deliberately brought racial slavery to Virginia.

Edmund Morgan argues that, from the standpoint of the English in Virginia, they did not have to actively enslave anyone: "they converted to slavery simply by buying slaves instead of servants" (1975, 197). Indeed, they often placed the blame for slavery on the English government, which, after all, permitted the traffic in slaves. Yet it is quite evident that the colonists felt the need to concretize their practices and the customs developing around them in law by passing dozens of statutes and regulations that hemmed in the Africans with increasingly tighter restrictions. Englishmen in Virginia, as in Maryland, South Carolina, and other colonies, actively passed numerous laws separating out Africans for special treatment and institutionalizing permanent hereditary slavery for them and their descendants. Although these acts contradicted prevailing English laws governing servants and their treatment, it is obvious that the Virginia planters expected no reaction from the English government. The Africans were different; they were heathens and they were already slaves, it was argued, and to some they were a "brutish people" whom English laws need not protect (Morgan 1975, 314). Thus it became easier to think of them solely as slaves and property purchased for an obvious good.

The substitution of slaves for servants, Morgan tells us, gradually eased the threat posed by unruly, aggressive freed servants driven by desire for land and contemptuous of authority (Morgan 1975, 308). A clearly demarcated category of slaves allowed freed European servants new opportunities to realize their own ambitions and to identify common interests with the wealthy and powerful. Allen has built on this analysis to demonstrate with meticulous evidence and admirable logic that the reduction of Africans, especially those newly arriving, to permanent lifetime slave status was a social control mechanism, one he believes was deliberately and consciously contrived.

The implication of his argument is clear: although the colonists recognized the physical diversities in their population, until the end of the seventeenth century they had not yet imposed *social* meanings on them. Allen's fundamental argument is that by dividing the laboring class along color lines, by allocating privileges and rights to poor European freedmen, and by abrogating the rights of Negroes and by relegating them to permanent bondage, the bourgeois plantation owners diminished the possibility of the kind of "class warfare" that Bacon's Rebellion had portended. By passing laws offering material advantages (land, tools, and equipment) and opportunities to the freed European poor, opposition to official policies was muted. There were few to oppose the enforcement of permanent slavery on Africans. Written expressions of the colonists' motivations and intentions in letters and the records of the colonial assembly were unambiguous (see Allen 1997; Parent 2003).

Wealthy planters were also doing something else in what appeared to be a calculated manner. They were creating a sort of "consciousness of kind" that eventuated in the formation of the "white race," out of a heterogeneous and motley collection of Europeans *who had never before perceived that they had anything in common.* As they were diminishing the rights of all blacks, free and enslaved, the political leaders of the colonies, all great planters, began to homogenize all Europeans, regardless of ethnicity, status, or class, into a new category. The first time the term *white* rather than *Christian* was used for Europeans was in a 1691 law prohibiting the marriage of any "Englishman or other *white* man or woman" to any "negro, mulatto, or Indian man or woman" (Epperson 1999, 160; see also Parent 2003).

A watershed in the developing ideology was reached when in 1723 the General Assembly of Virginia passed an act ostensibly designed to promote better government and social control. One of its most significant articles states that "no free negro, mulatto, or indian whatsoever, shall have any vote at the election of burgesses, or any other election whatsoever" (Allen 1997, 242). By such disenfranchisement of people who had been free for upward of five generations, according to Virginia's governor at that time, William Gooch, the assembly sought "to fix a perpetual Brand upon Free Negros & Mulattos" (245). Allen's analysis of the significance of Gooch's letter, often overlooked by historians, is critical to understanding the thinking behind the numerous acts leading to the creation of race ideology.

It was the political elevation of notions of separateness and difference that formed the substratum out of which were created the social categories that came to be designated as "races" in North America. For the next two centuries Americans continued to imbue these categories with social meanings and to act as if these meanings were tantamount to reality. The attributes embroidered for each social category were intended to forever maintain the inequality and power differentials that the colonists had established.

Black slavery in America, it should be emphasized, was an important economic institution. It was profitable for both the traders and those whose wealth was acquired from the labor of slaves.[14] But colonists of all sorts, slave owners and non–slave owners, did not seek to maintain slavery for merely economic reasons. It became predominantly a social institution, a mechanism integral to the structuring of the colonies' social system. It evolved simultaneously as a relationship of dominance and power and as a form of conspicuous consumption for the socially ambitious. Europeans of all social and economic classes and ethnic identities learned that they had the right to yearn for the plantation lifestyle, with its comforts, graciousness, elite mannerisms, and luxuries. Even if the economic efficiency of slavery declined or was subject to question at times, the structural relationships and social functions persisted and strengthened in the eighteenth and nineteenth centuries. Leaders in the South manufactured a "southern way of life" that was imbued with concepts of honor and grace and tightly linked to religion (Wyatt-Brown 2002). Historians who have treated American slavery as only an economic institution, as a mode of production, have often ignored or failed to perceive the importance of this social-cultural factor. It was this latter reality that generated the greatest resistance to ending slavery, as southerners and other proslavery advocates recognized that the social dimension in all its complexity was critical to what they saw as their way of life.

The process of creating this new slave system at the domestic level, the plantation production level, and the level of legislated decisions and public policy was cognitively connected to the physical differences between those who had the power to enslave and those, lacking power, who were enslaved. As I have already emphasized, the English, not unlike other Europeans of this era, had found it easy to treat the poor and powerless with contempt and indifference. When society was transformed so that indelible physical differences were linked to such victims, the situation literally called for the exaggerated degradation of all who bore such features. Thus even African Americans who were ostensibly, and legally, free were demarcated from the rest of society and gradually demoted to a status of permanent inferiority. A multitude of decisions made in the individual treatment of relatively powerless blacks resulted in, and reinforced, attitudes of contempt and denigration focused on the blackness itself.

Conscientiously moral human beings, however, do not conventionalize such habits of thought and behavior without formulating a rationalizing ideology. Even as laws were enacted and customs created, the colonists were inventing ideologies to mirror, explain, and justify them. After all, they told themselves in the beginning, Africans had been slaves in their homelands and ipso facto accustomed to much worse treatment. They were heathens and wracked with sin. How much better to be slaves in Christian colonies, where hard work would purify their souls and prepare them for Christian worthiness. It was in this manner that Africans soon became the new savages. Almost imperceptibly the status of "the Negro" in the gallery of interacting populations in the colonial world was lowered below that of Indians, most of whom were, after all, formally free. Indians gradually receded as the most savage creature; by the latter half of the eighteenth century a primitivistic view of the Indian, elevating him as a "noble savage," began to take hold in North America. A subtle reshuffling of the existing ranking system was taking place.[15]

In summary, in the process of advancing slowly along the road to a full-scale slave society, English colonists gradually transferred an institution (indentured servitude) into a form of permanent slavery for people of African origin. While doing so they initiated the development of a unique and subtle ideology about human differences, not the least of which was the homogenization of all Europeans into a "white" identity and of all those with African ancestry into an identity as "Negroes" and slaves.

As they were creating the institutional and behavioral aspects of slavery, the colonists were simultaneously structuring the ideological components of race. The practices and customs of black slavery and white freedom thus helped form the basis for the racial worldview. By the latter part of the eighteenth century we see "race" appearing not merely as a subdivision of interacting populations in the colonies but as (1) an intellectual construct about human differences and power relationships and (2) a novel and unprecedented quality introduced into the structuring of social status. This was the only slave system whose rationale became uninhibitedly and exclusively "racial." By increasingly limiting perpetual servitude to Africans and their descendants, the colonists were proclaiming that blacks would forever be at the bottom of the New World social hierarchy. By keeping blacks, Indians, and whites socially and spatially separated and enforcing endogamous mating, they were making sure that visible physical differences would be preserved as the premier insignia of unequal social statuses. In this way they institutionalized exclusive group membership and paved the way for later rationalizations of group distinctiveness in terms of natural, inbred inequality.

Throughout the eighteenth century even free persons of African ancestry were diminished and degraded into what some have called a "pariah" caste. Thus the creation of this new dimension of social difference went beyond the mere transformation of those who were already slaves. It helps us to understand the potentially autonomous nature of "race" itself, how it developed as an essential quality and came to persist as a form of social identity independently of slavery (see chapter 9).

On this point, we should again emphasize that there is no intrinsic relationship between slavery and the development of race and racism. Many find this difficult to comprehend, in part because the American experience has so dramatically intertwined the two in our historical memories.[16] But as shown in chapter 6, slavery existed long before race and racism. Whether race ideology could have evolved without black slavery is another question future scholars will no doubt explore.

Although we must separate conceptually the idea of race from slavery, for our present purposes we must acknowledge that historically the circumstances of black slavery provided the fertile soil out of which the English ideology of race evolved. It is in these unique components of North American slave practices and beliefs, especially as they evolved in the eighteenth century, that we penetrate to the core of the race idea. In the next chapter we take a closer look at the institution of Anglo-American slavery in the broader context of Old World slavery.

NOTES

1. In the sixth edition of his famous work, written in conjunction with Alfred A. Moss, John Hope Franklin refers to the works of Leo Wiener and Ivan Van Sertima, two scholars who have argued that Africans were in the Americas before the explorations of the Spanish and Portuguese. Because the theories and evidence offered by these historians have not been accepted by most scholars, Franklin notes that the "traditional story of the coming of Africans to the New World remains essentially unchanged" (1988, 30).

2. There were a few Africans in England following the wars with Spain in the late sixteenth century, who served primarily as personal servants to traders, military men, and for-

eign diplomats. Or they were entertainers or independent traders and were concentrated in London and other port cities (Fryer 1984). Numerous scholars have begun research on the history of Africans in Europe. Stefan Goodwin's two-volume work, *Africa in Europe* (2009), is the best and most comprehensive of these works and deserves close attention by new scholars.

3. Historian Colin Palmer acknowledges that there are no comprehensive statistics on the number of African slaves in Spain in the sixteenth century. Africans were not distinguished as a separate category of slaves. He records, however, that "in 1565 there were 6,327 slaves in Seville out of a total population of 85,538," and states that a majority were probably Africans. He notes further that Antonio Dominguez Ortiz claimed that there were about 100,000 slaves in Spain at this time, most of whom were not Africans (1976, 6). The Almoravids (followers of Ibn Yasin, a Muslim holy man residing in Sijilmasa) who conquered Spain during the last quarter of the eleventh century, and the later Almohades, included large numbers of supporters from the Senegal River area of West Africa (see Rotberg 1965, 39–40; also Hitti 1953, 540). These were mostly free people. During the Reconquest, when Christians ejected both Muslims and Jews from Spain unless they converted, their numbers dwindled.

4. Compare Nash 1982 and Handlin [1948] 1957.

5. Tocqueville had an amazing clairvoyance about the American experience. Writing about democracy and the potential for revolutionary fervor after his 1831 visit to the United States, he noted: "If ever America undergoes great revolutions, they will be brought about by the presence of the black race on the soil of the United States; that is to say, they will owe their origin, not to the equality, but to the inequality of condition" ([1831] 1945, 270).

6. The classic work of Eric Williams, for example, declares unequivocally: "Slavery was not born of racism: rather, racism was the consequence of slavery" ([1944] 1966, 7). Williams believes that the initial impetus for establishing slavery was economic and was unrelated to the physical features of the black population.

7. In 1547 a statute was passed in England inflicting slavery upon "vagabonds" and "runaways," but it proved unenforceable and was repealed in 1553. Laws of this sort contradicted the trend toward personal liberty that increasingly characterized English society (Jordan 1968, 51).

8. Similar values and associations for the colors black and white are shared in other European cultures. This raises questions about the real significance of the initial English reactions to skin-color differences and what such differences might have meant in the English interpretation of social status in the absence of slavery.

9. For further detailed descriptions of the relationships among blacks and whites during this period, see Morgan 1998.

10. Louis Ruchames cites H. N. Brailsford's description of the aftereffects of the English Civil War of 1648, in which he speaks of "the systematic sale of prisoners, Welshmen, Scots and Englishmen, to serve as slaves in all but name in the plantations of Barbados and Virginia" (1969, 7).

11. Allen has calculated that of "some 92,000 European immigrants brought to Virginia and Maryland between 1607 and 1682, more than three-quarters of them were chattel bond-laborers, the great majority of them English" (1997, 119).

12. Part of the larger ethical position of Protestants was a deep-seated and irrational hatred of the poor. In their view, men who were idle were also evil and sinful, and of course likely to be criminals. This accounts for the jailing of poor and destitute individuals, the establishment of poorhouses and workhouses under government sponsorship, and their harsh

treatment and unmitigated exploitation. This attitude provided a legacy that weaves throughout American culture down to the present time.

13. As should be well known, Africans did resist slavery and were sometimes successful in escaping. In some parts of Latin America and on Jamaica and other islands, some Africans escaped and founded remote villages replicating the villages of their African homelands. These Cimarrons frequently posed threats to Spanish settlements, often attacking supply stations and wagons as well as local militias. See, for example, Palmer 1976 and Bowser 1974. We saw in chapter 4 how Francis Drake made alliances with some Cimarrons, and he wrote admiringly of them.

14. Some recent publications have criticized Eric Williams's ([1944] 1966) principal theory that slavery generated the wealth for the development of modern industrial capitalism. Scholars may debate the point indefinitely, but when export crops produced by slaves, such as tobacco, sugar, and cotton, generated the greatest wealth, it is legitimate to raise the question of what the alternative may have been. In any case, social policymakers aiming at eliminating racism might consider the fact that when history finally gives the African slaves their due—by emphasizing the real contributions of their strength, skills, and knowledge to the building of America—we will have made a giant step toward transforming racial attitudes.

15. A good illustration of this subtle change is found in Thomas Jefferson's historical work on the state of Virginia ([1787] 1955). He staunchly defended the Indians' abilities while simultaneously diminishing those of Negroes. Jefferson was among many who held out the possibility that the Indian might ultimately be assimilated into colonial society. This was never considered an option for the Negro.

16. It is interesting that Moses I. Finley, writing on the topic of slavery for the *Encyclopedia of the Social Sciences* (1968a), felt it necessary to include a section on color prejudice, so closely bound together are these topics in the American mind.

CHAPTER 6

Comparing Slave Systems: The Significance of "Racial" Servitude

There can be no denying the fact that certain distinctive features of slavery in the English colonies had a direct relationship to the development of the colonists' ideology of race. One cannot explain American social structure and contemporary relationships without reference to the former enslavement of African Americans. Race ideology emerged during a period of intensified slavery; it formed its roots in North American attitudes toward slaves.

Slavery was an essential social institution with deep roots in Western history, not a mere aberration in the historical unfolding of Western society. Present-day democratic and egalitarian ideals have not persisted as untainted virtues of the West since ancient times; they are of very recent venue and, ironically, have been afforded to us principally because of the wealth created by slaves.[1] In the eighteenth century, slavery represented the epitome of inegalitarian and inhumane values at a time when social forces in the Western world were striving toward individual freedom, representative government, equality, and social justice.

It is arguable whether the components of race ideology could have been created without slavery. Indeed, historians of the Americas have explored and debated the linkage between race and slavery for over half a century. Much of the historical discussion has focused on explaining differences between Latin American and North American experiences of race in the context of their presumably different slave systems. Because of the importance of this background literature, I briefly examine their findings in the first part of this chapter.

On the other hand, slavery existed without "race" for several thousand years, so a broad look at slavery as a social institution seems useful to determine which features represented the general characteristics of all slave systems, and may be found anywhere, and which reflected the developing components of race in North America. Because many Americans know so little about the topic, I explore the probable origins and nature of slavery in those areas of the Old World (Europe, Africa, and the Middle East) where cultural precedents for much of New World slavery were established.[2]

Then, looking at the development of slavery in the Spanish and Portuguese (Latin American) colonial settings, I note some areas of continuity in the customs, laws, beliefs, and practices brought by these Europeans to the New World that persisted irrespective of phenotypic differences within these populations. At the same time, I briefly delineate certain features that may be useful diagnostic criteria for comparing, evaluating, or classifying slave systems.[3] I then look at the uniqueness of English attitudes and beliefs, noting how their practices differed from those in Old World slavery as well as its versions in Latin America.

The last section addresses the problem of the significance of North American slavery and its contributions to the idea of race. The evidence supports the argument that it may have been not so much the differences in the forms of slavery that evolved in the New World, but rather the preexisting cultural attitudes of the varying European colonizers toward human differences, that best explain developing ideologies of race during and after the slave era.

THE BACKGROUND LITERATURE AND THE ISSUES OF SLAVERY

Frank Tannenbaum was one of the first scholars to probe the differences between North American and Latin American slavery. Although he noted that Africans were brought nearly everywhere in the New World, he was struck by the absence of patterns of racial discrimination and clear-cut racial categories in those areas that came under Portuguese and Spanish hegemony (1947). Indeed, in most areas extensive intermating had resulted in complex mixtures of Indian, African, and European genetic elements in the populations, and physical boundaries became blurred or disappeared altogether. Hypothesizing that differences in the slave systems between North and South America were responsible for the variations observed, Tannenbaum presented evidence that Latin areas had high rates of manumission, that freed slaves were not barred from participation in the larger society, and that there were no legal barriers to manumission or intermarriage.

In searching for explanations of such different patterns of group interaction, Tannenbaum argued that cultural-historical differences in the backgrounds of the colonizing Europeans were responsible. In the Spanish and Portuguese territories, these were the paternalistic structure of Latin society, the church and its insistence on the moral personality of the slaves, the previous experiences of slavery on the Iberian peninsula, and the heritage of Roman law tempered by Christian ethics. These and many other elements of Latin culture protected the Negro slave and prevented the abuse and loss of his human personality and rights.[4]

Stanley Elkins ([1959] 1963) continued and extended the Tannenbaum thesis. Concentrating on variations in the systems of slavery, Elkins noted numerous differences in the slave laws of the Latin and English regions. He found that nothing—not laws, customs, church, or state—inhibited the plantation owners in English colonies from exercising total dominance over slaves and hastening their transmutation into chattel. Latin slavery, however, was circumscribed by traditional institutions; the authoritarian personal interest in the colonies shown by Spanish monarchs, the church with its numerous overseers of moral behavior, and the slave laws themselves were protective of the moral personality of the slaves and their legal rights. Elkins concluded that Latin slavery was less harsh and oppressive than English slavery and had fewer debilitating consequences for the slaves once they were freed.

Reactions to the Tannenbaum and Elkins theses stimulated much new research, especially on comparative slavery among European colonists, and inspired debates among scholars on such questions as which system of slavery was more severe, what impact different socioeconomic conditions had on slavery, and how the qualities of slavery in different eras should be assessed. Revisionist scholars rejected the notion that North American slavery was more brutal and exploitative, pointing out that it was only in the North American slave colonies that Africans expanded their populations by natural reproduction, whereas slaves on plantations in the Latin areas often died or failed to reproduce. Many scholars attempted to prove that there were more similarities than differences in the realities of slavery in all the New World colonies.[5]

Yet, as Peter Kolchin noted in his review of comparative studies (1982, 72), scholars have not been able to totally deny Tannenbaum's observations that there were and still are significant differences in race relations between the two continents. North American race categories are limited in number and are socially rigid, even though phenotypic traits vary enormously within each category. South American "racial" terms are not race categories at all, but tend to be descriptive of multiple variations in phenotype that presume random miscegenation and a range of ancestral mixtures in individuals. In North America's southern colonies, distinctions in attitudes toward and treatment of people in different race categories were institutionalized and rendered uniform by law.

Criticizing and often contradicting the cultural-historical explanations, recent scholars have posed alternative answers for the differences in Latin and English patterns of slavery and race relations. They point to the circumstances of contact, demographic realities, the nature of the local economies, differences between rural plantation areas and urban centers, and other economic and ecological factors. Some scholars feel that these factors alone, and not long-standing cultural orientations or values, may best explain the differences between Latin and North American forms of slavery. Other scholars do not deny the significance of cultural traditions, but believe that the arguments for the greater importance of economic and demographic factors are more persuasive (Nash 1982, 156–160). Gary Nash cites evidence explored in recent primary studies, such as the labor demands of different crops, the ratio of blacks to whites and males to females, the availability of new slaves through trade, and the effects of tropical diseases, as critical factors in the treatment of slaves.

Economic circumstances and ecological features are clearly important determinants of human actions and decisions, as many studies in cultural and human ecology have shown. And these must be factored in as critical to any analysis. But neither the colonial settlers nor the people they conquered and/or enslaved were totally deracinated individuals. We cannot ignore the fact that values and ideologies are strongly perduring aspects of culture. People adapt to new situations with the cultural equipment they already have. Prior values, habits, norms, customs, and beliefs function to guide and control people's behavior even in alien and unusual circumstances. The degree to which Latin American slavery reflected certain Old World traditions and behavior patterns is a case in point. The Iberian explorers brought with them knowledge of slave customs steeped in Mediterranean history, laws, and attitudes. The continuity of such elements of Old World culture can be identified not only in New World slave codes and laws but also in many actual practices.

First, Old World slave systems all acknowledged the slave as an unfortunate but nevertheless human being. There are few societies outside of North America in which the basic humanity of those in a slave category has ever been denied or even questioned. As we shall see later, North American science, and even the courts, provided a battleground for just this question in the nineteenth century (chapters 10, 11). And the practical consequences of scientific decisions on the problematic humanity of blacks reverberated throughout the

United States in the unqualifiedly demeaning, deliberately humiliating behavior of many whites toward blacks and Indians.

Second, some specific features of slavery exemplify the degree to which the dominant society understood and accepted the fact of the slaves' humanity. A complete analysis of these most common features would be far more elaborate than can be outlined here. But such features might well be used in combination as diagnostic tools or as a baseline for discussing the transformations in slavery in the New World that brought about what some historians see as a new institution in North America (e.g., Curtin 1977, 10). These are briefly identified and discussed in the following sections.

A third and final point is that levels of brutality and harshness are not necessarily indications of whether slaves are considered human. The acceptance of the slave as another human being did not inexorably lead to the amelioration of slave conditions or even diminish the levels of brutality meted out in any given society. Much scholarly energy and time have been expended debating the issue of which system was harsher, the Latin or the English. The question, however, seems moot and irrelevant, because examples of extreme cruelty as well as humane concern and treatment can be found in all systems. In any case, we may never have enough comparable evidence to accurately assess the levels of cruelty or severity found in any system.

History demonstrates, furthermore, that we humans did not need to invent slavery in order to brutalize and dehumanize one another. Modern warfare and oppression, torture, mutilation, and murder provide abundant evidence of our penchant for brutalizing one another, free people and slaves alike. Humans exhibit the greatest cruelty when they have the uncurbed power to do so, when individuals perceive some extraordinary psychic or material benefits from sadistic behavior, and when mob or group actions override individual judgment and sensitivity. Slavery satisfies all of these requisites and more, and the situation can be exacerbated when there are ethnic differences between slave and free. Interethnic hostilities and pejorative stereotypes are fairly persistent group experiences. But human cruelty need not have ethnic boundaries, as we all know. Moreover, it is a fact that owners of pet animals may treat such property—their horses, dogs, or cats—with a great deal of tenderness, love, and care, especially those living in close conjunction with them. In the North American colonies, slave children were often treated very kindly, literally as pets, while they were simultaneously considered subhuman. Many owners held their slave property as much too valuable to be mistreated. In other words, levels of violence and brutality alone are not the best indicators of the dehumanizing qualities of slave systems.[6]

An anthropological perspective does not attempt the difficult, indeed impossible, task of evaluating severity even if all data for making such judgments were available. This approach seeks only to specify the substantive areas in which institutions manifest similarities and differences. But first we must establish the common features, or baseline similarities, of Old World slavery by briefly examining its nature and history.

THE NATURE OF SLAVERY

Slavery is only one of a number of forms of servitude that are predicated on unfree, controlled labor. It is easier to characterize or describe slavery than to define it in a universally useful manner. Although a great deal of work has been done in the past four or five decades, scholarship on comparative slave systems is still in fairly early stages of research and theory development. This research has shown, however, that the diversity of forms of servitude and the customs associated with them have been considerable; a wide range of customs, practices, beliefs, norms, and values have been subsumed under the rubric of "slavery." Sometimes the dissimilarities between societies have been so great that they inhibit making generalizations acceptable to all scholars. Different scholars emphasize differing aspects of slavery, and they often disagree on how to translate terms in other languages into concepts meaningful for comparative study. The result is that there is only limited and somewhat tentative agreement on the empirical dimensions of slavery contrasted with other forms of servitude.[7]

Nevertheless, slavery has generally been defined as an institution in which some persons are legally owned by other persons just as a piece of property is owned. The slave exercises no will of his or her own, theoretically, but submits to the authority and domination of the master. Customs and laws in slave-owning societies permit a slave to be bought, sold, given away, inherited, bequeathed, used to pay debts, or used in any other way that personal property can be used. Thus the essential quality of slavery everywhere has been that an individual is defined legally as a thing, a piece of property owned by another, and physical force or some other form of coercion is the chief mechanism for maintaining this notion.[8] The power of the master-owner over the slave may vary in time and space, but it has always been one constant, and usually inviolable, fact.

But the slave is also a human being, with all the attributes of consciousness, sensitivity, and thought that characterize free persons, and this is where the fundamental contradiction unfolds. All slave-owning societies have had to deal with the paradox expressed by the question, How can a human being be both a person and a thing?[9] Throughout history, societies have devised several different ways of trying to resolve this question or at least of coping with the glaring contradiction that it tries to mask. I argue in this analysis that "race" evolved in the Judeo-Christian society of North America in large part as one way of dealing with this dilemma, by defining Africans and their descendants as something less than fully human, or as a form of human being different from and inferior to whites.

Slavery has sometimes been treated as if it were solely an economic institution, with emphasis on the productive activities of slaves. My analysis focuses on what I consider to be the most important aspect of all such systems, the social and human relationships. Whether or not systems of slavery were productive and profitable (as has been debated in studies of Greco-Roman slavery and some periods of North American slavery) is not relevant to this analysis. It is the consequences of slavery for human social systems and social relationships that matter; in this case, the manner in which slavery contributed to the concept of "race" and the postemancipation relationships between racially defined populations. There are elements of personal power and dependency; social identity and consciousness; prestige, status, and social distance; religious belief, morality, and ritualized interactive patterns; and many other factors, that cannot be subsumed under a limited vision of slavery purely as an economic institution. Like all human institutions, slavery has to be comprehended within a wider context. To this end, we need to examine, albeit briefly, its history and the ways in which the institution has functioned over time.

A BRIEF HISTORY OF OLD WORLD SLAVERY

Slavery (in its fundamental sense) originated in societies that were essentially kinship-based; that is, in which kinship structures, institutions, values, beliefs, and ideology were dominant forces in the social system. In such societies, the chief organizing principles were those of kinship; it was the foundation not only of people's identity but of their social, political, economic, and ritual status in society and their relationships to others. This was true even in the civil societies of Rome and Greece, where social identity came nearest to the concept of citizenship, a form of identity essential to modern nation-states and viewed as a contractual relationship between the state and the individual. The "paterfamilias" was the head of the Roman lineage or family; family members derived their social status, property, and identity—and thus a large element of their "citizenship"—from their relationship to him. Such was the power and responsibility of the pater that he "had the right to life-and-death decisions about his own children" (Curtin 1977, 4).[10]

In all such societies, the kin group, whether it was a large aggregate encompassing thousands or a small lineage of ten or twenty persons, was the sine qua non of the sociopolitical system. Without a kin group to support and fortify him, a man was essentially a nonentity. Even the poorest peasants were enmeshed in a complex of relationships, of which the vortex was the kin groups that socialized them, told them who they were, provided guidelines and sanctions for their behavior, and determined the course of their future lives. Genealogical ties, regardless of their biological accuracy, were a network of links that bound individuals (most importantly men) to one another and specified their rights, privileges, powers, immunities, and obligations.

In the urban city-states of the ancient world and in kingdoms and chiefdoms throughout history, kinship underscored the political-jural relationships among peoples and groups. The element of kinship as the universally recognized mechanism by which the most significant political relationships were established and maintained has been well established by anthropologists. All civil societies before the rise of the modern nation-state of the industrial world were in many ways elaborations on the principles of kinship. It is important to establish this point early, because slavery is best comprehended minimally as a nonkinship relationship, institutionalized in societies in which kinship provided the central principles of organization, particularly at the community or local level. As Paul Bohannan has observed, "slaves are essentially kinless people" (1963, 180); indeed, he claims, the institution of slavery itself is anti-kin. Patterson has likened this condition to one of social death.[11]

We will probably never know exactly when and where slavery first arose as a new concept of human relationships. Evidence indicates, however, that it came about only after the establishment of a mature farming way of life, with large stable populations and an emphasis on the aggregation of property and wealth. Such societies had already evolved groups and statuses that were unequal in their command over goods and services and in the degree of social-political power they could exercise. By the time of the first records on slavery, there were already small city-states with stratified social systems incorporating many specialists, such as farmers, herders, fishermen, traders, metalworkers, builders, carpenters, butchers, priests, administrators, bureaucrats, and military men. Differences in economic functions had given rise to social distinctions and to the further tendency to rank these different occupations and positions. Moreover, power and privilege had become politically concentrated in the hands of specific functionaries. Slavery arose, then, in inegalitarian societies in which the concept of one man having power over others was already developed.

Another characteristic of these societies was that some form of compulsory labor was also recognized. We know from many anthropological studies that in developed chiefdoms (an early stage of centralized governance), community members were required to allocate a portion of their labor or produce to the chief, as well as to his retinue and household. Young men, for example, who constituted the members of age-grade organizations (Age Sets) were required to clear land, footpaths, and roads; build bridges; erect granaries and other semipublic buildings; and serve in the armed forces. This was customary and expected, and young men had few or no options for avoiding such service. Other types of what we would call coerced labor have also been documented. What we should bear in mind when we look for comparative materials, however, is that these were societies in which there was no wage labor as we know it; wage labor is a phenomenon that developed in early capitalism. All labor, voluntary or compulsory, was invariably compensated through the reciprocal processes inherent in preindustrial economic systems where kinship values prevailed.[12]

Trade was a source of much of the wealth and the basis of political development of most ancient kingdoms. As various groups came into greater competition for trade, strategic resources, and raw materials, many also came into open conflict. Hostilities led to small- and large-scale battles, and eventually there came a time when one of the consequences of such warfare was conquest, the takeover of whole communities, and the subjugation of their people. It was without doubt in answer to the problem of what to do with these "foreigners" that slavery developed. The first recorded instances of slavery represent the slaves as products ("booty") of war. And warfare was to remain throughout much of human history a major source of slaves (Finley 1968b). Slavery was an alternative to extermination.

Slave men and women could be put to productive work, augmenting the resources and wealth of their masters. Those with special skills were more valuable than simple laborers. Women could be used as domestic workers, prostitutes, or child bearers, creating more workers for their masters. Both domestic and industrial enterprises benefited from this unpaid labor, who needed only to be fed and clothed with minimal material comforts, which they themselves often had to produce. Slaves thus liberated free men and women from productive labor. They also became a source of prestige to the wealthy and powerful; owning slaves was a symbol of status and affluence, a form of conspicuous consumption.

Several other factors facilitated the conquering societies' treatment of alien human beings as objects, property, and beasts of burden. First of all, from the earliest settled Neolithic farming way of life some 10,000–12,000 years ago, when defined groups of people became associated with demarcated plots of land, property relationships factored into all human relationships. In such societies, groups of people formed by kinship principles came to be identified with property, and specific kinds and pieces of property became symbols of social relationships among and between individuals and groups.[13]

In probably all human societies, some aspects of persons have been interpreted as being exchangeable for some form of property. Bridewealth is a recognition of the fact that women have value as wives. Prostitution is an ancient institution that focuses on a woman's sexuality as an asset, exchangeable for some other form of property. Children were and still are frequently pawned, sold, and adopted via the exchange of some valued good. And of course, wage labor is a prime example of the exchangeability of certain facets of human beings—their time, skills, talents, abilities, strength, senses, and attention—for property. Yet the differences are clear: Under most forms of slavery, the total person becomes a commodity, and the exchange is mostly involuntary and often permanent.[14]

Second, in kinship-based societies, particularly where the kin group is a corporate, estate-owning entity, an ethos already exists expressing the concept that both individuals and groups have rights-in-persons over their members and one another.[15] This means that individuals belonging to the kin group, and the group itself through its representative or headman, can make demands of its members and can dispose of them according to their judgment of what is best for the group. This is manifest in the high degree of control and power that kin groups exercise over members' behavior in such transactions as the arranging of marriages; the adoption, sale, or pawning of children; the allocation of labor and resources among members; and the imposing of penalties for wrongdoing. The group may also make demands for expenses accompanying all rites of passage (births, puberty ceremonies, marriages, and deaths) and other ritual occasions. Some of these rights are exchangeable, as in virilocal marriages, in which men of one kin group relinquish certain rights over their daughters or sisters, "giving away the bride" to another kin group. In most societies, before the imposition of state-level laws protecting the individual, kin groups had the sole power of life and death over their members.

Slavery evolved, then, in traditional societies where the concept of "rights-in-or-over-persons" was part of a nexus of understandings, customs, and beliefs about human relationships.[16] The extension of some of these values to the resident stranger(s) was probably an inevitable outcome of the adjustment of the host society to the presence of unfree aliens in their midst. There is of course a theoretical if not always pragmatic distinction between rights in people as property and rights-in-persons, a point that Suzanne Miers and Igor Kopytoff do not address (1977, 11). But the notion of power and rights over others clearly forms the backdrop for the transformations that gave rise to slavery.[17]

As strangers, the conquered aliens had no kinship ties among the conquering group, and thus they were not a part of the ongoing social system.[18] Though the norms, etiquette, and values of kinship and community demand that proper behavior be accorded to all members of one's own society, there were certainly in the early stages of its development no laws, customs, or religious proscriptions governing the treatment of aliens as the spoils of war. As "enemies" who were no longer a threat and no longer free to pursue their old way of life, captive persons were without any viable position or status in their new setting. Their very existence, as Patterson (1982) has noted, was as an option to physical death. In the absence of any previous guiding experiences, an avenue was open for these conquering societies to create a whole new system of relationships, a new set of attitudes, customs, habits, and patterns of interaction. The conquering people, given unrestrained power, could theoretically formulate their own policies and laws to suit their own purposes and from the standpoint of their own group or self-interest alone.

It was probably at the juncture at which decisions were made about how to treat these marginal human beings that variations in the institutionalization of slavery began to take place. The variables that influenced the developing system related to the economic and sociopolitical complexity of the host society, the nature of the domestic situations (in which most slaves were placed), already existing customs governing the behavior of persons in the stratified society, the economic factors of production and distribution, and perhaps a host of other features as well. It is impossible at this stage to determine this precisely. What the evidence shows, however, is that certain trends began to develop, many found within the contexts of quite different societies. One of these was the habit of absorbing individual slaves into the masters' kin groups.

Most preindustrial or peasant societies valued large kin groups for the prestige, protection, and power that they provided. Beyond normal reproduction, one of the chief ways of enlarging one's kinship unit was to incorporate other individuals through adoption and/or marriage. This process was particularly common in those societies in which there were few slaves, in which the economy could not sustain or had no need for slave labor, or in which there were slaves with unusual talents or skills. Throughout Africa, in regions where traditional slavery was practiced, there is considerable evidence that enslaved persons were frequently absorbed into the kin group of their conquerors (Miers and Kopytoff 1977; Watson 1980). In many societies, including the ancient Mediterranean states and the Muslim world, such adoptions became an important device for freeing slaves. Once kinship had been created, obviously an individual's slave status ceased to exist.

In a different context, where agricultural and manufacturing activities could be enhanced with additional labor, slavery was institutionalized as pure manpower, and there grew a demand for slave labor on farms and plantations; in mines, manufacturing industries, and commerce; as well as in the domestic setting. Because warfare and conquest are unpredictable and unreliable ways of obtaining slaves, other mechanisms appeared to fill the demand. Slave raiding and trading are described in the early literature of the Mediterranean and Babylonian peoples. Phoenicians and Greeks raided for slaves along the Mediterranean coast and inland as far as the Danube River and the coasts of the Black Sea. In Asia Minor, where some of the largest trading centers developed, records show that Syrians, Germans, Thracians, Greeks, Jews, Egyptians, Ethiopians, Arabians, Persians, Spaniards, and North African peoples were sold in the slave marts. In Roman times, the Greek islands were a favored source of slaves, but many came from what is now Spain, France, Germany, and the British Isles. The Germans raided their neighbors and the people around the Black Sea to obtain captives for Muslim markets.[19] Once the trade in slaves had been established, it became an end in itself as a source of wealth for merchants.

Slavery subsequently became a very flexible institution, which could be molded to fit many kinds of social exigencies. As such, it was perceived as essential and necessary. There were many poor but free men, for example, who could barely eke out a living in the farmlands and towns. So it soon became a custom for men who had become impoverished to sell themselves or their children into slavery. Men would voluntarily enter into servitude for a period of time to work off their debts, after which they or their family members would regain their freedom. Debt slavery became quite common and was widely recognized as an accepted variant of slavery. In addition, slavery as punishment for crimes committed by free men evolved as a way of dealing with miscreants. Individuals were sometimes sentenced to enslavement for a given period of time or for life and might be sold away to a foreign land as an extreme form of punishment. And of course persons identified as enemies of those in power were sometimes ambushed, captured, and sold into slavery, thus helping to stifle political dissent. Debt slaves, dissidents, and criminals were usually (but not always) of the same ethnic group as the slave owners, a fact that may have tended to modify the nature of slavery itself. Moreover, these variations of slavery enlarged the numbers and sources of slaves, further entrenching the institution into the existing sociopolitical system by making it more of a functional necessity.

From their beginnings, the Roman Catholic and Byzantine Churches were major slave-owning institutions, as had been their ancestral pre-Christian temples of the ancient world. They were also major forces for improving the conditions of slaves, and they frequently manumitted their own slaves, often with the purpose of incorporating them into the clergy. Some high church officials, including a few popes, were descendants of slaves or were themselves born into the condition of slavery. There were state-owned slaves, who were often men of great training who kept the books, prepared documents, and wrote and even administered the laws. There were industrial slaves who worked in the mines, craft shops, and local factories; domestic slaves, the largest category of all, were owned by individual families. Many ancient and medieval states employed slaves as part of their military forces. Slaves were even appointed as leaders of the armed forces. Some of these military leaders achieved greatness through their own talents and were able to gain their freedom because of their exploits and successes on the battlefield.

Most of the ancient and medieval states depended to a greater or lesser extent on slave labor for some facets of their economic production and trade. Not only was slavery extensive in the Old World, but the slave trade continued throughout the Mediterranean, the Indian Ocean, and the Black Sea until modern times. David Brion Davis points out that the "great Mediterranean slave trade reached its peak in the fourteenth and fifteenth centuries" (1966, 58). Christians enslaved Muslims, and Muslims in turn captured and enslaved Christians. Davis tells us that Swedish merchants traded captive Russians down the Volga and Dnieper river valleys along with furs and wax. Merchants and nobles of medieval Russia saw the export of slaves as a principal source of wealth. Men from Genoa and Venice established slave trading posts in ports along the Black Sea, where they did a thriving business. "Tartars, Circassians, Armenians, Georgians and Bulgarians flowed into the markets of Italy and Spain" (Davis 1966, 58).

At the height of the Muslim Empire, some of the caliphs of Baghdad, the political and religious center of the Islamic world from the eighth to the thirteenth centuries, were importing tens of thousands of slaves, many from Spain and a few even from the Far East. When sugar production was established on islands in the eastern Mediterranean, a new impetus was given to the slave trade, and a new structuring of slaves on plantations took place, despite the fact that slavery was declining in western Europe. Slavery was thus an institution that not only was widespread in the Old World but was intertwined with virtually all aspects of culture: political, religious, economic, and social. Just as in Old Testament days, slavery was recognized as a necessary, normal, and proper component of the social system. There were those who condemned the immorality or brutality of slavery, but they did not question or object to the legality of the institution.

Yet slavery was never considered a "nice" institution, even by those who believed it to be right and proper. The fundamental dilemma of slavery has frequently intruded into human consciousness, as evidenced by the fact that during its development some felt the need to attempt to justify the institution. They were bothered by the disturbing reality of treating people as objects and took great pains to rationalize this paradox and make it acceptable to themselves and others.

Early in the history of the Greek city-states, slaves were thought of as normal human beings who had had the misfortune of being taken into slavery. Later the beliefs evolved that some occupations were only fit for slaves and that conquered peoples were suited only for servile tasks. Greek ethnocentrism depicted all alien peoples as barbarians, uncivilized and deficient in governing themselves. Like some English two thousand years later, Greek apologists for slavery argued that the institution was just, legitimate, and proper and that the Greek states should enslave barbarians and provide law and order throughout the Mediterranean world. In this context, it was the superiority of Greek institutions of government, not the biological superiority of the Greek people, that provided the rationale. In Rome, those persons who accepted the Latin language, customs, and laws ceased being barbarians and could ultimately be accepted as full citizens of the state.

Much has been made of the fact that some Greek philosophers, notably Aristotle and Plato, formulated the argument that some individuals were "natural slaves." But it is important to realize that this categorization, though sometimes referring to specific ethnic groups, was a general statement about differences of personality and abilities among individuals: specifically, what these philosophers thought was the power to reason. The distinction was applied to other Greeks as well as to non-Greeks (Cuffel 1966).

Independent of the attempts to rationalize slavery, and much more frequent in expression, were periodic efforts to improve the conditions of slaves. Perhaps because it was viewed as part of the natural order of things, the morality of slavery was not widely questioned until the rise of antislavery sentiment in Western culture in the eighteenth century. During the most oppressive periods, such as in Rome under the Republic several centuries before Christ, masters had tyrannical powers over their slaves. Slaves had no civil position and could be punished, or even killed, by their masters with impunity. Industrial slaves working in mines received the harshest treatment of all. They were frequently beaten or worked to death and merely replaced by newer slaves, who could be purchased cheaply. The sheer brutality of such conditions inspired some to apply pressure to ameliorate the slaves' situation. But this was not just a reaction to the harshness of the treatment of slaves. Some people soon realized that slavery appeals to the most base, corrupting, and degrading of human inclinations. Both free people and slaves are brutalized under slavery, and each suffers a loss of freedom and human sensitivity and compassion. The unchecked power of slave owners sometimes led to unspeakable cruelty, and no one was exempt from the consequences.

Other factors provided a dynamic social tension that periodically served to curtail or inhibit the abuse of slaves. Practical self-interest led slave holders to moderate their behavior, if for no other reason than that one cannot get good work out of a skilled and intelligent person who is treated merely as a "thing." Many slaves of Roman times, for example, were highly educated, well-trained Greeks and Egyptians. In many instances the masters soon recognized the superiority of the slave. This helps to account for the fact that in different areas and different circumstances, the treatment of slaves and other unfree labor varied enormously.

The fact is that no matter how ruthless and brutal the practice of slavery in different periods may have been, inevitably the slave holders could not ignore the humanity of the slaves. But recognizing people as human beings is not tantamount to showing kindness and compassion. (From the standpoint of contemporary moral values anchored in humanitarian ideals, all forms of slavery are tyrannical, brutal, and oppressive in that they deprive other human beings of their basic freedoms. This was not always the case; the moral arena in which evaluations and judgments are made today differs greatly from that of antiquity.)

A variety of customs, habits, and conventions developed affecting the sale and treatment of slaves and the relationships between slaves on the one hand and masters and other free persons on the other. Some of these soon became codified into bodies of laws, like those found in the Codes of Hammurabi of Babylon eighteen centuries before Christ. In societies without written literature, codes for managing slaves were part of a large oral repertoire of customs and traditions that were handed down from one generation to the next and maintained as general guidelines for behavior.

These ancient bodies of laws, customs, legal precedents, and traditions recognized the paradox of people being defined as things. Lawmakers, writers, and philosophers grappled with the finer points of cases in which distinctions had to be drawn between the slave as property and the slave as human. One distinction, expressed in the law codes from Augustinian times to those of Justinian, was that between *ius gentium* (law common to all people) and *ius naturae* (natural law). The law of nature, some Romans argued, declares that there are natural rights inherent in mankind that cannot be denied under slavery. According to the law of nature, every man is an equal. When the law of nature comes into conflict with civil laws or laws of property, it is the law of nature that must prevail. Thus law codes, though dominated by considerations of the owner's property rights, provided an out by which the human rights of slaves could be given precedence over the property rights of masters.[20]

The Justinian Code expressed existing standards of Roman law and thought at a time when slavery in much of western Europe was being gradually transformed into a new type of servitude, villenage, or serfdom. Historians disagree on the distinctions between the conditions of serfs and slaves, but they do agree that both institutions continued side by side in many parts of Europe up until the fifteenth century and even later in some places. Slavery and serfdom gradually declined and disappeared in western Europe from about the thirteenth century on, although Jordan notes that laws relating to villenage as a form of unfree labor remained "fossilized" in the English legal system (1968, 50).

Slave codes, customs, and actual practices reflected the degree to which societies were willing to give cognizance and priority to the human rights of slaves. Of significance for this study is the fact that prior to the eighteenth century, there appears to have been no society that categorically denied the humanity of slaves in law and social beliefs, even when their treatment appeared most brutal.[21] That is, no society felt the need to rationalize slavery by denying that slaves were fully human. Virtually all societies viewed them as unfortunate, inferior, and powerless, although their status varied widely.[22]

Scholars from Tannenbaum on have identified some of the pragmatic social features that are indicative of a society's recognition and acceptance of the slave as a human being. These include the possibility of manumission, the right to marriage or some form of connubium, the right to hold or own property (and to use it to purchase freedom), access to training or education in some skill, and some form of special rights or protection for slave women and their children by their masters or other free men. These are the most frequently found customary rights permitted to slaves in Old World societies, and they were sometimes expressed in the written law. It should be obvious that these rights and privileges were not all equally and fully available to slaves in all societies and at all times. But evidence shows that they were accepted as normal aspects of slavery in the Middle East and Africa, and in Greco-Roman times, throughout much of the Mediterranean.[23] It is not clear whether such rights were always protected under the law, given the perversity of human behavior, but it seems to me they reflect the dynamic nature of slave systems and of attempts at the resolution of, or compromise between, the property rights of slave owners and the constant reminders or assertions of the slaves' humanity (Barrow 1928).

Slaves have had other rights accorded to them, such as the right to seek legal redress from cruel and unusual punishment, to be sold to another master, to some degree of physical and social mobility within the slave status, to enter into contracts and to conduct business, and to religious instruction and to worship the gods of the dominant society. These rights were probably less commonly implemented in the Old World than the rights cited earlier, but it is significant that they are also found in the literature on Latin American slavery at various times and places (see Bowser 1974; Rout 1976; and others).

Of greater importance is the fact that Old World slavery never developed as "racial" slavery, although the potential ingredients were there.[24] Peoples of all physical variations and ethnic groups have been subject to enslavement since ancient times. The only restriction was the prohibition against enslaving one's coreligionists: Christians theoretically did not enslave other Christians, or Muslims other Muslims, a situation likely honored more in its breach than its observance.

On the Iberian peninsula, dark-skinned Africans arrived as part of the Muslim conquests, as we have seen.[25] But slavery had existed there since Roman times and by the end of the fifteenth century comprised such varied peoples as Armenians, Bulgarians, Circassians, Greeks, Jews, Lebanese, Syrians, Russians, and even other Spaniards (Bowser 1974). Peoples from sub-Saharan Africa were not unknown in this medieval world; some records of Africans traded in Portuguese and Spanish ports go back as early as the thirteenth century (Rout 1976, 4), but many were certainly there even earlier. Snowden has documented the even more ancient presence of dark-skinned Africans in the Greco-Roman world (1970, [1970] 1983).

After Portugal established trading ports along the West African coast beginning in the 1440s, and Turkish forces conquered Constantinople in 1453, effectively cutting off trade with Black Sea ports, slave traders turned to West Africa. This greatly increased the numbers of African slaves bought during the latter part of the fifteenth century. The Portuguese initially monopolized the trade to West Africa, whose peoples supplied spices, ivory, gold dust, and animal skins, as well as slaves, to Europe. Lisbon and Seville evolved as major trade centers. Of the estimated 100,000 slaves in Spain during the latter part of the sixteenth century, many were of African origin, including some who were descendants of the Moors (Palmer 1976, 6). They were primarily domestic slaves, but many also served in more public functions as soldiers, laborers, porters, and trash collectors. There were also free people of African background on the Iberian peninsula, so that dark-skinned, negroid-looking people were not unfamiliar to the Spanish and Portuguese even before they began directly importing Africans to the New World colonies in the early sixteenth century. Herbert Klein, speaking of the intimate contacts between the Spanish and African peoples, claims that "the Iberian peoples had long accepted the individuality, personality and co-equality of the Negro." Africans had mixed freely in slavery with them and all other Europeans, slaves and free, and "there was no reason for the white Iberians to conceive of these Africans as anything but normal human beings" (1971, 141).

Leslie Rout Jr. notes that more female African slaves were imported than male, and they functioned as domestic workers and concubines. "As a result, a number of mulattoes were to be found in al-Andalus (the Muslim term for Spain), and several of them allegedly enjoyed positions of importance in the national aristocracy and bourgeoisie" (1976, 14, 18). Thus we perceive customs and practices already in place, involving not only slavery but also patterns of interaction with diverse human populations that subsequently would appear in Spanish and Portuguese America.

Certain codes of law had systematized and distilled many characteristics of Old World slavery as they were manifested in Spain and Portugal. Las Siete Partidas, a body of legal and moral principles enacted in Castile in the thirteenth century, governed slavery in Spain, and like its predecessor, the Justinian Code, it placed restrictions on the behavior of both masters and slaves, decreed appropriate punishment for offenses, and specified the rights and entitlements of slaves. It provided, among other things, for the manumission of slaves and the recognition of the rights of slaves to marry, earn wages, have instruction in religion, and be protected and represented in courts of law.

The continuity of slavery in the western Mediterranean meant that the institution's customs, laws, practices, beliefs, and habits were already established precedents for the New World conquerors. These precedents formed part of the cultural knowledge that was transmitted to the New World by the conquistadors and others. Elements of Las Siete Partidas were carried across the Atlantic and instituted in the New World colonies under the supervision and sanctions of the Crown and the church. They were designed to serve as guidelines for the legal regulation of slavery among both indigenous peoples and later imported ones. However, historians such as Magnus Mörner, Colin Palmer, and Leslie Rout Jr. have warned that strict supervision of the relationships between masters and slaves in the New World context could hardly have been very efficient, and adherence to Las Siete Partidas was most likely only minimal in many areas. They suggest that local laws enacted to deal with particular circumstances often superseded or contradicted the laws of the crown or colonial governments.

Nevertheless, Las Siete Partidas and the *cedulas*, or decrees issued by the monarchy and backed by the Catholic Church, provided standards and guidelines for slave–master relationships as reflected in Old World customs. If nothing else, they were reminders of the human personality and inviolable rights of the slaves and undoubtedly protected them in many instances from excessive brutality and abuse. In the structure of colonial society, representatives of the Crown and members of the church functioned to monitor the behavior of slave owners; these men often had considerable power, especially in the towns (Klein 1971). But custom and habit more than anything else probably functioned to provide adherence to the tenets of slave laws.

COLONIAL SLAVERY UNDER THE SPANISH AND PORTUGUESE

Unlike the English settlers, the Spanish had conquered lands in New Spain (Mexico) and Peru with armies of men and established an elaborate colonial bureaucracy that eventually controlled huge territories encompassing large numbers of indigenous peoples. Under instructions from the Crown and the mandates of the Catholic Church, they set about immediately, not only to impose their laws on the heterogeneous populations within the regions under their control, but to convert the Indians to their religion and monitor their moral behavior. Their primary aim as conquerors, however, was to exploit the wealth in gold, silver, and precious stones so abundant in the Aztec and Inca worlds.

Cortés set out to conquer Mexico in 1519, and within a decade Pizarro formed a company in Panama to explore the wealth of Peru. According to Frederick Bowser, "blacks figured in all the expeditions undertaken by the company between 1524 and 1528" (1974, 3). In 1534 Pedro de Alvarado sailed from Guatemala with two hundred Africans in his company to claim some Peruvian territory. After the conquest of the Incas, when the followers of Pizarro and Alvarado came into conflict and civil war ensued, blacks were important in the battles on both sides. "Even more significant was the role played by skilled Africans in the supply of the royal army. Black artisans were employed to manufacture harquebuses, swords, and lances, and an African woman was commissioned to supply the force with rosaries" (Bowser 1974, 9).

These first Africans to come to the New World, having been brought from the Iberian peninsula, were already Hispanicized, that is, acquainted with the Spanish language and culture. Although most were probably slaves, some were free men and women serving as retainers and employees of the conquistadors or church officials. When Africans served outstandingly in battles or as scouts, they were often given their freedom along with land and other spoils of war, much as under Old World slavery.

Bowser claims that Africans in Peru "profited by the free-and-easy atmosphere of the conquest period to gain their freedom" (1974, 273). Many more, he points out, came as free men on their own. They soon became an important component of coastal towns. All of this suggests that in the early years of colonization, the lifestyle that developed in Latin America was much more like that of the Old World ports and cities, including the ease with which individual slaves could purchase or attain their freedom by virtue of their services.

Initially it was the Indians whom the Spanish planned to use as slave labor in the mines and in food cultivation and provisioning. Colonial settlers everywhere applied the argument of the conquest of indigenes in "a just war" to justify their actions (much as their northern counterparts would later do). But within decades the decline of the Indian population from disease and maltreatment by their Spanish overlords became disturbing to the Spanish Crown and threatening to the labor supply. By 1550, the Crown had outlawed Indian slavery, although subsequent patterns of wage labor using the *mita* system (by which Indian districts or provinces had to provide laborers) and the organization of large haciendas reduced most remaining Indians to impoverished peasantry under the nominal protection of the Crown.

As the Indian population declined, a growing demand for labor resulted in decisions to import more Africans, who had already demonstrated their viability as workers in tropical zones.[26] Beginning about 1518, the Crown allowed slaves to be imported directly from Africa. These formed a new category of slaves (*bozales*), who initially spoke no Spanish and were not yet acculturated to the European way of life. After the establishment of the African–Atlantic trade, Peru and Mexico received the bulk of the slaves brought over during the first two centuries (Palmer 1976). It was in these territories that the dominant patterns of New World colonial slavery were first established. The numbers of African slaves increased steadily throughout the first century and much more dramatically after 1580, when the Spanish and Portuguese empires were united under Philip II, and Spanish ships became directly involved in the slave trade.

Colonization and interaction among the Spanish, Africans, and Indians differed in many ways from the patterns later established in the English colonies. Demographically, the number of Iberian colonists in any area was never very large except in a few cities. In most rural areas, not only did native peoples outnumber their conquerors together with their followers and slaves, but in certain regions the slave population eventually equaled or surpassed that of the Europeans, who were concentrated in the cities.[27] Spanish efforts to govern and control the two major viceroyalties, with capitals in Lima and Mexico City, entailed strategies that either attempted to keep ethnically distinct populations separated or pitted some groups against others. Whenever Spanish officials dealt with incidents involving Indians, for example, they were always accompanied by their black slaves, whom they armed. In addition, the Spanish in both areas frequently passed laws that attempted to prevent contact between the *bozales* and Indians in order to insulate the latter from alien and sometimes heretical (such as Muslim African) influences and to preclude any possible unity among them.

All conquered regions came under the direct control of the colonial administration, involving both church and state, and the administrative bureaucracy was spread widely and thinly over all territories.[28] This meant that in towns, mining settlements, agricultural plantations, and rural districts, a Spanish minority governed an increasingly heterogeneous society. The social structure that the Latin rulers envisioned and tried to achieve was one in which clear status differences between the visibly distinct populations could be retained to facilitate the organization and efficient governance of the colonies. Their vision followed the model of estates that had been developed in Spain under the Catholic kings, in which a system of *castas* distinguished Jews, Muslims, and Christians. The *castas* system was transmitted to the New World colonies, but ultimately the term itself came to be used to specify people of "mixed blood," the mestizos, mulattoes, *zambos* (African Indians), and various subsequent mixtures among these. The social structure was further complicated by class and status divisions and internal rankings within the European, Indian, African, and mixed groupings.[29]

A variety of civil laws were passed to keep the Africans, Indians, and mixed bloods apart. They were often separated into distinct residential areas and to some extent by the kinds of occupations open to them. Sumptuary rules placing prohibitions on dress, occupations, access to the military, universities, and hospitals, and restrictions on marriage were repeatedly promulgated. But efforts to enforce these laws were ineffectual or only weak attempts.

Because both the Spanish and their slaves were predominantly male, and the slaves identified with the Spanish as conquerors, both turned to Indian women for sexual partners. In Mexico, Palmer (1976) relates, frequent complaints were lodged throughout the sixteenth century against Africans who absconded with Indian women and who often mistreated and intimidated the Indian men with whom they worked in the mines or on haciendas. Similar processes took place in Peru. Blacks assumed a position of superiority over Indians and often forced the latter to serve them. The Crown imposed harsh penalties on Africans who mistreated Indians, attempted to prevent sexual relations between slaves and

Indian women, and tried to bar blacks from carrying arms (Bowser 1974, 154). The government appointed an Indian agent (*corregidor de indios*) to protect the Indians and prevent contact with black slaves. Despite official government policies, none of these numerous efforts at social control worked. The African slaves preferred to mate with or marry Indian women because their children would then be free, and Spanish men exercised their dominance as conquerors by mating with both Indian women and their female African slaves. This sexual intermingling between the different populations began early and continued right through the colonial period and beyond, following customs very much like Old World slavery.

On occasion, intermarriage with Indians was encouraged by the Crown, such as when Spanish men were pressured to establish strategic marriages with high-status Indian women. On other occasions, local attempts were made to prevent the mixture of peoples because of the confusion of status that resulted. But none of the Latin colonies passed laws, as did the North Americans, strictly prohibiting intermarriage on pain of legal penalties. The church was responsible for more than a few marriages, as it periodically forced Spanish men to legitimize their unions and their children by Indian, mestizo, and mulatto women (Klein 1971). As in the Old World, marriage was considered a normal state for men and women. Colonial laws permitted slaves to marry, while both custom and the Catholic religion pressured slave owners to recognize such marriages.

Well before the eighteenth century, according to Leon Campbell, "miscegenation had caused racial lines in Peru and elsewhere to become hopelessly blurred" (1973, 324). But it was not "race" that was blurred; it was the biophysical variations that the Spanish had tried to use to structure a society in a hierarchy of social categories. In Peru, Campbell asserts, the hierarchy placed Spaniards on top, mestizos next, then Negroes, and below them the large mass of "Indians" who retained much of their traditional culture and communities.[30] With the confounding of physical distinctions, new social criteria for signifying status had to be adopted. These allowed for a certain fluidity in the social hierarchy, so that some wealthy *castas* could purchase certificates of "whiteness," and children could be registered at birth in higher social strata for a fee (Campbell 1973). Wealth and/or occupation alone was often the catalyst of change in *casta* identity and further complicated the social status of mixed groups (Mörner 1967; Rout 1976). Moreover, some who were phenotypically recognizable as white also sank in status as their fortunes declined.

An important feature of these societies was the number of Spanish or high-status men who recognized their children by Indian and African-descended women.[31] Bowser notes that "sexual contact between Spanish men and

African women was widespread and persistent throughout the colonial period" (1975, 347). These preferences of Spanish males for such women were observed earlier in Spain (Rout 1976, 14). Their children were frequently freed, often provided education and/or training, bequeathed estates or some form of wealth, and permitted to hold significant positions in the colonial hierarchy. In a process of "whitening," some mestizos and mulattoes were allowed to inherit the social status of their European fathers, despite the even greater burden of illegitimacy in some cases. Whiteness, or being of "pure" Spanish ancestry, because it symbolized the conquerors, represented the pinnacle of the social system.

In both Mexico and Peru, "whiteness" was a social category that provided numerous privileges and advantages, and families in this numerically small upper crust continued to preserve as much of their declared "purity of blood" as possible. But it is clear that the elite assimilated considerable numbers of mixed persons. At the same time, the great masses of indigenous people absorbed both Spanish genes and those of the Negro population, so that in most of Peru and Mexico the combination of distinctive African negroid physical characteristics virtually disappeared as they were blended into the dominant mestizo population.[32]

Similar processes took place in Brazil, where a genetically mixed population soon came to predominate, particularly in the northern state of Bahia. Both Donald Pierson (1942) and Carl Degler (1971) describe a colonial society sensitive to the multifarious intermixtures of peoples and offering special benefits and higher status to mulattoes. The "mulatto escape hatch," as Degler called it, allowed those of mixed backgrounds to function in the interstitial areas of the economy, to have training and skills not available to freed blacks, and to achieve levels of political and social status closer to that of whites.

In all of Latin America, the European colonists not only recognized the intermixture of peoples but allocated distinct names to the various combinations and attempted to utilize their gradations within the social structure. Rank often came to depend on to what degree Spanish or Portuguese ancestry was manifest in one's phenotype, even though early in the conquest period negative connotations were associated with *castas*, primarily for their supposed illegitimacy. The social hierarchy, however, was a complex one, not easily fitted within parameters familiar to North Americans. Prejudice and discrimination against individuals with dark skins, which reflected their slave ancestry, characterized all of the Latin colonies in various forms and intensities. The value hierarchy ensured the persistence of color preferences, which were exacerbated in the postcolonial period. What some have called a "pigmentocracy" emerged slowly, according to Mörner (1967), and became more rigid as the colonial system matured. Black, Indian, and white, and every mixture among them, became not "racial" classifications but synonyms of individual social rank. As a consequence, before the end of the colonial period in the nineteenth century, some degree of fluidity had allowed mixed persons to achieve high status, wealth, and even fame, while poor whites declined in status. As Emilia Viotti da Costa and others have revealed, "the society was in fact structured according to criteria of wealth, rank, color and legal status" (1977, 297). Da Costa further argues that in Brazil, "money and status could change black, or at least mulatto to white" (298). In none of these Latin areas was there a stigma attached to elite individuals or families for having had African ancestors, although recognition of such ancestry declined with increasing interactions with North Americans in the twentieth century.

In summary, the documented evidence from a variety of sources on Latin America suggests that whereas minute physical variations and admixtures were recognized and utilized to create an ideology of social inequality, they were not homogenized and translated into specific, exclusive, and distinct groupings. And even the names and categories invented to try to represent every possible ancestral combination were not associated explicitly with stereotyped behavior or institutionalized as dogma about innateness. The continued reproduction of genetically mixed people ensured that easy boundaries could not be drawn on physical traits alone, and individuals shifted about within various social strata on the basis of criteria other than what would have been considered "race" in North America. Instead, the criteria were markedly varied and included education, social class, family background, occupation, and wealth as well as color and physiognomy. Moreover, as da Costa also tells us, in Brazil, blacks, slave or free, had a wide variety of personalities reflected in literature and in the minds of whites. Their image was never relegated to the "Sambo" or "Nat" that dominated white minds in nineteenth-century North America (Fredrickson 1977; da Costa 1977). We would expect this to be the case throughout Spanish America.

The fundamental question raised by extensive miscegenation and its social recognition in the Latin colonies is whether the attitudes and practices of discrimination against dark-skinned or more negroid-looking people is reflective of the existence of "race" and "racism." Campbell (1973) implies that in Peru there was racism without race due to the fact that visibly clear-cut, nonoverlapping, exclusive groups did not and could not easily have emerged. Recalling that exclusiveness is a major component of race in North America, as we here define it, the query rises to central importance.[33] We need new conceptual tools and a more refined vocabulary with which to denote these subtle differences.[34]

UNIQUENESS OF THE ENGLISH EXPERIENCE OF SLAVERY

All forms of colonial slavery bore numerous institutional similarities in the use and treatment of Africans as slaves. Modern historians have argued that every colony differed in some respects from others, whether Latin or English. Plantation societies, whether in Brazil, on the Caribbean islands, or in the southern United States, and whether producing tobacco, sugar, or cotton, were more similar to one another than they were to urban societies in their own territories; it was on plantations that slaves everywhere worked hardest and received the most inhumane treatment. Urban centers also tended to manifest, inter alia, similarities in the kinds of work that slaves did and in the nature of personal relationships between slaves on the one hand and slave owners and other free persons on the other.

But differences in the colonizing powers' varying historical experiences with human heterogeneity and older forms of slavery led to their devising different cultural stratagems for coping with current realities. In other words, the differences between English American and Latin American slavery relate most directly to the retention of Old World customs and habits in the Latin areas, irrespective of the physical diversity in the population.

On the important issue of manumissions, for example, we have seen that there were always substantial numbers of free blacks and mixed peoples in the Latin colonies; no laws prevented the emancipation of slaves. On the contrary, the laws and customs of the Iberians assumed that freedom was the natural and normal desire of human beings, and moral pressure was put on those recalcitrant slave owners who denied freedom to their slave(s) when it could be purchased. According to Bowser, the principles of Las Siete Partidas "viewed slavery as a necessary evil, as a transitory condition that did not alter or diminish the nature of the slave" (1974, 273). Thus manumission was not only possible but, at least in Peru, the old Roman *peculiam* (property or wages earned by slaves) was restored to provide slaves a means of income (278). Spanish American practices relating to the purchase of freedom, Bowser further tells us, were "more liberal than that envisioned by the Partidas" (1975, 343). Moreover, several historians have noted, Latins did not fear their freed slaves. Although most were poor, large numbers of freedmen worked in important crafts and professions. Many were mulattoes who did not identify with slaves or blacks.

In North America, numerous legal and customary prohibitions made private manumission difficult or increasingly impossible from the late seventeenth century up to the Civil War period. North Americans everywhere feared the consequences of freeing large numbers of slaves, a fear that peaked in the first half of the nineteenth century, when, as will be argued, "the Negro" was becoming viewed and defined as subhuman, as a species apart.

North American slaves had no refuge from, and no rights to redress against, cruel or unusual punishment. And they could not sue through the courts and request to be sold to another master, as was often the case under Old World slavery and as was found in the Latin colonies. In North America, from the early eighteenth century on, outside of the northern colonies, slave marriages were not considered legitimate or legally binding on the master, and there was no institutionalized religious pressure to recognize them. It was an arbitrary decision on the part of an owner to permit slaves to enter into any form of connubiality. There was indeed no acceptance of the need for affective relationships between male and female slaves. On the contrary, slave women were thought of only as workers or as breeders and concubines at best. The slave codes gave the master complete discretion in the matter of separating "husband" and "wife" or mother and child and virtually total control over the welfare of the slaves.[35]

It was in the matter of female slaves and their children by their masters or other white men that North American racial slavery contrasted most sharply with the practices and customs of the Old World and the slavery of the Latin American colonies. Historical records, from the biblical accounts of Sarah and Abraham to the laws of Islam, show that it was customary for a woman slave who had a child by her master to be protected from further sale and even to be allotted heightened status within the household.[36] It comes as no surprise that "Brazilians and foreigners alike acknowledged that the offspring of unions of masters with slave women were accepted as part of the family" (Degler 1971, 234). Nothing prevented Portuguese or Spanish settlers from recognizing their children by Indian or African women except their own personal inclinations and values.

This was not so in North America, although miscegenation manifested itself early in the history of the colonies and, by the first part of the eighteenth century, mulatto offspring constituted a sizeable and recognizable demographic reality, albeit not nearly as substantial as in Latin America. There was no customary provision for a slave woman's security or that of her children, and the system did not permit a change of her status under law. Indeed, North Americans obfuscated the facts and denied any separate social recognition to offspring of "mixed" parentage. Such children were not permitted by law or custom to be liberated, be acknowledged by their fathers, or be claimed as their heirs. In very few instances in the South or North did the mulatto descendants of white slave masters have legal access to the status or property of their fathers, even on those few occasions when they were emancipated, a clear indication that the ideology of race superseded other status dimensions.

The economic and social implications of this prohibition (or taboo) on paternal recognition have been far reaching. The North American black population today derives an average of about 30 percent of its biogenetic ancestry from Europeans, due initially to the matings of masters and slave women.[37] When we remind ourselves that it was not the poor whites who owned slaves, and that the slaves produced enormous wealth for their owners and for the nation as a whole, then the demands made during the 1960s by some black groups for reparations do not seem that specious.

This critical difference in the attitudes of Latin American and North American slave masters and overall society toward their offspring by slave women cannot be fully explained by the demographic and economic facts adduced by recent scholars, who relate the frequency of sexual unions with Indian and/or African women to the ratios of white men to white women. In the Latin colonies, men came to explore and exploit the land and people for wealth and generally did not bring their women with them. Consequently, it is argued, they established sexual liaisons with Indian and African women. Because of their fewer numbers, European men in the Latin colonies often elevated their children by these women to freedom (and freed other blacks) in order to fill "the innumerable petty jobs, the interstitial work of the economy, that the constraints of slavery would not permit the slave to perform and that white men were insufficient or unwilling to man" (Degler 1971, 44).[38] In contrast, the argument continues, Englishmen came with greater numbers of their own women, whose higher position and greater influence in English society made it possible to thwart any recognition of slave children (232).

Yet Nash reminds us that until about 1620, white women were generally unavailable in Virginia, and English males still took "little recourse to Indian women" (1982, 276). Nash cites a contemporary of this period, who thought that the Englishmen were "imbued with a false delicacy . . . and could not bring themselves to sleep with Indian women" (276). Nash finds it difficult to believe that such squeamishness characterized the generally lower-class Englishmen and argues that the cause probably lay within the Indian communities, which felt no need to give up their women.

But overall patterns of European relations with Indians tell us a somewhat different story. In the early sixteenth century, both the Portuguese and the French cultivated alliances and cooperation with the Indians. They sent boys and young men to live with the Indians and learn their languages (Dickason 1979, 189). All the Latin peoples assimilated some Indians into their communities, although sometimes attempting to separate them residentially and by occupations. They vigorously converted them and transmitted to them their languages and lifestyles. The English, on the other hand, systematically excluded Indians from the very beginning. Nash says of this circumstance that "the general lack of red-white sexual intermingling forecast the overall failure of the two cultures to merge" (1982, 278).

The Latin colonies, in contrast, produced and incorporated large mestizo populations, out of which came many outstanding cultural and political leaders. Not only was there genetic fusion, but the syncretism of Indian, Latin, and African cultures was extensive. Talented mestizos and mulattoes were coopted into the elite Latin community, many holding professional and skilled occupations. Of the English colonies, Nash states, "the half-Indian, half-white person, usually the product of a liaison between a white fur trader and an Indian woman, remained in almost all cases within Indian society . . . [and was] the most alienated of all people from white society" (1982, 279). What Marvin Harris calls the "rule of hypo-descent," whereby children were accorded the lower status of their mothers, obtained in the cases of both Indian and black mixed offspring among the English (1964, 56).

We have seen that some scholars have argued against the importance of Europeans' previous cultural attitudes in determining their patterns of colonial interaction (Nash 1982, 284). But we are reminded of the Statutes of Kilkenny, which forbade the intermarriage of English settlers with the Irish, and the general English cultural predisposition, seen in previous chapters, to keep themselves apart. It was not primarily the presence, or lack, of English women that generated Englishmen's indifference to their children by nonwhite women. Nash comes much closer to the truth when he states that Englishmen objected not so much to sexual relations with dark-skinned women but to conferring status on them "by accepting such intermingling as legitimate or by admitting its product to white society" (1982, 284). It was exclusion from English society that was the goal. The Portuguese and Spanish were also protective of their status, but they never erected exclusive categories and were much less rigid in their proscriptions.[39]

It seems, then, that the worldview of Latin colonists was from the beginning very different from that of the English, primarily because of their varying experiences with human diversity. The Latin colonists accepted Africans in a wider variety of roles, from free men of diverse social status to the lowliest of slaves, just as they had in the Old World. With the passage of time and increased importation of Africans, Latin colonists came to associate dark skins with slave status, but the correspondence was neither precise nor comprehensive. In the nineteenth century, Latin Americans came under the influence of the race ideology of North America. But because of the extensive intermixture of peoples, among other historical and cultural factors, it was impossible to incorporate all of the ideological components of "race" as they had developed in North America.

Because of the inability to structure phenotypically based separate and exclusive groups, none of the other components of race were institutionalized in Latin America as formidably and as widely as in the United States. Ranking and inequality were (and still are) heavily predicated on social factors, including income, education, inherited wealth, language, occupation, and lifestyle, which long predated the tricontinental mixing of peoples. This is so despite the retention of linguistic evidence suggesting phenotype-based categories. Postcolonial developments reveal clear preferences for "whiteness," in emulation of European and American values, but the race concept was never as rigidly and firmly established in the Latin colonial world as it was in pre–Civil War North America.

All of this suggests the need for rethinking and reformulating our understanding of attitudes toward human differences, not so much in terms of "race," using a lexicon specific to the North American situation, but in more precise terms derived from comparative studies of the ideological components of different societies' worldviews, at different stages of their development.

THE SIGNIFICANCE OF SLAVERY IN THE CREATION OF RACE IDEOLOGY

What the English were developing, concurrently with slavery, was a new criterion of status, the idea of race, whose rationale could be situated in the "natural divisions" of mankind. But these divisions were not historically recognized as natural and relatively insignificant, as they were in the Old World. Instead, they were compounded into autochthonous taxonomic population units and ranked so that the lowest acquired questionable human status.

The imposing of subhuman status, within the slave context, required the denial of any recognition of the human rights of the slaves. Nash portrays this phenomenon in terms of "the psychological compulsion to dehumanize slaves by taking from them the rights that connoted their humanity. It was far easier to rationalize the merciless exploitation of those who had been defined by law as something less than human" (1982, 151).

That "something less than human" is the critical element. The institution of slavery facilitates the dehumanization process in a logical manner by posing the contradiction that a human being is simultaneously both a piece of property, a "thing," and a person. This permits emphasis on the property element and the prioritizing of the rights of owners to their property. It also allows gross subjugation and brutality on a large scale, while obviating the possibility of guilt. The dynamic tension inherent in this dilemma has always in the past provided fluid space for preserving the human rights of slaves. American slave owners, however, steeped in English legal history and traditions regarding the overarching importance of property and its connection to individual liberty, reversed this trend. They never came to accept fully the concept of slaves having natural rights that might supersede the property rights of the master. When they confronted the age-old dilemma of slavery, they chose to emphasize the slave as a piece of property first and foremost. It was the strongest and most successful assimilation of human beings to property that has ever been made.

The evidence for this is clearest in the numerous judicial decisions that fortified property rights. It is also found in many of the laws that were enacted after the turn of the eighteenth century, especially the fugitive slave laws, the various legal codes controlling the movements and behavior of slaves, and the lack of specification of slaves' rights in any of the relevant legal documents. It is manifest unmistakably in the customs and social habits that developed governing the treatment of slaves and the interactions of slaves and masters. However, before complete assimilation could be accomplished, as Nash so clearly recognized, the slave had to be defined first as a creature who was not fully human.

There were, as we have seen, already existing tendencies in English culture that promoted and ensured this cognitive transformation and provided a kind of cultural validation for it: a hierarchical view of the world, the pseudoscientific-religious notion of the Great Chain of Being, and an extreme form of ethnocentrism emanating from long-antagonistic relationships with other neighboring groups. The English had an elaborate conception of what "savagery" was all about, and most important was its "subhuman" nature. We will recall that, in the late sixteenth century, some Englishmen were beginning to believe that the "wild Irish," their prototype savages, were inherently inferior and could never become civilized. Paralleling the promotion of black labor as the only viable and suitable labor force that could be totally controlled in the context of colonial development, the English increasingly fitted the Africans into the mold that the Irish had once occupied in the dreams of the Sidneys, the Gilberts, the Raleighs, and like-minded others. It was fortuitous for the English that (1) the new labor force happened to be not only culturally different but physically distinct and not easily mistaken for any of the other populations in the new colonies, and (2) the African–Atlantic trade provided an unlimited supply of this labor.

Several observations should be made with regard to the complexity of the processes taking place and of the dynamic nature of the interplay of ideological beliefs impinging on these processes. One is that it was ironically the context of a developing Christian world that virtually required the transmutation of the Negro's human status. Christianity was a doctrinal religious movement that emphasized humanitarian and spiritual concerns over material ones. Certain sectors of Christian European society were, throughout the centuries, progressively elaborating and expanding on the themes of Christian brotherhood, human rights, and the elevation of the good of the many over the privileges of the few. European Americans were virtually all exposed or conditioned (at one level and to a greater or lesser degree) to the virtues of selflessness, charity, compassion, and brotherly love. Within their own communities, certain standards of social behavior, shared systems of etiquette and politeness, and shared attitudes toward proper social graces all exemplified, at least minimally, the Judeo-Christian values governing human interactions. Theoretically, those who failed to adhere to the Ten Commandments and the Golden Rule, to treat others as they would like to be treated, would experience divine retribution, if not here on Earth, then in the next world. Such a sanction was strong in a world where religious faith was still a significant aspect of a peoples' social well-being.

But greed and the great drive to accumulate wealth, which were the engines of the new economic order, required increasing deployments of forced labor and a callous indifference to human suffering. The psychological and physical violence against other human beings that is inherent in the use of forced labor called for some justification that would inhibit or assuage any guilt, for guilt was an interloper and an obstacle to the spirit of a growing capitalism. Donald Noel, responding to his own query asking why exploitation should cause racism, answers: "It does so, paradoxically, only if the values of the exploiting society are such that its members have misgivings about the justice of their actions" (1972, 164).

Given the degradation of slavery, it took only a minor cognitive transition to focus on the obvious physical and behavioral differences between Africans and Europeans and reach the conclusion that Africans were somehow not quite human like themselves. With this conclusion, all moral and ethical problems receded, and there remained only the pragmatic ones of selective perception, namely, the obliteration from one's daily experience of any consciousness of the slaves' human qualities. Because the new definitions depended upon the very visible differences of the blacks, this psychological mind-set had to be extended also to those free blacks whom one might encounter. This accounts for the growing patterns of behavior and their corresponding attitudes, deeply humiliating and degrading, that Europeans showed to all blacks, especially in the southern English colonies. However trivial, every act symbolically had to remind both masters and slaves, whites and free blacks, of the subhuman status of the blacks. It also explains the increasing focus on the physical attributes of "the Negro."

This concern for the physical differences of blacks was to grow and intensify throughout the eighteenth century. It attracted the attention of learned people and scientists even as it was evolving as the basis for social, political, and economic discrimination. Jordan notes that there was a rapid growth of interest in the "anatomical investigations of human differences" in both America and Europe toward the end of the eighteenth century (1968, xiii). Two things are striking about this development. One is its indication of the direction that rationalizations of slavery were beginning to take. The other is the degree to which it coincided with the heightening of antislavery sentiment in both England and the colonies and with the independent, mushrooming revolutionary spirit on both sides of the Atlantic. As will be seen in chapter 9, the growing antislavery movement was an inadvertent catalyst for the final synthesis and elaboration of those elements represented in the popular culture explicitly by the term *race*.

We can conclude that slavery was seminal to the creation and development of the idea of race in the North American colonies. First, it gave the colonists, individually and collectively, the unrestrained power to create their own savage. They fabricated and imposed their ancient image of savagery over an easily distinguishable, and powerless, category of people, making it possible to view them as subhuman. Second, because slavery always exacerbates cultural-behavioral differences between the free and the enslaved, black and white behavior grew even more divergent, especially on those plantations where slaves were forced to survive under brutish conditions. When people were treated like beasts, they inevitably behaved accordingly. The slavish, cringing behavior forced on the slaves, the stumbling and awkwardness, the inability to remember simple directions, the feigned ignorance or ill health, all were postulated as innate. This belief was then used as justification for the further indignities and brutalities of slavery. It was a cycle that more deeply imbedded in the white mind the idea that behavior and biology were conjoined and inseparable.

Third, slavery enabled the colonists to maintain "the Negro" as a separate and discrete social category, imposing laws that preserved their distinctiveness. Although some miscegenation occurred, it did not approach the degree of genetic mixture of African, European, and Indian people found elsewhere. Legal prohibitions against intermarriage and fornication, along with the "rule of hypo-descent," meant that the pigmentation and physiognomies of the original populations could be preserved intact, for the most part, and thus be utilized for the critical function of maintaining easily perceived social categories. Fourth, slavery facilitated the establishment and maintenance of unequal social rank even after emancipation. It created gross cultural differences between whites and blacks and left the latter as a largely illiterate population without property or status and ignorant of prevailing political and economic processes. Because of its unequivocal linkage of social identity to physical characteristics, all people could easily be conditioned to such inequality. The ranking was implacable and permanent. All whites, regardless of social status, income, education, occupation, or social refinement, would always be on top, and all blacks at the bottom.

NOTES

1. See Morgan 1972, 1975 and the works of W. E. B. DuBois ([1935] 1985, 1965), who was one of the first to recognize this connection.

2. Philip Curtin notes that "the popular image of slavery is still pretty well confined to slavery in the United States, an image dominated by Uncle Tom's Cabin and textbook accounts of the cotton kingdom and the Civil War" (1977, 3).

3. The effort here is brief and not at all intended to be exhaustive. We need much more research that attempts to systematize comparative studies.

4. Tannenbaum was not the first to note and investigate this phenomenon. Sir Harry Johnston's book, *The Negro in the New World,* pointed out that travelers in the past had often observed differences in the treatment and conditions of slaves in Latin and English areas. Many writers and travelers pronounced Latin American societies, especially Brazil, as free of racial discrimination. See, for example, Pierson 1942. This may indeed be true for the early colonial period, but evidence suggests that by the mid-nineteenth century, the ideology of race had emerged in Latin America, and it continued to develop in the twentieth century.

5. See Davis 1966; Degler 1959–1960, 1970, 1971; Harris 1964; Lane 1971; Mintz 1961; Mörner, de Vinuela, and French 1982; Noel 1972; Sio 1964–1965; Skidmore 1972; and others.

6. Eugene Genovese's award-winning study (1976) argues that southerners did recognize the human personality of slaves, and this was manifest in the paternalism of the master–slave relationship. But there are many circumstances that reveal some telling truths about what owners really thought about blacks. For example, if slaves were accepted as human, why the shock, anguish, and feelings of betrayal, which "reverberated across the South," when the "most trusted and pampered slaves" promptly deserted their former owners after the Civil War (98)? Slave owners appear to have expected the loyalty of dumb animals from their former slaves and not the most human of all desires, to be free, which they would certainly have accorded to themselves.

7. For much of the material that follows, I have relied primarily on Davis 1966, 1975; Degler 1959–1960, 1970; Elkins [1959] 1963; Finley 1968a, 1968b; Mörner 1967; Mörner, de Vinuela, and French 1982; Noel 1972; Patterson 1982; Tannenbaum 1947; Watson 1980; Westermann 1955; and various articles from Foner and Genovese 1969, Miers and Kopytoff 1977, Mintz 1974, and Rubin and Tuden 1977. But the reader should be aware that there are other works on slavery too numerous to mention here.

8. A definition that is at greatest variance with the classic ones of Moses Finley (1968a) and others is offered in Orlando Patterson's remarkable study (1982), in which he attempts to identify the "constituent elements" of all systems of slavery. Patterson defines slavery ("on the level of personal relations") as "the permanent, violent domination of natally alienated and generally dishonored persons" (13). It is a definition that might well apply to others, for example poor blacks in the South after Reconstruction and convicts and prisoners in certain well-known circumstances. Patterson also characterizes slavery in ways utilized by other scholars. Domination and powerlessness seem to merit his greatest emphasis, but he also claims that slavery was tantamount to social death, in that the slave has no social status or human ties beyond his identity as an extension, and property, of the master. In the end, Patterson analyzes all slavery as a relationship of human parasitism (chap. 12) in which the slave's dependence on the master for all that he is and does is in some existential way countered or matched by the master's dependence on the slave, not only for his labor but for the honor that accrues to him as the owner and master. Honor and social death, however, are not clearly empirical and therefore are not easily documentable qualities.

My concern, of course, is not the commonalities among slave systems but those features that differentiate one from another. The Patterson work, however, provides enormous amounts of information and great insights into slavery in general.

9. The most articulate and important exploration of this problem in recent literature is the work of David Brion Davis (1966). See also his study of slavery during the Revolutionary War period (1975), in which he discusses among other things the "remarkable shift in moral consciousness" (41) that ultimately helped to bring about the end of slavery.

10. Wiedemann claims that "slaves were seen as similar to children; they were addressed as children" (1987, 25). See also Hopkins 1978; Watson 1987; and Weaver 1972.

11. Bohannan provides a good, brief discussion of this point (1963, 179–183). Most analysts have recognized this aspect of slavery. It is critical to understand what the absence of genealogical links means in such societies. See Finley 1968b.

12. For elucidation of these points, refer to the classic works in economic anthropology. A good single-volume collection of such material is Dalton 1967.

13. See Gluckman 1965, especially chap. 2, for insightful comments on the role of property in tribal and early state-level societies.

14. Finley argues that the uniqueness of slavery "lay in the fact that the labourer himself was a commodity, not merely his labour or labour-power." This meant that he suffered "total loss of control over his person and his personality" (1980, 74–77).

15. See the discussion by Miers and Kopytoff (1977) about "rights-in-persons" as it is applied in Africa, where the question of defining slavery has been the focus of some debate.

16. I am extending the argument from the African materials here, but Chinese, Arab, and Asian Indian kinship structures from many areas had similar controls over their members.

17. Curtin follows Kopytoff and his predecessors in identifying slavery as the "legitimate exercise of a bundle of different rights over another person" (1977, 4) and speaks of it as a form of social control. It was just one of "many kinds of bundles of rights," he notes.

18. Miers and Kopytoff, in the introduction to their book (1977), provide a brief discussion of the issue. Their notion of the marginality of the slave is well taken, but it is questionable that such slaves were considered "non-persons." With few exceptions, slaves could be set free in most systems and either incorporated into the host society or returned to their native land. In Africa, slaves were frequently incorporated into the kin groups of their owners and treated as any other kinsperson.

19. The term *slave* as used today comes from *slav*, a term applied by Muslims to prisoners captured by the Germans from among the Slavonic tribes of northern Europe and sold to the Arabs (Hitti 1953, 525). Davis also points toward a German origin, with the term *sclavi* applied to foreign slaves to distinguish them from slaves of German ethnicity (1966, 68). These are not inconsistent explanations, because Arab dealers may well have picked up the term from their German partners in the business.

20. It is this understanding that may be fundamentally responsible for the contradictions between the firm identification in laws of the slave as property and the social practices that recognized slave marriages, income and property *(peculiam)*, education, training, and so on. See Barrow 1928; Buckland 1908; Hopkins 1978; and Watson 1987; among others.

21. Early in the conquest period, some Spanish conquistadors and some Englishmen questioned the humanity of Native Americans. Largely because of the advocacy against Indian slavery of Bishop Bartolomé de Las Casas, Pope Paul III, as early as 1537, declared that the Indians were fully human with souls worthy of saving.

22. As in all human institutions, there are always exceptions that render the making of generalizations extremely difficult. Power has to be ascertained within specific contexts. Throughout the Middle East, Muslim North Africa, and much of the rest of Africa, many individual slaves held great political, economic, and social power, sometimes by virtue of being appointed as military or political leaders by their masters, sometimes as a result of revolts against existing political systems. Well-trained or educated slaves sometimes exercised more power than their masters. In Muslim history, many sons of slave mothers ascended to the high positions of their fathers. See Campbell 1974; Cuffel 1966; Hitti 1953; and Rotberg 1965; among others.

23. The most obvious exception to the custom of slave marriage was the large number of eunuchs created in many slave systems, a condition designed to preclude marriage and procreation. In Africa, master-owners were expected to provide male slaves with wives as a normal condition for all men.

24. See Campbell 1974 and Cuffel 1966. Moses Finley "insists" on the term *racism* to characterize Greco-Roman slavery because, he claims, slaves were considered barbarians and aliens in ordinary discourse, and ancient writers rationalized that they were inferior by nature (1980, 118–119). But his certainty is undermined by an earlier discussion in which he asks us rhetorically to contrast the fate of freed slaves in Rome with that of freed blacks in America (97). A Roman freedman "automatically acquired Roman citizenship," and his descendants suffered no stigma. For Finley, the difference was obvious.

25. It is well to be reminded, as Snowden (1970, [1970] 1983) has documented, that dark-skinned peoples from the African interior have interacted with southern Europeans and Near Easterners in the Mediterranean since ancient times. They were hired as mercenaries in the Persian and Peloponnesian Wars (see Herodotus, in Godolphin 1942). They were frequently found in the military forces of the Arab and Muslim world, from Spain and Morocco to India (Hitti 1953). However, the intermixture of peoples in the Mediterranean never led to an ideology of race or to institutionalized color prejudice.

26. Indians forced into labor by the Spanish began to be perceived as "weak and of little strength" (Palmer 1976), so the demand for black labor was made known early in the sixteenth century. Beginning in 1501, the Crown periodically allowed some black and mulatto slaves to be sent to the colonies. In 1517 Las Casas sent his famous request to the king for African slaves to be substituted for the Indians, a request that he later regretted.

27. See tables 11 and 12 in Palmer 1976, which show population estimates for the Mexican territories in about 1570. Comparable data for Peru seem not to be available, but

Bowser reports that after 1593, during the height of the African slave trade, the population of Lima, the capital city, "was half African and remained so until 1640" (1974, 75).

28. All of the Spanish territories were organized under political divisions called viceroyalties and governed by a viceroy from the capital city. Mexico City was the capital of New Spain, which included what is now California, New Mexico, Arizona, and Texas, as well as most of Central America. Other, smaller territories, called "captaincy generals," were ruled by special governors who were theoretically answerable to the viceroy.

29. Colonists born in Spain of Old Christian backgrounds set themselves above those Spaniards born in the colonies (the Creoles), and wealth and titles distinguished individuals within the colonies. Among Africans, those acquainted with Spanish culture and language functioned in roles superior to those of African-born blacks *(bozales)*, among whom were further ethnic divisions. Free blacks held higher status still, with wealth, occupation, and residency functioning as additional social dividers. See Mörner 1967 and Rout 1976.

30. Bowser explained that "the black man rapidly came to occupy an intermediate position between Spaniard and Indian rather than the place beneath the Indian to which the law had consigned him" (1974, 7). Some free Africans had Indian slaves or employees. The rapid increase in the "mixed" population resulted in many mestizos, mulattoes, and persons of more complex combinations often settling into Indian communities. What came to define "Indianness" was not biology, but culture and language. The same is true of mestizos. By living in the cities, speaking Spanish, and worshipping in the Catholic Church, Indians often changed their category of identity. See Mörner 1967.

31. See Bowser 1974, 1975; Mörner 1967; Palmer 1976; and Rout 1976; among many others. Some historians disagree on the extent and nature of this phenomenon, but none denies its existence, despite the evidence of discrimination against such illegitimate children.

32. Small pockets of more or less negroid-looking peoples have remained in largely isolated areas of such Latin American countries as Peru, Chile, and Venezuela. Recent literature suggests that, as a result of the civil rights and "black power" movements in North America, a consciousness of "blackness" as a biosocial category has emerged in Latin America. It appeared among some of the predominantly negroid peoples in Brazil's lower economic classes, where, as elsewhere, most people are of mixed genetic background and are not identified as black unless they show very little mixture. See Fontaine 1985 and Graham 1990.

33. "Racial" prejudice, as opposed to color preferences, particularly against blacks or negroid-looking people in Latin America, increased in the nineteenth and twentieth centuries in direct proportion to the numbers of Europeans immigrating to these areas, bringing with them an evolved racial ideology. In the twentieth century, increased interaction with, and influences from, North Americans amplified and intensified the racial ideology of the "white" upper crust. Thomas Skidmore argues that Brazilians were vulnerable to European theories of innate biological differences among people, in part because of their own feelings of inferiority vis-à-vis Europeans (in Graham 1990, 10). Space does not permit exploration of the diffusion of the race concept from North America, but this is a fertile territory that needs extensive investigation. See also Knight 1970; Drake 1987; and the other essays in the Graham volume (1990).

34. Michael Banton has suggested several schemes for making these distinctions, derived in part from Charles Wagley, an anthropologist who has studied in Latin America. Banton argues that racial identity in North America is based on ancestry; in central America, on sociocultural status; and in Brazil, on appearance (1983, 19). Although there may be merit to such a scheme, it may not reflect all the complexities of the varying ideologies about human differences prevailing in these regions.

35. Richard Sutch (1975) has addressed one of the "seeming paradoxes" in the comparisons of American slavery with slavery elsewhere. Blacks in the American South, he claims, "seem to have been better cared for in terms of food, living conditions, and medical attention than slaves in other systems. Yet the American slave, unlike his counterparts in most other countries, was stripped of his humanity" (174). Most North American slave owners regarded their slaves "solely as capital assets, no different in kind from acres of land, from farming implements, or from work animals" (173). Like all capital goods, they best met market conditions for profitability when they were in good condition and could be sold for high prices. In addition, particular slave-breeding plantations may account for some of the good care and the high rates of reproduction of North American slaves.

36. Under the Code of Hammurabi of Babylon, if a slave woman bore a child by her master, she could no longer be sold away, and she and her child were set free upon his death. If he called the child "my child" during his lifetime, that child could share equally in his estate. Among the Muslims, the slave woman became *umm walad* (mother of children) and, like her Babylonian sister, her position was made secure. She "could neither be sold by her husband-master nor given away and . . . at his death was declared free" (Hitti 1953, 236).

37. See Glass 1953. Estimates of the non-African genetic mixture in the ancestry of African American populations have varied considerably. See also Reed 1969 and Goldsby 1971.

38. Although appearing reasonable, this explanation does not account for the fact that slaves in other societies worked at petty jobs, highly skilled crafts, and all manner of jobs in between. I suggest that Latin slave owners freed their slave offspring because this was the known custom from biblical times on, and there was no reason (no legal prohibitions or social pressures) not to do so. For a fuller discussion of sexual relations in the Latin colonial setting, see Mörner 1967.

39. Englishmen in the West Indies, particularly Jamaica and Barbados, demonstrated a pattern more similar to Latin customs because of special circumstances. Some were absentee owners, and the managerial staffs who ran their large plantations were not encouraged to marry. The result was sexual intermingling with black and mulatto slave girls and the production of a mixed population, some of whom achieved freedom and/or privileges through their paternity. See Fredrickson 1981, chap. 11.

CHAPTER 7

Eighteenth-Century Thought and the Crystallization of the Ideology of Race

Throughout the eighteenth century, European nations were involved in a worldwide competition for colonial territories and trade. The Portuguese, the French, the Dutch, the Danish, and the British sent ships to explore Asia and establish colonies. Hundreds of trips brought them into contact with increasingly varied peoples who were physically and culturally unlike Europeans.

A variety of beliefs about human differences emerged and became fused together in the popular mind to form a seemingly internally consistent cosmological system. As a folk system of thought, this system represented a way of looking at the world's peoples that reflected the cultural values of expanding European polities and the relationships that Europeans engendered with indigenous populations in the process of expansion. *Race* became a potentially comprehensive worldview evolving out of and compatible with the power relationships, political goals, and economic interests of European colonizers.

New trends in social and scientific thought were germinating as a result of technological, demographic, economic, and political changes. A crisis in relations with the English government resulted in the birth in the American colonies of revolutionary social philosophies, radical conceptions of the nature of government's relation to its citizens, and ultimately the American Revolution. Within the same period, concerns about the moral rightness of slavery periodically arose, reaching a crescendo during the Revolutionary War era. In the wake of accusations of colonists' hypocrisy in owning slaves while advocating freedom, a hitherto insignificant rationale for black slavery—the argument of the Negroes' natural inferiority—was planted in American social thought, synthesizing irretrievably with existing presuppositions about human differences. With this synthesis, race ideology and the racial worldview came fully into existence. Its basic features were already intact by the end of the eighteenth century, but the social implications and wider ramifications were to reach fruition in the nineteenth century.

This chapter examines the historical and cultural matrix in which this transformation took place, identifying those aspects of North American thought that were most relevant to this worldview. American society in the pre– and post–Revolutionary War era was in a state of great economic and social flux, with diverse religious and social movements reflecting a search for order and stability. This may help to explain why the American vision of the world permitted for many the total displacement of any comprehension of the moral dilemma of slavery in a free and democratic society. The contradictions in American ideology coexisted without much trauma, as if they occupied separate spheres of the mind and never connected at any level. One level of ideology rejected undemocratic divisions of class and ancestry; the other prefigured individual and group identity and unequal placement in society on the basis solely of "race."

Beginning with a discussion of significant social values in the colonies, we next look at the emerging hierarchy of races, specifically the status ascribed to Indians and blacks. Historians agree that during the eighteenth century the gulf between blacks and whites continued to widen. More Africans than Europeans arrived on these shores during most of the century. Brought directly from Africa, these people were more culturally distinct, often speaking languages unknown even to those who had arrived earlier.

We then focus on certain other features now deeply imbedded in North American thought: the idea of races as separate and exclusive groups, the linkage in white minds of the slaves' blackness and their degraded condition, and the beginnings of racial determinism in explaining history and culture. Next we examine the function of the Anglo-Saxon myth in the construction of English identity and its transmutation into an ideology of innate white superiority. Finally, in this era of Jeffersonian influence and ideals, we look at the representative and somewhat transitional role that Jefferson himself played in the cultural construction of race.

SOCIAL VALUES OF THE AMERICAN COLONISTS

Ever since the Glorious Revolution of 1688, when James II was overthrown and prevented from reestablishing absolute monarchy, English society and its offshoots in the Americas had experienced a sense of "people power" unexcelled in any previous era of European history. That "people power," however, was limited to the middle classes and gentry, who opposed the unlimited power and privilege of monarchy. They were able through the restructuring of Parliament and the establishment of political parties to carve a voice for themselves in government and business affairs. The vision of a people having a role in their own governance was a novel paradigm about society. Its roots rested deep in English history, but its eighteenth-century philosophical manifestations lay in the writings of such men as John Locke, whose idea of government as a social contract became a useful political device to opponents of royal despotism. It was a philosophy highly compatible with the rough-and-tumble individualism, aggressive competitiveness, and volatile ambitions of the American colonists.

The history of the peopling of the North American colonies by Europeans, we have been taught, was often one of flight from repressive authoritarianism; resistance to legal and religious constraints; and striving for freedom of expression, thought, and action. Self-determination, along with efforts at self-discipline, provided the dynamic tension in the lifestyles of the colonies. The Calvinist ethos, shared in varying degrees by all the Protestant groups, undergirded much of the process of expansion. The widely held belief in the autonomy and rights of the individual was strengthened and expanded. Hard work, ambition, thrift, and perseverance were the qualities that brought success. And success was measured by the acquisition of property in land and slaves. Individual freedom and unimpeded property rights were bound together in the American mind, reflecting the persistent theme of possessive individualism. The focus on property rights prevented planters from comprehending the moral arguments against slavery.

The restlessness that prompted the push westward to the Mississippi after the end of French dominion in the Midwest (1763) could only find expression among a people who felt themselves liberated from political and social restraints. Nathaniel Bacon's rebellion against the Virginia governor in the late seventeenth century was an early example of the extreme individualism and contempt for authority that was to characterize so much of eighteenth-century behavior. It also exemplified a cultural predisposition to uninhibited ambition and recklessness that continues among some Americans to the present time. The aim of most immigrants was to make their fortunes, and the American frontier was where many sought them. An extreme outcome was that expansion westward created lawless frontier areas from Michigan to Louisiana, where every man was a law unto himself and the exploitation of others was a common phenomenon. The bourgeois ideology of early capitalism, indeed a history of highly individualized social and political conflict and attendant values, had predisposed many of the English to think of all those beneath them, and even their equals, in a competitive and exploitative manner. Many saw nothing wrong with impoverishing others while enriching themselves. They had already institutionalized the rationalization that the poor and powerless get what they deserve. Rapid social mobility, unbridled greed, and social instability had a powerful impact throughout the colonies.

One source of traumatic social disturbance was the appearance of a series of religious revivalist movements referred to as the Great Awakening. Beginning about 1740, itinerant evangelists preaching doctrines of rebirth began spreading rapidly throughout many of the colonies, attracting large numbers of people in a mass movement that reflected a personal searching for stability, order, salvation, and inner contentment. Charismatic fundamentalist preachers appealed widely to the masses, who were quickly drawn to the near hysteria and emotionalism of the events. Their preaching tended to be antiestablishment and thus gained the attention and sympathy of small farmers, ordinary laborers, and petty tradesmen. Some preached a "radical egalitarianism" (Nash 1982, 220), excoriating the extremes of wealth and poverty. They also frightened into conformity large numbers of people with their descriptions of hellfire and damnation. Those who were swept up in the movement split from their Anglican, Presbyterian, or Congregationalist backgrounds and formed new congregations, the largest of which were the Southern Baptists and Methodists. These latter were democratically run organizations, composed predominantly of the working class and poor. They were thus among the first populist movements in the colonies to function effectively without traditional elite leadership. The leaders of the Great Awakening, mostly from England, held antislavery views and preached to mixed congregations, which greatly angered slave owners.

In the coastal towns, a small elite class of wealthy landowners, merchants, planters, and traders had already emerged. Although their lifestyles varied from region to region, they had common pretensions to influence and power. An older gentry and the newly rich were distinguished from the small farmers and servants by their wealth and lifestyles. They or their representatives in the colonial assemblies controlled the finances, made the laws, and often enforced them (Morgan 1975).

In the southern colonies, particularly Virginia, the most influential men were those descendants of early planters who owned most of the land and slaves and could afford lives of leisure and travel. They had the time and the wealth to dabble in politics, read the classics, send their children to school in Europe, and emulate the European aristocracy. Although they were upright and often sanctimonious supporters of traditional values, they were also molded from the wellspring of individualism. Most important, they had worked to gain close supporters and associates from among the smaller planters, whose interests they also claimed to serve.

These large plantation owners were powerful enough to become formidable opponents of English colonial policies. They resented, among other things, taxation; control of exports and imports; and interference with their business enterprises through numerous, vexatious laws, particularly the arbitrary setting of the price of tobacco and the attempted regulation of the slave trade. In their confrontations with England, the plantation owners developed an ideology of republicanism to promote their cause, inspired by John Locke's view of liberty and society. Every man, they argued, had the right to life, liberty, and property. Liberty was construed generally as freedom from governmental interference in private lives. Property was construed, as we have seen, as an inalienable right equivalent in profundity to life itself. Government should exist, the colonists insisted, only to protect people in the exercise of their proprietary rights and from foreign invasions. When government exceeds these mandates, it becomes tyrannical and oppressive.

These were political and social values with which even the poorest landowners (or would-be landowners) could identify. All concurred in the belief that the man who owned his own property had the God-given, natural right to protect it. In this freedom, with responsibility, he was the equal of every other man with property. In this, and in other economic matters, the small landholder recognized common interests with the large planter. A growing republican philosophy bound them together, especially as opposition to English policies grew. Edmund Morgan noted that small and large landholders were equal in another way, of which most had daily reminders. They were not slaves. Republican equality, Morgan claimed, rested on slavery, at least in Virginia (1975, 381). Indeed, it rested on more than that; it rested on a growing racial stratification, for it was infinitely easier to perceive equality with members of one's own "natural" category, or so people were told. Barbara Fields (1982) expands on Morgan's arguments, implicating the intricate linkages between the concepts of slavery and freedom in North American thought.

Despite obvious differences in wealth and standing, eighteenth-century white Americans proudly envisioned their society as one "where a wealthy aristocracy did not dominate and no masses of poor whites were ground into the dust" (Nash 1982, 214). America, they thought, did not present the great extremes of wealth and poverty commonly seen in Europe. So it was not difficult for settlers to conceive of America as a land of essentially "middling" folk who lived in comfort with sufficient food, housing, fuel, transport, and clothing, such that no one faced abject penury. For Europeans, North America became the land of abundance, wide-open frontiers, unlimited opportunity, and vigorous growth. An egalitarian value system for white males propelled rich and poor alike toward the establishment of the democratic republic.

Certain trends of thought about Indians and blacks and their place in nature and society illuminated this period. In thinking about these matters, European Americans had begun to see themselves not so much as ethnic entities (English, Swedes, Dutch, Germans), but as a common group vis-à-vis Indians and blacks—an identity, as we have seen, that began to be greatly fostered by plantation owners during the last decades of the seventeenth century (Parent 2003; Morgan 1998). They brought to bear long-standing folk ideas, including beliefs about savagery and savages, in their assessments of social realities. Such ideas became major themes in the structuring of racial identities.

One of the dominant themes was the separation and ranking of those groups whom they increasingly saw as ineligible for the powers and privileges that white men could claim. To many, the status of Indians as a conquered and oppressed population manifesting few tendencies to transform themselves into "civilized" beings was very clear. They would ultimately become extinct with the advance of white civilization. The removal of Indians from their lands became virtually official policy, one that contradicted numerous treaties established to protect such lands. But the justifications for such actions were already becoming couched in the name of progress. The Negro, however, was an invaluable adjunct to the development of the colonies, but his very difference precluded his aspiring to the beneficence of white civilization. So his unquestioned inferiority had to be established, as this became the new basis for his allocation to permanent servile status.

Because this ideology promised no redemption or escape, the justification for black inferiority had to be impeccable. Arguments for the unique and lowly ranking of blacks were taken up on both sides of the Atlantic as the potential usefulness of these very physical differences became manifest. One of the first ideas propelled to center stage was an ancient one about the natural ranking of all living beings.

NATURE'S HIERARCHY

Most writers of the late eighteenth century who had anything to say about the nature of human differences operated from a theoretical-ideological assumption that governed all the biological sciences. This was the Great Chain of Being, which was a powerful world model of the relatedness of living forms to one another. It was a quasi-scientific, quasi-theological scheme that propounded a hierarchy of all living things from the smallest insect to the most complex animal forms. God was at the apex, but human beings ranked higher than any other living forms, just below the angels. Originating in the philosophical speculations of ancient Greek writers, this notion of a natural, unilinear scale along which all beings could be placed and graded, and on which they were linked together often by minuscule degrees of difference, persisted throughout the Middle Ages. It was familiar to most scholars as a speculation of interest, but not necessarily as an issue of great controversy. Although it had resurfaced periodically over the centuries, this element of Western cosmology was resuscitated as part of the growth of science. When the concept and the principles behind it reappeared in the eighteenth century, they "attained their widest diffusion and acceptance" in quite a different setting from their origin (Lovejoy 1936, 183).

Grandiose and comprehensive schemes like the Chain of Being function as unquestioned assumptions about the nature of the world, and because virtually all laymen and men of science are conditioned to them as part of their earlier enculturation, such schemes rarely become hypotheses requiring testing or proof. On the contrary, they insinuate themselves into the thinking patterns of scientists and laymen alike as accurate models of world reality. They can be maintained for long periods of time unaffected by either training or empirical research, both of which may tend to reinforce the prevailing worldview. The result is that scientists can be compromised in their levels of detachment and objectivity until a revolutionary new paradigm supersedes the existing one.[1] In the case of the placement and gradations of human groups on the Chain of Being, social, political, and economic realities had already decreed the ranking system. Thus, the preexistence of a grand theoretical scheme of nature that was already a part of folk culture and was consonant with these realities provided the model for the ranking, and affirmed the naturalness, and the God-given nature, of the inequality of human groups.

The Status of the Indian

Eighteenth-century thought turned to the physical characteristics of the Indian as well as the black population. By midcentury, most of the Indians of the east coast, from Maine to South Carolina, had either died of disease and warfare or been reduced to pitiable remnants on the outskirts of white civilization. Native Americans continued to pose a problem, however, in the frontier areas, where white expansion was displacing them and causing great social turmoil.

The apparent unwillingness of the Indians to either transform themselves culturally or submit to the depredations of white settlers and traders came to be interpreted by many as evidence of an inferior racial character. In some areas, a growing stereotype of the native as given to despair and addicted to alcohol, wantonness, wildness, and violence helped to perpetuate the conviction that the Indian was not capable of being assimilated. As with the Negro, white Americans looked for explications and justifications for their practices and policies in what they thought were the intrinsic characteristics of the Indians themselves.

Roy Pearce claims that in the American mind of the revolutionary era, the Indian was a "symbol for all that over which civilization must triumph." He was not a person but a type, not a tribesman but a savage (1953, 73). Drunken, diseased, and degraded, he was headed for inevitable extinction under the advance of white civilization. It was this view, with its foregone conclusion, that governed most of the relationships that the new U.S. government and its citizens had with the Indians. Because they were savages (the stereotype held that all Indians were nomadic hunters and gatherers), they had no right to exist on lands that God had given to white men.

After 1785, the Continental Congress established a policy for distributing lands in Western territories to white farmers. Although these were lands still occupied by Indians, it was widely assumed that white advancement was inevitable. The ideals of republican government required widespread ownership of property, since only with property in land could white men realize democratic and egalitarian principles. "Property was connected with life and liberty because its ownership was the surest guarantee of those other inalienable rights" (Berkhofer 1978, 137). A new Indian policy had to be created that would deal with the implications of this reality. Ostensibly the policy protected the interests of the Indians with the objective of civilizing them. But the underlying and contradictory belief was that such an aim was hopeless. Thus, "treaties were made, and boundaries were set by the new American government; and treaties were promptly broken and boundaries disregarded by frontier citizens who had little respect for their government and less for what Hugh H. Brackenridge termed in 1782 'the animals, vulgarly called Indians'" (quoted in Pearce 1953, 54).

Toward the end of the century, many other tribes beyond the Appalachians had been forced to surrender their lands as settlers pushed westward, but not without sometimes fierce resistance. In some cases, land was openly and violently expropriated from groups such as the Delaware, the Chippewa, the Shawnee, and the Ottawa because many of them had sided with the British in the conflicts with the colonies. In the southeast, only the "Civilized Tribes"—a loose confederation of Creeks, Choctaws, Chickasaws, Cherokees, and Seminoles—had been able to retain some degree of identity and autonomy. But they held twenty-five million acres of land in what is now Georgia, North

Carolina, Tennessee, Alabama, and Mississippi, which they had farmed since early in the eighteenth century. And there were increasingly large numbers of white settlers and land speculators who coveted this land (Hoover 1976).

Although a few whites believed that the Indians of the southeast could be assimilated into white society, others preferred not to wait for such a process to occur. Many thought that these Indians would simply die out as had previous groups. After the Louisiana Purchase in 1803, greater attention was focused on the southeast Indians, who as sedentary farmers had absorbed much of the cultural trappings of whites. But some had refused to give up aspects of their tribal culture, and as a result the whites frequently suggested that they should be dispossessed of their lands. Of the public leaders who had opinions about the future of the Indians, Thomas Jefferson was the first to suggest that they be forcibly removed beyond the Mississippi, prognosticating a new policy brought to fruition after his death.

As Dwight Hoover and others have convincingly argued, the Indian removal policy was instigated by white fear and, especially, by greed (1976, 83). Despite numerous treaties before and after the creation of the Indian Department in 1787 under the federal government, most of which were designed ostensibly to protect Indian rights, their days were clearly numbered.[2] The policy of separation, so intrinsic to the ideology of race, was easily reconciled with white avarice and ambition. The expulsion of most Indians from territories east of the Mississippi was eventually accomplished following the passage of the Indian Removal Act in 1830 under President Andrew Jackson, who held the "generally accepted view" that they should be settled in what was then called the Great American Desert, "which white men would never covet since it was thought fit mainly for horned toads and rattlesnakes" (Tindall 1988, 423). Between 1830 and 1844, "some 70,000 Indians were removed from their homes in the South and driven west of the Mississippi River" (Takaki 1987, 63). In the hardship and brutality of the process, nearly one-third died.

We must remember that nascent views about the incapacity of "savages" for achieving the levels of progress of civilized Europeans date back at least to the Irish–English conflicts of the sixteenth century. The continuity of this rationalization made it a prominent part of the ideology about human differences. Once "race" became the major mode of thinking about group differences, history received its simplest (and most distorted) explanation for all human achievements. Thus, any society composed of "inferior races" lost the potential for social, economic, and political advancement in the minds of whites. Cognitive perceptions and understandings of the nature of cultural differences were reduced to a single causative factor: race. The future of the native peoples of North America was thus predetermined within the context of white expectations about their behavior and development. Because by the nineteenth century the Indians were a totally conquered and powerless race, white expectations were never very high.

Black Inferiority: The Lowest of Them All

As early as 1680 in the colonies, Winthrop Jordan notes, the Reverend Morgan Godwyn attempted to refute an allegation that Negroes were not truly men (1968, 229). What had prompted this speculation was that both the apes of Africa and African peoples had been discovered by Englishmen at about the same time, and in the minds of some imaginative travelers and writers of tall tales, the two had been subtly linked together. In some circles, it was held that ape males and black females in the wilds of Africa sometimes copulated (Jordan 1968, 236). Englishmen were obviously titillated by the presumed lewdness and promiscuity of Africans; and this imagery has persisted throughout the twentieth century and into the twenty-first.

Jordan believes that the "handful of assertions" that Negroes were not truly human were not advanced seriously (1968, 231), largely because of the strength of Christian tradition. Humans differed from beasts in that they had speech, were capable of rational thought, and possessed souls waiting to be saved. The Negro was indubitably human, but this did not prevent the growth in the eighteenth century of the perception that blacks were closer to the apes than to other human groups. As the barbarities of slavery progressed, it was easier to seize upon such speculations about the physical resemblance of Negroes to apes to diminish the humanness of the slave.

Belief in black inferiority increased throughout the eighteenth century; it came to be expressed in a variety of forums and among some individuals who had quite legitimate claims to scholarship and erudition, as we have already seen. Edward Long, a jurist and planter for twelve years in the West Indies, published a volume entitled *History of Jamaica* in which he revealed a doctrinaire set of beliefs about Africans that English planters in Jamaica and elsewhere accepted as explicitly and as tenaciously as they held to biblical history. The volume was first published in 1774 in England, and sections of it attracted greater attention in the United States after they were reprinted in 1788 in *The Columbian Magazine*, which also published excerpts from Jefferson's writings. Long's book was designed primarily as a justification for slavery in Jamaica. Although at first a treatise of little significance, in the nineteenth century it had major influence on southern proslavery thought.

Long's rationalization for black slavery was one of the first popular ones that incorporated some of the speculations and language of the developing sciences of humankind. He argued that the Negro was a separate species from white men and described their physical differences in terms that made them appear closer to beasts than to humans. Instead of hair, they have a head covering of wool, "like the bestial fleece." They differ also in the "roundness of their eyes, the figure of their ears, tumid nostrils, invariable thick lips, and general large size of the female nipples, as if adapted by nature to the particular conformation of their children's mouths" (Slotkin 1965, 209). The lice that infest their bodies are black, and they have a bestial or fetid smell.

However, it was in the faculties of the mind that the Negro showed the greatest disparity. "In general," Long argued, "they are void of genius, and seem almost incapable of making any progress in civility or science. They have no plan or system of morality among them . . . it being a common known proverb, that all people on the globe have some good as well as ill qualities, except the African" (Slotkin 1965, 209). He then went on to rank the Negro and the orangutan on the Chain of Being in a position intermediate between man and the lower primates, stating: "That the oran-outang and some races of black men are very nearly allied, is, I think, more than probable" (210). The gradation rises from monkey to ape, to orangutan, to the Guinea Negroes, "and ascending from the varieties of this class to the lighter casts, until we mark its utmost limit of perfection in the pure White" (211).

Long's characterization of the Negro was a subjective exegesis, harboring and enhancing folk stereotypes that became a significant part of the American heritage. In his view "the Negro," in addition to being devoid of intellect, was given to excesses, lacking in moral restraints, and prone to idleness and thievery. Dwelling on what he thought were the lascivious and rapacious tendencies of this creature, Long averred that it was the Negro's uncontrolled sexuality that was most troublesome, a quality that made him most like a beast. In his assertions about the Negro's affinity to the ape, or "oran-outang," Long played up the theme of the male of a lower species having a "passion" for the female of a higher form. "Ludicrous as the opinion may seem, I do not think that an oran-outang husband would be any dishonour to an Hottentot female" (quoted in Jordan 1968, 490). The simile of an ape male passionately embracing a black woman was not lost on white society, which showed a growing, but baseless, fear of black male rape.

For about a century, a small minority of individuals had continued to believe that the major groupings of humankind represented distinct species. Among the notable and influential scholars of the eighteenth century were the philosopher Voltaire and the jurist Lord Kames, who provided not scientifically based arguments but what they thought were rational ones for the separation of blacks and Indians as distinct and inferior species. Both reasoned on the basis of differences in physical features that there must have been unique creations for the three or four major races. It was the Negro, however, who provided the significant foil against which the contraposition of the white appeared immeasurably superior. Said Voltaire of Negroes: "They are not capable of any great application or association of ideas, and seem formed neither for the advantages nor the abuses of philosophy" (quoted in Gossett 1965, 45). It should be noted that Voltaire had investments in the slave trade.

The Scottish philosopher David Hume was among the first to suggest, in 1748, what was to become in the nineteenth century a dominant theory of history. "I am apt to suspect," he said, "the negroes, and in general all the other species of men (for there are four or five different kinds) to be naturally inferior to the whites. There never was a civilized nation of any other complexion than white, nor even any individual eminent either in action or speculation. No ingenious manufactures amongst them, no arts, no sciences" (quoted in Jordan 1968, 253). He believed that even the most primitive whites, such as the ancient Germans and the Tartars, had some positive qualities that redeemed them. The only rational explanation for these striking differences was that "nature had . . . made an original distinction betwixt these breeds of men" (253).

The works of these European scholars were widely read by the educated American public. Intellectuals in both North and South converged in their thinking, particularly about the nature of the Negro and the causes of his inferiority. So great had the distinction between whites and blacks become in the collective consciousness that toward the end of the eighteenth century a major controversy began taking shape, comprehending both public sentiment and scientific speculations. This was the great debate between the polygenists and monogenists over the origin and taxonomic status of "the Negro," which received inordinate attention for several decades in the mid-nineteenth century. The debate became the central focus of developing sciences in the United States and involved biologists, anatomists, physicians, antiquarians, politicians, social theorists, and others. We turn to this debate in chapter 10.

One perceives during the mid- to late eighteenth century a tremendous acceleration in the thrust to magnify the differences between blacks and whites. As Jordan notes, "a few men . . . were so intent over distinguishing Negroes from whites that they proceeded to invent the facts they were unable to discover; they claimed variously, that the Negro's blood, brains and skull were black. Cornelius de Pauw announced in 1770 that the Negro had dark brains, blood and semen" (1968, 249). The term *race*, with its basis in heredity and descent, cohered as the symbol of all these differences. Although it may have appeared ill defined, its cognitive correlates were increasingly specific and tangible in the mental images held by whites.

Jordan claims that the term *race*, at the time of Jefferson, was "characterized by total absence of any precise meaning" (1968, 489). But the evidence that he himself provides of the range of white beliefs and attitudes shows a far more concrete conceptualization of race and race differences than he would allow. Jordan even recognizes Jefferson's "axiomatic" acceptance of the Great Chain of Being in the latter's *Notes on the State of Virginia* and his even more significant adhering to the "objectively hierarchical character of natural variation" (490). The point is that *race*, a term that had come into widespread use, already referred to unequal groups; the inequality had been established even before the application of the term.

In the writings of proslavery individuals, and even of some individuals who were antislavery but viewed "the Negro" as a being apart, we see the nearly complete transformation of "the Negro" into a subhuman creature. This grotesque monster, more ape than human, was perpetuated as much by the writings of scholars as by members of the white public, whose repugnance toward blackness was in turn increasingly fueled by such writings. In the eyes of many whites in both the North and the South, the Negro had been transformed into a degraded and contemptible creature by the turn of the nineteenth century (Fredrickson 1977).

DOMINANT THEMES IN NORTH AMERICAN RACIAL BELIEFS

The major themes, what I have called the constituent components of North American race ideology, came into clear relief before the beginning of the nineteenth century. The first and clearest theme expressed in the beliefs and practices of Europeans was that races were exclusive groups.

Races as Exclusive Groups

The element of race that holds that different human groups constitute separate, discrete, and exclusive entities, differing in important qualities from other groups, was fashioned from earlier antecedents in the folk practices of the English. One may see its elemental nature in the policies of the first colonists who segregated "missionized" Indians in their church congregations and established separate villages for converted Indians. It is also evidenced in the many statutes forbidding intermarriage, prompted by the desire not to confuse distinctions of social status between servile and free populations. But such exclusiveness and insularity was an established custom in English culture. In chapter 3, we saw that the English from the thirteenth to the sixteenth centuries fulminated against a practice that they found both menacing and malignant. This was the habit among proper Englishmen of settling in Ireland and "going native," taking on the language, customs, dress, hairstyles, and general behavior of the "wild Irish." Just as aggravating and incomprehensible were the same processes occurring with the savages of America. Why was it that white men, women, and children were so attracted to the Indian way of life that, once exposed to it, many refused to return to civilized society?

The facts, as we saw earlier, are suggestive of a disquieting uncertainty and apprehension about the English sense of their own identity. The posing of this question by writers of the colonial period suggested that deep-seated doubts existed about the value and worthiness of English culture. It may be that the more threatening this reality, the more attenuated the sense of self and society, the more rigidly insular and introspective the English felt it necessary to become. Could it also be that the Englishman's burning need to associate himself with property and power was, in part, a desperate effort to construct and preserve a sense of self? Both Jordan (1968) and Margaret Hodgen (1964) infer that the English may have had a psychological need for the existence of the "savage," to affirm their own virtues and stand as a symbol of what they must not become.

Racial Determinism

The idea that biological variations account for differences in cultural behavior did not appear suddenly in the eighteenth century. An incipient sense of biological concomitants to, if not determinants of, human behavior is found in a few of the early writings and philosophical and scholarly musings of certain individuals who were among the intellectual leaders of the seventeenth century.

By the mid-eighteenth century, the considerably broader experiences of Europeans in trade and colonization had led to far more complex perceptions and evaluations of non-European peoples. Variations in material cultures, languages, and beliefs among peoples of the colonized territories were sometimes recognized. But the myriad of impressions reaching the European mind could only be processed and comprehended in terms of antecedents within its own culturally prescribed sets of meanings. There were existing categories, imprecise and value-loaded, that could be employed not only to identify all newly discovered sociocultural realities but to give meaning to, and literally "read," the panorama of humanity.

The terms *barbarian*, *heathen*, and *savage* had been invariably applied to most non-Europeans, from Africans to Turks, Chinese, and Native Americans. These were ethnocentric terms that reflected the most striking contrasts with the Europeans' views of themselves as people who were both Christian and civilized. All of these terms had in common the implication of the inferiority of the cultures of non-Europeans. Until the eighteenth century, no clear connection had been made between the biophysical features of the different human groups and their specific cultures. That is, no causal link was assumed to exist between their differing physical characteristics and their habits, customs, beliefs, values, and behavior. If anything, the extrinsic nature of cultural behavior should have been recognized, since both Indians and blacks had long been observed to learn Spanish, English, or Portuguese (and sometimes all three) and to be able to function as cultural beings in European contexts.

Earlier in the century, some scholarly writers had begun to speculate on the material causes of cultural differences and to pose cultural-historical theories about the reasons for certain practices, beliefs, and developments. The beginnings of cultural evolutionary thought had already made an appearance in the literature of some learned men. The idea of environmental causes for human differences had long precedents in the sixteenth- to eighteenth-century writings of Europeans such as Montaigne, Thomas Hobbes, and even John Locke. Such theories of external causation persisted in Europe, albeit in limited circles, into the nineteenth century and beyond.

However, a central ideological component of race, hereditary determinism, was soon to take precedence over other explanatory models, particularly external, environmental, and material explanations of human history and cultural diversity. This new causal theory appeared in the writings of a number of scholars beginning in the latter part of the eighteenth century who, without hesitation, linked physical features with cultural behavior. What emerged was a comprehensive ideology with the capacity to inform all understandings, and all queries, about the nature of human groups everywhere. It was manifest in an expanding consciousness, and a widening interpretation, of all cultural-historical features as due to "race"—a process that Marvin Harris and others have called the "biologization of history" (1968, chap. 4). It obscured all possible perceptions of similarities among individuals and groups and distorted the meaning of behaviors that in modern times we have come to understand as part of our universal primate, and human, nature. By the early nineteenth century, racial determinism was a dominant ideology; it had become the central key to the interpretation and explanation of all human achievements and failures.[3]

ANGLO-SAXONISM: THE MAKING OF A BIOLOGICAL MYTH

In chapter 3 we saw that the sixteenth-century English, partly to justify their break from the Roman Catholic Church, sought a new historical identity that could rival the glories and accomplishments of the ancient Romans. Turning to the tribal histories of pre-Roman, and pre-Norman, times, they fabricated as part of a national identity a myth of an Anglo-Saxon people who had a pure religion and free political institutions. The invention of distinguished ancestry was not merely a political action of Henry VIII's followers, but was part of the broader pattern of cultural chauvinism, intolerance, and ethnic conflict that accompanied the emergence of nation-states in Europe from the sixteenth to the nineteenth centuries. During this period, the English solidified their identity as Anglo-Saxons, further distinguishing themselves from the Celts, Vikings, Normans, and others who also had composed the mélange of peoples in England.

The Anglo-Saxons, it was said, had developed advanced political institutions before the Norman conquest. They were a "freedom-loving people, enjoying representative institutions and a flourishing primitive democracy" (Horsman 1976, 388). English scholars spent lifetimes researching this history and concluded that their Anglo-Saxon ancestors had derived the excellence of their social system from German forebears. Glorification of the German past became a prelude to the history and greatness of the Anglo-Saxons.

Reginald Horsman (1976, 1981) and L. P. Curtis (1968) agree that such chauvinism was not initially racial but was focused instead on reconstructing the continuity of institutions. However, they both found a change occurring in the mid- to late eighteenth century that transformed ideas of Anglo-Saxon ethnic superiority into a philosophy of racial superiority. According to Horsman, "not until the 1760s and 1770s did a variety of new tendencies foreshadow a shift in emphasis from the continuity of free institutions to the inherent racial traits which supposedly explained them" (1976, 390). It is no mere coincidence that this transformation paralleled the rise of racial ideologies on the North American continent.

There is, it should be noted, a theory that racial ideas in Europe may have evolved independently of those in North America, with origins quite distinct from English sources. Jacques Barzun (1965) and Hannah Arendt ([1951] 1968) observed the germination of racial thought in the works of Count Henri de Boulainvilliers (1658–1722), a French nobleman and apologist for the aristocracy. Barzun noted that Boulainvilliers's writings, published in the 1720s and 1730s, were widely read in England because of his connections with the Freemasonry movement (1965, 19). Boulainvilliers argued that the noble classes of France were not originally Gauls but Germanic Franks, who after conquering the inferior natives, established themselves as the ruling class. They derived their laws, pride, individualism, and love of liberty from their Germanic ancestors and ruled by the right of might. Arendt claims that in Boulainvilliers's representation, the Franks, like all racists, were antinational, having more in common with other ruling castes than with the French people ([1951] 1968, 43).

Boulainvilliers's diatribe against the native Gauls, whom he saw as peasants and slaves, was a political tract, designed specifically to promote the interests of one class over the others. What concerns us here is that both he and the proponents of Anglo-Saxonism in England based their claims for the superiority of the Germanic peoples on a single source. This was the second-century Roman historian and early anthropological writer Tacitus, whose essay on the German tribes represents one of the few recognized ethnographic descriptions of what was then a primitive people.

Tacitus praised the Germans as a primitive, crude people who led simple lives, adhered to pure values, loved freedom, practiced monogamy, and were courageous and warlike. Tacitus's purpose in extolling the simple virtues of German culture was to contrast their pure and unadulterated lives to the corruption and decadence of Rome, the sophisticated, civilized state whose evils he abhorred. Those who mined his work to argue for Germanic purity and superiority tended to ignore his less flattering characterizations of Germans. He claimed that not only were they intensely warlike, they actually hated peace and would always find some occasion to continue fighting. German warriors despised work, opting to sleep or lie about idly when off the battlefield. They gave blind obedience to their chiefs and had an ignoble passion for gambling and drunken fights. Large, awkward, and rough, with hair the same color as their reddish faces, the Germans, Tacitus observed, clothed their ugliness with the skins of wild animals.[4]

Nothing in Tacitus's descriptions of the Germans resembles the diagnostic features proposed here for recognizing the modern idea of race. Roman writers, like others who followed them, were not reluctant to make ethnocentric or subjective assessments of the "barbarians" they encountered. The primitive German tribespeople were, in fact, the first of the "noble savages" whom some "civilized" peoples have sometimes viewed as living pure and idyllic lives. They were not, however, the stuff of which ideologies of racial purity and superiority can be made.

The highly embroidered Germanic myth, nevertheless, had a tenacious following both in England and on the continent. In the nineteenth century it became the crux of the Nordic myths of Comte Joseph-Arthur de Gobineau and Houston Stewart Chamberlain, who easily assimilated it to contemporary race thinking. The twentieth century was to find the greatly enlarged Germanic myth transferred in a full-blown version in Nazi notions of racial superiority.

Transatlantic intellectual discourse meant that ideas about race were transmitted back and forth from Europe to the Americas throughout the eighteenth and nineteenth centuries. Before the Revolutionary War, Americans conveyed their ideas about the inferiority of Indians and blacks to European intellectuals, and Europeans began to see themselves and others in similar racial terms. The influences were pervasive and ramified beyond the boundaries of immediate social circumstances. Thomas Jefferson, for example, had an intense interest in Anglo-Saxonism and was well aware of developing ideas of the superiority of Anglo-Saxon history, religion, and language. Such was his obsession that he actually tried to learn the ancient language. He and other Americans accepted the myth of Anglo-Saxon racial purity and superiority because it was so consonant with prevailing beliefs and so comforting to those whites who might on occasion be smitten with moral doubts about slavery and the exploitation of indigenous peoples.

The idea of innate Anglo-Saxon superiority was nurtured by, and became an integral part of, American racial ideologies of the late eighteenth and nineteenth centuries (see Gossett 1965). It also became part of American mythology associated with republicanism, Protestantism, democracy, laissez-faire economic theory, progress, and empire building. The presumed superior "racial" traits of Anglo-Saxons became a stimulus for American expansion. Indeed, the myth was at the heart of the doctrine of Manifest Destiny, by which some white Americans expressed belief in themselves as a "chosen people" destined to dominate others. Although this doctrine was utilized in the late nineteenth and early twentieth centuries as a justification for preventing the immigration of southern and eastern Europeans, over time, many non-English whites also assimilated this myth of Manifest Destiny, as it provided the foundation for the general ideology of white supremacy.

By the turn of the nineteenth century, the vision that Americans shared about human group variations had taken on full racial coloration. Their characterizations of racial groups demonstrated that the authors of such theories thought of races as homogeneous biophysical entities. Non-European races were considered to be fundamentally and intrinsically different from, and inferior to, Europeans. There were few attempts to ascertain or establish similarities among human populations, and even the possibility of similarities was precluded by the growing belief that each race had a unique racial character granted by God or nature.[5]

This "unique" racial character reflected the fusion in white minds of distinct intellectual, moral, temperamental, and physical characteristics. Other than a few Enlightenment writers whose materialistic philosophies emphasized the power of education, and whose influence had waned by the end of the century, no significant voices contradicted this idea. Even the writings and speeches of Dr. Samuel Stanhope Smith, Presbyterian minister and professor of moral philosophy at the College of New Jersey (later Princeton), tended to associate refinements of culture among blacks with a change in their physiognomy (Gossett 1965, 40). Smith, who later became president of Princeton University, believed fervently in the potential equality of all men, a rare stance with few progeny in the early nineteenth century.

Before we consider the full flowering of race ideology in the nineteenth century, it is important to recognize the dilemma that the growing concept of race posed in the context of the democratic ideals of the revolutionary era. No one reflects the emergence of this peculiarly American paradox better than Thomas Jefferson. We examine facets of his life that are emblematic of this dilemma in the next section.

THOMAS JEFFERSON AND THE AMERICAN DILEMMA

Winthrop Jordan, in his classic study *White Over Black* (1968), rightly focuses on Jefferson to illuminate some of the problems of race and slavery that confronted the incipient nation during the Revolutionary War period. Jefferson's life spanned not only the drama of this era and the birth of a new nation, but the maturation of a new worldview often vividly expressed in his own writings. As a young man, he inveighed against slavery in powerful language, but once elected to public office, he took a position as a Virginia planter that John C. Miller describes as "utilitarian," "pragmatic," and "prudent," even once advocating the extension of slavery into the western territories (1977, 18, 37, 39).

Jefferson's life exemplifies the agonizing ambiguities and contradictory impulses that came to warp American thought. Indeed, he was central to the formulation and dissemination of American attitudes about race, as we will see. Specifically, he was instrumental in casting the whole question of racial inferiority into the arms of science. But Jefferson represented a great deal more than that. He articulated better than almost anyone else the concepts of human rights, individual liberty, and justice—an enlightened ideology diametrically opposed to the ideology of race. As a slave owner, he vividly reflected and internalized these opposing forces.[6]

The questions of personal freedom, the rights of men (not women) within the state, and human liberty in all its forms and manifestations constantly occupied Jefferson, and not just on account of political conflicts with England. We see it clearly in the turmoil and ambivalence that characterized his early writings on the subject of Negroes and slavery. We are told by his biographers, and apologists, that he hated slavery with a passion.[7] But since he participated fully in the plantation slavery system, buying and selling slaves on occasion, and could not bring himself to free his own slaves, who often numbered upward of 200–250 on his plantations, one has to either question the verity of this passion or speculate that it was merely the abstract idea of slavery that he hated.[8] He apparently never ceased believing that slavery was ultimately doomed to extinction, but he made few efforts to accelerate this process in his own lifetime.

What is so striking about Jefferson on this score is that he was one of the few men who put into writing some of his anguish over the issues of slavery and freedom. Other men, such as Thomas Paine, an impoverished English-born revolutionary leader, wrote brilliant and inspiring passages on the nature of slavery, freedom, and the rights of man. But Paine, who also wrote against the extremes of wealth and poverty, never owned a slave, and his soul was never scoured by a confrontation with the realities of his own duplicity and hypocrisy. Jefferson, on the other hand, faced enormous inner contradictions. His actions in many areas of politics and social affairs often seemed to lend little veracity to his words. Even his written statements, especially on the matters of slavery, the Negroes, and the Indians, contaminate one another with their sophistry.

Nevertheless, Jefferson was one of the most brilliant men of the American colonies, and his writings on slavery, the Indians, and the Negroes reveal much about the thinking of the times and of the men and women who, like himself, were caught up in the controversies over slavery and the rights of mankind. David Brion Davis claims that in Jefferson we see a microcosm of the conflicts permeating American culture (1975, 166). It was these controversies and conflicts that deeply influenced the man, swirling around him and prodding him unsuccessfully to face the world that the colonists had made, with all of its evils as well as its potential for human good.

Like all men of conscience who owned slaves, Jefferson was faced with a double-pronged dilemma, with both intellectual and moral implications. The first was that existential Gordian knot that we have already encountered. A slave was conceptualized as being property, in a very real sense tantamount to a "commodity." But the slave was also a human being—a talking, walking, thinking, living organism no different from the slave owner. Although it appears that this was the source of some of Jefferson's pain and anguish, he could never confront the implacable contradiction, the monumental paradox of the simultaneity of both the animate and inanimate, personhood and commodity, consciousness and unconsciousness.

There followed from this dilemma the equally troubling problem of the development of relationships between master and slave, between free and unfree persons. The double identity raised the kind of question for which there is no logical or suitable answer: What kind of behavior is required or necessary in order to treat someone as both a human being and a commodity, a thing? It was the kind of dilemma that generates ambivalence, inconsistency, and indetermination, to say nothing of confusion. Fawn Brodie's intensive research into the personal life of America's third president (1974) shows that all of these qualities were characteristic of Jefferson.

As already indicated, on the question of the double identity of slaves, Americans gave greater weight, stature, and legitimacy to the property rights of slave owners. Many statutes and judicial decisions clearly underscored this fact. Constant references in court documents to slaves as property, the according by decree and by legislative action of absolute power to masters over this property, and the enactment of fugitive slave laws on the state and federal levels for recapturing slaves are just some of many examples. Despite the occasional use of the word "persons" in laws designed to control the movements, activities, and potential manumission of slaves, it is very clear that the overwhelming reality of the legal status of black slaves was that they were property, not persons.[9]

Legal decisions and interpretations nevertheless cannot set precedents or procedures for all the activities of daily life. Jefferson, like all large-plantation owners, had to manage a variety of workers. A few white men provided some of the skilled labor, and whites had jobs as managers and overseers. But most of the skilled laborers were slaves—blacksmiths, bridle makers, carpenters, grooms, cooks, spinners, weavers, mechanics, brick makers, and bricklayers. They were distinct from the larger body of field hands and the special group of drivers and foremen who kept the field slaves in line. A few of the slaves had renowned skills, even in such areas as midwifery and healing, and they were sometimes contracted out, with their services sold for cash. It may have been easy to maintain indifference toward the humanity of remote field hands, but Jefferson, like all slave owners, must have been forced to come to terms with the diverse humanity of those workers with whom he had more intense interaction. These would have included slaves who tended to his most personal needs as well as those who cooked, washed, scrubbed, waited on tables, tended the fires, spun the cotton and wool, wove the cloth, and made the clothing for the household. Among this group was the young woman who was to share his bed for more than two decades, who gave up a chance for freedom during more than two years with Jefferson in Paris and returned to slavery at Monticello, probably pregnant with her first child, Tom.[10] That Jefferson often vacillated or was indecisive about matters, that he frequently had bouts of deep depression, may have been one of the by-products of the morally duplicitous life of a slave owner in a "free" nation.

As a political and intellectual leader in the newly independent United States, Jefferson faced tremendous pressures. Critics throughout Europe and in some northern states confronted the nascent new nation with a damning question: How can the American revolutionists speak of liberty, justice, and the rights of man and still keep large numbers of their fellow human beings in slavery? As a young man still in his twenties, Jefferson had purchased a three-volume French edition of Montesquieu's *De l'Esprit des lois*, and he was in Paris on the eve of the French Revolution. He was much affected by the ideas of Enlightenment thinkers, especially their condemnation of the abuses of authority and the evils of injustice and oppression. He was also aware of the growing abolitionist movement in England and the United States, which endangered the very foundations of the new state.

Nevertheless, on the question of slavery, Jefferson shared with his fellow planters the anguishing realization that it was an entire lifestyle itself that was at stake. Jefferson knew as well as anyone the overpowering dependence of white planters on slave labor. It was their belief that without the slaves there could not have been the critical commerce on which the new nation depended or the great wealth that was accruing in both North and South. Over 80 percent of the nation's overseas trade was in products produced by slaves: tobacco, rice, cotton, sugar, and indigo. Manufacturing, transport, banking, shipbuilding, and road construction were stimulated by and benefited from the profits of slavery.

In a very personal manner, Jefferson agonized over this unhappy dependence on slave labor, realizing that his own lifestyle would be impossible without it. As all of his biographers recognized, he was much obsessed with the life of opulence that his status provided, even though later in life he excoriated young men for their greed and materialism. He mused that the southern economy would be in shambles were all slaves to be immediately freed (this accounts for his belief that it might be possible to gradually emancipate the slaves). It is indeed highly relevant that, while he owned at one time over 15,000 acres of prosperous plantations, he remained in debt much of his life because he persistently overextended himself. The productivity of Monticello and Popular Forest seemed never to reduce those debts, in part because Jefferson took on the debt responsibilities of others. He became as ambivalent and evasive about his debts as he was about the subject of freeing his slaves.

Jefferson's ambivalence did not cease on the matter of economic dependence. He was implicitly aware of the deficiencies in the rationalization that Africans could rightly be held in slavery because they were heathens. Consequently, he was among the first to embrace, albeit tentatively, an intellectual argument that was much more devastating than any previous ones: the claim that the Negro was an inherently inferior form of human being. Jefferson found himself one of the foremost spokespersons of this view in America.

Jefferson's ideas, published materials, speeches, letters, and actions had enormous influence over other men and women. Jordan pointed out that Jefferson's *Notes on the State of Virginia*, when published in the United States in 1787 (it was first published in Paris two years earlier), "helped generate a lively discussion of the Negro's nature" (1968, 547). It was he more than anyone, Jordan tells us, who framed the terms of the debate on Negro intelligence. When he first wrote this manuscript (in 1774), and up until the Revolutionary War, Jefferson indeed was the only southerner to speak out publicly on the subject of the Negro's intellectual inferiority. Moreover, Jordan explained, "until well into the nineteenth century Jefferson's judgment on that matter, with all its confused tentativeness, stood as the strongest suggestion of inferiority expressed by any native American" (455). John Hope Franklin's observation is even more damning: "From the time that Jefferson's *Notes on Virginia* was made public, Southern leaders did not hesitate to use his work to strengthen their contention that Negroes were by nature an inferior race and therefore should be enslaved" (Franklin and Moss 1988, 172).

Jefferson's book contained descriptions and speculations about "the Negro" that made it clear that Jefferson was equivocal, at best, about the blacks' humanity. He asserted that in memory blacks were equal to the whites, in reason they were much inferior, and in imagination they were dull, tasteless, and anomalous. Nature itself had produced a great distinction between the races, not only in physical features but in temperament and mental endowment. Later, he corrected the absolutist tenor of such statements and posed this qualification: "The opinion, that they are inferior in the faculties of reason and imagination, must be hazarded with great diffidence." And he offered some redemption by suggesting that assessing mental ability was a difficult matter. He even conjectured an alternative explication that the "conditions" under which the Negroes lived (as slaves) may have a determining effect upon their character. Yet he was quite capable of writing later, "I advance it therefore as a suspicion only, that the blacks, whether originally a distinct race, or made distinct by time and circumstances, are inferior to the whites in the endowments both of body and mind" (Jefferson [1787] 1955, 143).

Alternatively, Jefferson asserted that the Negro's "moral sense" was as "fully developed" as that of whites. When he was not contradicting himself, on a number of occasions he made the prophetic suggestion that it must be left to science to determine the true nature of the Negro's inferiority. On this matter, Merrill Peterson has offered the most revealing statement: "Many of his [Jefferson's] observations, paraded as scientific, were but thinly disguised statements of folk belief about Negroes" (1970, 262). These folk beliefs have been the very substance of the idea of race from the very beginning.

Jefferson's general orientation toward liberal and Enlightenment thinking (he was a disciple of John Locke, a friend of Condorcet, and widely read in philosophy and history) was subverted by his role as plantation owner. As such, he shared the general values, beliefs, and conditioning toward blacks that characterized his social class. Born into a world in which he was forever surrounded by slaves, Jefferson seemed never to have considered them except as "the other." Indeed, he believed "that an indelible color line had been drawn by Nature between the two races and that this line determined the rights and liberties to which they were entitled in America" (Miller 1977, 17). To resolve the contradictions, he "reached a tentative conclusion on the Negro that he knew to be indefensible morally and unproven scientifically," (Peterson 1970, 264).

George Havens (1955) suggests that Jefferson was "confused," while Dwight Hoover declares only that Jefferson "could not make up his mind" (1976, 75) about black inferiority, intelligence, or sexual appetites. Dumas Malone (1962, 1970, 1981) rationalizes Jefferson's dilemma, preferring instead to emphasize his generous and humane treatment of his slaves. Fawn Brodie, who has delved into Jefferson's life with microscopic candor, tells us that he was a man in deep conflict, "ambivalent not only about love but also about revolution, religion, slavery, and power" (1974, 7).

The fact is that Jefferson, like so many other men of his times, was ready and willing to accept the argument that blacks were a separate and permanently inferior "race" because this assertion provided an intellectual, seemingly rational, defense of slavery and the way of life to which he was deeply committed.

After he came into public office, Jefferson personally managed to avoid much of the controversy over slavery and the questions of Negro inferiority. Though in his early years he had written scathing passages about the evils and immorality of slavery, especially its malevolent effects on slave owners (see chapter 8), he never publicly condemned it after his rise to political prominence, and he did not support any of the abolitionist movements or publications. He was caught in the quagmire of growing racist sentiment as the role of the ideology of race was coming into focus in the minds of those leaders who were committed to preserving slavery in the age of revolution. Although Jefferson showed honest ambivalence and was perhaps even tortured by the reality of slavery in the "land of the free," like most other individuals (in both North and South), he seemed ultimately able to resolve his internal conflict only by increasingly projecting the African as something subhuman.

It may never be possible to fully comprehend the workings of the slave owners' minds. That they were able to successfully dichotomize their daily experiences and perceptions of reality and avoid confronting their own hypocrisy is readily apparent. The most tragic instances of these mental gymnastics was their treatment of the offspring they had by slave women. Visitors to southern plantations were often struck by the frequency of such "mixed" offspring among the other slaves. Whether sired by the owners, the white overseers, or other white men, these children constituted a growing population. By defining Negroes, indeed creating them, as subhuman creatures, white Americans precluded all possibility of claiming such children as their own or even establishing a relationship with them on a human level. As shown in chapter 6, this most extraordinary feature of slavery in North America set it apart from all other contemporary and historical systems of slavery. It was a feature that had significant implications for the future relationships of all peoples in the new nation. And it was critical in constructing the exclusionist components of race ideology.

North Americans apparently found it not only socially and ideologically necessary, but easy, to distance themselves from any consciousness of connectedness to their slave offspring and kinspeople. Once racial slavery had become fully institutionalized in the eighteenth century, public paternal recognition of slave children by their white fathers became increasingly rare during the later eighteenth and early nineteenth centuries.[11] The result was a strangely irrational social reality, of which Jefferson's own life appears to provide a fascinating example. When, during his presidential campaign, his opponents accused him of having fathered children by "Dusky Sally," Jefferson responded with silence, even though at least one alleged son was said to greatly resemble the master.[12] One of Jefferson's legal grandsons, Thomas Jefferson Randolph, many years later admitted to an interviewer that one of the slave sons (either Madison or Eston, with whom he grew up) looked so much like Jefferson that in the dusk or at a distance he might have been mistaken for him. When asked why Jefferson did not remove these children who so closely resembled him from public sight by sending them to his Bedford estate, Randolph replied that Jefferson "never betrayed the least consciousness of the resemblance" (quoted in Brodie 1974, 322; see also Malone 1970, app. 2).

This suggests that Jefferson had developed a mechanism for so compartmentalizing his consciousness that the dichotomy of free and unfree was totally synonymous with white and black, and the barriers between them were so indelible that he could not even recognize his own children, emotionally, psychologically, or socially.[13] In the orderly world that he wanted to create, the fuzziness of genetic mixture had no place. Apparently, Jefferson could only tolerate the slave situation if he could retain the conviction that slaves, even his own children, were qualitatively different and inferior kinds of being. The ideology of race as formulated in his mind required that the white population retain its identity unthreatened by any of the uncertainties that miscegenation represented. He was no doubt aided in this philosophy, in this mode of thinking, by his enormous concern (or growing obsession) with Anglo-Saxonism.

The idea of a pure Anglo-Saxon people and culture was one of the major sociocultural themes to find nurturance on the American continent, though, as we have seen, the notion emerged independently in Europe. It gave added strength to the idea of racial purity and the need to protect whites from contamination by blacks. Culture and biology became so intricately interwoven that the biological processes of intercourse and reproduction were considered threatening to "white" culture!

Gary Nash believes that, at a much deeper level, such beliefs were a question of power. The prohibition against interracial sex ran only one way, he notes, since sexual relations between white men and black women "were frequent and usually coercive throughout the eighteenth century" (1982, 283). White men, Nash argues, banned interracial marriage as a way of declaring legally that the Negro, even when free, was not the equal of whites. "But white power was also served by sexually exploiting black women outside of marriage—a way of acting out the concept of white domination. Racial intermingling, so long as it involved free white men and slave black women, was a way of intimately and brutally proclaiming the superior rights and strength of white society" (283). Thus the offspring of such unions had to be morally, psychologically, and legally invisible. Jefferson and his compatriots set the stage for the dichotomy of consciousness, the moral duplicity and hypocrisy in many areas of life, that still haunt many white Americans today.

Jefferson's role in the evolution of the concept of race was that of the institutional mediator through whom popular beliefs and attitudes toward human diversity were meshed together with, and confirmed by, a growing body of "scientific" judgments. In Jefferson there occurred the amalgamation of pseudoscientific truths, folk beliefs, and stereotypes, and this was transmitted to a populace that desperately needed a way out, a new justification for the economic and social system on which it depended for survival and its way of life. From then on, throughout the nineteenth and well into the twentieth centuries, science was to provide the guidelines for the ideology of race, the data to confirm racial differences, and the arguments justifying racial ranking.

As the medium through which science and popular images were conjoined, Jefferson played a critical role in the growth of American science, and not just because he was admired by his compatriots for his knowledge and intellect. According to John Greene, Jefferson was a practitioner and promoter of science in an age of seminal developments in American science. He "participated in one way or another in nearly every field of scientific inquiry, stimulating his compatriots with his ideas and researches and inspiring them with the knowledge that their efforts were appreciated at the highest level of government" (1984, xiv).

In his *Notes on the State of Virginia*, Jefferson brought together his research on the flora and fauna of his home state. He established himself as a creditable scholar by his careful research, including descriptions and measurements of all manner of phenomena. He successfully defended the animals of the New World against the charge by Buffon that these creatures had migrated from the Old World and subsequently degenerated in size and vigor because of the influences of the American climate. He also defended the Indian population against similar charges of lacking vigor and sexual ardor. In fact, Jefferson's attitude toward the Indians, whom he thought might become assimilable, was inconsistent with his attitude toward blacks, which was a reflection of the different roles they played in his life. In the Scale of Beings, Indians clearly ranked higher than blacks. Page Smith believed that Jefferson had a romantic infatuation with Indians (1976, 266).

As an activist, Jefferson participated in the excavation of an Indian mound, collected fossils of ancient animal forms, was instrumental in the development and distribution of a smallpox vaccine, organized and provided the guidelines for the Lewis and Clark expedition, and promoted other such scientific explorations (Greene 1984). His personal library, which contained one of the largest collections of scientific works in the nation, became the nucleus for the Library of Congress. Greene claims that Jefferson became "a national symbol of interest and faith in science" (35). Because of Jefferson's centrality in its formation and establishment, Greene designates this period in the history of American science as the "Age of Jefferson."

By virtue of his great reputation, whatever pronouncements Jefferson made on moral, political, philosophical, or scientific matters would have been both widely known and respected as authoritative. They would have functioned as guideposts for the thoughts of others. Whatever was left unstated and whatever was absent in his philosophy, ideals, and judgments would also have had an impact. When the author of the Declaration of Independence compromised on the ideals of the American Revolution and failed to extend his advocacy of the rights of man to the internal situation of slave labor, this did not pass unnoticed by the public.

In Jefferson's lifetime, the transformation of Africans and their descendants in the American colonies into subhuman creatures was to a great extent completed. From that time and well into the nineteenth century, the term *race* had a consistent and well-understood meaning. Its various elements had been consolidated into a worldview that had undeviating clarity, which in the nineteenth century was to become total. The role of science was to become critical to the elaboration of the ideology of race. "Race" as a new and infallible truth had to await the development of a proper substitute for religion, and science became that substitute. It provided an intellectual response tailored to the needs of a materialistic, pragmatic society that had elevated greed to a holy passion and made property and the acquisition of property an unassailable and sacred right, superseding even the right to life, liberty, and the pursuit of happiness.

The entire revolutionary period—its causes, motivations, and objectives—was permeated with this prime consideration, the rights of property. Jefferson's silence on the subject of slavery and Negro rights to life and liberty, to say nothing of happiness, conveyed just this fact—the primacy of property rights among men who reckoned their wealth and status primarily in terms of two forms of property, slaves and land.

As an esteemed political leader and a chief advocate and promoter of science, Jefferson helped introduce to the American public what was to become the supreme justification for treating the African Americans in their midst however they chose. When he suggested that the question of the Negro's intellectual inferiority be put to the scrutiny of science, he opened the way to the documentation of assumed black inferiority and the widespread acceptance of such inferiority, not only by Americans with an interest in preserving slavery and the privileged positions it brought, but also by the world at large.

NOTES

1. See Kuhn 1962 for one view of the processes of scientific growth. This view and model has its critics. Greene 1981, for example, poses a much broader paradigm that includes the importance of cultural traditions and preexisting worldviews as well as challenges to them from outside the scientific establishment (e.g., political economy) for generating new scientific theories.

2. Hoover 1976, 59. The first Indian Department was established as part of the War Department, under the secretary of war, a telling comment on white attitudes toward Indians as separate nations that had to be dealt with through violent means.

3. The linkage of biology and behavior is one of the components of race that appears so intractable and so aggravating to physically identifiable minorities. It homogenizes all individuals in a perceptible minority category and prevents the understanding of individual differences in culture and behavior. Benjamin Franklin's admonition against such a view is just as pertinent today as it was two hundred years ago: "If an Indian injures me, does it follow that I may revenge that Injury on all Indians? . . . It is well known that Indians are of different Tribes, Nation and Languages, as well as white people. In Europe, if the French

who are White People, should injure the Dutch, are they to revenge it on the English because they too are White People? If it be right to kill Men for such a Reason, then should any Man, with a freckled Face and red Hair, kill a Wife or Child of mine, it would be right for me to revenge it, by killing all the freckled red-haired Men, Women and Children, I could afterwards anywhere meet with" (quoted in Jordan 1968, 277).

4. From Tacitus 1942.

5. The interesting exceptions were those few scholars who concentrated their attention on the customs, beliefs, and traditions of "primitive" societies. As early as 1724, Father Lafitau studied the kinship system of Iroquois Indians and others and discovered the kind of similarities in kinship terms that later anthropologists were to call "classificatory." He saw value in comparing the customs of contemporary savages with those of ancient peoples. Later, William Robertson not only recognized similarities but suggested that they had been caused by independent invention and by developments along parallel lines. Both writers were expressing the early speculative evolutionary themes of eighteenth-century anthropological thought, which presaged fully mature nineteenth-century theories of sociocultural evolution.

6. It is instructive that, perhaps because they could not directly come to terms with their own hypocrisy, Jefferson and many other planters placed the blame for the origination and persistence of slavery on the English king, George III (see Miller 1977.)

7. The classic biography of Jefferson is Dumas Malone's six-volume work under the general title *Jefferson and His Times*, published from 1948 through 1981. Another well-known biographer is Merrill Peterson (1962, 1970). John Chester Miller's work (1977) deals specifically with Jefferson and slavery. The most controversial and perhaps best-known work is Fawn Brodie's best seller (1974), which has often been scorned by more conservative historians. New books on Jefferson appear with somewhat predictable regularity.

8. There were several rare circumstances, perhaps not so unusual during the times, under which a few of the slaves in Jefferson's household were permitted to obtain their freedom. One was the proviso in his will that freed five slaves, all members of the Hemings family, which included two of his own sons by his slave concubine, Sally Hemings (whom he did not set free in his will). The earliest known instance relates to his stay in Paris as U.S. representative (1785–1789). All of the slaves whom he took with him became technically free once they set foot on French soil. But Jefferson apparently persuaded James Hemings (Sally's brother), who had learned French cooking, to return to Virginia with him to instruct some other servants in the preparation of French food. In return, Jefferson promised him his freedom. It was not granted, however, until seven years after his return (Brodie 1974, 303).

9. See Loren Miller 1966, and also John Chester Miller 1977, who explicitly observes that while black slaves were "admittedly human beings, they were also property and where the rights of man conflicted with the rights of property, property took precedence"(13).

10. Many American historians have long denied that Jefferson had such a "miscegenous" relationship with a slave. Peterson says the allegations, which came out in local newspapers at the time of Jefferson's first presidency, were groundless and scandalous. "Such a mixture of the races, such a ruthless exploitation of the master-slave relationship, revolted his whole being" (1970, 707). John Chester Miller feels that such a relationship would have contradicted the ideals by which Jefferson lived, especially his moral sense and his "loathing of racial mixture" (1977, 176). Malone concurs and denies the relationship in every volume of his exhaustive biography, arguing that the "vulgar liaison" cannot be proved, but was "distinctly out of character" and "unthinkable in a man of Jefferson's moral standards and habitual conduct" (1970, 214).

Jefferson is a true and revered hero of the revolutionary era and an honored founder of the American nation, but he was not a saint. And he was most definitely a product of his times and culture. Two facts about Jefferson's circumstances should be considered. One, he was a widower before the age of forty and never remarried, and there is no reason to believe that he remained celibate. Two, in all slave-owning societies, without exception, masters have taken advantage of the power inherent in their role and engaged in sexual relationships with their slaves with total impunity. In the United States, such relations might have been distasteful to those who focus on the racial element, but it was a natural concomitant of slavery. Adultery was considered a much worse offense, and historians report with little hesitancy about Jefferson's overtures to several married women (which apparently Malone does not consider "vulgar"). Nor have they been reluctant to expose the fact that Sally Hemings was the slave offspring of John Wayles, Jefferson's white father-in-law. Thus she was a half-sister to Jefferson's own wife and considered very beautiful. My contention is that Jefferson was human, not a sacred legend. His biographers provide abundant evidence in many aspects of his life that he did not in fact live according to the ideals he so eloquently espoused; keeping slaves was the most obvious and glaring example.

11. Historians such as Joel Williamson have recently found evidence that "on the eve of the Civil War . . . some eminent white men were having not only one child by a Negro woman but several children" (Williamson 1984, 41). Moreover, Williamson claims, they tended to recognize the relationship and to will property to these children. Until 1850, the U.S. census did not even count mulattoes.

12. Dumas Malone and others have suggested that Sally Hemings's children were fathered by one of Jefferson's nephews, Samuel or Peter Carr (or both). See Malone 1970, app. 2. However, DNA evidence contradicts this, as the Y chromosomal characteristics only follow the male line; the Carrs would have inherited it from their father. DNA evidence now shows that the male descendants of Sally Hemings were fathered by Jefferson.

13. Page Smith observes that Jefferson had a "strange capacity for compartmentalizing his emotions" (1976, 59). Speaking of Jefferson's sexual overtures to Betsey Walker, a friend's wife, Smith says that "far more than most historical figures, [he] is constantly stepping 'out of character'" (60).

CHAPTER 8

Antislavery and the Entrenchment of a Racial Worldview

The rise of antislavery sentiment early in the eighteenth century implied worrisome doubts about the moral rightness of slavery. It prompted a reassessment of the economic and social value of slavery, moved some slave owners to free their slaves, and inspired organized movements to end the slave trade. It also simultaneously provoked in the South a hardening of resistance to antislavery pressures and an increased tendency to denigrate "the Negro," helping to more deeply embed the ideological components of race in American culture.

Donald Noel has suggested that the antislavery movement was the catalytic agent that conjoined "the material fact of gross exploitation with an egalitarian value system to produce racism" (1972, 163). Racism, he continued, "emerged from the 'necessity' to defend a profitable institution which was under attack because its gross exploitation of human beings was sharply at odds with emerging Western values" (165). That antislavery pressure was seminal to important transformations in ideas about human differences in the late eighteenth and early nineteenth centuries should not be in doubt. The context within which the antislavery movement functioned, an expanding democratic and humanitarian ideology, clearly conditioned the proslavery response.

This chapter explores some of the implications of this development, further elucidating the components of the race identity imposed on blacks. Focusing on some of the main thrusts of the antislavery movement, I briefly outline its history and the diverse motivations of its participants. Following the detailed analysis by David Brion Davis (1966), I identify two major sources of antislavery thought—religious inspiration and Enlightenment ideology—although the differences between them were probably irrelevant to the galloping advance of racial ideology. Many opponents of slavery were themselves deeply influenced by their conditioning to the racial worldview and antagonism to blacks.

The chapter then examines the often extreme reaction to abolitionism on the part of proslavery forces, delineating the realities of southern economic, social, and psychological dependence on both race and slavery. The idea of race differences had become an instrumental part of American social structure, molding values and lifestyles. Southerners, including those who never owned slaves, saw race and racial differences as critical to their way of life, and they were much more comfortable when gross physical variations clearly delineated the status of free persons and slaves. They came to see free blacks as an anomaly, a contradiction of their vision of what the natural state of things should be. Antislavery sentiments endangered their perception of what was essential to their culture, in part because of the very real economic changes abolition would entail, but also because it threatened to disrupt the status and power relationships to which many whites had become addicted. Unmitigated power permitted the whites' racial hostility and sense of superiority to flourish with impunity. It also allowed the fabrication of a vicious and devastating image of "the Negro," which precluded the acceptance of blacks as potential equals.

Finally, I consider the autonomous nature of the concept of race, arguing that it was created as a qualitatively unique social phenomenon. Abolitionism undergirded the development of race as a cognitive social domain distinct from other forms and patterns of social stratification, because it compelled proslavery forces into an extreme defensive posture from which there was no retreat. In its uniqueness, race solidified and rigidified the social hierarchy, permitting fluidity in a class system preserved only for whites. Since the end of the eighteenth century, "race" and "class" have represented separate and distinct social domains; one is not reducible to the other, although an obvious relationship and similarities between the two domains should be recognized.

A BRIEF HISTORY OF ANTISLAVERY THOUGHT

There had always been some men and women, both in England and the colonies, who expressed varying degrees of opposition to slavery. Many were merely uncomfortable with the idea of one human being having total, forcible control over another. Others accepted slavery and even recognized some basis for it in the Bible and the writings of the ancient Greeks and Romans, but they argued that the course of human history had advanced beyond such practices. Human progress in the future would be based on free labor, which would ultimately prove more productive. Such views were influenced by the ideology of capitalism and the growing urban and industrial development in the North that depended on free wage labor.

Some critics of slavery recognized an implacable reality: the corrosive effect of slavery on white attitudes toward all blacks. Even Thomas Jefferson, in his painful ambivalence, wrote one of the most eloquent expressions of such sentiments:

> The whole commerce between master and slave is a perpetual exercise of the most boisterous passions, the most unremitting despotism on the one part, and degrading submissions on the other. Our children see this, and learn to imitate it; for man is an imitative animal. This quality is the germ of all education in him. From his cradle to his grave he is learning to do what he sees others do. . . . The parent storms, the child looks on, catches the lineaments of wrath, puts on the same airs in the circle of smaller slaves, gives a loose to his worst of passions, and thus nursed, educated, and daily exercised in tyranny, cannot but be stamped by it with odious peculiarities. The man must be a prodigy who can retain his manners and morals undepraved by such circumstances. ([1787] 1955, 162)

Thirty years before Jefferson wrote these remarks, the great abolitionist John Woolman had observed how the "wrongful enslavement of Negroes . . . depraves the mind" (Jordan 1968, 274). Both Woolman and his fellow abolitionist Anthony Benezet decried how the minds of white children are conditioned to Negro inferiority. The Negroes, Benezet noted in 1762, "are constantly employed in servile Labour, and the abject Condition in which we see them, from our Childhood, has a natural Tendency to create in us an Idea of a Superiority over them, which induces most People to look upon them as an ignorant and contemptible Part of Mankind" (Jordan 1968, 275).

Woolman and Benezet were not alone in discovering the power of such conditioning and its corrupting effect on human relationships. Speaking about the "fallacious reasoning and absurd sentiments used and entertained concerning negroes," David Cooper declared: "The low contempt with which they are generally treated by the whites, lead children from the first dawn of reason, to consider people with a black skin, on a footing with domestic animals, form'd to serve and obey" (quoted in Jordan 1968, 276). A population so humiliated and degraded, overworked, sweat-drenched and filthy most of the time, and totally deprived of any form of self-esteem, could hardly have met the requirements of "civilized" appearance and comportment. Those whose perverse reasoning denied the effects of the slave situation and environment on blacks could accept with equanimity the equally perverse belief that such behavior and appearance were "natural" to all those with black skins.

Despite such critics, during the long decades when the institution was being solidified, few voices opposed slavery, although some men like Morgan Godwyn were critical of the greed and materialism of slave owners (Davis 1966, 369). In the eighteenth century, the moral problems inherent in slavery became more acute, with antislavery sentiment emerging out of what Davis sees as a new ethic of benevolence (378). This was an era of rising humanitarian concerns, of revolutionary ideas about human nature as rational and/or governed by natural laws, the application of which would lead to improvement of the human condition. As Europeans were reconceptualizing the functions and limits of government and ruminating on the nature of life, liberty, economics, and politics, they speculated on the equally critical meaning of Christian living. Sensitivity, compassion, the expansion of moral feelings, and the idea of public duty appeared as common topics of sermons and written literature, providing a fertilizing milieu for antislavery thought.

The Religious Inspiration

There was considerable debate over the issue of converting and baptizing slaves. On the one side were those who felt that it was civilized man's obligation to instruct the heathen Africans in Christianity. Such men were disturbed by widely accepted proscriptions, dating from medieval times and earlier, against the enslavement of fellow Christians. They were matched against those who were opposed to conversions, for much the same reasons. As long as the slaves remained heathen, Christian qualms about their continued enslavement would be largely abated. The strongest negative reactions to exposing slaves to religious teachings were found primarily in those states where the largest numbers of slaves were concentrated. The New England colonists, for the most part, seemed generally to favor missionary activity and even the establishment of schools for instructing servants and slaves.

In the coastal and southern colonies, where dependence on slavery was greatest, proselytizing among the poor and servant class was perceived as a problem. When it proved impossible to control either the proselytizers or their influences, proslavery forces turned to alternative strategies. As early as 1664, some colonies began to enact laws declaring that baptism could not affect the status of the slaves or require their manumission (Jordan 1968). In this the colonists were following precedents established in Latin America, where baptisms were virtually universal and the church also owned large numbers of slaves.

Early in the eighteenth century, various religious groups in England and Europe, mostly Protestants and including some men and women of prominence and wealth, began to press more vigorously for the conversion of slaves. In 1701 the Society for the Propagation of the Gospel in Foreign Lands was formed, which eventually gained the support of the Church of England. Although its success was at best questionable (it found itself the heir of a large plantation with four or five hundred slaves and soon succumbed to the lure of profits), it kept alive the obligation to proselytize and exemplified the ways by which Christian duty could be rendered compatible with slavery.

Actual arguments against slavery itself appeared to surface slowly in the Christian community. The earliest, and the most vociferous and persuasive, of all the religious groups were the Quakers, and for the next 150 years theirs was the strongest and most consistent voice in the antislavery movement in England and the colonies. When George Fox, the Quaker leader, began his campaign in the 1650s, he argued that slavery was inherently evil and repulsive to Christian principles. But many Quakers owned slaves or were involved in trade that was dependent on slave labor, so the response was slow.[1] Soderlund (1985) observes that it took a hundred years of deliberation before the Quakers could convince their fellow religionists to give up their slaves. Wealthy Quaker slave holders acted to hold on to their laborers, insisting on their own benevolence as sufficient for Christian redemption. In 1776 the Quakers finally prohibited all slave ownership.

During the Great Awakening, as we have seen, evangelical preachers penetrated the South, and many preached against slavery. If this movement appealed to the poor, the uneducated, and the dispossessed, it was no less attractive to black slaves, who found in it a soothing balm for the psychic wounds of slavery. Blacks took to the revival movement with a vigor and vitality that could not be expressed in other forums. For a time early in the movement, blacks and mostly poor whites worshipped together in open-air meetings. They shared a common experience of being "born again" with a living Christ who saw their spirits, if not their bodies, as equal in the divine light. This experience of shared rebirth may have ushered in a new and revolutionary ethos, but the implications of transforming personalized evangelical zeal into a social movement were never realized (Mathews 1980). By the 1790s, white and black churches in the South began to emerge as separate and segregated congregations under the power of expanding racial ideology.

Although antislavery sentiments were expressed in tones of moral outrage, particularly by those whose views stemmed from religious piety, it should not be assumed that these sentiments reflected egalitarianism. Most opponents of slavery did not advocate the total equality of blacks, although many individuals, like

Samuel Stanhope Smith and Benjamin Rush, held to the view of their potential equality. Products of their time and culture, eighteenth-century Americans were increasingly socialized to believe that there were profound differences between races and to accept the developing negative stereotypes of Africans.

External pressures, often only for the humanization of slave conditions, were perceived as threatening to the plantation system and caused considerable uneasiness. For one thing, the process of conversion continued to raise the question of the legitimacy of slavery itself. For another, conversion and baptism often carried in their wake a requirement for some degree of literacy in order for the converted to read the Bible. Early missionaries and educators, concerned for heathen souls, frequently established schools for blacks and Indians specifically for the purpose of teaching them the scriptures. But even minimal literacy was seen by slavery proponents as dangerous to the preservation of a caste of ignorant, dependent laborers. Equally threatening of course were the subversive ideas that slaves might inculcate from written sources, including the Bible. Moses leading the Israelites out of bondage was not considered an appropriate model for black slaves in America.

Far more fundamental was the nagging question that followed the unexpected logic of missionary zeal. If the black slaves were capable of being converted to Christianity, would not that mean that they had souls? And if this were the case, then surely they would have to be accounted as fully human men and women like their owners, with all of the subtle sensitivities, passions, reasoning abilities, and spiritual needs of others. Some slave owners thought, rightly as it turned out, that literacy would encourage conspiracies and rebellion among the slaves. It would give them pride and too great a sense of themselves. It would, indeed, make them more like their masters.

The slave owners' dilemma was expressed poignantly in Jordan's words: "For if the Negro were like themselves, how could they enslave him? How explain the bid on the block, the whip on the back? Slavery could survive only if the Negro were a man set apart; he simply had to be different if slavery was to exist at all" (1968, 183–184).

Despite much initial resistance on the part of slave owners and many of the organized Protestant churches, the majority of slaves, in time, converted to Christianity. Most became Baptists or Methodists, and some became members of the churches of their masters. The revivalist fervor of the Great Awakening era may have underscored the spiritual equality of blacks and whites, but this had little impact on the slave condition. Although many evangelists were or became abolitionists, others placated slave owners who objected to conversion by arguing that the effect of Christianity upon slaves would be a mollifying one, conditioning them to proper Christian humility and willingness to serve their masters.

In any case, the black presence was no longer an alien one; there were already in many areas blacks descended from seven or more generations of laborers on American soil. The African Americans and their masters had learned much from each other, and the very intimacy of their lives in the South no doubt led to many breaches of the customs that were designed to underscore their differences. Life in the South for both blacks and whites had taken on an interactive pattern and rhythm that was not to be broken until the Civil War; and then, some might say, only temporarily.

It seems oddly incongruous that the more culturally adjusted these populations became, the more the dominant whites simultaneously focused on and emphasized their differences, even to the point of inventing some.[2] The insistence on a wide cultural gap between themselves, blacks, and Indians was a mental construct, created to provide whites with a defensible justification for the exploitation of these peoples. Were they to admit to any similarities, "then the entire rationale of domination and exploitation would crumble" (Nash 1982, 292).

The alternative to admitting similarities was to conceptualize the fabricated sociocultural gap as biologically determined, in other words, as part of the different inborn natures of blacks, Indians, and whites. Proslavery Christians thus invented a cognitive protective mechanism to justify and preserve their privileged status, one that required avoiding the reality of blacks as full human beings. Dwight Dumond, observing this process, said: "The denial of emancipation by conversion to Christianity had shifted the basis of slavery from heathenism to race" ([1961] 1966, 62). In the creation of the racial domain, the moral dimensions of slavery and exploitation could be projected to a different plane, thereby acquitting Christian consciences.

Enlightenment Influences

The second source of antislavery values emerged from the maturing political and social consciousness of the English regarding the nature of freedom in a culture that claimed to greatly value the rights of individuals. English thoughts about the meaning of a free society were clearly products of revolutionary political changes over several centuries, the rise of bourgeois capitalism, and Enlightenment history and philosophy. The English constitution (or common law) since the seventeenth century had been characterized by increasing emphasis on human and civil rights and the growth of sentiments for the advancement of popular democracy and political liberty. Many Englishmen were enjoying more freedom and opportunity than ever before. The constitutional guarantees that the middle and upper classes had wrenched from the monarchy were praised and emulated on the continent. English settlers in the Americas saw themselves rightfully as heirs of this tradition, although not necessarily of all Enlightenment thought.

By the last quarter of the eighteenth century, some Englishmen took the argument against slavery to political forums, claiming that the history of the development of English laws was reflective of the unfolding and strengthening of human liberties. Slavery, they said, was a regressive institution inherently incompatible with this tradition. In 1772, Granville Sharp was instrumental in securing a judicial decision that West Indian planters could not hold slaves in England, as slavery was contrary to English law. Within a few years, English Quakers began a vigorous campaign for the complete prohibition of the slave trade. In 1787 the primarily Quaker British Abolition Society was organized, and its leader, William Wilberforce, led the campaign against slavery in Parliament. Others, like Thomas Clarkson, spent many years gathering evidence against the slave trade in courts, anticipating that if the trade were banned, slavery itself would eventually disappear. The inexorable progression of antislavery sentiment reached its height in England as the issue of slavery became the focal point of parliamentary debates. People from virtually all segments of English society supported the abolitionist movement.[3] Petitions by the hundreds of thousands poured into Parliament. Both traditional congregations and radical dissenters joined together in support of the cause.

Some opposition to slavery came from Enlightenment writers in Scotland, England, and France. We noted previously that radical new currents of social thought, as well as new perspectives and developments in science, reflected a liberalizing atmosphere of inquiry and speculation. The thinkers and writers of this period appealed above all to reason, denied the traditional emphasis on supernatural revelation, and created a milieu for the triumph of empiricism. Some argued for the recognition of scientific principles governing all the processes of nature and extended this model to human societies. Many also turned to notions about the perfectibility and progress of humankind, speculating on what would become in the nineteenth century a full-blown evolutionary paradigm. Focusing on the quest for freedom from both secular authority and stifling tradition, some Enlightenment writers made a clear connection between the abolition of slavery and the expansion of English values of liberty and equality.

Enlightenment writers provided nourishment for the growth of liberal ideologies in the colonies. By emphasizing that people were rational beings who should be free to make choices and decisions about their own destiny, by raising questions about democratic reforms and human rights, and by awakening intellectual thought to new possibilities, they fostered bold and novel ideas for political and social reforms. Consistent with their progressive social philosophies, most Enlightenment writers were generally opposed to slavery. Yet as we have seen, some were ambivalent on the question of equality and expressed doubts that blacks were the equal of whites. Many also promoted the value of property rights, which inherently contradicted according human rights to slaves. Opposition to slavery was not necessarily predicated on belief in the natural equality of all humankind.

In the American colonies, Enlightenment thinkers gained sympathetic audiences from a populace who shared their optimism and advocacy of freedom and who strove to emulate their sophistication. When Thomas Paine set about to write his famous paean to human freedom, *Common Sense,* it was the views of Enlightenment thinkers that informed his positions and arguments on liberty, equality, justice, and the rights of mankind. Like Rousseau, Paine was against concentrations of power, privilege, and wealth in the hands of the few and the less-than-coincidental impoverishment of so many.[4] His advocacy of the rights of ordinary citizens fed the spirit of revolution in the colonies as well as in France.[5]

Throughout the revolutionary era, Americans were sensitive to the many charges of hypocrisy. Few critics failed to emphasize the blatant inconsistency that, while the colonists were struggling for freedom from English domination, they were holding hundreds of thousands of people as slaves. Disturbed by the naggings of their moral consciences, some people did free their slaves. For a few brief years, individual acts of manumission increased, and all northern states eventually outlawed slavery.

When the Constitutional Convention met in 1787 to frame a new federal document, its members debated, often passionately, prohibiting the slave trade. Antislavery advocates offered moral and practical arguments for gradually eliminating slavery, and even some delegates from slave states like Virginia conceded that slavery was a fundamental evil, a canker on the body politic. But majority southern opposition to emancipation was intransigent. In the end, members deferred to southern interests and prohibited terminating the slave trade for twenty years. The Constitution did not directly refer to slavery, but some of its provisions tended to lend implicit protection to the slave system. Article IV, for example, provided that fugitive slaves be delivered back to their owners, and Article I prohibited Congress from taxing slavery out of existence (Miller 1966, 20). In fact, no southern state would have ratified the Constitution if the convention had attempted to eliminate slavery. Men who were ostensibly antislavery capitulated in the compromise; all were aware that slavery was an important foundation of the American economy and society and a major source of overseas income.

When dealing with the question of the bases for taxation and representation in the House of Representatives, an even stranger compromise was effected. Southern leaders insisted that "the Negro" could not be recognized as a full citizen, but at the same time they sought to enhance their power in the new government. So some insisted on counting the slaves as persons, which would have boosted the population of the slave states and provided stronger representation in Congress of the planters' interests. The compromise resulted in a clause stating that slaves were to be counted as "three-fifths of all other persons" for the apportioning of representatives. Although it was understood that this was merely a formula for enhancing the power of southern politicians, this famous clause was to haunt some leaders of the federal government for decades to come, as their critics castigated them for what many saw as an ignoble definition of blacks. In fact, the news that the white power structure had defined them as three-fifths human swept through many African American communities.

These actions by America's first leaders demonstrated the extreme degree to which black slaves had come to be seen as mere property. The close interlinking of life, liberty, and the right to property has been a consistent and enduring theme throughout American history. When the country's leaders spoke of individual or private rights, they always meant rights of property, which tended to eclipse all others. Such actions also reflected the transparent ambivalence that we saw in Jefferson, and in many other minds, about the humanity of slaves. As Loren Miller observed, the "Founding Fathers were well aware of the contradictions implicit in recognition of slavery in the Constitution side by side with the guarantees of individual rights." Yet he claimed that their glossing over these contradictions should not be perceived as hypocrisy, for "the belief in the inferiority of Negroes was widespread and deeply rooted" (1966, 23). Indeed, these compromises reveal how remarkably and deeply entrenched slavery had become; so also was the system of ranked and unequal groups embraced in the idea of race that was evolving along with it.

The antislavery movement experienced a brief decline in the last decade of the eighteenth century. Much of its momentum had already dwindled during the convulsions of the Revolutionary War. Under pressure of British abolitionists, however, both the United States and England passed laws abolishing the slave trade on the high seas in 1807. Now fully committed to ending the slave trade, the English government devoted the full force of its navy to the battle against this commerce.

Meanwhile, a number of events and changing economic circumstances provoked an even greater commitment to slavery and the continued dehumanization of blacks. The first was the invention of the cotton gin, which made it possible to grow and process cotton at a hitherto unimagined rate. As a result, new territories were opened to cotton cultivation. From South Carolina to Georgia and eventually westward to Texas, cotton plantations sprang up all over the South. With them came an unparalleled demand for slave labor, as planters strove to expand production and feed the insatiable English textile industry.

Second, an increase in slave rebellions, some of which were of large scale, shocked and frightened Americans. The most dramatic began in 1791 in Haiti and ended with the stunningly successful overthrow of French dominance in that Caribbean nation. This was followed by Gabriel Prosser's conspiracy (1800), Denmark Vesey's rebellion (1822), and Nat Turner's revolt (1831), along with numerous other incidents. There had always been slave insurrections and conspiracies, but the Haitian Revolution was the first to meet any measure of success. It had come on the heels of, and was directly inspired by, the French Revolution; its meaning intensified the atmosphere surrounding all acts of resistance. It struck such fear in the hearts of slave owners on the mainland that it was a constant topic of conversation and caused panicked attempts to close state borders to immigrants from Haiti. The prospect of slaves gaining freedom, through emancipation or revolution, now seemed very real and very terrifying.

A new era of radical antislavery fervor was initiated in the 1830s when William Lloyd Garrison began publishing his famous newspaper, *The Liberator*, and the American Anti-Slavery Society was born. Opponents of slavery were now calling for immediate abolition, and some were prepared to take drastic actions to bring it about. The next three decades were punctuated by periodic demonstrations, public lectures and meetings, the organization of numerous antislavery groups, and widespread criticism of slavery in newspapers and magazines in the North and abroad. Dwight Dumond claims that Theodore Weld's *American Slavery As It Is* (1838) sold more copies than any other antislavery pamphlet, more than 100,000 the first year alone. When Harriet Beecher Stowe published her famous novel, *Uncle Tom's Cabin*, in 1852, it became a clarion call for antislavery action.

Such intensification of abolitionist activities often came in response to actions taken by the states and especially by the federal government to protect or extend slavery. Amid controversy over the institution and related stormy debates in Congress over proper constitutional interpretations of the powers of the legislature and federal judiciary, the federal government found itself unable to deal with the problem of slavery. Its actions were contradictory and often incoherent, leading ultimately to a situation that could only be resolved by violence.

The Fugitive Slave Law of 1850, when passed by Congress, generated a storm of protest. It mandated the retrieval and return of fugitive slaves to their owners, endangering many blacks who had lived unmolested for years in free territory. What was worse, it denied the right of suspected runaways to testify on their own behalf, presuming them to be guilty rather than innocent. The abrogation of the Missouri Compromise of 1820 had a similar effect. While allowing slavery in Missouri, the 1820 act prohibited it in the Kansas-Nebraska territory. In 1854 the Kansas-Nebraska Act repealed the compromise, opening an opportunity for the expansion of slavery. States passed numerous laws in an attempt to control or calm the slavery controversy, sometimes later repealing them. The arguments pro and con were strident and harsh. Abolitionists continued and strengthened their demands for the immediate freeing of all slaves. In 1859 the irascible John Brown dramatized the conflict and the antislavery cause for all time when he was elevated to martyrdom following his unsuccessful raid on the federal arsenal in Harpers Ferry, Virginia.

THE PROSLAVERY RESPONSE

Larry Tise (1987) notes that little was written or published in defense of slavery until the latter part of the eighteenth century, and each spate of proslavery writings thereafter was in response to an upsurge of antislavery activities. Toward the end of that century, white slave owners and proponents of slavery were caught in a quandary. With slaves in even greater demand for cotton production, yet increasingly feared and hated because of their frequent refusals to accept their degraded circumstances, the visceral reaction of slave owners was to increase discipline and control. In this context, the antislavery movement simultaneously forced slave owners and those who benefited from slavery to strengthen arguments to protect and preserve the system.

In the wake of such fervor there appeared, progressively, a more virulent mythicizing in popular literature of a creature called "the Negro." Some proslavery proponents turned again to the story of Noah and the curse placed on Ham's descendants through Canaan. Updating an older sixth-century interpretation of the Old Testament, they proclaimed that black slavery was merely the implementation of God's ordained punishment for Ham's transgressions on the ark. Who could argue with God's will or his plan for the different races? Although the appeal to biblical sanctions for slavery, along with the "Christian duty" to save African souls, may have satisfied the religiously oriented, more pragmatic and secular arguments were also put forth. Slavery was essential for the southern economy. But this argument had detractors even among some southern economists, who believed that cotton and other products could just as well be produced by free wage laborers. The argument that appeared to make more practical sense was that slavery was a means of controlling a savage, ignorant, irrational, and potentially violent population and bringing to it the blessings of civilization. Indeed, their ancestors, it was believed, had been slaves in Africa, and they knew no other condition.

In the decades that followed independence, argues Tise, Americans backed away from the revolutionary and egalitarian ideals of Jefferson, John Adams, and James Madison (1987, 191). Some intellectuals formulated a subtle new argument that sanctified inequality and made republican values consonant with slavery. Turning to history, especially Greek and Roman history, they argued that all great civilizations were built on slave labor; that inequality is normal and natural in humankind, just as it exists in nature; and that the possibility of justice and liberty for all is a myth. Led largely by New England–born clergymen, many Americans came to view abolitionism as a subversive and conspiratorial movement while extolling the benefits of conservatism and preserving the status quo.

Just as they retreated from the liberating and humanitarian ideals of the revolutionary era, many American social thinkers also turned away from the environmentalist explanations of the early Enlightenment and began to focus more on the inner qualities, and character, of "the Negro" as a way of explaining the predicament of slavery and the existence of white prejudice.[6] Reflecting the long-standing English discomfort with differences, some whites in both the North and the South, perceiving the end of slavery, advocated the forced removal and colonization of all blacks in some distant territory, along with continued reservations for Indians. But slave owners were understandably not enamored of the prospect of losing their laborers, and more rational people rejected such schemes because of the prohibitive costs to the federal government of resettling blacks in some as yet unknown territory. When confronted with the impracticality, the logistics, and the cost of removing nearly two million unwilling black Americans to some unspecified land, advocates of removal backed down. Nevertheless, the colonization effort reflected the concerns of those who had come to believe that blacks represented a danger to the order, stability, and progress of white civilization. It also represents irrefutable evidence of the whites' persisting belief that there were vast differences between themselves and the Negroes.

In 1828 white Americans elected to the presidency Andrew Jackson, a man widely known to be an Indian fighter and an Indian hater (he had fought in the War of 1812 and the Creek War of 1813–1814), who was also the proslavery owner of a Tennessee plantation with over a hundred slaves. He was a new type of politician, elected with a large majority of votes from the white male populace. Most states had eliminated voting requirements tied to property ownership and taxes, and suffrage for white males was now almost universal. A humble westerner, without aristocratic background or pretensions, who appealed to the masses, Jackson thus represented a democracy of the "common man." During this era, Americans were described by European visitors as crude, unrefined, ambitious, aggressive, prudish, and vulgar materialists whose great passion was money (Pessen 1985). They had no respect for tradition, laws, learning, or intellectual accomplishments. Jackson was the ideal role model for this "common man," inspiring a sense of identity and unity among them never seen before. His vice president was John Calhoun of South Carolina, one of America's most powerful defenders of slavery.

During Jackson's presidency in the 1830s, conflict over slavery reached a crisis. Abolitionist pressure had forced Americans to confront the very real problem of what to do with "the Negro" after slavery. Colonizationist proposals began to evaporate as the lines between pro- and antislavery forces hardened (see below). White Americans everywhere feared the consequence of huge numbers of black slaves being set free on American soil. Many who opposed slavery in principle could see no alternatives to maintaining the institution, and there ensued a massive eruption of writings in defense of slavery.

The 1830s also saw the beginning of Irish immigration. Dirt-poor, illiterate, half-starved Irish farmers appeared in the east coast cities with their families and began to compete for unskilled jobs with poor white Protestants and black Americans. Because of preferences for white workers, they soon supplanted the blacks in foundries, factories, and domestic services; in the trades; and as laborers on the canals and railroads. Hostilities among all three groups festered and became violent, leading to urban riots. The Irish soon learned that, as poor as they were, the blacks were even worse off and had no political voice in the Jacksonian world, which the Irish came to support.[7] It was not long before the Irish were acculturated to the racial worldview and took a proslavery stand to protect themselves from black competition.

In the meantime, proslavery forces marshaled every possible logical or reasonable argument in defense of the status quo; their arguments became even more extreme in the 1850s (Fredrickson [1971] 1987). Although some historians have observed consistency in proslavery arguments from the seventeenth century on (see Faust 1981; Tise 1987), one proposition assumed heightened significance in the nineteenth century. In an age increasingly harkening to the authority of science, the most powerful argument was that claiming the natural inferiority of the Negro, with all the malevolent implications of such a belief. This component of race ideology came to constitute the most enduring proslavery argument, superseding all others by midcentury and forming the basis for much public policy and social treatment of African Americans in the post–Civil War era. Its remarkably effective ally was the growing field of American anthropology, as we shall see in following chapters.

THE SOCIOCULTURAL REALITIES OF RACE AND SLAVERY

Some fundamental realities about racial slavery rendered the seemingly unassailable moral and legal arguments of the abolitionists virtually ineffectual, particularly in the South. One was the overwhelming dependence of white plantation owners on black labor. Another was the fact that the entire culture and social system of the South had evolved with race and slavery at its core. In the emergence of the southern lifestyle, race had added a new dimension of social differentiation to the structuring of American society, coinciding with a growing capitalist economic system.

Dependence on Black Labor

The dependence on black labor had become manifest within two generations after the first white settlements in North America. This reality is well documented in literature, letters, memoirs, diaries, the fiscal records of plantations, and other materials. It was most visible in the persistent demand for Africans, which increased toward the end of the seventeenth century and became all but compulsive in the eighteenth.

As early as 1645 Emanuel Downing, in a letter to his brother-in-law, John Winthrop, expressed the hope that the settlers could use Indians "captured in just wars" to exchange for Negro slaves from the West Indies, "for I doe not see how wee can thrive untill wee get into a stock of slaves sufficient to doe all our business" (quoted in Davis 1966, 146). This was a revealing statement of simple clarity, one echoed by multitudes of later settlers. Other such expressions reverberated throughout the Americas, in the Spanish and Portuguese colonies as well as in North America (Davis 1966, 148–150, 164). Davis's own cautious conclusion is that, given the mortality of Indians and the blockage of traditional sources of white labor, "it can be argued that the development of the New World as a producer of tropical staples would have been impossible without African slaves" (1984, 357).

The best example of this ineluctable dependence on black labor is the history of the colony of Georgia. Financed by wealthy philanthropists in 1730, the colony was deliberately planned as a social experiment; its settlers were to be refugees, orphans, and convicts, often men who had been imprisoned for debts. Its organizers were also idealists, many of whom believed, as did their leader, John Oglethorpe, "that a colony founded to bring relief to the distressed of Europe should not be the cause of enslaving thousands of free Africans" (Davis 1966, 166). Although this was only one of a number of reasons given for the policy, in 1732 Georgia became the first and only non-slaveholding colony.

Within a few years, however, members of the colony began to petition the trustees to alter this policy and allow slaves. The experiment was not working. Each year they begged for relief. The white workers would not, perhaps could not, produce the food and export crops needed. Hunger, disease, poverty, and death ravished the settlement. When settlers saw the tremendous wealth being produced by slaves in neighboring South Carolina, the remedy for Georgia's predicament seemed self-evident. The colony needed slaves or it would not survive. Even the "Great Awakener," George Whitefield, "was convinced that Georgia could not subsist without slaves" (Tise 1987, 21). During the long controversy that ensued, black slaves began to be illegally brought into the colony. By 1750 the act prohibiting slaves had been repealed. From then on, Georgia prospered. Even poor white men firmly grasped the connection between owning slaves and advancing oneself individually along with the colony's overall prosperity.

The Culture of Racial Slavery

The second reality, the creation and reification of race as a new form of social stratification with all its cultural integument, is somewhat more complex to delineate, yet is at the heart of this analysis. It involved the differentiation of blacks as distinct beings, a magnification of the social distance between blacks and whites, and the formulation in the white mind of a stereotype that became a caricature known as "the nigger." We have seen that the dichotomy between slaves and free men had become established in the American mind as concomitant with physical differences. It is based on this fact that Davis concluded, "In no ancient society was the distinction between slave and freeman so sharply drawn as in America" (1966, 62). White Americans had come to express this distinction by defining blacks as a race apart and ranking them as the lowest of all groups in a racial "scale of being."

Once reified, that is, crystallized and rendered as substantive reality, the folk idea of race assumed an identity and autonomy of its own, aided by the authority of learned opinion. The autonomy of any aspect of culture is, of course, relative. But ideas and ideologies, when institutionalized in people's minds, often develop a fluidity and refractivity that allow them to persist even in drastically altered situations. In this case, the amorphous nature of race meant that the ideology could transcend the sources of its origin, and race classifications could be logically extended to any populations where inequality and a sense of unbridgeable differences were desirable. Such populations could be identified by color or other physical features, and their relative ranks be established accordingly.

In the nineteenth century, relationships between whites and Native Americans were changing dramatically as white dominance crippled the ability of Indians to resist their cultural encroachment. Views about the Indians also shifted as what some historians have called "romantic racialism" replaced images of bestiality and savagery (Berkhofer 1978; Fredrickson 1971; Nash 1982, 1986), and blacks became the new savages. Indians were ranked higher than blacks in the ordering system. Asians, when the need arose later, were variously located, depending on who was constructing the gradations, either between whites and Indians or between Indians and blacks. In the eyes of its formulators, the ranking was based on each group's presumed capacity for civilization.

There is no doubt that, whatever the strength of their attitudes toward human variation, the originators of race perceived it as a mechanism of social stratification. They argued from a simple logic. Someone had to be the "mudsill," to do the mean, dirty, dangerous, and difficult work in civilized society. And others had to be the leaders, thinkers, planners, creators, and administrators of high culture. The use of original physical differences to structure such social ranks, for those who had the power to do so, was perhaps a logical consequence of the conquest situation and the enslavement of physically differing populations.

It is in the treatment of nonslave blacks that the element of race as the premier determinant of social position is best viewed. The free Negro contradicted the white image of those who by their very racial definition were not entitled to freedom. If slavery was the natural and normal condition of Africans, and they were happiest and freest when subordinate to and in the care of whites, then free Negroes were an abomination, a threat to the social system and a danger to themselves. In both North and South, the lives of free blacks in the late eighteenth and nineteenth centuries were hemmed in by numerous and onerous restrictions. Their mobility was limited, they could not vote or hold public office in most states, they could not own or bear arms, and they could not testify against a white man. They had no right of assembly (except in churches), were forced to observe curfews, and often had to carry certificates confirming their free status. In both North and South, the free Negro was perceived as lazy and improvident; prone to crime and general depravity; and unworthy of white respect, fair play, or justice. Simultaneously, they were also being displaced from skilled jobs in favor of white workers.

The cultural behavior prescribed by an ideology of inequality and exclusiveness meant that everywhere the rank of white was given precedence. Even where there were no strict laws of segregation, the black presence was downgraded. In religion, recreation, and economic and social life, blacks and Indians could be present only as subordinates, unseen and ignored. Only low-status occupations were open to low-ranked races; it was inconceivable that such persons could have any role to play in public life.

For all blacks, slave and free, repeated daily humiliations and unrestrained cruelties translated into conventional behavior and were perpetuated in each new generation. It takes little imagination to conjure up the proliferation of demeaning treatment targeted at "the Negro" and the consequent institutionalization of such practices. A variety of customs were originated and associated with the debasement of blacks. Acts of physical and psychological brutality were carried out with impunity. There should be no doubt that the degradation, dehumanization, and demeaning aspects of the slave relationship elicited from many blacks behavioral syndromes of abject subordination. On many plantations, slaves were broken in spirit; they were constantly fearful of the unmitigated power of their owners and other whites over them. Lower-class whites who would never own slaves debased and humiliated both slaves and free blacks, if for no other reason than to demonstrate their own superiority and power to do so.

As they were structuring a social hierarchy based on race, white Americans instituted patterns of etiquette, of demeanor and personal address, between racial populations that were to survive and become exaggerated in the post–Civil War period. The essence of racial inequality was distilled in the shuffling and subordinate behavior of blacks vis-à-vis whites, the lowering of the eyes, the avoidance behavior in public, the jocular acceptance of insult and humiliation, and the deference always to white opinion. Black subservience and control by whites was important, from the white point of view, not only to prevent riots and rebellions, but also to prevent race mixture and the subversion of white racial purity, a notion gaining currency with the ascendancy of racial Anglo-Saxonism.

The overarching vision of America for most whites became that of white advancement, privilege, and homogeneity, with inferior races kept at a distance in a state of permanent subordination. To this end, throughout the nineteenth century race hatred, fear, and contempt increased as commonplace sentiments. Numerous physical attacks on blacks, even in northern cities, attested to the intensity of race hatred instigated by those whites who felt threatened or insecure. All of the precursors of Jim Crow laws, enacted toward the end of the century, were already in place in the sense that white manipulation and control of blacks was an everyday, ongoing affair, fulfilling the explicit mandate to keep the Negro in his decreed place. The culture of race placement required embroidering a social tapestry replete with small acts and nuances that formalized and entrenched gross inequality.

In a society where personal acts of brutality and violence are often touted as bravery or courage or are tolerated as "human nature," unmitigated power becomes a dangerous instrument. Power corrupts, as Lord Acton observed so astutely. And absolute power is so bloating to the psyche that men and women who acquire it lose all rational perceptions and connections to reality. We saw in the twentieth century many examples of tyrants and despots around the world who have aggrandized excessive personal power (and wealth) and become addicted to its lure. There is no redemption from the corrosive consequences of absolute power. It is an addiction so complete that peoples' minds become warped. They can no longer comprehend limits of any nature and too often accede to extremes of brutality, avarice, and lust. They cannot relinquish the exaggerated levels of power and privilege or even think rationally enough to try. This is the sickness of excessive and absolute power. This sickness and the seductive nature of white power characterized the social reality of white–black relations in the nineteenth century. In many areas of the South, this situation continued throughout the twentieth century.

Some whites reveled in their power over blacks. It shored them up, gave them a feeling of mastery and grandness, and even seduced some into unspeakable acts of cruelty and sadism.[8] Every white person, slaver owner or not, could experience the lofty feeling not only of being better than any Negro but of having his power over blacks sanctioned by society. When Jefferson spoke of the depravity that whites derived from such power and transmitted unwittingly to their children, the "unremitting despotism," the "giving loose to his worst of passions," and the education in the "exercise in tyranny" ([1787] 1955, 346), he revealed the malignancy of such raw, insensate power. Jefferson was not a stranger to the brutalizing and odious effects of absolute power in the slave situation.[9]

The daily exercise of white personal power over black individuals had become a cherished aspect of southern culture. To abrogate it by emancipating the slaves was tantamount to giving up the "southern way of life," as the North was so frequently reminded during and after the Civil War. Wealthy plantation owners even convinced poor whites, who had never owned slaves, that they shared in this power relationship over blacks; indeed, they enlisted poor whites in the proslavery cause. The Southern concept of honor was predicated on maintaining the system. This was one issue that could and did bind together all whites. It became a cause that transcended their own cultural and class differences and provides clear historical evidence of the distinctiveness of the race domain and its priority over class.

THE PRIORITY OF RACE OVER CLASS

Events in the nineteenth century made it abundantly and irrefutably clear that race as a concept sui generis superseded social class as the dominant mechanism of social division and stratification in North America. But social science literature has been ambiguous about the relationship between race as an ideology of social division and social classes as empirical organizational features of the capitalist system. Put simply, the thesis of this section is that race differences in identity and social position were, and are, more important than class differences in American society.

Class analysis as a mode of accounting for race and racism is simplistic and bears little relationship to the complexities or the realities introduced by the racial worldview. It ignores or obscures the material circumstances and specific interests of the white working class, which has for more than a century benefited from diminished competition from other racial groups, who were barred, by custom and law, from jobs and positions available only to whites. By stressing the common exploitation that all working-class people experience at the hands of capitalists, class-based analysis precludes, indeed exempts, white working-class culpability in the preservation and continuity of racism. It ignores, and sometimes denies, an important reality: that the white working class shares the same exploitative, self-aggrandizing, and oppressive capitalist ethos as the bourgeoisie and essentially the same racial ideology.[10] Few white, or black, scholars have researched or documented the countless blatant acts of exploitation experienced by poor blacks at the hands of working-class whites, especially after emancipation, but these were (and are) common knowledge in African American communities across the nation. A regular feature of black life in the South was having to put up with humiliating, intimidating, and degrading acts from working-class whites on a daily basis. Such behavior was part and parcel of the corrupting nature of the unbridled power that even poor whites held over blacks as a consequence of the established racial ranking and associated habits of denigration.

Although the expressions of racism may have varied, whites of all social classes adhered to the racial worldview. Joel Williamson reminds us that the radical racists of the 1890s were of upper-class backgrounds, and the Ku Klux Klan during Reconstruction was organized and led by upper-class white men. He concludes that upper- and lower-class whites "functioned, not against each other, but both against the Negro, the intermittent, sporadic, open violence of one complementing the steady, pervasive, quiet violence of the other" (1984, 295).

Class analysis cannot explain the power that race has of eliciting a sense of vast difference. This power grew from the eighteenth to the late nineteenth centuries to the point where it became almost unnatural to even conceive of different races as potential equals. So strongly were Americans, and many Europeans, conditioned to the idea that the world's human population was constituted of distinct "racial" units that it became an indispensable way of looking at world realities. This helps us to understand why race became so much more important after the Civil War, whether applied to freed blacks or extended to new immigrants, such as the Chinese and Japanese or the "little brown brothers" from the Philippines. After 1865, emancipation may have brought freedom from formal slavery, but it did not bring freedom from the tyranny of the racial worldview.

After the brief but promising period of Reconstruction, race separation was built into the infrastructure of American society by law and white social preferences. In all areas of life, Americans were persuaded that the major races—black, Indian, Asian, and white—could not and should not live or work together and certainly not as equals. All blacks were homogenized, regardless of education, training, skills, religion, income, or place of origin, into a single category. With few exceptions, so were all Asians and Native Americans, regardless of differences of language, tradition, religion, education, or experience.

In contrast, class separation was temporal and situational, as so many Americans discovered. White Americans grew up with the vision that any young person who succeeded in business, politics, entertainment, the arts, or the professions automatically improved his class status and eliminated the barriers to most upper-class institutions. Class barriers can be transcended; race barriers cannot.

During the colonial period, the discriminating features and symbols of older social-class systems became blunted and imprecise. Although the Puritan communities sought to protect themselves as an exclusive social and religious entity, and a few of the settlers in Virginia and surrounding colonies were able to retain their middle- to upper-class pretensions, many others from the lower levels of society aspired to status and wealth.[11] Yeoman farmers grasped at the opportunity to become plantation owners. For some on the lower rungs of society—the ex-convicts, ex-thieves, and others who had come as indentured servants—their potential anonymity in a new and vibrant setting was a welcome and necessary protection. Many men sought to break with their past and start anew in the colonies without the restrictions imposed in England by language, family name, education, and class origin. They learned that not only were there great fortunes to be made, but the social dynamics in the fluid arenas of expanding, bustling towns and frontier areas obfuscated older class lines. An American atmosphere vibrant with energy and the spirit of adventure made the rigidities of class for whites less relevant. In an era of assertive individualism, energy and ambition counted far more than family and proper table manners.

A new American class system based on wealth and conspicuous consumption soon emerged, supplementing older class structures still retained in the collective mind. Several new phenomena, however, tended to undermine prevailing class barriers and encourage a flexible and dynamic stratification system that allowed white Americans to boast about their lack of class distinctions. One was the intermingling of European ethnic groups, rare in most of the initial settlements but increasingly more common as the settlements became more established. Scots, Germans, Irish, French, Danes, Swedes, Dutch, Belgians, and other Europeans mingled with the descendants of early English settlers. Within a few generations, intermarriages among these ethnic groups began to confound the trappings of traditional status. Thus, Europeans experienced radically different social motifs at work in the New World. Land and property were still requisites of status, but breeding, ethnicity, and genealogy no longer worked against an ambitious man. White Americans came to believe that any man who was healthy and driven could acquire property in land, livestock, slaves, business enterprises, and real estate and rise up the social ladder. The American colonies were indeed a land of freedom and opportunity unlike anything that had existed for them before.

A second phenomenon was the erection of racial barriers, which eventually led to the imposition of a firm castelike quality on all blacks and Indians, condemning them to perpetual low status while enabling white society to develop as fluid and dynamic "without the crippling apprehensiveness that proper social ordering was going entirely by the board" (Jordan 1968, 134). This new social order placed Indians and blacks in a context wherein services could be extracted from them, but social mobility for them was made impossible. With Indians kept at a physical distance on reservations and blacks defined as functioning only in a servile status, white society was free to develop among its members a strong sense of the equivalence of all white men (Allen 1997; Morgan 1972, 1975).

A third, related phenomenon was the emergence of a new value ethic about the power and importance of the "common man." Jefferson's ideals and the entire experiment in republican government after the Revolutionary War presaged an apparent commitment to an egalitarian ethos. This was an egalitarianism that included for the first time men of the working classes, but restricted to white Europeans. The fullest manifestation of this ethos was to come with the election of Andrew Jackson in 1828, inaugurating what contemporaries and later historians were often to call "the Age of the Common Man." The opening of voting and political rights to all white males further exaggerated the differences between them and the blacks and Indians, who had no civil rights. Later, with the organization of the first labor unions, black Americans were excluded at almost all levels, which made it possible for some employers to use them as scabs or strikebreakers, further exacerbating the divisions among all working-class people.

The transformations in worldview that restricted the definition of who would be full participants in American society were confirmed repeatedly by judicial decisions, legislative enactments, and scientific publications. They were reiterated in the daily activities of whites, who affirmed in their behavior the rightness of the racial ordering system. Race came to outrank all other considerations of social valuation, superseding class and adding a totally new essentialist criterion to the ways by which societies could be hierarchically structured.

Although visible differences in physical features were the initial criteria of racial rank, once instituted as a qualitatively different way of categorizing people the idea of race ceased to require significant overt biophysical differences. Race differences could be imputed or external symbols could be utilized to denote the unbridgeable chasm. Race quite simply was a matter of human inventiveness, a fact most vividly manifested when Europeans began to apply the racial worldview and racial categories to themselves in the nineteenth century.

NOTES

1. For more detailed study of the significance of Quaker involvement in slavery, see Davis 1966 and Soderlund 1985.

2. Until recent decades, many historians seem not to have recognized the inevitable cultural assimilation that must have taken place between people who lived in such close juxtaposition as did slaves and masters in the South. Despite the status differences, blacks and whites came to share elements of a common southern culture. The myth that blacks constitute an "ethnic"

group in the United States operates to prevent sociological acceptance of the reality of cultural similarities among blacks and whites. It is only in highly segregated northern cities that blacks have developed unique cultural forms, in such areas as music, language, personal behavior, art, literature, and so forth. White receptivity to black urban culture forms also demonstrates that cultural assimilation is not a one-way process. In the early twentieth century, it was common to find older blacks, born into slavery, explaining how much they once had to teach white folks in the South about ordinary ways of thinking and doing things. This sense of black history has rarely been captured by historians, although scholarship in this respect is changing.

3. See Walvin 1980. Drescher has dealt with the rise of abolitionism in Britain and argues that its causality rested in the expansion of capitalism and political liberalism (1986).

4. The growth of moral consciousness and introspective disquietude about the extremes of wealth and poverty seems a seldom studied aspect of Western history. It parallels the development of the American nation and is at the heart of many contemporary humanitarian concerns. Rousseau, from a middle-class background, was shocked by the atrocious inequality that saw the building of a Versailles but left peasants starving. He even had to put his own five children (by his mistress) into a foundling home because he was too poor to feed them.

5. *Common Sense*, published in January 1776, sold over 500,000 copies. Paine's booklet *The Rights of Man*, advocating aid to the poor and unemployed, education for all, a progressive income tax to be used for public benefit, and the destruction of monarchy in favor of a republic, was banned in France during the French Revolution, and Paine was tried for treason.

6. See Fredrickson [1971] 1987 and Jordan 1968, and their treatment of transformations in social thought in the decades around the turn of the nineteenth century.

7. For a good introduction to the culture of the Jacksonian world, see Pessen 1985.

8. Descriptions of such acts can be found in Blassingame 1979 and Elkins [1959] 1963. Dumond ([1961] 1966) provides examples gathered by abolitionists of personal acts of unbridled cruelty toward slaves.

9. Two of Jefferson's grandsons beat a slave to death over a broken cup.

10. The great American historian W. E. B. DuBois recognized the superior significance of the racial divide, especially in his studies of black and white labor ([1935] 1985). Fredrickson, like other historians taking a cue from DuBois, acknowledges the dual forms of stratification (1988). The race hatred of poor whites had little to do with class conflict with the elite. Poor whites tended to identify with the elite and derived psychic, emotional, and often material benefits from their outbursts of violence against blacks. See also Williamson 1984.

11. According to Morgan, among the first Virginia pioneers there was "an extraordinary number of gentlemen," members of the gentry and nobility and their personal attendants, who were ill suited to the rigors of pioneer life (1975, 83–84). Nash concurs and adds that "almost nobody" came from the top layers of European society during the eighteenth century (1982, 201). Howard Mumford Jones points out that a whole class of the American elite disappeared when the loyalists returned to England during the Revolutionary War period (1964, 316). These observations imply that there was greater homogeneity of class status among early Anglo-Americans than perhaps has been realized, and the later emergence of a new and fluid class structure with an egalitarian ethos may be in part a product of this lack of rigid class differentiation.

CHAPTER 9

The Rise of Science and Scientific Racism

By the end of the eighteenth century, a whole new body of intellectual endeavors called "science" had begun to emerge as a distinct domain of Western culture, one that would have great prestige. When Thomas Jefferson raised questions about the "true" nature of the Negro and declared that we should leave it to science to ascertain the Negro's position in nature, he may well have speculated that science would respond in ways that would affirm southern pro-slavery beliefs. As will be shown in this and later chapters, science indeed came to play a major and important role in defining races and the relationships among them. Science has been a critical institution in perpetuating the racial worldview.

From the beginnings of European expansion and colonization, questions had been raised about the identity of the indigenous peoples discovered around the New World. Were they truly human? Did they have souls? Were they rational beings? Until well into the nineteenth century, the major sources of knowledge and explanations of the world and its complexities were the biblical interpretations and inferences made largely by men of the church. To be sure, the Enlightenment period in Europe, which spanned most of the eighteenth century, produced scores of scholars who objected to the often dogmatic positions of the church and sought to free scholarship from its restrictive doctrines. This period is well known in Western history for the rise of naturalistic explanations, confrontations between science and theology, and advances in empirical research and experimentation that are at the heart of modern science. It was through the efforts of scholars who dared to question theological positions and assumptions that the growth of Western science took place. By the mid-eighteenth century, science was well on its way to becoming a full-blown and distinctive ingredient of Western culture.

We should be very clear, however, about the nature of science and its position and functions in Western culture. Both naturalistic and supernaturalistic knowledge, as well as the application of this knowledge to solving human problems and explaining world realities, are found in all human societies. Throughout human history, naturalistic knowledge—the pragmatic information and understandings that peoples have about the world around them and the practices they undertake to modify that world—and supernatural or religious beliefs have been intertwined. Naturalistic knowledge is supplemented by a culture's religious explanations for things and events that are otherwise inexplicable.

Western science arose, gradually evolved, and became self-consciously dissociated from religion and other supernaturalistic perspectives. Science became a peculiar epistemology arising out of a distinct philosophy about the acquisition and manipulation of knowledge. Enlightenment writers saw science as an endeavor emanating from man's rational mind, unfettered by superstition or blind emotion.

Today, modern science comprises those ways of knowing and understanding that theoretically exclude the supernatural and the mystical; that is, it is based fundamentally on empirical knowledge, independently and objectively acquired through normal human sensory faculties or mechanical techniques. It is guided by a body of concepts, formal procedures, specific rules, methodologies, and perspectives that carry the presumption of objectivity and neutrality. We are conditioned to view it as a separate sphere of culture and its findings as products of strict empiricism and rigid procedures.

Yet from its beginnings, certain theologically based assumptions and propositions survived undiluted in early scientific thought. These assumptions related to the underlying cosmological and ideological themes of European cultures, specifically values, beliefs, and "revealed" knowledge about God, nature, the world, and humankind. In its early stages, the Judeo-Christian idea of a single creation and the story of Noah's ark as the explanation for human diversity were some of the main survivals of biblical thought in science. Their persistence was based on unquestioning acceptance of the scriptural representation of human beginnings, but they also reflected the church's pragmatic commitment to spreading Christian doctrines.

The book of Genesis provided a divine explanation of human origins as well as the main impetus to proselytize. In one broad episode of creation, God (always identified as male) gave life to man, located him in the Garden of

Eden, provided him with a female mate, and charged him to be fruitful, multiply, and subdue the earth. God also cautioned this first man, Adam, in obedience, admonishing him that he could eat all the fruit of the garden except that of the tree of knowledge of good and evil. But the reality of sin intruded in the form of a snake, who tempted Eve (the woman and rib-mate of Adam) to eat the forbidden fruit. She found it so delicious that she shared it with her mate. Subsequently Adam and Eve fell from the grace of God and were banished from Eden for their disobedience.

One aspect of this story had extraordinary relevance for those who grappled with the identity and meaning of the "savage" peoples of the colonies. In their state of ignorance, before they tasted the fruit exposing them to knowledge of good and evil, Adam and Eve were naked, innocent, and unashamed. But after eating the banned fruit, they not only became conscious of their nudity but also experienced shame. Thus, nudity in the Judeo-Christian world became associated with a state of sinfulness, with the condition of Adam and Eve after the fall; it became a sign of their disobedience to God's commands. Previous chapters showed how this cultural value about nudity prompted the English in particular to develop hostility and contempt for Irish and Native American peoples and to see in their absence of clothing reflections of the original sin and of bestiality.

As the biblical story continues, generations later the descendants of Adam had multiplied on the face of the earth, but they had also become wicked and corrupt in the eyes of the Lord. Repenting his creation, God decided to destroy humankind and most of life on Earth. But Noah, a descendant of Adam, had found grace in the eyes of God, who determined that, Noah, along with his sons, their wives, and representative pairings from the animal and plant world, would be saved from destruction to renew and replenish the earth. In a covenant with God, Noah built an ark for his family and assorted living things, and in it they rode out a massive storm of forty days and nights, which destroyed all other life on Earth.

After the flood, the descendants of Noah prospered and proliferated. They formed the new nations of the earth, all of whom spoke the same language. However, not content with things as they were, the ambitious descendants decided to build a city and in it a tower so tall that it could reach to heaven. For reasons not clear in the biblical text, God was not pleased with this. He descended from the heavens, confounded their language (gave them plural languages that were mutually unintelligible), and scattered the people upon the face of the earth (Gen. 11:7–9). The tower that the people had erected was called "Babel," and since then the term has been used to refer to situations characterized by a confusion of languages and an inability to communicate. This passage was interpreted, allegorically if not literally, as the source of the origins of different peoples, languages, and cultures.

The vast majority of peoples known to Europeans before the age of discovery could be fitted into some lines of descent, following the genealogical schemes of the Bible. Thus Shem, one of Noah's sons, was the ancestor of the Shemites (Semites), and Japheth was the founder of lines that led to Christian Europeans. Later, Ham came to be interpreted as the founder of the darker-skinned peoples known to the Hebrew tribes, the Cushites, Canaanites, and others not always fully identified. The task of scholars concerned with origins was to trace which of the three sons of Noah gave rise to the various other ethnic groups. Central to the paradigm was the idea, and the Christian ideal, of the universality of the fatherhood of God and the brotherhood and oneness of humankind, deriving from the single creation.

We should not underestimate the influence of biblical theology and the interpretations of world history and relationships provided by the church. Until the second half of the nineteenth century, only a minority of men, and even fewer women, were literate, much less well educated. Nevertheless, virtually all were familiar with the basic tenets of scripture, so that even those involved in the natural sciences operated from the same widely held presumptions of human origins. Among the literate elite, as well as the larger populace, biblical passages were taken literally as unerring explications of contemporary events and conditions and of moral righteousness. The "truths" extracted from scriptural sources were considered infallible and were rarely questioned before the eighteenth century. The scriptures were the authoritative source of information about the world and everything in it. As A. deWaal Malefijt has aptly summed up, "whatever God had wanted man to know about nature and society was revealed in the Scriptures, and whatever was not so revealed was intended to remain hidden" (1974, 25).

Some Renaissance writers, under the influence of the materialistic and naturalistic approaches of the ancients, developed a healthy skepticism about scriptural explanations. By the sixteenth century a few writers had begun to speculate on the possibility of more than one creation. Such skepticism reflected the broadened horizons of European learning during the early era of exploration and colonization.

From the sixteenth century on, one trend of scholarship followed a trajectory that increasingly veered away from orthodox explanations of natural phenomena toward material and secular ones. This movement paralleled the growth of a natural philosophy that required and emphasized objective, empirical studies and the search for the causes and origins of natural phenomena in elements of the environment.

Meanwhile, the authoritarian hold of the Catholic Church over men's minds had begun to decline as a lingering consequence of the Protestant Reformation and the breakaway of various sects from the mother church. In the wake of much political upheaval in Europe—widespread civil wars, numerous schisms, and factionalism in both church and state—the power of the church was greatly diminished. The rise of merchant capitalism and significant changes in class structure brought new social forces into power. An accelerating quest for knowledge resulted in the formation of private schools and academies, learned societies, and universities, some of which arose spontaneously in the colonies. Increasing wealth permitted some young men to devote their lives to research and writing, much of it on the amazing new discoveries in areas opened to European exploration. Writings and publications about aboriginal peoples expanded, providing much new information about the world's peoples.

Commitment to the idea of a single creation persisted with virile strength, even down to the present. Scientists as well as nonscientists adhered tenaciously to this belief, not just for its position as a fundamental element of religious faith, but for its philosophical significance in giving meaning to human existence. Rudimentary speculations on the possibility of multiple creations aside, the dominant religious and philosophical themes of the age of discovery made all the newly discovered peoples part of the great human family. This was particularly evident in the earliest attempts by scientists to identify and classify the newly discovered varieties of human beings.

EARLY CLASSIFICATIONS OF HUMANKIND

In the early stages of the development of science, the most fundamental operation was the collection of data and the subsequent examination, description, and arrangement of the data into categories according to certain explicit principles. Those persons who accumulated and often published data on the flora and fauna of strange lands and peoples came to be known as "naturalists." Others were writers, geographers, and curiosity seekers who simply wanted to inform a widening circle of literate persons about the wonders of foreign lands.

Many persons acquired material objects from cultures around the world, forming collections that became the bases of the great ethnographic museums of modern times. Others accumulated descriptions of alien peoples and their customs from travelers, commercial traders, missionaries, geographers, and adventurers. The invention of the printing press in the mid-fifteenth century had greatly aided the sorting and organization of descriptive materials and their dissemination. Based on these collections, enormous compendia of natural phenomena were published. The men involved in these activities became known as classifiers and systematists, noted for organizing specific sets of data into logically comprehensible schemes. This was the beginning of a new trend in which the collecting activities were deliberate and a wide range of materials were organized for systematic and comparative study to provide answers to fundamental questions. Taxonomic systems for the world's flora and fauna multiplied, as did efforts to identify and classify human groups. A scientific perspective on the world's realities thus began to emerge.

Most historians of science consider that modern classifications of human populations began with Carolus Linnaeus, a Swedish botanist, who in 1735 published *Systemae Naturae*, the first version of a vast classificatory scheme. In later editions Linnaeus included humankind not only within the larger classification of all living things, but for the first time in specific relation to the apes and monkeys. He grouped human beings with the higher primates under the order Anthropomorpha and divided the genus *Homo* into four basic varieties—*Europeaeus, Americanus, Asiaticus, and Africanus*. Considered the founder of scientific taxonomy, Linnaeus is best known for having originated the binomial nomenclature still used today that denotes all living forms by genus and species.

Like most scientists of the eighteenth century, Linnaeus had a precise understanding of "species" as distinguished from "varieties." He saw species as distinct primordial forms dating from creation that remained essentially the same throughout all time, whereas varieties were clusters within a species that had acquired superficial differences in appearance. Species were fixed and unalterable in their basic organic plan, whereas varieties reflected changes caused by such external factors as climate, temperature, and geographic features. It was the general and widespread belief that all humans were members of the same species, as they had descended from a common original ancestry and were capable of intergroup mating and reproduction.

In later editions of his work, Linnaeus elaborated on his classifications of both apes and humans. Significantly, and like earlier classifications, his descriptions of the four human groups indiscriminately mixed physical features with supposed traits of character, disposition, and behavior, features we would see today as specifically external and cultural. His groups were:

> *Americanus:* reddish, choleric, and erect; hair—black, straight, thick; wide nostrils, scanty beard; obstinate, merry, free; paints himself with fine red lines; regulated by customs.
>
> *Asiaticus:* sallow, melancholy, stiff; black hair, dark eyes; severe, haughty, avaricious; covered with loose garments; ruled by opinions.
>
> *Africanus:* black, phlegmatic, relaxed; hair—black, frizzled; skin—silky; nose—flat; lips—tumid; women without shame, they lactate profusely; crafty, indolent, negligent; anoints himself with grease; governed by caprice.
>
> *Europeaeus:* white, sanguine, muscular; hair—long, flowing; eyes—blue; gentle, acute, inventive; covers himself with close vestments; governed by laws.[1]

Linnaeus's commingling of physical features with behavioral and psychological traits shows the growing influence of a certain type of thinking that presumed that each species had innate qualities of behavior or temperament. He included in his descriptions opinions and observations about character, dress, customs, and behavior as if these were linked to the physical features. Like all his European contemporaries, Linnaeus acquired the vast majority of his data from the writings, descriptions, commentaries, speculations, musings, opinions, and beliefs of travelers, explorers, traders, missionaries, plantation owners, and the like with experience of the New World, parts of Africa, or Asia. Their perceptions of "savages" with accompanying mystical interpretations and fantasies flowed into the scientific establishment and fueled its speculations.

Walter Scheidt (1950) credits Louis Leclerc, Comte de Buffon, with introducing the term *race* into the lexicon of the natural sciences in 1749, although clearly the term was used by scholars before Buffon. Moreover, his use of the term was not significantly different from uses of the term *variety*. His varieties included Laplanders or the "Polar Race," Tartars or Mongolians, southern Asiatics, Europeans, Ethiopians, and Malays. Buffon, however, was less interested in classifying than in explaining the varieties of humankind, whom he saw as a single species. He offered what we now see as a modern theory of human diversity:

> Whenever man began to change his climate, and to migrate from one country to another, his nature was subject to various alterations. . . . The changes he underwent became so great and so conspicuous, as to give room for

> suspecting that the Negro, the Laplander and the White were really different species, if, on the one hand, we were not certain, that one man only was originally created, and, on the other, that the White, the Laplander and the Negro, are capable of uniting and of propagating the great and undivided family of the human kind. Hence those marks which distinguish men who inhabit different regions of the earth, are not original, but purely superficial. (in Slotkin 1965, 185)

Buffon had reasoned that climate was the "chief cause of the different colours of men" and that food, soil, air, and the earth's topography have an influence on the form of the human body. A third area of causation was culture, habits, customs, beliefs, and practices, which he speculated must have affected physical features. Such naturalistic elements were then the prima facie causes of human differences. Buffon concluded: "Upon the whole, every circumstance concurs in proving, that mankind are not composed of species essentially different from each other; that on the contrary, there was originally but one species, who after multiplying and spreading over the whole surface of the earth, have undergone various changes by the influence of climate, food, mode of living, epidemic disease, and the mixture of dissimilar individuals" (in Slotkin 1965, 185). J. S. Slotkin holds that this relatively modern sense of race, which converges with much of twentieth-century understanding, originated with Buffon. But belief in the natural, environmental causes of human variation was widespread among the learned people of Europe during the Enlightenment.

Toward the end of the eighteenth century Johann Blumenbach, a professor of medicine in Germany, emerged as the most important of the classifiers for later scientists. Between 1770 and 1781, he proposed the division of humankind into four, later five, "varieties" associated with the major regions of the world. These five (Caucasian, Mongolian, Ethiopian, American, and Malay) came to be widely accepted by the educated community, and most continue in use today. Like the majority of scientists, Blumenbach worked within the single-origin (monogenetic) framework, holding to the biblical version of human creation. The unity of the origin of humankind is either explicit or implicit in all of these cited works. The groups named, however, were not considered equal except in a general spiritual sense; their ranking along a scale determined by their closeness to "civilized" status gained currency during the late eighteenth century, becoming a prominent feature of the comparative sciences.

On this score, Blumenbach was responsible for promoting a major and familiar theory of the monogenists, the argument that degeneration, caused by climate, food, and living habits, accounts for the external differences among human groups. Although not a new idea, Blumenbach's sophistication and reputation elevated it to a fundamental deterministic principle of science. His theories of causation were thus similar to those of Buffon and others, proposing external environmental factors as responsible for the state of civilization of different human groups.

To his credit, Blumenbach emphasized the difficulty of setting boundaries around human populations, observing that the varieties of humans blend "insensibly" into one another (Slotkin 1965, 189). Here he recognized a reality that Americans rarely expressed or even perceived. Such thinking suggested a kind of arbitrariness about human classifications that contradicted the trend in the American colonies toward establishing rigid and exclusive categories.

Nevertheless, all seventeenth- and eighteenth-century scientific classifications were burdened by the heavy weight of ethnocentrism, or cultural chauvinism, and subjective judgments on the physical features of non-Europeans. Blumenbach, for example, like the vast majority of his contemporaries, believed that the original human form was that of European whites. To him, they were the most physically attractive of the varieties of humankind. If God had made humans in his image, this surely was the variant he would have chosen. Blumenbach selected the term *Caucasian* for this classification because he felt that the skull of a woman of the Caucasus region in Russia was the most beautiful of his collection. Value judgments about other human groups varied insofar as they departed from this ideal.[2] Blumenbach was not alone in his willingness to impose his aesthetic judgment on the physical features of different peoples. Buffon and Linnaeus had done so, as well as many others. It was part of the general cultural values of the European world that people with dark skins, thick lips, and wooly hair compared unfavorably with those who had white skins, straight hair, and narrow features. This was acceptable scientific commentary in the eighteenth century, demonstrating the degree to which scientists shared the cultural values and preconceptions of their times (Greene 1981).

These scholars were all working at a time when the African–Atlantic slave trade was increasing, indeed reaching its peak in the eighteenth century. All that most scholars learned about Africans during these two centuries was compressed into the reality that Africans were the premier slaves of the Western world. Most European societies were involved in African slavery in one way or another. In general, the image that most Europeans had of Africans was that of slaves, of subordinate and powerless peoples. Similarly, their knowledge and understanding of Native Americans was distorted by the facts of their conquest and apparent demise. By then it was widely accepted that the indigenous peoples of the Americas were weak savages who had to be conquered to make way for superior civilization. The scholars and scientists of Europe could hardly have attitudes toward these peoples or make judgments about them that were uninfluenced by these social, economic, and political realities.

THE IMPACT OF EIGHTEENTH-CENTURY CLASSIFICATIONS

The consequences of these classifications were far reaching and perhaps unanticipated, with implications that went far beyond the immediate taxonomic problems. The fundamental error was to assume that the human species was divided into clearly demarcated subgroups, such as subspecies.

1. They gave an aura of permanence and rigidity to conceptions of human group differences. Once something is classified, it is set irretrievably in time and space, with a tendency to be transmitted to others as a fixed and unalterable entity. This interpretation was compatible with the growing American conception of race.
2. The categories, as drawn up, seem to accept without question the linkage of physical characteristics with behavioral ones, along with such psychocultural features as temperament, disposition, and moral character. Such fusion, we have seen, was a trend in the general popular thought of the times; hence it documents the growing strength of this component of the racial worldview in the minds of both the classifiers and their readers.
3. As Jonathan Marks has pointed out, the categories ignored "the geographically gradual nature of biological diversity" (1995, 52) as well as the cultural realities that do not accord with presumed biological boundaries.
4. The classifications lent themselves to hierarchical structuring, fostering an impression of inequality among the different groups, with the most positive and progressive cultural features associated with Europeans and the least positive ones associated with those called "savages." This clearly fit well with the still expanding racial worldview and accorded with social, economic, and political realities.
5. Finally, such classifications by reputable and widely renowned scientists (naturalists) such as Linnaeus and Blumenbach made humankind part of the natural order of things. They thus legitimized as "natural" and as God-given the inferior qualities ascribed to non-Europeans and helped

> to justify their lower positions in world societies. In other words, they tended to provide scientific sanction and scholarly credibility for prevailing popular images and stereotypes of non-Europeans.

All of the scholars who produced classifications of human groups, we will be reminded, were Europeans. None had extensive experience with diverse human groups; most had never even seen a "savage." Furthermore, it bears reiterating that the materials on which they based their classifications were far from impeccable. They came not from modern trained researchers but from ordinary people preoccupied with other interests and purposes. They came from the writings and verbal descriptions of men operating from a position of dominance—slave traders, sailors, slave owners, merchants, and others who were sometimes the social equals of the systematizers. Today, such descriptions of the "dispositions" and habits of "savages" strike us as at best naive. But the reality is that to the eighteenth-century mind, "Satyrs," "Troglodytes," "Giants," and "Dwarfs" were very real populations. So was the still-evolving belief in the innate foundations of all human behavior.

Educated people in the American colonies were not excluded from the scholarly activities and knowledge that were diffusing through the universities and learned societies in Europe. Intellectual interest in the American Indians increased during the eighteenth century, and some of the writings of Americans found their way to Europe. Various travelers from Europe had also published descriptions of Native Americans, so European classifiers had considerable materials to use. The taxonomies of scholars such as Linnaeus and Blumenbach were known and discussed by educated men in America. They became part of their knowledge systems and were assimilated into American views about human differences.

To their credit, most of the classifiers accepted the principle of the unity of the human species, if for no other reason than adherence to scriptural requirements. Most also expressed a belief in the potential improvement of savage peoples that was consonant with Enlightenment ideas about environmentally induced change and human progress. That the human animal was plastic, flexible, and capable of progress was not in much doubt among those influenced by Enlightenment thinking. Blumenbach in fact argued against the notion beginning to penetrate European intellectual circles that the different varieties of humans were unequal and should be ranked accordingly (see note 2). His positions reflected the continuing influence of early Enlightenment thought and the general position of educated Europeans who had accepted the presence of individuals of African ancestry in Europe, some of whom achieved fame for their abilities and talents.[3] In the late eighteenth century, the hard currency of racial ideology had not yet settled on the European mind as it had in North America.

However, toward the end of the century polygenesis, the theory of multiple creations, reappeared, emerging from its subordinate role among philosophical theories. Among the European scholars who suggested that the major variants of humankind were separate species, created at different times, was the French philosopher and dramatist Voltaire (1694–1778). Not a scientific researcher but an opponent of the dogmatic positions of the church, Voltaire simply believed that the differences in physical characteristics as well as the "state of civilization" of Africans and Indians were sufficient evidence to categorize them as species distinct from Europeans. He thought of black Africans as mere animals who mated with orangutans.[4]

Voltaire, more than most of the Enlightenment writers, was an "establishment" man. He lived in England for several years and became an admirer of English laws and concepts of property and their linkage to freedom. He also invested heavily in commerce and trade, which he saw as the lifeblood of a free society. He thus had vested interests in maintaining the colonial system, slavery, and the slave trade. Voltaire's influence among the educated classes on both sides of the Atlantic was powerful. Leon Poliakov observes that "no writer of the Enlightenment had as many readers—or as important ones—as Voltaire" (1982, 56).

Voltaire was joined in his view of separate origins of the races by Henry Home (Lord Kames), a Scottish jurist who also wrote about a great variety of topics and was widely read on both sides of the Atlantic. Kames scoffed at Buffon's definition of species in terms of their mating behavior and reproductive isolation; denied that climate was responsible for the great variations in biophysical characteristics; and insisted that fundamental and primordial differences in innate behavior, as well as in overt physical traits, were indicative of species distinction. His *Sketches of the History of Man*, published in 1774, was looked upon, even by some monogenists, as providing authoritative arguments for the separation of the races. His pronouncements on the inferiority of blacks and Indians could have been favorably received by both monogenists and polygenists without disturbing their respective positions on human origins. But a little more than fifty years after the publication of Lord Kames's work, a new group of writers and scientists began an unparalleled debate in science over the very questions raised by Voltaire and Kames.

The question must be posed. Why, after over a century of Africans, Indians, and Europeans (and various mixtures of the three) interacting in the American colonies, should there still have been doubts about the classifications and relationships in nature of these three originally separate human groups? What was there about the nature of the relationships to prompt such energetic attention to questions of classification and difference? Was it merely a product, or by-product, of the growth of science, or were there deeper, hidden meanings in the desperate attempt to ascertain the different places in nature of various peoples?

NOTES

1. Linnaeus had several other categories for human types that included *Homo ferus*, or wild men, and *H. monstrosus*, a category that included dwarfs and "large, lazy Patagonians." He accepted popular myths regarding the existence of "Troglodytes," humanlike creatures that lived underground and hunted at night. The tenth edition of *Systemae Naturae* in 1758 classified these creatures in the genus *Homo*, noting that they were also called "Orang outangs."

2. The influence of earlier writers and philosophers such as Montaigne, and especially writers of the early Enlightenment, can be seen in the thinking of most of the classifiers, who generally thought that the inferior races could also advance and improve themselves. At the same time, we see the growing influence of the racial worldview in their writings, which appears to oppose some of their liberal views. In the case of Blumenbach, there were apparent contradictions in his public statements and writings. According to Thomas Gossett, Blumenbach criticized those who thought that different "races" could be ranked as inferior or superior or judged by a common standard of beauty. And he "collected a library of books written by Negroes, to demonstrate that they are not inherently stupid" (1965, 39). This was hardly in keeping with the theory of degeneration.

3. In the nineteenth and twentieth centuries, virtually all knowledge of people of African ancestry in European history was obliterated by the many writers of history who took the ideologically acceptable position of denigrating all black achievements. Thus St. Maurice (a leader in the Children's Crusade), Alessandro di Medici, Alexandre Dumas, the Russian poet Aleksandr Pushkin, and other outstanding Europeans of African ancestry ceased to exist, or were ignored, in the history books (see Goodwin 2009).

4. Despite his progressive and tolerant views on other matters, Voltaire, according to Leon Poliakov, was strongly anti-Jewish as well as antiblack (1982, 56).

CHAPTER 10

Growth of the Racial Worldview in Nineteenth-Century America

It was no coincidence that at the height of the abolitionist movement in the 1830s, certain scientific developments occurred that attempted to provide greater legitimacy to the folk beliefs we have seen as the ideological components of race. This chapter looks at the processes by which scientific and folk ideas on human variability converged with legal decisions and buttressed the autonomy of race as a generic natural category.

Nineteenth-century scientific contributions to ideologies about human differences were critical not only to the affirmation of the existence of races and race differences as natural and inborn, but also to the formulation of public policies and the treatment of various immigrant groups still to come. Scientists constructed definitions and characterizations of each racial population, focusing especially on the identification of "the Negro" in the context of what had come to be defined as white civilization. Some turned to science because it was the one institution that could claim neutrality. Science was objective and detached, at least by reputation, and people looked to it for those truths that resonated, unsullied by politics or religion. Because the elements in the idea of race were so largely compounded of myths, there was a need for their persistent reiteration. Most important, due to the strength of the countervailing pressures of abolitionists and the growing humanitarian sentiments associated with democratic ideology, it was necessary to continuously seek ways of magnifying the presumed differences between races, thereby underscoring both their scientific validity and their social inequality.

The dominant view of human origins until the mid-nineteenth century accorded with the biblical vision of a single creation. All species were created in their present forms by an omnipotent being who fixed their characteristics from the beginning. Because of their known interfertility, all human groups belonged to a single species, whose design emanated from the Maker himself. Two explanatory paradigms operated as philosophical guidelines for comprehending the intraspecies diversity. One was degeneration, which was compatible with biblical history in that it could be interpreted as a consequence of the fall from grace. The other was the Great Chain of Being, which served as a model of God's hierarchical plan for the world.

In 1799 Dr. Charles White, a noted physician from Manchester, England, published a volume that was important for claiming scientific support for existing race ideas but that also contradicted the Christian theory of origins. Entitled *An Account of the Regular Gradation in Man*, it proposed the evidence for the differential status on the Great Chain of Being accorded by the supreme being to Africans, Asians, Indians, and "white Europeans." White concluded that the Negro was an intermediate form between true human beings (white Europeans) and apes. Other races were assigned positions intermediate between the Negro and the European. Like Lord Kames and Edward Long before him, White rejected the Christian and Enlightenment notion of the unity of the human species. He found differences between geographically separated races to be sufficiently great to counter the idea of a single species. White postulated instead that each race was a separate species, a product of separate creation, specifically preadapted by God for the geographic area in which it was found.

With the early attention that taxonomists and systematists had focused on human diversity and the unremitting moral and ethical problems of slavery, the search for a scientific authentication of folk beliefs about human differences was a rational option. But to propose the idea of separate species as products of separate creations was a remarkable position for a scientist to take, especially in light of the unsuccessful history of polygenist ideas over the previous two centuries and of commonly held understandings of what species were all about. The strength of the theologically based idea of a single creation, or monogenesis, was such that it was considered almost unassailable. The vast majority of scientists, even most of those who identified themselves as deists, adhered to the powerful principle of human unity. Whether for romantic, idealistic, or religious reasons, or those based entirely on rational considerations of empirical data, the idea of multiple creations was anathema to most learned people.

Yet, given the ever-expanding focus on human differences during the late eighteenth century and the potent motives of the proslavery establishment,

White's position should not have been totally unanticipated. There were precedents, as we have observed, and it seems quite clear that polygenesis had remained a subdued minority viewpoint for several centuries. But the most important factor about White's publication that brought it exalted recognition among the educated population was that it signified a new development. It took the widely held folk belief about the Negro's place in the natural scheme and placed it unambiguously in the realm of science. His conclusions were based on comparative studies that he had made on the anatomical features of Negroes, Europeans, and apes, and they were presented in a seemingly objective, erudite fashion. White demonstrated what he thought were unvarying constitutional differences between black and white races in skeletal structure, muscles, tendons, cartilage, skin, hair, and the size of the sex organ and the brain. He also claimed differences in sweat and body odor, and in reason, speech, and language. Most important, he declared that the different gradations of human beings "were endued with various degrees of intelligence" (Greene 1954, 390).

White's publication brought considerable reaction, in part because he made significant use of Thomas Jefferson's descriptions and evaluations of Negroes in Virginia. It promoted a curious phase in the history of the concept of race in the form of a major intellectual controversy.[1] The question, simply put, was whether Negroes were a product of the same act of creation as whites and thus members of the same species, but an inferior variant, or whether they were the result of a separate act of creation. It should be stated from the outset, however, that, contrary to most historical accounts, the debate that ensued was only superficially a debate about origins. At bottom, it was a debate about the meaning of race, especially about the place of "the Negro" in the context of racial ideology and about the magnitude of the differences between black and white that the dominant society had already decreed and accepted.

POLYGENY VS. MONOGENY: THE DEBATE OVER *RACE* AND *SPECIES*

In the early eighteenth century, before the term *species* came into widespread general use by naturalists and taxonomists, it was sometimes used interchangeably, as we have seen, with *race*, and both had much the same connotations as *type* or *kind*. But the essential meaning of *species* in biological thought, even before the term itself became fixed as the significant semantic unit in taxonomic language, was understood in modern Europe certainly as early as the sixteenth century. Montaigne, for example, in his conclusion that all humans were of one species, based this belief on a presumptive understanding of the ability of all known human populations to interbreed (Slotkin 1965, 61).

When two contiguous populations that are otherwise similar physically and morphologically do not intermate naturally and produce viable offspring, they are identified as separate species. "Reproductive isolation," as this phenomenon is now designated, was widely acknowledged as a critical divider separating species both implicitly and explicitly in the works of the ancient Greeks, and it still prevails.

Until the acceptance of Darwin's *The Origin of Species* (published in 1859), the predominant view was that species were created in their present state at the beginning of time and were fixed and unchanging. This was consonant with prevailing theological beliefs about the origin of all living phenomena and with the existing state of knowledge about the immutability of all natural forms. There is no doubt but that, after several hundred years at least of solid work by systematists, the idea of species as animal (or plant) breeding populations clearly distinguishable from one another on the basis of reproductive isolation was well understood in the scientific and literate world.

Yet White's assertion that the races of men were created as separate species was not dismissed out of hand or ignored as nonsense contradictory to well-known facts. On the contrary, it polarized much of scientific opinion on the issue of human origins. The polygenists, who argued for multiple creations, generally started with the enumeration of differences between racial groups. The monogenists, on the other hand, acknowledged and accepted most differences, but cited biblical sources for their adherence to belief in a single creation followed by diverging descent. With over three hundred years of "racial" intermixture on the American continents and throughout the world, during which viable "hybrids" had been produced and reproduced, there should have been no doubt anywhere in the world as to the inclusion in the species *Homo sapiens* of any known human population. How then do we account for the seeming retrogression in scientific thought and development represented by the debates of the mid-nineteenth century over whether or not blacks were of the same species as whites?

To understand this development, we have only to realize that this period was characterized by the intensification of efforts to maximize the number of scientific ways by which races could be differentiated. This was the "central theoretical concern of pre-Darwinian anthropology" (Stocking 1968, 40). That these efforts were aimed specifically at setting apart the Negro population is readily ascertained by the circumstances, the men involved, and the contents of the debates themselves. The focus on the one issue—the Negro's place in nature—was overwhelming. There should be no doubt that such intensity of attention was a besieged culture's response to the rise of militant abolitionism, the threat of emancipation, and its own fear of irrevocable social changes.

Shortly after the radical abolitionist movement had gained momentum and national recognition, and, significantly, after Nat Turner and Denmark Vesey had inspired infamous slave revolts, an American physician, Dr. Samuel Morton, produced his major contributions to the controversy. In two publications, *Crania Americana* (1839) and *Crania Aegyptiaca* (1844), he set forth his views on the nature of racial differences and their possible origins. Working initially within the limits of accepted biblical chronology, he did not at first claim species distinctions. But he based his conclusions about the enormous differences between the races on quantitative studies of human crania, for the measurements of which he himself had developed sophisticated scientific techniques.[2] For these developments he became known as the founder of the science of craniometry and of the first American school of anthropology.

Morton concluded from his study of cranial capacity that different races had distinct skull shapes and sizes. The Caucasoid brain was the largest, followed by the Mongoloid, Malay, American Indian, and the Negro, in that order. He assumed that brain size directly correlated with intelligence. Moreover, he went on to describe not only the physical traits of each race but also their moral and intellectual concomitants. The "joyous, flexible and indolent" Ethiopian was contrasted to the Caucasian with his "highest intellectual endowments" (quoted in Stanton 1960, 33). He argued that these racial characteristics were permanent, as each race had been adapted for its peculiar habitat from its origin. He denied the possible effects of climate and geography on physical characteristics.

Native Americans (Indians), Morton believed, were lacking in intelligence and capacity for "a continued process of reasoning on abstract subjects" (Stanton 1960, 34). They were inherently savage, and it would be difficult, if not impossible, for them to survive under the onslaught of European superiority. He was writing at a time when the Indian Removal Act of 1830 was being implemented, and thousands of Cherokee, Choctaw, and Creek Indians were being forcibly resettled in Oklahoma territory west of the Mississippi. Morton's interpretation of the internal qualities of the mind, judged solely from the skull, was well in keeping with the increasingly popular tendency to embrace beliefs about innate sources for all talents and abilities that became widely disseminated with the phrenology fad.

Among the more important of Morton's conclusions, noted in many journal articles in the latter half of the century, was his claim that the ancient

Egyptians were not Negroes but merely dark-skinned Caucasians. This assertion was necessary because prior to and during the Napoleonic years, French scholars, some of whom had accompanied Napoleon on his conquest of Egypt in 1798, had described the peoples associated with the ancient ruins recently discovered as *noires* (blacks) and their cultures as "les civilizations Nègres."[3]

By 1817 the great French zoologist Baron George Cuvier, who had corresponded with Jefferson and no doubt was influenced by Jefferson's views on blacks, had concluded that the ancient Egyptians could not have been Negroes. The Negro, with his low cranial capacity, was incapable of creating such a great civilization (Stocking 1968, 35). Morton based his argument on the same premise. In *Crania Aegyptiaca* (1844), Morton retreated a bit from this position and claimed that the ancient Egyptians were neither Caucasian nor Negro, but a blend of "several distinct branches of the human family."[4] But he maintained that Egyptian slaves were all Negroes, which was intended to prove the constancy of their lowly status from the beginning of history.

Toward the end of his career, Morton became convinced that the races represented "primordial" differences and had been created separately in different environments. But in order to advance this argument of separate species status, he had to deal with the problem of "hybridity," the ability of the several races to mate and produce viable offspring. Morton intuited that human hybrids somehow contradicted the law of nature. Eventually he concluded that interfertility did not prove the unity of the human species. He finally arrived at what Louis Agassiz was to praise as a "true philosophical definition of species, the first to bless the world of science." A species, said Morton, was a "primordial organic form" (Stanton 1960, 141).

Morton's works were read and widely applauded in the southern states. When he died in 1851, the *Charleston Medical Journal* published a biographical memoir stating: "We can only say that we of the South should consider him as our benefactor, for aiding most materially *in giving to the negro his true position as an inferior race*" (Stanton 1960, 144). This was an open and unequivocal recognition of science's role in the construction and affirmation of folk beliefs.[5]

Dr. Josiah Nott of Alabama took up the polygenist cause, pushing his theories at a time when proslavery forces were most vigorous in their reaction against the abolitionists. In numerous talks and publications, beginning in the 1840s, Nott promoted the belief in the debilities and the degeneracy of Negroes and especially of "hybrids" (mulattoes), arguing that the latter were unnatural offspring of two species and analogous in their nature to mules. Nott carried the argument further, however, emphasizing the degree to which the

Negro experienced well-being under slavery. Like children, he argued, Negroes required care, direction, and control. If manumitted, they would soon perish because of their inability to endure the "ravages" of freedom. This theme was embraced and widely perpetuated by many members of the educated public during and after the Civil War.

In 1854, the year of the formation of the antislavery Republican Party, Nott collaborated with the notorious George Gliddon to publish a work, *Types of Mankind*, which "was designed as a compendium of all anthropological evidence that had been brought forward in support of the specific diversity of mankind" (Stanton 1960, 163). One of the most popular works of its time, *Types* went through nine editions by the end of the century. Although some theologians condemned it for its apparent negation of revealed religion, few criticized its arguments on behalf of the inequality of the races. It brought together all of the data of the polygenists—Morton (to whom it was dedicated), Nott, Gliddon, and others—and included a chapter by Agassiz (see below). Numerous tables of statistical data collected by Morton, both previously published and some unpublished, were included in its contents.

This was perhaps the single most important book to set the issue of race in a peculiarly scientific context for the general public. It was the culmination of a trend begun in the latter part of the eighteenth century and was encouraged by the tremendous growth in the reputation of science. For the next few generations, *Types of Mankind* was used by students and laypersons alike as a major source of descriptive, statistical, and other quantitative data on the different kinds of human beings. Presented as the fruit of extensive, objective research, it succeeded in backing with the awesome prestige of science what were actually folk views of the Negro in the nineteenth century, transformed into racial ideology.

Louis Agassiz, a Swiss naturalist whose fame as an ichthyologist derived from his major investigations on fossil fish, had been invited in 1846 to pursue research at Harvard on the fish of the New World. Until that time he had held the monogenist position of most European naturalists—that all humankind comprised one original species. But in the United States between 1846 and 1850, he underwent a remarkable conversion to polygenism, to which several elements contributed.

One was his strong adherence to creationism, the idea of independent creations of all animal species, and their immutability through time. Another was the influence of Morton, whom he visited in Philadelphia. Agassiz was impressed with his collection of skulls; his apparently careful, precise, and objective methods of measurement; and his arguments on the significance of these metrical differences.

The final element in Agassiz's conversion was unrelated to his religious convictions, the scholarly evidence and arguments, or the academic milieu. In Philadelphia and later in Charleston, South Carolina, the site of most of the polygenist–monogenist debates, Agassiz saw Negroes for the first time, having contact with them as domestics in his hotel. In a letter to his mother (resuscitated from Harvard's Houghton Library by recent scholars), he expressed his shock at their features, their black skin, their thick lips and "grimacing teeth," their peculiar limbs, and the "wool" on their heads. He admitted that when a Negro waiter approached him in the hotel dining room, he wanted to bolt from the room. "What unhappiness for the white race," he exclaimed, "to have tied their existence so closely with that of negroes in certain countries! God preserve us from such a contact!" (quoted in Gould 1981, 45).

The experience convinced him, he wrote, that though the Negro was human, he was not of the same species as whites. "I experienced pity at the sight of this degraded and degenerate race, and their lot inspired compassion in me in thinking that they are really men" (Gould 1981, 45). This was, as Gould has recognized, a visceral judgment, one that had no basis in reason or objective examination of fact. It is curious that Agassiz should have had such a reaction of personal revulsion, linked with an instant perception of the "ugliness" of the Negro. He had spent much of his life studying and identifying thousands of species of fossil fish, ancient animal forms not generally lauded in Western cultures for their beauty.

Within months, Agassiz was lecturing in both the South and the North that the Negro and white races were morphologically and physiologically so distinct as to constitute separate species. He also published numerous articles in which he elaborated this argument. In the chapter he contributed to Nott and Gliddon's *Types of Mankind*, Agassiz identified eight primary human types that "inhabited specific zoological provinces." He argued for the primordial qualities of their differences, as determined by the will of their Creator. "I am prepared to show that the differences existing between the races of men are of the same kind as the differences observed between the different families, genera, and species of monkeys or other animals. . . . Nay, the differences between distinct races are often greater than those distinguishing species of animals one from the other" (Nott and Gliddon 1854, lxxiv).

Thus it was that Agassiz lent the weight of his scientific reputation and status to the likes of Nott and Gliddon and the championing of the southern cause. In these activities, however, he believed that he was supporting the cause of scientific freedom against dogmatic theology. Agassiz was also personally opposed to evolutionary theory, as was Cuvier, particularly criticizing the Lamarckian notion of the inheritance of acquired characteristics. Following the publication of Darwin's *The Origin of Species* in 1859, Agassiz became one of the most important leaders of the opposition to evolutionism (much to the pain and embarrassment of some of his students and colleagues).

Within a few years Agassiz, who as an impecunious young student had been partially supported in Paris by his great friend and mentor Cuvier, became one of the most famous professors and scientists at Harvard. He revolutionized teaching methods in the natural sciences; founded the Museum of Comparative Zoology; and raised large amounts of money for buildings, collections of natural phenomena, and publications. He also married Elizabeth Cabot Cary, a descendant of the wealthy and prestigious Cabot family, after the death of his first wife. Through her social contacts, his reputation became widespread, not only among the "Boston Brahmins" but to a larger public. A brilliant and scintillating lecturer and a charming companion, Agassiz was lionized by the eastern establishment and university circles. More important, he passed on his racial views and theories on human species to generations of students. According to one source, "every notable teacher of natural history in the United States for the second half of the nineteenth century was either a pupil of Agassiz or of one of his students."[6] Two of his students, Nathaniel Shaler and Joseph Le Conte, also became outstanding late nineteenth-century promoters of the idea of the inequality of human races.

The mid-nineteenth century was a period of major discoveries of new species and extinct animal forms. An enormous amount of attention and resources were focused on the collection of new data and the establishment and refinement of new classifications and taxonomic methods. With Darwin's and Alfred Russell Wallace's virtually simultaneous discovery of the chief mechanism of biological evolution, natural selection, attention was diverted from older issues and debates. Evolutionary theory raised the question of diachronic relationships among animal forms, and one effect of this was a greater preoccupation with phylogeny. The debate over single or multiple origins of human groups soon languished with the acceptance of evolutionary theory and the dynamic perspective that it fostered.

As George Stocking has demonstrated, however, polygenist beliefs persisted long after Darwin because of their grounding in fundamental social values and a deeply rooted racial worldview. He observed, "the external forces which nourished a broadly polygenist point of view were if anything intensified: the gap between civilized white and savage black men, and the need to justify the white man's imperial dominion, were both becoming greater than ever before" (1968, 47). Both the biological and social sciences reflected attitudes that Stocking saw as survivals of the polygenists' perspective, implicitly if not explicitly, and regardless of whether their practitioners were theoretical monogenists or not. Indeed, for certain sectors of the scientific establishment, Darwinism provided an even more potent vehicle for arguing that black and white races had evolved as separate species.

With a few exceptions among some of the monogenists, virtually all those involved in the controversy fully accepted the prevailing belief in the inferiority of "the Negro." John Haller characterizes the era with this statement: "Almost the whole of scientific thought in both America and Europe in the decades before Darwin accepted race inferiority, irrespective of whether the races sprang from a single original pair or were created separately" (1971, 77).

However, the debate was spurious. Human "races" and the differences between them had been so magnified by both popular and scientific characterizations that the argument over the taxonomic levels was redundant and irrelevant. *Race in the American collective consciousness had already assumed the same dimensions of differentiation as "species," even without a change in the terminology.*[7] It really did not matter at what taxonomic level scientists saw fit to allocate the differences.

In retrospect, the evidence for this is overwhelming. It is revealed in the scholarly writings of learned men and women, in the images expressed in popular media and literature, and in social practices and public policies. Scientists expressed it in their continuing concern, down through the first half of the twentieth century, to ascertain the "Negro's place in nature." Their publications and speeches had a powerful influence on other scholars, popular writers, educators, politicians, and others.

George Fredrickson has observed that polygenism, although overtly decried by Christians in the South, "did speak to certain Southern needs. . . . [It] raised prejudice to the level of science; thereby giving it respectability" (1971, 89). Not only was the South affected, "a substantial segment of Northern opinion was prepared to welcome the biological theory that the Negro belonged to a separate and inferior species" (90). Thus was the groundwork laid for the racial exclusion and segregation that appeared after the Civil War and continues into the twenty-first century.

After the Civil War and emancipation, numerous writers continued to propose theories on whether Negroes could survive as free people. But now the theories were couched in Darwinian terms. In the competition for existence, only the fittest would survive; the Negro was deemed among the unfit. A derivative postulate, widely believed, was that "the Negro" had not evolved to the same degree as whites.[8] Thus stunted in development, their natural inferiority did not equip them for success in the "struggle for existence." An inherent inclination toward crime, debauchery, and sloth would cause them to degenerate even further. Extinction was obviously to be their lot, just as other species had disappeared due to "lack of fitness." Darwinian evolution was thus made compatible with the ideological components of race, with a vocabulary that "reflected the country that bred it and, in reflecting it, wore the prejudices of the land that gave it birth" (Haller 1971, 94).

Caricatures of "the Negro" abounded in popular literature, and no characterization seemed too extreme. Clergymen, scholars, educators, politicians, and publicists justified their calls for total segregation of blacks from whites out of fear that the inherent degradation and barbarism of blacks might contaminate white society. Following the brief and anomalous Reconstruction era, state and local legislatures responded with segregation laws and statutes that aimed to isolate this inferior species from all unnecessary access to white institutions. Thomas Gossett tellingly summed up the sense of race differences in the decades that spanned the turn of the twentieth century: "American thought of the period 1880–1920 generally lacks any perception of the Negro as a human being with potentialities for improvement" (1965, 286).

THE UNNATURAL MIXTURE

Perhaps the clearest and most obvious example of the degree to which subhuman species status had been conferred on blacks was the now widespread belief that interracial sex or marriage was not only wrong socially, but sinful and unnatural. One of the strongest advocates of this position was Josiah Nott. One would have thought that a physician from Mobile, Alabama, where intermarriage was illegal but where there was a long history of creating "mulattoes" both on and off plantations, would have been highly knowledgeable about such matters. But Nott gave expression to beliefs that seemed, especially in that context, awkwardly unreal. He joined a number of polygenists in arguing that the mulatto was a degenerate and abnormal hybrid. This hybrid might be slightly superior intellectually to the full-blooded Negro but still remained much inferior to the true white. Physically and morally, hybrids lacked the vigor of the pure types and, if left to themselves, would soon become extinct. The fame and fortune that attended Nott's lectures were indicative of public concurrence on this matter.

Louis Agassiz was even more convinced of the degeneracy of the hybrids. His assertions that they either were sterile or suffered from diminished fecundity as a result of their unnatural ancestry should have evoked some shocked reaction, but there is little evidence that they did. For the wider public, as well as for declared polygenists and most monogenists, the mulatto was a tragic product of the unrestrained lust of black men, or of white morals gone awry. Even more forbidding was the possibility that some black "blood" might contaminate the white race and cause the deterioration of all that was noble, pure, and superior.

Antipathy toward interracial unions was not new. We have seen evidence that some colonists expressed this sentiment quite early. By the mid-eighteenth century, legislation designed to prohibit interracial unions had been passed in all of the southern colonies and several northern ones, at various times covering both fornication and marriage (Jordan 1968, chap. 4). Such prohibitions did not entirely prevent interracial liaisons, but they did inhibit or restrict legal marriages.

Public aversion to interracial unions and the imposition of such sanctions as social ostracism for white women who married black men grew during the eighteenth century. After blacks had been reduced to slavery, virtually no marriages took place between white men and black women, although the slave–master relationship spawned large numbers of "colored" slave children. In the nineteenth century, sexual congress between black and white underwent even greater castigation and vilification; its sinfulness and unnaturalness became part of public consciousness and values on matters of race.

The children of such unions were sometimes called "spurious issue," but antagonism toward them seems to have been minimal or absent during the colonial period. It was not until the nineteenth century that public hostility to interracial sex and the resulting offspring became virulent, emotional, and malevolent, as the statistical and other documentation of Negro inferiority proliferated. One has only to read some of the hundreds of publications on the subject from midcentury on to realize the perversity of the charges against miscegenation and of the many newly invented beliefs about the abnormality of the offspring.

That an accentuated degree of attention was paid in the nineteenth century to those persons regarded as mulattoes was signaled by the fact that they began to appear in the census in 1850. They were also differentiated in the studies done by the United States Sanitary Commission and the Provost Marshal General's Office during and after the Civil War.[9] However, the general currents of the times argued against the establishment of a "mixed-race" classification, as occurred in South Africa. Historically, as we have seen, such a category of people had had no separate social role to play in the North American colonial situation, as they had, for example, in the West Indies and Latin America (see chapter 6). Although in the late nineteenth and early twentieth centuries laws in some southern states attempted to ascertain varying degrees of mixture, from one-half to one thirty-second black "blood," such refinements were socially useless to most whites. They were overshadowed by the more fundamental dichotomy revealed in the debate over the race versus species question. The utilization of "hypo-descent" (by which a child was given the identity of its low status parent) not only militated against the creation of a special "mixed" category but had the added feature of better preserving the value of "pure" white "blood," which became an obsession in Anglo-Saxon America.

SCIENTIFIC RACE IDEOLOGY IN THE JUDICIAL SYSTEM

Long before the codification in law of what came to be accepted as a policy of official segregation of freedmen (the Black Codes of 1865–1866 and the Jim Crow laws of the 1890s), an important judicial decision had become a symbol of the influence of science on the wider public consciousness. The well-known Dred Scott decision of 1857 was ostensibly about a fugitive slave who, having twice been taken to free territory, sued in the courts for his freedom. Scott received conflicting decisions in the state and lower federal courts. Because a number of constitutional issues were perceived to be involved, and the issue of federal versus state control of slavery was crucial among these, Scott's lawyers, backed by abolitionists, took the matter all the way to the Supreme Court.

The case was argued twice before the Court in 1856 before a final decision was rendered. It was written and presented in March 1857, by Chief Justice Roger B. Taney, a Jacksonian democrat and a man known to have proslavery sentiments. Taney was joined by six other justices, each of whom wrote opinions clarifying his points of concurrence. Taney posed the major issue in its broadest context, going beyond the more limited problem of fugitive slaves. He addressed the whole matter of the constitutional right to the maintenance and perpetuation of slavery itself. Expanding this scope, he examined the more profound issue of the social and legal status of all Negroes. His decision first addressed the question of whether or not blacks could be citizens:

> The question is simply this: Can a negro, whose ancestors were imported into this country, and sold as slaves, become a member of the political community formed and brought into existence by the Constitution of the United States, and as such become entitled to all the rights, and privileges, and immunities, guaranteed by that instrument to the citizen? One of which rights is the privilege of suing in a court of the United States. (Bell 1980, 1)

Taney went on to point out that the case applied to "that class of persons only whose ancestors were negroes of the African race, and imported into this country, and sold and held as slaves . . . and the descendants of such slaves." He answered the question of citizenship by asserting that "people of the United States" and "citizens" are synonymous terms that apply only to those (whites) who were citizens of the several states when the Constitution was adopted. Negroes, he claimed, were seen only as property (they "were never thought of or spoken of except as property" [Bell 1980, 9]) and were not intended by the framers of the Constitution to be included in the category of citizen. "On the contrary, they were at that time considered as a subordinate and inferior class of beings" (3), and it did not matter whether or not they later obtained freedom.

Stretching and distorting history, Taney continued by arguing that Negroes "had for more than a century before been regarded as beings of an inferior order, and altogether unfit to associate with the white race, either in social or political relations; and so far inferior, that they had no rights which the white man was bound to respect. . . . This opinion was at that time fixed and universal in the civilized portion of the white race" (Bell 1980, 6).

This stigma, he went on to say, "was fixed upon the whole race." Taney's use of such language as "scale of created beings" here indicated that he was familiar with the arguments on human differences of the biological sciences, and he assumed his audience was as well. To support his position, Taney cited two laws of the early eighteenth century (from Maryland and Massachusetts) that showed, in his words, "that a perpetual and impassable barrier was intended to be erected between the white race and the one which they had reduced to slavery, and governed as subjects with absolute and despotic power, and which they then looked upon as so far below them in the scale of created beings, that intermarriages between white persons and negroes or mulattoes were regarded as unnatural and immoral, and punished as crimes, not only in the parties but in the person who joined them in marriage" (quoted in Bell 1980, 7).

Taney cited other laws in the nonslave states that suggested to him that the Negro was not a citizen or considered of the same order of human beings even when ostensibly free. He also noted that there are two clauses in the Constitution that "point directly and specifically to the negro race as a separate class of persons" who were "not regarded as a portion of the people or citizens of the Government then formed" (Bell 1980, 10). The framers of the Constitution had in fact used the word *persons* (after much debate) to avoid inserting the word *slave* and thereby institutionalizing slavery itself in the Constitution.

The Dred Scott decision strengthened the idea that the property rights of white men superseded in importance the human rights of nonwhite individuals. But Justice Taney, in addition to misrepresenting the history of Africans in the early colonies, in effect declared a great deal more than that. He concluded that Negroes, either free or slave, were not citizens and could not be made citizens by either the state or the federal governments. And he formulated in legal terms what the folk beliefs and scientific pronouncements had already expressed very clearly: The Negro was not fully human, but a separate and distinct class of being, isolated from whites by an "impassable barrier."

Although the issue in the Dred Scott case was without question a matter pertaining only to blacks who were slaves, Taney had made a sweeping declaration about the status of all blacks. The most important phrase in the text of the decision is: "[The Negro] had no rights which the white man was bound to respect." In this statement, Taney went beyond affirming that slaves were mere property; he asserted a social value about a whole category of people that was an unambiguous statement about their status in the larger racial scheme of things. This was a far more damning and meaningful conclusion than the actual decision about Dred Scott's slave status or the legal standing of the Missouri Compromise, which was upset by this decision. This statement was not even pertinent to the legal decision; indeed, it was irrelevant for the testing of the legitimacy of the fugitive slave laws. It was a far more powerful reflection, and ultimate denouement, of prevailing social beliefs and practices. Going beyond slavery or the concept of property rights, it captured the essence of the American perspective on race differences between blacks and whites. Thus it was perfectly consonant with, indeed a product of, the racial cosmology that had been evolving during the past century, illuminating the exaggerated sense of difference that the term *race* then conveyed.

America's racial ideology was institutionalized in the law from Dred Scott onward. Congress passed the Thirteenth, Fourteenth, and Fifteenth Amendments, which emancipated the slaves and gave them the rights of citizenship. It also passed the Civil Rights Act of 1875, which theoretically accorded them "full and equal enjoyment of . . . public accommodations." With the end of Reconstruction, and northern forces abandoning the South, southern politicians regained power and raised powerful opposition to including blacks as free and equal citizens. In 1883 in a series of five civil rights cases consolidated into one, the Supreme Court held that Congress did not have the constitutional authority to outlaw racial discrimination by private individuals and organizations and overturned the Act of 1875. In 1896, in the famous case *Plessy vs. Ferguson*, the Supreme Court put a final stamp of approval on segregation laws and the disfranchisement of Negroes. The separateness decreed by popular beliefs was now enshrined in the law, and American whites made great strides to see and enforce segregation in local and state laws and virtually all social practices.

In midcentury the United States had become in world forums the citadel of democracy. It had evolved an ideology of the rise of the common man to standards of individual rights and liberties unmatched by any previous sociopolitical system. As Irving Bartlett (1967) has reminded us, Americans fervently embraced beliefs in moral laws and justice and religious-based ideas about human worth and made them part of the American dream. But as we have seen, they also had an unremitting drive for worldly success, and worldly success was most often accomplished by the exploitation of slaves and other poor labor. By diminishing the Negro to nonhuman status in their cognitive perceptions of the world, Americans had declared that democracy, freedom, opportunity, and justice were not to be made available to blacks. They had placed the Negro beyond the moral and ethical parameters that ostensibly guided what was appropriate and acceptable behavior between human beings, especially in a democracy.

It is of telling interest that the Fugitive Slave Act of 1793 made no mention of race or racial categories, using only the term *person* (tenBroek 1969, 57). Yet the unmistakable concern of the act was to protect the property rights of those who owned slaves, permitting them to reclaim fugitives without impediments, legal or otherwise. More than fifty years later, in the Dred Scott case, Justice Taney made "race" the specific arbiter of human, legal, and property status, overshadowing the status of slave. In so doing, he introduced and institutionalized the components of the idea of race in the law, giving legal stature to both the scientific presumptions and the folk ideology.

To the comfort of many, there was strong reaction against the Dred Scott decision and not only on the part of abolitionists. Justice Benjamin Curtis in his dissent denied that the Constitution was made exclusively by and for the white race. He pointed out that free blacks were citizens and voters in at least five states at the time of its adoption. He quoted a case from North Carolina in which the state supreme court "rejected the proposition that free Negroes were less than citizens and laid emphasis on the commonly held doctrine that there was no intermediate class between citizens and slaves" (Miller 1966, 78). He also disagreed with the majority view that persons of African descent could not become citizens of the United States. Justice John McLean, the other dissenter, opined that the Constitution did not protect slavery, merely tolerated it. He proclaimed that slaves were not simply chattel, but men made in God's image. Not everyone subscribed to the view that "the Negro" was a separate and inferior species.

Several northern legislatures passed resolutions denying the legitimacy of the Scott decision. The antislavery press was vehement in its anger and rejected the implications of the decision. It was clear that Justice Taney's position had brought the new nation closer to civil war. But it should also be clear that most Americans were little disturbed by the Taney declarations on race. The differences connoted by the term were deeply and solidly established in the American psyche. And the majority of Americans, including those who were opposed to slavery, were attuned to the real implications of these differences.

One inescapable fact of the nineteenth century was that many whites profited in a great many ways, from economic opportunities to psychic satisfaction, from the seemingly indelible barrier that had been erected between blacks and whites. This was especially true after the Civil War and Reconstruction, when blacks were systematically eliminated from skilled and unskilled employment to make room for white labor, particularly the new immigrants from Europe. Moreover, with the recession of the 1880s and a severe depression in the 1890s, whites were economically embattled, bitter, and enraged; they were more than willing to flay a scapegoat. The Negro became that scapegoat and for the next four decades endured an era of intimidation, torture, lynching, gross discrimination, and unheralded psychological brutality.

WHITE SUPREMACY

To a great degree, the debates between the monogenists and polygenists were an anachronistic diversion, a subtle obfuscation of the fact that a qualitatively new form of social differentiation had taken place in the human experience that superseded class and even nationality differences in its impact and significance. The logical outcome of the racial idiom in which human diversity was now being expressed was the distillation of a corollary ideology, white supremacy. Fed by a rampant Anglo-Saxonism that was to become transformed in Europe as Nordicism or Aryanism and by the fear of miscegenation, white Americans were exhorted to preserve the purity and sanctity of their race.

The sociopolitical conditions of the mid-nineteenth century lent credence to the belief in the innate superiority of Europeans. In the 1850s the illegal slave trade flourished in the United States as never before, with such vigor that some of the proponents of slavery suggested a return to legalization of the trade. This decade also saw the first significant penetration of Africa, by the explorers Barth, Speke, Burton, and Livingstone, which presaged the eventual conquest of the last of the overseas continents to succumb to European domination. In Asia, the Opium Wars of 1839–1841 had led to the weakening of the dynastic leadership of China, and the British now literally handled the trade and foreign affairs of that sleeping giant. Also in the 1850s, the long-drawn-out process of the conquest of India and Burma was completed. By 1859 all of the colonies and provinces of Australia had been founded and settled. From then on, Australia was spoken of as a white man's land. In the ten years between 1851 and 1861, the white population of that continent doubled.[10] In 1854 Louis-Léon-César Faidherbe began the fateful French penetration up the Senegal River in West Africa. In 1851 the British invaded Lagos Island in what is today Nigeria and effectively exercised power in that port city behind a titular ruler. In 1859 the construction of the Suez Canal was begun, and by the time Ismail came to power in Egypt in 1863, the British and French presence and influence in eastern Africa and the Middle East were already ineradicable.

In the 1850s, then, it was painfully apparent that Europeans (or at least some of them) were rapidly becoming dominant forces nearly all over the world, and for most whites there was no other explanation for this expansion but their "obvious" racial superiority. Thus when Robert Knox, a well-known professor of anatomy and ethnologist, proclaimed in 1854 that "race is everything: literature, science, art—in a word, civilization depends on it" (Gossett 1965, 95), he was expressing this new dimension of social differentiation as well as a new mode of interpreting history and new forms of power relationships that he and his contemporaries perceived as natural and universal. The "truth" of the ordering system denoted by race had been proved by science and by the political hegemony of a small group of nations from northwest Europe. For Knox and many others, the Anglo-Saxon race dominated all, beginning with the Celts and other inferior races of Europe.

During the latter part of the nineteenth century, an elaborate global edifice of social philosophy and theory was developed around the theme of white racial superiority. Theories of racial history were transformed into theories of world history. Facts that did not fit the racial worldview of white superiority and black degradation were ignored, deleted, distorted, or obfuscated. Typical was the widely read book by Dr. John Van Evrie, *White Supremacy and Negro Subordination* ([1861] 1969). Explaining the "magnificent structures" of the ancient cultures of Mexico-Guatemala-Yucatán and Peru, he reasoned that such high cultures were due to Caucasian adventurers or shipwrecked mariners who settled in these areas, became "undisputed masters, built cities, organized governments, framed laws and laid the foundations of a civilized society" ([1861] 1969, 46–47). Likewise, in Asia, Van Evrie continued, all of the great leaders were white—Attila the Hun, Genghis Khan, Tamerlane—all "pure" Caucasians. Confucius was also white, as were all the more progressive portions of Chinese society. Explications for advanced social systems in Africa, discovered or rediscovered in the late nineteenth century, were predicated on ascertaining the degree of Caucasian mixture in the aristocratic or ruling elements. Thus the Hamites, once the burnt-face sons of Ham and lineage founder of all blacks, were reinterpreted to be archaic Caucasoids who had conquered Negro tribes and provided them with whatever aspects of order, law, and civilization were discernible among them (Sanders 1969). According to Van Evrie, "progress and indefinite perfectibility are the specific attributes of the Caucasian" ([1861] 1969, 79).

IMMIGRANTS AND THE EXTENSION OF THE RACE HIERARCHY

Although the phenomena of slavery and the black–white social polarization were basic ingredients out of which the ideology of race was most visibly generated, it is clear that other peoples could also be racialized and fitted into the scheme. Wherever there were visible physical and/or cultural differences among new immigrants to the United States, the potential for the stigma of racial inferiority could be, and usually was, applied. For white Americans, power and status relationships had to be established.

Americans became even more conscious of having multiple racial populations with the immigration of the Chinese, which began in the 1850s following the discovery of gold in California in 1848. During the 1860s, the Chinese provided the bulk of the labor for the building of the Central Pacific Railroad. When this was completed in 1869, thousands of Chinese were out of work and thrown into an already depressed labor force, mostly in California (Daniels [1962] 1977). But antagonism toward the Chinese began as early as 1852, and by 1870 organized protests against the "mongolian hordes" were taking place in San Francisco. The racialization of the Chinese had begun.

Protests, demonstrations, and even massacres targeted against the Chinese increased in many regions after the Civil War. Thomas Gossett points out that the California Supreme Court barred Chinese people from testifying in court cases involving whites, for a reason that was incontrovertibly racial. The court claimed that since Indians were not allowed to testify against whites, and anthropologists had determined that the Chinese were of the same race as the Indians, the law should also apply to them (1965, 290). Arguments about the inferiority of the Chinese and fear of hordes of Asians taking over the western states were rampant. By 1882 Congress had passed the first of several Chinese exclusion laws designed to prevent further immigration. Throughout this time, violence against the Chinese left untold numbers murdered, and "incidental brutality and casual assault" were their "daily lot" (Daniels [1962] 1977, 17).

Japanese immigrants began to arrive gradually in the United States during the last quarter of the century. From 1890 to 1910, their numbers increased fairly rapidly. Although initially the Japanese were perceived by Americans as more acceptable than other Asians, opposition to them was considerable and became so strong that in 1909 an executive order, the famous "Gentlemen's Agreement," was promulgated to restrict immigration. By 1924 Japanese immigration was effectively terminated. But anti-Japanese sentiment increased between the two world wars, reaching a crisis in the 1940s (see Daniels 1975). The well-known removal of Japanese Americans to relocation camps during World War II was an unabashed example of the racial worldview at work.

In the cases of both the Chinese and the Japanese, objections to their presence in the United States were overwhelmingly racial. Though many employers accepted them as laborers during periods of heightened demand, organized labor unions, especially in the West, vigorously opposed their presence. Through their leaders, unions expressed the dominant themes of hostility toward, and fear of, "the yellow peril." From their point of view, the Asians as a racially distinct population were not assimilable. They were expected to live separate and indeed segregated lives, with their own habits, customs, and institutions. Their inherent inferiority prevented their accommodation to the American (white) way of life. Most important, their presence was a threat to the "racial purity" of white Americans. This was translated as a threat to democratic institutions, because only Anglo-Saxons (Nordics, Teutonics, Aryans) had the innate capability for creating and preserving democracy. The Asians, with their high birthrate, strange customs and rituals, and incorrigible habits, could only contribute to the demise of white civilization.

In 1913 and again in 1920, Congress passed two Alien Land Laws designed to exclude the "yellow peril" from white territories. Such groups as the California Oriental Exclusion League, the American Legion, and numerous other anti-Asian organizations lobbied to exclude all Asians from citizenship (see Daniels [1962] 1977 and Takaki 1989).

The irrational hatred and fear of these peoples also helped to establish a precedent for the treatment of others not so visibly distinct but nevertheless unwanted. In the late nineteenth century, Italians, Jews, Greeks, Slavs, and other peoples from eastern and southern Europe began to arrive in increasingly larger numbers, eventually outnumbering even the immigrants from northern Europe. Concern over these foreign elements led to the organization, by a group of Harvard alumni, of the Immigration Restriction League in 1894. The platform of this and other such organizations aimed to restructure immigration policy solely on racial grounds. By 1924 they were eminently successful in lobbying for immigration restrictions. Their success was due in large part to the arguments that they could adduce from a large repertory of scientific literature on race differences.

It would have been tantamount to a form of perversion had any reputable scientist in America at the turn of the century promoted the idea that the races of humans were equal in their endowments. The social and intellectual climate of the times mandated conformity to a racial worldview resolutely fixed in American culture and consciousness. It was a cosmological perspective that was compatible with European and American industrial and commercial dominance and with the accelerating exploitation of non-European lands and peoples.[11] With the takeover of Hawaii in 1893 and the Spanish–American War of 1898, a conflict permeated with racial elements, America entered into the colonial world and took upon itself some of the "white man's burden" in the form of the "little brown peoples" of the Philippines, Samoa, and Guam and the heterogeneous peoples of Cuba and Puerto Rico. After the Berlin Treaty of 1885, nearly the entire continent of Africa came under at least nominal European control, and the mantle of providing contrasting images of savagery and civilization fell almost exclusively to its indigenous population. Thus the sixteenth- and seventeenth-century Irish "savages" yielded in the nineteenth century to an even more invidious portrayal of the "wild men" of Africa (Curtin 1964).

Scientists, scholarly and popular writers, and other educated individuals directly reflected general folk perceptions and fears of Negroes, Chinese, Native Americans, and the southern European "types" who flooded the United States during the latter half of the nineteenth and early twentieth centuries. Science writers synthesized and articulated the hatreds, fears, and frustrations emanating out of explosive and unprecedented experiences such as race riots, labor conflicts, and the like. Race was the social doctrine that permeated them all and the dominant theme of the nineteenth century.

In bringing to bear the "objectivity," knowledge, methodologies, and authority of science, these "experts" advanced the racial worldview by (1) certifying and validating the incredulous beliefs of the public about racial differences and (2) providing material evidence and arguments on which public policies, such as the immigration laws, segregation laws, and discriminatory employment practices, came to be based. Mark Haller observed: "Between 1870 and 1900 educated Americans took giant strides toward a fairly wide acceptance of varying forms and degrees of racism" (1963, 50). These educated Americans were contemporaries, or social offspring, of Herbert Spencer and the Social Darwinists. They were students of Louis Agassiz such as Joseph Le Conte and Nathaniel Shaler, who thought that race prejudice was innate and who defended the lynch laws of the South (Haller 1971, 184–185). They were often men of wealth who also controlled the public media, such as Edward

Drinker Cope, editor of *The American Naturalist.* And they frequently published in the leading journals and popular magazines of the times, such as *De Bow's Review, North American Review, Atlantic Monthly, Science, Popular Science, Nineteenth Century, Arena, Nation, McClure's Magazine, Scientific Monthly,* and *Sewanee Review.*

The wedding of scientific and folk beliefs was now complete. From the mid-nineteenth century on, science provided the bases for the ideology of "race." Numerous scholars of the late nineteenth and early twentieth centuries occupied themselves not only in tediously researching the nature of human differences, but also in interpreting how these differences reflected the inequality of the races.

But the activities and findings of scientists were also to create the impetus for the contemporary rebellion against the idea of race. I turn to this development after examining the diffusion of race ideas in Europe and some of the ways by which European and American scientists influenced one another in the documentation of race differences.

NOTES

1. Stocking (1968, 45) holds that the speculations of Lord Kames may be seen as the beginning of the debate between polygenists and monogenists. Kames, however, did not have the "scientific" data that White had developed to support his theories.

2. See Stephen Jay Gould's review of Morton's works and documentation of his errors, omissions, distortions, and questionable techniques ([1981] 1996).

3. See Baron Denon, *Travels in Upper and Lower Egypt* (New York: Heard and Foreman, 1803); and Count Constantin Volney, *Travels Through Egypt and Syria* (New York: J. Tiebout, 1798). Volney is quoted in Diop 1981, along with others. See also Keita 1993a and Sanders 1969.

4. Quoted in Stanton 1960, 51. The debate over the "racial" identification of ancient Egyptians was renewed in the twentieth century and continues to have periodic efflorescence, such as in the two-volume *Black Athena* (1987, 1991) by Martin Bernal.

5. For those who find it of interest to speculate on cycles in history, it might be useful to compare Morton's role with that of a modern-day scientist, Arthur Jensen. Both men published scholarly works promoting the idea of black inferiority. In both cases, their major publications came in the wake of dramatic events that tended to advance the cause of racial equality: Morton in the wake of the abolitionist movement, and Jensen following the civil rights movement of the 1950s and 1960s. Both were impeccable scholars, having established their reputations in fields other than racial biology. Both were esteemed for their probity by their colleagues; neither had previously been known for harboring racist beliefs. Yet both achieved widespread fame for their support of popular race ideology. In like manner, *The Bell Curve* (1994) was written by outstanding scholars Charles Murray and Richard Herrnstein at a time when white dissatisfaction with affirmative action and other policies aimed at social justice for minorities was on the rise and when blacks had made great strides toward the middle class. Such historical patterns should provide stimulating material for new research.

6. *Encyclopaedia Britannica* 1: 290 (1971). See also Lurie 1954.

7. Long after I had come to this conclusion, I discovered a footnote in Greene 1959 that confirms this position. Writing about the midcentury debates, he states, "Although the racial interpretation of history was by no means confined to the polygenist camp, it is perhaps significant that the qualities of purity, permanence, and divine contrivance which later came to be associated with the idea of a 'pure race' were qualities which the eighteenth century attributed to species rather than to varieties" (371).

8. For discussion of late-nineteenth-century scientific speculations on the evolutionary position of the Negro, see Haller 1971; Frederickson 1971; and Gould 1981.

9. See Haller 1971, especially chaps. 1 and 2, for a description of the role of these agencies in the study of racial differences.

10. In that same period, forty thousand Chinese arrived in Australia, having been recruited to work in the gold mines, and the first serious "race" riot occurred in 1861 between the Chinese and white populations.

11. For discussions and analyses of the relationship between racism and colonialism, see Bolt 1971; Curtin 1964; Davis 1966; Hammond and Jablow 1970; Robinson, Gallagher, and Denny 1968; Ross 1982; and Williams [1944] 1966.

CHAPTER 11

Science and the Expansion of Race Ideology Beyond the United States

The cultural construction of the ideology of race culminated in its institutionalization as a worldview in the nineteenth century. At its developmental peak in the latter half of the century, it achieved systemic autonomy and uniqueness as a mechanism for the hierarchical structuring of society and as a rationalization for imposed inequalities. The degree to which economic competition could be thwarted and access to privilege and power limited to members of a "superior race" were lessons available to all. The components of race ideology had potential applications that transcended group relations in the North American setting. Allegations of racial superiority and inferiority could satisfy the private interests of certain powerful groups in Europe. And European scholars were prepared to substantiate theories of intra-European races and their inequality with measurement techniques and arguments similar to those used in the United States.

This chapter briefly locates European race thinking in the evolving spectrum of racial attitudes. It focuses on how European science complemented the developing ideology and had further synergistic influences on American thought. Evidence of the appearance of race as a generic, autonomous, and essentialist idea with universal application is shown in the proliferation of arbitrary racial classifications in Europe during the latter part of the nineteenth century. Ideas from Europe diffused to and from the United States, further nourishing racial thought, and helped to condition American reactions to the massive immigrations of "inferior" southern and eastern European "races" beginning in the last decades of the century.

The nineteenth century also saw the transmission of the ideology of race to Europe's colonial outposts and other areas of the world. Recent explorations of race ideology have turned attention to the global manifestation of "race" and "racism." Some scholars have maintained the position, as we saw in chapter 1, that race and racism are universal, that other people in other societies have invented or recognized racial populations. Looking at this issue, recent scholarship has begun to unveil new facts about the history of the idea of race in other areas of the world.[1] Some of the findings from this research are examined in the last section of this chapter.

THE CONTINUING POWER OF POLYGENIST THINKING

Nancy Stepan observes that when the nineteenth century began, scientists in Great Britain were still "firmly monogenist in outlook" (1982, 2). The liberal and monogenist views of such outstanding thinkers as Dr. James Cowles Prichard and Sir William Lawrence still swayed most scientific thought on human variations. Like most monogenists, Prichard accepted the notion of European superiority, but as Stepan notes, this was not based "on the idea of permanent, unchanging physical types, and his ethnocentrism was tempered by his moral disgust for slavery, his belief in the essential humanity of the African, and his Christian faith in the psychic unity of all the peoples of the world" (1982, 44). After 1859 the identification of natural selection as the fundamental mechanism of biological change signaled the eventual triumph of evolutionary theory in the biological sciences and the end of the polygeny–monogeny debate. The introduction of a dynamic element to the understanding of biological processes should have advanced the understanding of human biological variation and directed attention away from the rigid conceptions of race that had developed. However, Stepan claims that evolutionary thought actually strengthened racial ideas and "provided them with a new scientific vocabulary of struggle and survival" (1982, 49).

The earliest ideas about human evolution were first put forth by scholars who focused on human cultures. The discovery of similarities in technologies, rituals, folklore, origin myths, kinship patterns, and many other features of culture among peoples widely separated from one another geographically stimulated a number of hypotheses about their origins. As early as the eighteenth century some scholars had begun to speculate on, and build theoretical models of, a developmental history that would encompass all of the world's societies.

Theories about the development of various institutions such as marriage, kinship, law, and religion were frequently published, and scholars began to debate the merits of various schemes of human development. Many saw a kind of order and sequence to the emergence of different kinds of human societies, and the growing body of archeological evidence suggested similar patterns of development in different parts of the world. What crystallized out of this intellectual endeavor were schemes of universal history that suggested a developmental sequence from a small-scale hunting and gathering stage, to a stage of food production, to a gradual accumulation of wealth and technological knowledge, culminating in the industrial civilizations. Over time there was some agreement among these theories on the three major stages of human social development—"savagery," "barbarism," and "civilization"—and this became the pattern of conjectured history most familiar to learned men and women during the late nineteenth and early twentieth centuries. Scholars persuaded by Enlightenment values were sufficiently optimistic about human progress to believe that even lowly primitive man, with education and training, could some day rise out of his barbarous state and achieve the stage of civilization. The material evidence that human groups in Europe had done so, from similar stages of savagery, had already begun to accumulate.[2]

Because of the many similarities among widely separated populations, some scholars arrived at the conclusion that the human mind was the same everywhere. The notion of the "psychic unity" of all humankind was compatible with monogeny and the Enlightenment belief in progress. It suggested that savages were not essentially different from civilized men in the workings of their minds, and that they had the potential for acquiring knowledge and achieving civilization.

But this changed with the influence of polygenist thought and the overwhelming force of the racial worldview. In the latter part of the nineteenth century, instead of exploring the continuously mounting evidence of the psychic unity of humankind, intellectuals turned their interests to exploring the mind of "primitive man." The dissemination and acceptance of racial ideology had now determined that this "mind" was vastly different from that of rational civilized man. The rising evolutionary theories, rudimentary though they were, soon froze primitive man into stages of savagery and barbarism from which his mind, now seen as stunted or stagnant in its development could not save him.

EUROPEAN CONTRIBUTIONS TO THE IDEOLOGY OF RACE

Race emerged in European consciousness as a worldview that affirmed the division of Europeans into "racial" groups and the inherent superiority of certain of these "races" over others. But the ideology was refashioned for quite different social circumstances, with the result that a peculiarly intra-European version of race was created out of what traditionally had been class and ethnic differences. That is, Europeans began to interpret their internal group differences in terms of permanent, innate endowments, ignoring and dismissing their historically deep awareness of such cultural distinctions as manifestations of learned (acquired) behavior.[3] Simultaneously, the new racial ideology provided rationalization and justification for further conquests abroad, satisfying the elevated imperial ambitions of politicians, military adventurers, and commercial interests.

Not surprisingly, many Europeans turned their racial imagery toward, and began to racialize, those minority ethnic groups within their own borders with whom there had been conflict or competition. Defining such groups as separate races became the new raison d'être for imposing harsh restrictions and repressive practices. This was particularly hard on largely endogamous groups such as the Jews, who in many areas suffered the ignominy of being defined as racial inferiors. The power politics within European nations took on a whole new spectrum of racial incompatibilities. By taking ethnic or class stereotypes and making them biological givens, Europeans transformed the complexion of political realities, structures, and processes and exacerbated existing conflicts, regardless of their origin.

It is important to emphasize that *race* was a particularly useful term when a rationale based on descent, unequal rank, and inheritance of social status was sought. Aristocratic, upper-class elements in human societies tend to have a penchant for thinking of themselves as innately superior, if not divinely endowed. Defenders of the rights of the aristocracy during the revolutionary eighteenth century in France found in the ideological components of race a perfect, and expedient, paradigm for their entrenched class structures, interests, and beliefs. The racial theories of the French nobleman Henri de Boulainvilliers, for example, were essentially rooted in the class conflicts of his times, but they carried the invidious notion that each class had distinct and unalterable hereditary qualities derived from separate origins.

Nurtured by the growing glorification of Germanic origins among English writers and historians, some French writers began to extol the virtues of the Franks, the Germanic tribe that had defeated the Gauls. They introduced into the consciousness of the French people the notion that they comprised three separate racial strains: Nordics, Alpines, and Mediterraneans. Each had different physical characteristics and correlative differences in temperament, mental acumen, and natural abilities, such as leadership, economic resourcefulness, progress, inventiveness, and moral and aesthetic sensitivity. The tall, blond

Nordics, descendants of ancient Germanic tribes, were the originators of all civilization and the only individuals capable of effective and efficient leadership in a rapidly changing world.[4] Indeed, they were seen as recipients of a "Divine Right" to rule over the Alpines and Mediterraneans who constituted the lower classes. But the Divine Right was no longer couched in theological terms; it became identified in terms of the inherent biological superiority of those groups already in power. The weaker classes were naturally inferior to the stronger and owed obedience to them.

This French upper-class conception of internal racial divisions was vividly expressed in Comte Joseph-Arthur de Gobineau's famous *Essay on the Inequality of the Human Races* (four volumes published between 1853 and 1855). Gobineau worked in Germany, in Hanover and Frankfurt, as a diplomat, and it was from his experiences with certain German intellectuals that he developed his racial views. He divided all of the world's people into three major racial groups—the white, the yellow, and the black—with the white races as the superior races. In fact, he claimed that the key to all history and civilization was race, and it dominated all other explanations in history. All civilizations were the product of the white race, and no civilization could exist without its cooperation (Shirer [1959] 1988, 103).

Gobineau was especially concerned with the peoples of Europe and the decline in its "high civilizations." He was a major advocate of the natural superiority of the aristocratic or noble classes, who he thought derived from an Aryan origin and were the purest of the white races. Working from the premise that such classes were responsible for all great works of civilization, he proposed what he thought was a natural law of the decline of great nations: Civilizations fall when the aristocratic classes intermarry with the lower classes and dilute their superior blood (Chase 1980, 91).

Gobineau's publications were among the best known of a number of writings on racial populations in Europe at a time when the anthropological sciences were becoming consolidated in learned societies and academies. The composer Richard Wagner, strongly anti-Semitic and racist in his personal beliefs, introduced Gobineau to the German public, among whom "he was revered as a prophet and as the great forerunner of the truths of racialism" (Snyder 1962, 49). His ideas rapidly diffused among the German people, who in turn established many Gobineau societies to proselytize such views.

According to Hannah Arendt, German race thinking differed from that of the French in that its purpose was to unify, rather than to divide, the nation ([1951] 1968, 45). It appealed to nationalism rather than to class interests. Its advocates sought to awaken the peoples of disparate German states to a "consciousness of common origin" (45). After the Franco-Prussian War (1870–1871), such consciousness was fully developed in the form of a new dogma of Aryanism that Gobineau's ideas had played a major role in establishing.

It is highly significant that Gobineau was very much aware that the racial attitudes of his times were unique to the western European nations. His friend Alexis de Tocqueville, who traveled widely, disagreed with his racial views and criticized their moral and political effects. In a letter to Gobineau, written from Tehran, Persia (now Iran), in 1856, Tocqueville wrote: "I confess that after having read your book I remain, as before, opposed in the extreme to your doctrines. I believe that they are probably quite false; I know that they are certainly very pernicious" (1959, 227). He accused Gobineau of fatalism, arguing, "What purpose does it serve to persuade lesser peoples living in abject conditions of barbarism or slavery that, such being their racial nature, they can do nothing to better themselves, to change their habits, or to ameliorate their status?" Later he pointed out, "In no way, either tribal or aristocratic, does the Persian nation have any racial prejudices. She is too mixed for that, and she carries her own indifference so far that the numerous Negroes here are considered on a basis of perfect equality" (1959, 276). But Gobineau clearly understood the political nature of his writings, and he seemingly reveled in the fame and fortune that they brought him.

After 1890, Houston Stewart Chamberlain, the British-born son-in-law of composer Richard Wagner, became the chief proselytizer of German racial superiority. Although Chamberlain published a number of books, his most influential work, *Foundations of the Nineteenth Century*, appeared in 1899. This was to become the bible of the National Socialist German Workers (Nazi) Party early in the next century. Like Gobineau, Chamberlain extolled the virtues of the superior races; he explained the entire history of the nineteenth century in terms of the racial accomplishments of Germanic peoples like the Teutons. According to him, nations rise and fall in relation to the amount of Teutonic blood in their population. Like many of his compatriots, Chamberlain had also developed a virulent anti-Semitism, claiming that Jews had a moral defect as part of their racial character. Hatred of the Jews increased out of opposition to what was thought to be their liberal political ideas and the growing belief that they were dominating German culture.

HERBERT SPENCER AND THE RISE OF SOCIAL DARWINISM

A more powerful influence on the world of scholarship in both Europe and America, including the new fields of sociology, anthropology, and psychology, was the work of Herbert Spencer, who began publishing in the 1850s. Spencer was unique among the learned men of England and Europe. He did not come from the wealthy elite strata, and although he undoubtedly had a brilliant mind, it was untrained and undisciplined.[5] He never went to college and was basically self-taught. Working as an editor for *The Economist* magazine, he began a series of writings in the 1850s that were eventually to make him famous. He was a prolific writer and covered such topics as the origin and development of human societies, including language and social systems, religion, politics, forms of marriage, and other institutions. Like many intellectuals of his times, he was an evolutionist, but he was distinct in that he tried to develop a synthetic theory that would connect both biological and cultural evolution.

According to Spencer, evolution and progress had come about because certain groups (races) had, in the struggle for existence, achieved higher levels of fitness and perfection. This was seen as compatible with the Darwinian theory of evolution by natural selection (but was in fact a distortion of Darwinism). Those who lacked fitness would be extinguished, just as the American Indian tribes had been and just as other "savage" tribes would suffer in the future. Spencer's broader vision linked biological evolutionary changes with the mental and moral development of human groups and the material achievements of the Western industrial societies. Such a synthesis elevated the racial worldview to a fundamental and virtually undeniable truth and helped to justify the imperialistic expansion of the European nations.

Although he came from a middle-class background, or perhaps because of his class position, Spencer became a proponent for many of the interests and beliefs associated with the upper classes. He ingratiated himself with people from this class, and they in turn showered him with honors and awards, especially when he visited the United States. More than anything, he preached and made part of popular wisdom the importance of heredity as the cause of a peoples' or an individual's status and performance in life.

Spencer was even more widely read in the United States than in Europe. His views harmonized perfectly with the prevailing imagery of the world that most white Americans shared. Although his socioeconomic class values were particular to the English social structure, they also influenced American thinking about the poor, especially in the next century. The economic disparities among white Americans would be reinterpreted to accord with the hereditarian doctrines of Spencer and his followers, beliefs that would be identified as Social Darwinism in the twentieth century. It was Spencer who first coined the phrases "struggle for existence" and "survival of the fittest," before Darwin. Spencer saw competition and struggle as the lifeblood of all animal and human systems; for this reason he opposed all activities that eliminated or restricted competition. He was an extreme proponent of laissez-faire capitalism, a defender of the rights of private property and of imperialist exploitation of indigenous peoples. He opposed public education, women's rights, child labor laws, taxation, the regulation of industries, and sanitation laws. He opposed all interventions to help the poor (cf. Herrnstein and Murray 1994).

Spencer collected data from a wide range of sources and recruited many people to assist him. But because of his lack of formal training, he could not assess evidence or data with a critical eye, which led him to accept all kinds of extreme, mistaken, or distorted ideas and beliefs, especially about "primitive" peoples, for which no confirmation or authentication existed. Like his contemporaries, he held firmly to a racial interpretation of all human institutions. Primitive people had primitive cultures because they had the least developed minds (their minds were like those of children). With their limited intelligence, he believed, they communicated through snarls, gestures, and facial contortions; their languages were so poorly developed that they could not understand one another in the dark (Leslie White, personal note, 1957).

Spencer's negative attitude toward preindustrial societies mirrored that of most of the writers of the times. One is startled by the degree of "otherness" projected onto these societies by nearly all who had something to say about humankind or human nature. Spencer characterized "the savage" as being close to nature. He had acute sensory perceptions, but "his mental processes rarely rose above the level of sensation" (quoted in Stocking 1968, 117). The primitive mind could not formulate abstract thoughts; rather, it functioned impulsively and without much forethought. The "savage's" nervous system was simpler than that of civilized man, and hence he was limited in his creativity and higher intellectual faculties. (It is unfortunate that such beliefs have been retained even into the twenty-first century and are widely held by many Europeans and their compatriots throughout the world.)

Race had become an extraordinarily comprehensive and compelling worldview in its explanatory powers and rationalization of social inequality. It is little wonder that it spread so rapidly among European nations and into their overseas territories. Its basic components left little or no room for doubt.

It was not a long step to take from theories about superior and inferior races and classes to the dogma that a particular superior race has the right to rule the world. Theories about the purity of the German race, its greatness and militarism, and its destiny in history flourished from the writings of these and other thinkers. In the early twentieth century they had a major impact on Adolf Hitler and the National Socialist Party. But they also deeply influenced American writers Madison Grant and William Z. Ripley, who extolled the virtues of

Nordics and actively opposed the immigration of southern Europeans. Both Gobineau and Chamberlain had identified the southern Europeans, the peoples of the Mediterranean lands, as inferior races. They claimed that Rome had declined and been destroyed because the Latin world had incorporated so many inferior races. In attacking and conquering the remnants of the Roman Empire, the Germanic groups had proved their superiority and their right to rule the world.

THE MEASUREMENT OF HUMAN DIFFERENCES: ANTHROPOMETRY

Like their American counterparts, many Frenchmen invoked the techniques and findings of science to reveal the specific qualities of each racial group, qualities that had already been incorporated as stereotypes into a popular worldview. Thus it was that some French scientists were among the first to develop techniques for measuring differences among any human groups to whom they had applied the classification of "race" and to use these measurements to justify social inequality.

To identify these internal "racial" types, Europeans paid close attention to such physical features as hair and eye color; shape of head, chin, and nose; and stature as signifiers of race identity. In the process, scholars invented a variety of techniques to measure even minuscule variations in such features and establish classifications of European races. The basic assumption was that each of these "types" was once a pure race; statistical data would help to establish what these racial populations were and something about their history.

Because of frequent discoveries of fossil materials, beginning in the late eighteenth century much attention was paid to the skull. Among these finds were skulls that had obvious humanlike features. More significant, however, was a popular synthesis of ideas about human mental processes and certain associated features of the skull or cranium, which led to the so-called science of phrenology. Phrenology purported to demonstrate "that different parts of the brain each had their own mental function, and that the relative size of these parts determined the degree of development of their respective faculties. Observations and measurements of 'bumps' on skulls and heads, it was thought, could thus provide accurate estimates of personality and character" (Malefijt 1974, 260). Phrenology thus inspired scientists to study skulls for the purpose of assessing the character, personality traits, and talents of individuals and the national character of ethnic populations. Everything from aesthetic sensitivity to mathematical ability, musical and other talents, moral character, criminality, frugality, and other personality traits became presumably measurable products of the mind. The potential usefulness of this approach for establishing or demonstrating racial distinctions was obvious. During the 1830s phrenology as a faddish form of scientism, as well as an interesting parlor game, found its way into the United States.

It was, however, a Frenchman, Paul Broca, who made the most extensive use of quantitative methods for classifying races as well as for promoting phrenological assumptions in the sciences. Broca, a polygenist and one of the founders of the Anthropological Society of Paris in 1859, invented a number of instruments used by craniometrists and accumulated over 180,000 measurements on different populations. Anthropometry (the science of measuring human bodies) and anthropometrists proliferated in Europe and America. According to Haller, "the hallmark of anthropology in the 19th century was anthropometry" (1971, 71), and its primary objective was to identify, document, and measure physical differences among human groups. The greater the number of variables that could be quantified and measured, the stronger was the argument for a vast gulf between the races.

The instruments of the growing fields of anthropology and human biology came to be utilized abundantly, from the middle of the nineteenth century on, to support the principles of racial determinism and racial separation. Those who argued that the Negro was nearer to the ape than to Caucasians found much support in anthropometry.[6] Marvin Harris's observation sums up the significance of these endeavors: "Prior to the nineteenth century, nations had never rewarded their wise men to prove that the supremacy of one people over another was the inevitable outcome of the biological laws of the universe" (1968, 81).

After the Civil War, many claims for the scientific verification of racial inequalities rested on wide-ranging anthropometric studies of Civil War soldiers and sailors made by two government agencies, the United States Sanitary Commission and the Provost Marshal General's Bureau. In 1862 the U.S. Sanitary Commission commenced large-scale studies of military recruits to identify the extent of differences among the races (Haller 1971). The idea was to construct an "average man" for each group, determined by numerous measurements.

Using the increasingly more sophisticated techniques of anthropometry, the commission tested and measured thousands of white soldiers, white sailors, and marines; "full-blooded" Negroes; and several hundred mulattoes and Indians. They took measurements of body dimensions throughout, from head size to toe length. They tested physical strength, vision, respiration, and pulmonary capacity. Their results, and later interpretations of these data, were published over a period of several decades following the war. Explicit in these works was the preordained conclusion that in virtually all ways that mattered to a civilized world, "Negroes" were inferior to whites, and so were their mulatto offspring. They had smaller brains, being closer phylogenetically to the apes, although their strong physical endowment made them capable soldiers and workers (Haller 1971, 191).

Even though the varied findings of these commissions and physicians were questioned by other scientists, and census data were shown to be erroneous, continued interest in the measuring of racial differences persisted well into the twentieth century. Some scientists, dissatisfied with the apparent subjectivity and inaccuracies of older anthropometric work, proposed innovative new methods for measuring and differentiating races. Elaborate techniques for observing and reporting skin color, for example, were developed early in the century.

TYPOLOGICAL MODELS OF RACES

All of the measurement activities in the late nineteenth and early twentieth centuries fostered thinking about races as "racial types," both in the biological sciences as well as in the popular mind. The essential elements in the typological scheme were voluminous statistics derived from external measurements of groups of individuals. Quantitative measurements were supplemented by morphological observations; in other words, by purely visual impressions. From the quantitative data, means, averages, and standard deviations were computed, which provided a statistical profile of the population. This profile was purported to represent, in objective and quantitative terms, the type characteristics of that population as abstracted from the real data. That the completed profile may not have corresponded to any individual in the population was irrelevant. The profile of each group conveyed the point that each was a distinct morphological type. When profiles of different groups were compared, the differences between them would be interpreted as the degree of their racial differences (Hunt 1959, 66). Associated with these abstractions was the notion of "pure" and "intermediate" types (Bean 1926; Hooten 1926, 1936). It was assumed that all races were originally pure and unmixed. The problem was to discover those clusters of traits that made each race, or at least each "pure" race, distinct.

The procedures and findings appeared to validate the image of races as discrete and internally homogeneous, obscuring all of the variability in the original data. By extrapolation and creative interpretations, some scholars used such data to confirm the assumption that some races were more developed than others. Frequent assertions were made that some races actually constituted primeval primitive types that had not evolved, or at least not as rapidly as the more advanced races.[7] Lending a theoretical framework to the absolutism inherent in this perspective were the late nineteenth-century generalized theories of evolution, both biological and social, especially those proposed by Herbert Spencer and his ideological compatriots. Clearly, if some people were able to evolve more complex and sophisticated social and political institutions, laws, and technologies, this was indicative of their superior intellectual endowments.

Americans and many Europeans of the nineteenth and early twentieth centuries were even more convinced that there were fundamental and ineradicable differences among racial populations, equivalent, as we have seen, to those used to identify separate species. However, a new element soon developed in the racial cosmology on both continents, which held that every race has a distinct "racial essence." This idea was necessary in Europe because populations there were not as easily distinguished from one another on physical grounds alone. North Americans required the concept because of the presence of persons of mixed ancestry who were phenotypically ambiguous. *Racial essence* is based on the presupposition that distinctive temperament and character, moral proclivities, and intellectual capabilities are bound and inherited together regardless of superficial physical features. Despite the lack of empirical evidence, these abstracted qualities of racial uniqueness persisted in the mental imagery. It was presumed that such qualities were also amenable to measurement, and it was up to science to discover, measure, and document these realities.

In a general sense, the distance between races as expressed by the measurements of physical features was compounded (metaphorically) in the interpretations of the psychological and intellectual differences that the metrical evidence was thought to mirror. At bottom, the real key to the differences that denoted a race's ranking and capacity for civilization rested in ascertaining these mental, psychological, and intellectual traits. By the end of the nineteenth century, new modalities were operating that attempted to isolate the psychodynamic aspects of race differences and to calculate and measure these independently of the anthropometric findings.

THE MEASUREMENT OF HUMAN DIFFERENCES: PSYCHOMETRICS

Anthropometry, with its multiple measurements of body parts, could not be definitive in its efforts to prove white superiority. Metrical measurements merely demonstrated average statistical differences. Moreover, it was discovered that there was greater variability within the defined racial groups than originally had been assumed. And there were no answers to such questions as whether Negroes with large brains were more intelligent than whites with smaller ones. Values and meanings had to be placed on the numerical findings, and there were clearly limits to the interpretations that could be imposed on such data. Science had exhausted all of the interpretations; thus one could conclude that all nineteenth-century attempts to measure the physical character of races and relate this to the ranking system had ended in failure (Gossett 1965, 77). Raciologists needed some other mechanism for ascertaining racial character and demonstrating both inequality and the appropriate ranking of human groups.

Increasingly, the brain was seen as the site of moral, intellectual, and temperamental qualities. The idea of measuring the contents of the skull—determining the presumed racial variables in the size and weight of the brain—and the success of certain craniometric endeavors prompted the development of a new field that aimed at the measuring of mental, intellectual, and/or psychological processes. New techniques were needed for examining the workings of the human mind and appraising the quality of its output.

The field of psychology had begun to take form during the early nineteenth century. It also had its roots in the growth of science during the Enlightenment and in the writings and speculations on human nature produced by philosophers, sociologists, physiologists, and physicians. In developing the field that later came to be called phrenology, Franz Joseph Gall had done much to focus on the probable physiology of the brain and its correspondences to mental functions. He is rightly seen by many as one of the founders of the field of psychology. His legacy underscored two things: his focus on individual differences and his belief in the correspondence of certain behaviors with different regions of the brain. He also believed that talents and faculties of the mind were innate, and this put his interests squarely within the tenor of the times.

Another major figure in the history of the sciences, Sir Francis Galton, demonstrated that extraordinary skills and talents ran in family lines. A half-cousin of Charles Darwin, Galton came out of the same aristocratic British background that produced a disproportionate number of scientists and intellectuals in nineteenth-century England. In 1869 he published *Hereditary Genius*, a landmark volume partly designed to convince everyone of the superior hereditary endowment of certain eminent British families. Arguing that there is a physiological basis for psychological traits, he invented techniques for measuring what he thought was intelligence, along with the bell-shaped curve for demonstrating its "normal distribution." Galton also introduced such concepts as "regression toward the mean" as a way of explaining the stability of the normal distribution curve in light of the flux found within a population and even among individual members of the same family. These are still basic models for twentieth-century psychology.

Although he never fathered a child, Galton had an almost fanatical concern with "superior" heredity, as evidenced in two of his other famous books, *Human Faculty* (1883) and *Natural Inheritance* (1889). He is especially remembered for having coined the term *eugenics* to denote efforts to improve racial stock by selective mating, thus founding the first scientific movement to overtly implement hereditarian beliefs (see chapter 12). In addition, Galton wrote much on mental defectives, the criminal mind, color blindness, and other traits that he believed were differentially inherited in inferior races. More important, Galton discovered the hereditary significance of the study of twins and is thus the intellectual predecessor of Sir Cyril Burt, the recently discredited English "twin expert," and Edward Lee Thorndike, originator of the first important American study on twins. Galton not only suggested the need to observe the differences between fraternal and identical twins but also recommended the study of twins reared together as distinct from those reared apart.

In Europe, Alfred Binet, director of the Sorbonne psychology laboratory in Paris, was requested by the French government to establish some means of testing and discriminating among the differential capabilities of Parisian schoolchildren. Both Galton and Binet thought that they were measuring intelligence. But neither ever defined it, nor did they approach an operational characterization of what they thought they were measuring. However, unlike Galton, Binet never argued that intelligence was a single, innate, unitary entity. Because his main concern was to improve the performance of schoolchildren, he advanced no determination as to the cause of poor performance. According to Gould, "Not only did Binet decline to label I.Q. as inborn intelligence; he also refused to regard it as a general device for ranking all pupils according to mental worth" (1981, 152). Thus, Gould continues, Binet avoided the fallacies of reification and hereditarianism.

When mental testing was introduced in the United States in the 1890s, some of the first experiments involved attempts to determine race differences. The first tests were not strictly mental tests, but rather assessments of physiological reaction times in which subjects responded to a number of stimuli and their responses were measured. Galton had pioneered the development of many of these types of tests. Among the first were the experiments of R. M. Bache; his tests were designed to ascertain "quickness of sensory perception." Bache administered the test to twelve whites, eleven Indians, and eleven Negroes to see which group had the quickest reactions. Indians turned out to be first, Negroes second, and the whites the slowest. Bache's interpretation of these conclusions was that whites were superior. Their reaction times were slowest because "they belonged to a more deliberate and reflective race" (Gossett 1965, 364). When in later tests whites had the quickest reactions, again this was interpreted as evidence of their racial superiority.

In another example, some five hundred black children and five hundred whites were given a test that evaluated memory. The black children scored slightly higher than did the white. But the interpretation given to this result was that sometimes blacks may excel over whites in "mechanical intellectual" processes that require no extensive mental activity (Gossett 1965, 364–365). Such results should be seen, in retrospect, as early prognostications of what mental testing was to be all about: confirmation and validation of the already established presumption of white superiority. No matter what the outcome of the tests conducted, the conclusion was foregone. We shall see more about the use of such tests and the American fascination with IQ as a measure of intelligence in the next chapter.

EXTENSION OF RACE IDEOLOGY OVERSEAS

Race is just one way of looking at and interpreting human phenotypic differences. During the nineteenth century, European intellectuals assumed that all societies recognized races, with much the same ideology of difference and inequality. However, recent scholarship has suggested that nothing relating to the Western concept of race existed in the indigenous societies before they came under colonial rule. On the contrary, scholars now argue that European colonial powers transmitted the ideology of race throughout the Third World, especially during the nineteenth and early twentieth centuries (see endnote 1).

Not only did colonists perceive the peoples whom they conquered or dominated as racial inferiors, but in large territories where there were already considerable physical variations, such as in India, the English colonists also expected that these peoples had already established racial categories among their populations. Because skin color had figured so prominently in the racialization of Africans and Native Americans, the British assumed that variations in skin color in India would also carry social meanings reflecting race divisions, with lighter skin colors valued over darker colors. They interpreted the Hindi term *varna* to mean skin color, which it does not, and even assumed that the term *jati*, used for *caste* (a term introduced by the Portuguese) could be equated with the Western idea of race with the same element of rigidity and concreteness. But none of the Hindi terms carried meanings that were even similar to race (Chana 2002, 2003; Klass 1980). The Indian view of human differences was based in religious beliefs. And dark skin historically had had positive meanings, as reflected in the Indian deities, Shiva and Vishnu, and his incarnations, the Gods Rama and Krishna (Chana 2003).

Nevertheless the British tried to impose racial categories and racial meanings on the peoples of India and Burma. By the early twentieth century, British anthropologists had imported anthropometric techniques for measuring heads and bodies to ascertain racial divisions. It was clear that they envisioned the caste system as rigid, with clearly bounded social groups (Chana 2002). They even trained some Indian students to gather vast numbers of measurements from various populations. However, the number of races that scientists invented were arbitrary and without consistency; some found as many as thirty-six races in India. Needless to say, they had no meaning to the Indian people.

The British succeeded to some degree in transmitting European aesthetic values and preferences for Caucasoid appearance. As Chana notes, "aesthetic values or what constitutes 'superior looks' is a reflection on who has the power and who controls the dominant discourse in that particular place or time" (2003, 3). Light-skinned Indians were more susceptible to and accepting of the ideology of race. Today skin-lightening products are widely sold in India, particularly in many urban areas, attesting to the widespread conditioning to Western values.

After Admiral Matthew Perry had forced Japan to open its ports to trade in the mid-nineteenth century, race was imported into Japan along with other Western scientific ideas (Tomiyama 2002). Japanese intellectuals found a general categorizing term in their language (*jinshu*) to equate with the Western concept of race (Katayama 2002). Beginning in the late nineteenth century, Japanese scientists were trained in the Western traditions of anthropological scholarship. Thereafter, they began to racialize peoples on their borders, such as the Koreans, Okinawans, and Ainu, with whom they had had conflict. Under the influences of Western science, they even tried to use craniometric techniques to distinguish these populations.

The Chinese had long engaged in conflict and competition with peoples on their borders whom they had identified as "barbarians." Frank Dikötter claims that this was cultural prejudice or ethnocentrism up until the Opium Wars, when British influence was imposed (1992). Subsequently, the stereotypes became "racial" (1992, 44). When the idea and ideology of race were introduced to China, Sakamoto observes, "it was through missionary publications and Japanese books" that presented translations of the racial works of Gobineau and Blumenbach (2002).

Anthropologists who have worked in Africa have also seen the degree to which European colonists conditioned these peoples to perceive themselves and others in racial terms. I have heard British colonial officers speak of the Hausa as a "superior" race to the Ibos and Yorubas, and in East Africa colonists favored certain ethnic populations, such as the Tutsis, over the

Hutus and other groups. The Baganda in Uganda were especially separated from the rest of the population and provided with education and positions in the colonial administration. The notion that they were "racially different" was instilled into these populations, a fact that exacerbated any conflicts that might have existed and led to the current tragedies in this area. This may have been a "divide and conquer" tactic, but it left a residue of "racial" mistrust among many peoples.

American missionaries were particularly influential in teaching racial ideology in Africa. The Sudan Interior Mission (SIM), for example, established churches, hospitals, and schools in several West African nations. Many of the missionaries were little educated white southerners from the American Bible Belt. They maintained segregated facilities in towns such as Jos, their headquarters. Such was the strength of their racial ideology that they would not even allow fellow Americans who were black into the white schools and hospitals. Black Americans who sought American medical treatment had to go to the much inferior hospitals designated only for black Africans.

Global comparative studies of attitudes toward and beliefs about human differences, particularly as expressed in the ideology of race, are still in their infancy. We do know that most societies around the world have been influenced by American and European racial values, which have often been incorporated into historical indigenous conceptions of differences among human groups. It might be extremely difficult to ascertain the nature of indigenous beliefs before Western influences.

Yet, as we will see in chapters 13 and 14, gradual modifications began to occur in race ideology during the first half of the twentieth century. With the rise of Hitler's Germany, even the term *race* itself took on nuances for the first time that conveyed to an increasingly receptive public its malignant and corrosive influences on human society.

NOTES

1. In 2002, the first international meetings of scholars dealing with the question of "race" globally were held in Japan. The first meeting, a two-day conference, was held at the University of Kyoto, where international scholars addressed the question, "Is Race a Universal Idea?" The second was a symposium on "The Racialization of the Human Body" under the auspices of the Inter-Congress of the International Union of Anthropological and Ethnological Sciences. In both meetings papers were read by scholars from Japan, England, India, and the United States.

2. As early as 1809 a curator at the Danish Museum, C. J. Thomsen, had sorted through a massive amount of archeological materials collected from European sites and had established the now well-known sequence of the Stone, Bronze, and Iron Ages.

3. Because of their proximity to one another, Europeans have always been aware that individuals, families, and even larger groupings often migrate and change their language and culture; that is, changes in ethnicity, nationality, and even class are unrelated to the biophysical characteristics that an individual or family may have. The components of the ideology of race transform this kind of consciousness in subtle ways.

4. This triadic paradigm and the resulting stereotypes in European racial myths have stubbornly persisted. In a 1927 publication entitled *The Racial Elements of European History*, H. F. K. Gunther described the characteristics of these three presumed races without equivocation as to their innateness. The Nordic, he believed, has a strong urge toward "truth and justice, prudence, reserve, [and] steadfastness," exhibiting calm judgment, fairness, and trustworthiness. The Mediterranean, in contrast, is "strongly swayed by sexual life." He is not as continent as are Nordics, for whom "passion has little meaning." Alpines are "petty criminals, small-time swindlers, sneak thieves and sexual perverts." Nordics are "capable of the nobler crimes." See Tobias 1972, 27.

5. Personal notes from Leslie White (1953).

6. Stephen Jay Gould (1981 [1996]), we are reminded, has examined the original data of many of the outstanding nineteenth-century anthropometrists involved in race and gender studies. He has shown how their blind commitment to race and other hereditarian differences led these scientists to fudge, finagle, and misconstrue their own data in order to support the fundamental assumptions and myths of their culture.

7. For accounts of this theory and of the notions of other scientists, see Chase 1980 and Haller 1971.

CHAPTER 12

Twentieth-Century Developments in Race Ideology

In this chapter I explore some of the developments in the twentieth century that promoted, preserved, and enhanced the racial ideology of the nineteenth century. I briefly examine social, political, and economic developments, particularly those that heavily impacted the low-status races. I look next at the way science evolved in a manner that perfectly paralleled the collective consciousness about matters of race. Anthropometric measurements gave way to intelligence testing, which was to become the most powerful tool of the advocates of innate race differences. Then I take a brief look at the eugenics movement and its promotion of hereditarian values. The next section examines the rise of Nazi Germany and the manifestation of extreme race ideology in Europe. The chapter ends with a brief exploration of continuing modern attempts by some scientists to promote and prove the racial superiority of whites and the inferiority of blacks.

SOCIAL REALITIES OF THE RACIAL WORLDVIEW

In the United States, the racial worldview promoted the belief that all racial groups should have their own institutions, lifestyles, and communities. Segregation of all facilities, public and private, was seen as normal and desired, especially in the cases of the white and black racial groups. The most extreme forms of segregation were found in the local laws of southern states, where separate waiting rooms, water fountains, washrooms, and the like proclaimed the undesirability of "the Negro." Black Americans could not eat in the same places as whites or try on clothing in the same stores; and in some places they had to purchase food from a separate counter. They were excluded from skilled trades, and in unskilled jobs they were commonly the last hired and the first fired. Education for blacks was haphazard at best, although black schools and universities managed to offer the best education available to them (Berry and Blassingame 1982). In most places in the South, survival for blacks depended upon assuming a servile manner and accepting any job, no matter how demeaning. Most whites continued to concur with the views of James Hammond, who had declared in the U.S. Senate in 1858: "In all social systems there must be a class to do the menial duties, to perform the drudgery of life. This is a class requiring but a low order of intellect and but little skill. . . . This class constitutes the very *mud-sill* of society. Fortunately . . . we have found a race adapted to that purpose (the negro)" (Fredrickson 1988, 23).

By 1910 the nation saw the complete disfranchisement of African Americans throughout the South, despite the progress they had made in the decades after the Civil War. According to John Hope Franklin and Alfred Moss, "The new century opened tragically with 214 lynchings in the first two years. Clashes between the races occurred almost daily, and the atmosphere of tension in which people of both races lived was conducive to little more than a struggle for mere survival, with a feeble groping in the direction of progress. The law, the courts, the schools, and almost every institution in the South favored whites. This was white supremacy" (1988, 238).

Many of the attitudes and beliefs about inferior races were expressed in literature and increasingly in the new entertainment media of radio and the movies. As Fredrickson points out (1971), a great deal of literature written during the first quarter of the century consciously exaggerated black bestiality, degeneracy, crime, and sexuality, especially the lust for white women. These stereotypes help to explain the increasingly extreme white hostility, policies of segregation, avoidance of contact with African Americans even in northern cities, and burgeoning hatred of blacks among all levels of society. Such attitudes were prime conditions fostering the construction of isolated urban black ghettos and the increasing institutionalization of black poverty.

Certain popular works perpetuated the common themes of this era. Charles Carroll's *The Negro a Beast* (1900) continued the polygenist tradition and enlarged upon the then widely accepted argument that the Negro was in reality an ape. Thomas Dixon's popular novels terrorized their readers with their portrayals of lust-driven black males attacking virginal white women. When his book *The Klansmen* was made into a movie, *The Birth of a Nation* (1915), it inaugurated the development of a new facility for portraying racial differences and proselytizing the racial worldview: the graphic medium of film. Tragic scenes revealing the horrible consequences of Reconstruction governments on innocent southerners, the corruption of these governments "run by illiterate blacks," and the final suicide of a young white virgin (rather than submit to rape by a gorillalike black male) were cleverly designed to turn the emotions of the audience to the southern cause and vitiate black aspirations. The film also provoked mob violence and unspeakable acts of brutality and intimidation in local regions of the South.

The period between World War I and World War II in the United States was punctuated by outbursts of intense racial hatred that took various forms. Some of the most violent resulted from the reinvigoration of the Ku Klux Klan under a dogmatic leadership that was relentlessly committed to the preservation of "Anglo-Saxon civilization." Klan leaders saw the restlessness of African Americans emigrating from the South and the onrush of different immigrant peoples from southern and eastern Europe as threats to the dominance of the white Anglo-Saxon establishment. Throughout the South and in some regions of the West and North, the Klan turned to intimidation and threats to maintain the subordinance of the undesirable groups, which now included people from the Roman Catholic areas of Europe.

Between 1890 and 1930, more than twenty-three million immigrants, mostly from southern, central, and eastern Europe, arrived in the United States, with only a brief cessation during World War I (Steinberg 1989, 33). This was one of the largest migrations in history, and it changed the character of American society. When the first of these immigrants began to pour into the United States, the juxtaposition of such culturally different groups caused many old-stock Americans to react strongly to perceptions of their "otherness." At the same time, Italians, Greeks, Armenians, Russians, Jews, Poles, Yugoslavs, Czechoslovaks, and a miscellany of other ethnic populations were welcomed by some for their labor.

One of the strongest reactions was fear on the part of the older Protestant populations that their own economic and political positions were endangered. Language, religion, and other cultural differences were now so persistently seen as innate and permanent that any consideration of the acculturation of these groups was muted. Older white Americans began to believe that their world was changing, and for the worse. They cast the newcomers as racially distinct and inferior, and they were aided in this perception by the newly emerging science of IQ testing (see below). Caricatures of these new immigrants in newspapers and journals fed the xenophobia of older northern European immigrants.

Those immigrants from Catholic countries (Italians, Poles, and Irish) were seen as a particular threat because of the fear that their presence might enlarge the power of the Catholic Church and the pope in American life and politics. These groups tended to have more children, and because they were mostly poor, it was thought that their lifestyles and habits would diminish the quality of the country's social fabric. Age-old antagonisms toward Jews also began to surface. The general thinking was that these groups could not be assimilated into American (white Protestant) society. Anti-Jewish and anti-Catholic sentiment reached new heights in many parts of the country as membership in the Ku Klux Klan peaked at over six million persons during the mid-1920s. Under pressure of such opposition, Congress passed the immigration laws of 1921 and 1924, sharply limiting the immigration of southern and eastern Europeans.

The eventual acceptance of the new immigrant peoples into the dominant society made it possible for them ultimately to identify as "whites" and to assert their superior position over and above blacks and Indians. Their skin color and common continental origin may have been important factors in their assimilation. They soon learned English, and their children were rapidly socialized to American lifestyles. But more important was the existence of an already entrenched low-status population, more or less clearly set apart by physical characteristics, whose presence dramatized the often antagonistic role of the new immigrants. One factor of great significance was that employers preferred to hire immigrant Europeans over blacks. Immigrants easily obtained the best jobs, displacing unknown numbers of black workers. This was a pattern that was only interrupted for a few years during World Wars I and II, when for the first time blacks were hired in larger numbers in industry, because of the declining availability of whites. After the wars, when immigration picked up again for a brief while, competition between immigrant whites and blacks came to a head. Blacks were beginning to complain about their loss of jobs or their inability to obtain jobs because of the preference for European immigrants, and the tension between these groups sometimes led to violence (Berry and Blassingame 1982).

The Second World War opened opportunities for African Americans to a degree not even imagined in the earlier conflict. Black workers became necessary because of the large mobilization for the war effort and the millions of men and women who were conscripted away from jobs in the larger industrial economy. The defense industry gradually opened its doors, and the auto and steel industries followed suit. But the entry of blacks into the more desirable manufacturing jobs did not proceed without conflicts. Race riots in Detroit in 1943 exemplified the painful process that culminated in the unions capitulating to economic realities. As a result, blacks were formally integrated into some unions and into the industrial economy as a whole. Almost always the jobs most readily available to them were low wage, dirty, and difficult. Even blacks who had skills found that sweeping floors, hauling waste, or doing various tasks in the foundry around hot molten steel were the best jobs they could obtain.

Meanwhile, dramatic demographic changes were occurring in the major cities. Middle-class whites had begun moving to the suburbs as early as the 1930s, and the inner cores of most large cities were becoming more and more occupied by blacks migrating from the South and by some of the ethnic populations from Eastern Europe. Uneasy though the relationships were, there was comparatively little friction between whites and blacks during the 1950s. But the dispersal to the suburbs on the part of middle-class whites continued and in some cases was accelerated by the disturbances of the 1960s.

During all of these changes, science played a peculiar role in the lives and consciousness of Americans. Many scientists were conditioned to hereditarian beliefs, which, as we saw earlier, were essential to the ideology of race and during the nineteenth century had been elevated to a higher level of authenticity and respectability by some of the intellectuals of Europe. Heredity as an explanation for human social behavior became, and still is, a powerful dogma. It is facile, simple, and easily grasped by virtually everyone. More important, it does not require intricate or tedious examination of detailed facts and does not demand proof. So willing were Americans to subscribe to the doctrine of innate differences and causality that one could attribute all kinds of social facts to heredity with the safe assumption that it might obviate all further query or investigation. For those unwilling or unable to accept social change, hereditary explanations clearly worked to ensure the status quo and promote stability.

It is little wonder that some American scholars began to argue that the existing inequalities, even among the European American populations, were the result of hereditary differences. Under the influence of Herbert Spencer, Francis Galton, and others, many Americans came to accept a society composed of naturally unequal citizens. Social class differences were deemed the product of differential intelligence, and as we will see, some American scientists worked hard during the twentieth century to propagate the idea that intelligence was a unitary characteristic that was inherited from parents to children, that it was not subject to modifications through external influences, and thus that no social interventions would change the class (or racial) structure of America. One simplistic technique was called upon to proclaim this reality for race and class differences: the IQ test.

PSYCHOMETRICS: THE MEASURING OF HUMAN WORTH BY IQ

With the emphasis being placed at the end of the nineteenth century on processes taking place in the mind, it seemed predictable that scholars and scientists in the growing field of psychology would turn to the issue of race differences. The task of documenting inequality among races became one of the most important concentrations in this new field. What was necessary was the development of new methods of ascertaining not only the processes but the products of mental activity.

The most important work at the end of the nineteenth century that set precedents for future developments in the study of mental differences was the tests devised by Alfred Binet and his colleague Theodore Simon in France. It was noted that Binet and Simon never defined intelligence, although they did believe that their tests measured intelligence to some degree. But differentiating children into groups by some presumably innate criteria, based on their performance on these tests, was not their purpose. Both men understood that a child's environment and educational opportunities affected his performance on tests. Binet died in 1911, and there were few further developments on intelligence testing in Europe outside of Great Britain.

Americans, on the other hand, were quickly attracted to the possibilities inherent in the use of such tests.[1] A number of psychologists in the United States began experimenting with mental testing, taking much of their cues from European developments. In 1908 Henry Goddard began testing on four hundred inmates of a home for feebleminded boys and girls in Vineland, New Jersey. The tests he used were adapted from those created by Binet and Simon, but they were modified in such a way as to reflect American schooling and his own social beliefs. He believed that intelligence was inherited as a single, unitary faculty and that performance on the tests directly mirrored this reality. Goddard was also one of the earliest psychologists to identify with the eugenics movement, which had originated in England but achieved its greatest strength among American and German scientists (see below).

In 1912 Goddard turned to immigrant populations arriving at Ellis Island in New York Harbor and began testing them. His conclusions were publicized in scientific journals and shocked most educated Americans. He found that incoming European immigrants were indeed an inferior lot. Seventy-nine percent of Italians were feebleminded, as were 83 percent of Jews, 87 percent of Russians, and 80 percent of Hungarians (Chase 1980, 228). Goddard was the expert on feeblemindedness; it was he who established the categories and the criteria for mental deficiencies, assigning them terms such as *moron*, *im-*

becile, and *idiot*. His fame and standing in the profession grew when he published a book detailing the hereditary pattern of feeblemindedness for three generations in a family to whom he gave the pseudonym Kallikaks (Chase 1980; Gould 1981; Kevles 1985).

Goddard came to believe, without any direct scientific evidence, that feeblemindedness was inherited as an element in the brain (or the absence of some normal hereditary feature) that followed a Mendelian pattern. As a mental defect, it explained the behavior of social misfits, inmates of prisons, prostitutes, criminals, the mentally retarded, and paupers, among others. In 1914 he published his findings in a book entitled *Feeblemindedness: Its Causes and Consequences*, which had a strong influence on scientists involved in the growing field of genetics as well as on the public at large.

Lewis Terman, a professor at Stanford University, adopted Binet's mental testing techniques, revised them, and proceeded to further develop "intelligence" testing in the United States. The tests he and his colleagues devised and published became known as the Stanford-Binet tests and were later used widely as the foundation of IQ testing programs all over the United States. Terman concluded that the average American tested at a mental age of sixteen years. Moreover, his tests showed that children from upper-class homes had a higher average mental age than children of the "laboring classes." This outcome confirmed Terman's belief that test performance reflected natural hereditary (genetic) abilities. He claimed that it was a gratuitous assumption to hold that nurture (a child's environment) had anything to do with "the qualities of intellect and character" (Chase 1980, 234). And he argued that "opening up avenues of opportunity to the children of lower socioeconomic groups probably made no sense; they did not have the IQ points to compete" (Kevles 1985, 83). (By the 1940s, Terman had changed his beliefs and concluded that environmental factors had more to do with a child's learning than his or her original genetic equipment.)

American psychologists took advantage of the drafted military men of World War I in 1917 to experiment with IQ tests on a massive scale.. The army Alpha and Beta tests were devised and used on nearly two million recruits between 1917 and 1919. The Alpha tests were designed for literate recruits; the Beta tests were developed for those who were illiterate or did not speak English. The outcome of these tests was foreboding. The published report showed that the average intelligence of white military men put them on a par with a child of a little over thirteen years (13.08); only 4.5 percent of the men were intelligent enough to be trained as officers. The highest-ranking draftees were of English descent. These were followed by the Dutch, Germans, Scots, and Danes. Descendants of peoples from eastern and southern

Europe (Russians, Greeks, Italians, Poles) ranked much lower, with Russians highest at a mental age of 11.01 and Poles lowest at 10.74. At the very bottom were Negroes, with a mental age of 10.41.

The fact that Negroes from four northern states—New York, Pennsylvania, Ohio, and Illinois—scored higher than whites from the southern states of Mississippi, Kentucky, Arkansas, and Georgia did not appear to contradict or even raise questions about the findings. Neither did the other numerous findings that showed that northern draftees of all races scored much higher than southern ones, or that those with more education scored higher than those with little education. Rather than conclude that the army tests measured the degree of formal education and cultural familiarity that recruits had, psychologists reached the immediate interpretation that they reflected innate or hereditary intelligence.[2]

The outcome of the army tests alarmed Americans concerned with progress and the educational system. But few scholars raised criticisms of the tests or questioned their validity. Indeed many, such as Dr. Carl Brigham, used the data from these tests in his own popular book, *A Study of American Intelligence* (1923), which, Gould says, "became a primary vehicle for translating the army results on group differences into social action" (1981, 224). Brigham attempted to estimate the amount of "Nordic blood" in the recruits using only their name and background. His findings were that Sweden had 100 percent Nordic stock; Norway had 90 percent; Denmark, Holland, and Scotland 85 percent; England 80 percent; Wales and Germany 40 percent; France and Ireland 30 percent; Poland and Spain 10 percent; and Italy, Russia, and Portugal 5 percent (Gossett 1965, 375). His effort was intended to prove the superiority of Nordics. However, in 1930 Brigham repudiated his own work as racially biased, but it had already had significant influence on the American public and scholarly writers.

Later the army tests were revised for civilian use and became virtually universal instruments for measuring racial differences in mental processes. They were used in a wide variety of settings by psychologists as well as by schools, businesses, and other institutions as a way of sorting out individuals according to their supposed innate abilities. As a result, most Americans accepted IQ testing as a positive scientific instrument that accurately recorded native intelligence. Many schoolchildren learned that their IQ scores were a set and unchanging aspect of who they were.

Jack Fincher points out that the scientists involved in developing these tests held personal views on heredity that justified inequities not only of racial treatment but also of class differences (1976, 176 ff.). But it is Gould's indictment that penetrates to the proverbial bottom line:

> American psychologists perverted Binet's intention and invented the hereditarian theory of IQ. They reified Binet's scores, and took them as measures of an entity called intelligence. They assumed that intelligence was largely inherited, and developed a series of specious arguments confusing cultural differences with innate properties. They believed that inherited IQ scores marked people and groups for an inevitable station in life. And they assumed that average differences between groups were largely the products of heredity, despite manifest and profound variation in quality of life. (1981, 157)

After World War II, the army developed more sophisticated tests designed to identify disparate aptitudes of recruits and volunteers for various jobs in the military. This was known as the Armed Forces Qualification Test (AFQT). Dr. Bernard Karpinos, one of its administrators, emphasized that the results of these tests really measured the level and quality of education and experiences outside of school, not native intelligence. Discrepancies between blacks and whites were noted, but in a curiously strange way, as Allen Chase observed when he examined these tests: White American males had strong minds but weak bodies; black Americans, on the other hand, had strong bodies but weak minds (Chase 1980, 433). He maintains that the entire findings of these tests were questionable because they contradict the well-documented understanding that strong bodies make strong minds. Massive surveys of millions of American children show a clear relationship between poverty, disease, ill health, malnutrition, and low school achievement.

At a much deeper level was the broader, more fundamental query that all such tests raise: What are the causes of human behavior? This raises the *nature* versus *nurture* controversy (heredity versus environment) that continues to periodically insinuate itself into the public consciousness. Those who believe in biological determinants (nature) insist that most behaviors, including intelligence, are innate and determined by one's genes. In a consistent manner, they also adhere to the components of the racial worldview. Those who find biology less significant in human affairs argue that we are all products of our environments—family, school, personal experiences, religion, and so forth (nurture). These scholars see sociocultural forces as the main determinants of human behavior.

Both of these groups bring forth evidence drawn from various scientific fields to support their claims. The IQ tests became the favorite technique of pro-heredity advocates, and their success reflects the fact that their findings and interpretations have been highly compatible with the racial worldview to which Americans in general have been conditioned. Major proponents of this view included Dr. Henry Garrett, a professor of psychology for many years at

Columbia University, and his student, Dr. Audrey Shuey, who taught at Randolph-Macon College in Lynchburg, Virginia. They were among many whose theoretical, social, and philosophical positions continued the polygenist trend in American science.

Chase points out that Garrett authored the *Encyclopaedia Britannica* article "Differential Psychology" in 1929, in which he used the findings of the army World War I tests as the basic source of information for comparing different groups. It was reprinted in subsequent editions of the encyclopedia for the next thirty years. Among its conclusions were the following statements:

> These tests [World War I Army tests] indicated a superiority of those foreign-born men from northern countries of Europe over those from central and southern Europe. . . . Intelligence tests given to large groups of whites and negroes in the American army place the negro below the white both in tests of language and non-language variety. [Investigations] have shown the negro to be more overtly emotional and less inhibited in his reactions than the white. . . . The American Indian ranks consistently below the white man on tests of mental capacity; the greater the admixture of white blood, the smaller the deviation from the performance of the white. (Chase 1980, 454)

In *The Testing of Negro Intelligence* (1958), Audrey Shuey brought together several hundred studies with statistics and other data that supposedly represented original investigations of Negro intelligence. Chase claims that her research protocol had a fatal flaw: She omitted those tests done exclusively on whites that gave proof of "socioeconomic and socio-biological factors known to be involved in the IQ test scores of all ethnic groups" (Chase 1980, 451). She also took at "face value" all of the statements made by Brigham in his 1923 book and dismissed or made light of the fact that he had repudiated them in 1930. Her conclusions were as expected; all of the tests "prove" innate (genetic) differences in intelligence between Negroes and whites.

It is of no small significance that Shuey's book came in the wake of the 1954 U.S. Supreme Court decision (*Brown* v. *Board of Education*) that called for the desegregation of schools nationally and the events in Montgomery, Alabama, in the summer of 1955 that gave rise to the civil rights movement. A similar situation can be seen in the work of Arthur Jensen.

As late as the early 1960s, Jensen was a proponent of this belief. In an article in a British journal, *Educational Research*, he stated: "The fact that Negroes and Mexicans are disproportionately represented in the lower end of the socio-economic-status scale cannot be interpreted as evidence of poor genetic potential. . . . Since we know that the Negro population for the most part has suffered socio-economic and cultural disadvantages for generations past, it seems a reasonable hypothesis that their low-average IQ [test score] is due to environmental rather than to genetic factors" (quoted in Chase 1980, 461).

By 1968–1969, however, Jensen had been converted to the views of Garrett, Shuey, McDougall, and other hereditarians. In his now famous (or notorious) article published in the *Harvard Educational Review*, "How Much Can We Boost IQ and Scholastic Achievement?," he took the position that all the compensatory government programs had failed (Head Start was then only a few years old) and that we cannot change the IQ of poor black children and other minorities, so we should cease spending "vast sums" of money on remedial programs (1969). He had become convinced that heredity had more to do with performance on intelligence tests than learning, individual experience, and other nonbiological environmental factors.

As Richard Lewontin (1970) noted, this article created a furor, especially among scholars who had focused much research on child development. Critics lambasted Jensen, but the media made sure that his name was in every newspaper and was mentioned frequently on the radio and TV, and that his basic ideas were profoundly simplified for the lay public. Again, a scientist with an impeccable reputation had confirmed for the mostly white public one of their most cherished beliefs. It should be noted that Jensen was at that time supported by the conservative Pioneer Fund.

Jensen, Garrett, Shuey, William Shockley, Carleton Putnam, and a host of other promoters of hereditarian ideology have worked hard to maintain the racial worldview. Both Shockley and Putnam were independent businessmen who invested in publishing ventures to proselytize their views. And Chase claims that Garrett and Shuey both wrote materials on race differences for publication and dissemination by the white citizens' councils that were formed, beginning in the summer of 1954, to oppose the changes taking place in the South.

After World War II, American society began to undergo some fairly rapid and dramatic changes. Millions of young men used the G.I. Bill to further their education, and a new generation of college-educated people began to settle down and have families. They became concerned with their children's growth and development and began to educate themselves on matters of sanitation, hygiene, food, and nutrition and their impact on their families. Particularly, they learned about how important it was to have good schools and to create culturally rich environments to stimulate their children. Authorities on child rearing and children's health published numerous guides and studies detailing the influences of environment on children's growth and mental development. This new, large body of middle-class Americans came to accept without fanfare that a good environment was more important than the genes a child inherits. Nurture was far more important than nature when the focus was on their children.

THE EUGENICS MOVEMENT

The new understanding of heredity occasioned by the rediscovery of Mendel's experiments, and the inspiration provided by the potentials of mental testing, also helped to inspire the eugenics movement, whose influence rose early in the century and diminished fairly quickly, but did not disappear, in the 1930s.[3] Eugenics was the handmaiden of hereditarian theories. It held as its basic premise that all kinds of human frailties and debilitating propensities such as crime, sloth, poverty, immorality, prostitution, alcoholism, pornography, and various other diseases were for the most part inherited, predominantly among the poor. The generalized philosophy and abstract goal of the movement, dating back to Galton (who coined the term *eugenics*), was to improve the race by selective breeding.

The person most responsible for the development of eugenics in the United States was Charles B. Davenport, a Connecticut Yankee who studied biology at Harvard and then went on to the University of Chicago in 1899. He corresponded with Galton and his disciple Karl Pearson and introduced Pearson's statistical methods to American universities. In 1904 he received money from the Carnegie Institution to establish a biological experimentation center at Cold Spring Harbor on Long Island. As director, he acquired considerable fame and prestige. Much of his early work involved breeding experiments on small animals, but he began to focus on human heredity in 1907. Thereafter he became actively engaged in expanding the study of human heredity with the support of the American Breeder's Association and wealthy individuals such as Mrs. E. H. Harriman. In 1910, with her help, he established the Eugenics Records Office, which became the center for all of the work and publications of the eugenics movement.

Davenport's general philosophy was based on his commitment to the idea that most human personality traits were products of simple Mendelian patterns of inheritance. Criminal and antisocial behaviors, musical ability, shiftlessness, and even wanderlust were caused by either recessive or dominant traits. Mark Haller claims: "All sorts of mental diseases, quirks, and eccentricities were lumped together and traced to the action of a single gene, despite the fact that the conditions were biologically unrelated or not biological conditions at all" (1963, 69). Most of the characteristics that eugenicists deplored were found predominantly among the poor, and this may be one reason for its rapid and widespread acceptance among some of America's most outstanding social, intellectual, and political leaders.

As Daniel Kevles notes: "Eugenics enthusiasts in the United States and Britain were largely middle to upper middle class, white, Anglo-Saxon, predominantly Protestant, and educated. . . . Fully half the membership of the British eugenics society consisted of women. . . . In the United States, women played an insignificant role in the national society but a prominent one in local groups" (1985, 64). The health and development of children had always been a women's issue.

Members relied for scientific evidence not only on IQ tests but on the very rudimentary field of genetics. At that time the only traits amenable to study by the techniques known were those determined by single genes, expressed in a number of allelic variations. The majority of known hereditary traits were various types of abnormalities (Ludmerer 1969; Marks 1995). Concentration on such traits tended to retard theoretical interest in "normal" traits, maintain focus on a small range of variation and limited generational depth, and emphasize the evaluation of a few characters for "fitness" within a single generation.

Eugenicists advocated sterilization of those individuals who carried "defective" genes (which could include any imagined hereditary trait such as criminality, feeblemindedness, tuberculosis, epilepsy, various mental diseases, and poverty). Some outstanding members of the American political system adhered to eugenic beliefs, and they supported policies of sterilization. So did most of the American public, according to a poll reported in *Fortune Magazine* in 1937. "Sixty-three percent of Americans endorsed the compulsory sterilization of habitual criminals and . . . sixty-six percent were in favor of sterilizing mental defectives" (Kevles 1985, 114). The result was that a number of states passed laws allowing the enforced sterilization of individuals deemed by the state to have defective genes. California and Virginia were the leaders in these actions. By 1941, nearly thirty-six thousand people had been sterilized (Kevles 1985, 116).

The idea of ridding a population of inferior and/or deleterious traits by selective breeding and of improving the "racial stock" by controlling the reproduction of only those individuals with supposedly superior inheritance appeals to a great many people. Although the logic is misplaced, and the ideas have no basis in scientific facts, there are still many advocates of producing a "super" race through special breeding (see Chase 1980; King 1981; Ludmerer 1969). With the eugenics movement, the hereditarian component of racial ideology was now greatly enhanced and refashioned to apply to members of what was the superior white race. The vast majority of individuals sterilized were white. So obsessed were the proponents of race superiority and purity that they could not tolerate presumed innate imperfections or inferior traits within the white race.

The primary legacy, then, of the nineteenth-century science of "raciology" (as it was called) as it redounds to us in the twenty-first century is not merely the penchant for measuring differences between groups called "races." It is the whole engorged mind-set that sought to explicate differences in behavior, real and imagined, in terms of heredity. The hereditarian component in the world-view of race has become the major argument of those who continue to adhere to the ideology of race and race differences; IQ is the idiom of its expression. The emphasis on differential intelligence and the array of inferences about innate qualities of which this was the center are the direct outgrowth of a late-eighteenth-century concoction that contradicted and distorted a fundamental human reality—the extrinsic, nonbiological causes of human behavior.

THE RACIAL WORLD OF THE NAZIS

By the time of the Third Reich, an elaborate variation of the ideology of race had been embroidered for Nazi consumption. Although the central figure in the policies and activities of the Nazi establishment was Adolf Hitler, he was clearly not alone in promulgating the German variation of the racial world-view. Hitler absorbed the works of the nineteenth-century race advocates and wrote his own guide to race thinking while in prison. *Mein Kampf* was Hitler's masterpiece, and it became the bible of the German nation.

Hitler grew up in the late nineteenth and early twentieth centuries imbued with a sense of German nationalism. This was also a time when antagonism toward Jews was rising in many areas of Europe. As a young man he lived for a time in Vienna, where he developed a visceral hatred of Jews. As William Shirer observed: "He buried himself in anti-Semitic literature, which had a large sale in Vienna at the time" ([1959] 1988, 26). In *Mein Kampf*, Hitler wrote that he went out into the streets to be able to observe and distinguish who were the Jews. "I began to see Jews, and the more I saw, the more sharply they became distinguished in my eyes from the rest of humanity. . . . Later I often grew sick to the stomach from the smell of these caftan-wearers. . . . Gradually I began to hate them" (Shirer [1959] 1988, 26). Shirer adds that he continued this blind and fanatical hatred to the bitter end.

Hitler joined the military in Germany and served in the First World War. While still in the army, he turned to politics and soon learned that he could be a very effective speaker. He became an early member of a new political party, the German Workers Party (which later became the National Socialist German Workers [Nazi] Party), and thus was formed the basis of his rise to power. Among the major points of the Nazi program was the unification of all German people, including those living outside of Germany, into a "Greater Germany"; the creation of a strong centralized state; and the denial of citizenship and the right to hold office in the new Germany to Jews. They were to be excluded from the press and ultimately to be expelled.

Hitler took over the leadership of the Nazi Party in 1921, and his philosophy became the party's philosophy. Essentially, his beliefs were the legacy of the Social Darwinists and other nineteenth-century writers on race superiority and ranking. He "saw all of life as an eternal struggle and the world as a jungle where the fittest survived and the strongest ruled" (Shirer [1959] 1988, 86). He conceived of a master race, called the Aryan, which was the creator of all science, arts, industry, and technology. It was the Aryans who laid the foundations for every great structure in human culture and were destined to be the masters of the world. The Aryans only lose when they pollute their blood with that of the lesser races. The Germans were the modern Aryans, the master race, and the Nazis forbade the intermarriage of any German with a member of an inferior race, especially the Jews and the Slavs. And of course Hitler would lead the Germans to their destiny.

In 1932 the Nazi Party was voted into power in Germany as the dominant party. That same year, the national army swore allegiance to its leader, Hitler, who now was strong enough to demand the chancellorship. By the time Hitler was appointed chancellor in January 1933, he was already the most powerful man in Germany. He began to promulgate policies that raised to its zenith the theory of the aristocracy of the German race. In doing so, he took the myth of superior and inferior races to a logical extreme, proclaiming the Germans as the "master race," destined to rule the world. From his point of view, it was also logical that inferior races, the destroyers of civilization, should be exterminated; and this he systematically began to accomplish.

What of those members of the German "race" who had physical deformities or other evidence of inferior traits? The lessons of the eugenic philosophy of the Americans and British were not lost on the Nazis.[4] Among the first legal acts of the Nazis was the passage of a Eugenic Sterilization Law in 1933, which made sterilization compulsory for all people who suffered from presumed hereditary defects. This included the feebleminded, the blind, drug and alcohol addicts, schizophrenics, epileptics, and those with physical deformities considered "grossly offensive." Within three years Germany had sterilized two hundred twenty-five thousand people in order to improve the German race (Kevles 1985, 116–117). In addition, the Third Reich provided loans and subsidies for increasing the reproductive activities of those couples considered of good genetic quality and established special homes for superior women to bear children for members of the S.S. (*Schutzstaffel* or blackshirts, the special police who came to dominate Nazi Germany).

By 1939 the German government took the next logical step—it began a program of euthanasia on some people in asylums who were either disabled or had mental diseases. Kevles claims that seventy thousand people were put to death under this program. The next step, as we are all aware, was the gas chambers.

Nazi race ideology contained the basic ingredients that we first saw appearing in the late eighteenth century and that constituted the racial worldview. The concept of exclusive groups having some biological and heritable essence that made them distinct from all others, the inequality and ranking of such groups as superior and inferior, the notion that each has peculiar behavioral characteristics, and the belief that differences among them cannot be bridged or transcended were constant elements of racial thought and provided the underbelly of Nazism. Hitler added to these beliefs the glorification of the state as the supreme power and the notion that "inferior races" could be exterminated without moral qualms. Indeed, the preservation of civilization, predicated on world dominance by the Aryan race, could only be achieved by eliminating the destructive forces of the inferior races.

The logical outcome of the race ideology first developed in the eighteenth century was an extraordinary principle, that human physical and cultural differences need not, and in fact could not, be tolerated. And the most horrific outcome of this history was that the rationalization processes of racial ideology had led some members of the human species to believe that they had the right to annihilate others.

The Western world retreated from the extremes of Nazism. But the populace at large in Europe may not have been prepared for the vast movements of Third World peoples into its homelands. The racial worldview still flourished in North America and captured the attention and consciousness of western Europeans when these nations experienced waves of African and Asian immigrants after the war. For the first time, some Europeans had to deal with large numbers of people in their territories who were both physically and culturally different from themselves. This has led to the rise of racism in countries where such sentiments had been muted or had never really found much of a berth. Because of limitations of space and subject matter, this volume cannot explore this subject, but we should note that hostile racial attitudes and extreme ethnocentrism in Europe are increasing, especially in the former colonial nations. Incidents of "race" hatred have been coming under increasing scrutiny by scholars as we continue to move into the twenty-first century.

THE CONTINUING INFLUENCE OF RACIAL IDEOLOGY IN SCIENCE

Despite opposition to Nazism, the racial worldview remains essential to the social system in the United States. There are still scientists, after two world wars and numerous conflicts in Asia and Africa, who have found it necessary, and often profitable, to buttress the racial worldview with documentary evidence. Beginning in 1969 with an article in the *Harvard Educational Review* by Arthur Jensen, as we have seen, some recent scholars, deeply steeped in the folk race tradition, have reinvigorated the arguments for the inequality of races. Jensen, William Shockley, Hans Eysenck, Philippe Rushton, and others have garnered considerable public attention with their arguments propounding innate intellectual differences between blacks and whites. Although often met with opposition or skepticism, they tour the universities, feed their ideas frequently to the media, publish many books and articles, and give numerous talks proselytizing their beliefs. The extent of their influence has not been fully studied, but it is no accident that their publications have appeared in the wake of the civil rights movement and the continuing revolutionary social changes begun in the 1960s.

One such work, *The Bell Curve* (1994), authored by Charles Murray and the late Richard Herrnstein, received extraordinary public attention, almost predictably appearing simultaneously with the rise of antagonism toward affirmative action programs. Although most of the book's chapters represent a heinous insult to poor whites, whom the authors consider to be of low intelligence, what the public and publicists retrieved from it has been its seeming confirmation of popular beliefs (stereotypes) about blacks and the new Hispanics. No new ideas or evidence was introduced by these authors to back up their conclusions; in fact, the book reads much like earlier works of the late nineteenth and early twentieth centuries, focused on hereditary causes of human behavior.

Race and class differences, Murray and Herrnstein argue, are caused primarily by genetic factors. The upper classes are blessed with high intelligence as expressed in IQ scores, which is why they are successful; the lower classes score lowest on IQ tests, which leads to lack of success. Moreover, blacks score lower than whites on average, which explains their low socioeconomic status. Since these features are innate and immutable, no form of compensatory training can bring such low intelligence people up to normal functioning.

All of these ideas have been contradicted by modern scholarly and scientific works, but the large number of critics of *The Bell Curve* never received the kind of media attention that the book itself attracted. Its political nature has been made very clear by its critics, and scientists and scholars throughout the nation have been distressed by its reception. It reached the top of the bestseller lists within months of its publication.

J. Philippe Rushton, a South African–bred psychologist teaching in Canada, added a new dimension to the ranking of races when his book, *Race, Evolution and Behavior*, was published in 1994. He posits the same social Darwinist arguments, but focuses more on race differences than on class. Rushton, who claims to be an evolutionist, expands the racial worldview a step beyond the relatively unsophisticated ideology of the last century. He traces his intellectual lineage from Galton and emphasizes his belief in hereditary causes of human behavior. Environmental influences are added on, he claims, but for most of his book they seem irrelevant. His interest is in documenting hereditary differences in behavior among Africans, Asians, and Europeans, the "core" races. But he changes the racial ranking in response to some contemporary circumstances, the appearance of the "model minorities." Asians are intellectually superior to Europeans, who are in turn superior to Africans.

Rushton proposes that there are over sixty anatomical and social variables on which Asians and Africans consistently aggregate at opposite ends, with Europeans ranking consistently in between. The behaviors that he asserts have a genetic or hereditary base, in addition to intelligence, include altruism; aggression; criminality; social, political, and religious attitudes; dominance behavior; emotional reactivity; sexual habits; sociability; violence; marital stability; personality; and law abidingness. It comes as no surprise that Africans rank lowest (or negatively) on all of the character traits that are seen as positive or have some acceptable value in Western cultures, while Asians are highest.

Rushton's most innovative contribution is his application of r-K Life History Theory to human societies. This is a speculation about the relationship among brain size, intelligence, and reproductive behavior as evolutionary strategies. The r strategy is found among men who have small brains, large sex organs, lots of children, and low investment in child care. This is a strategy of Africans. The K strategy is found among Asians, who have large brains, small penises, lower sexual activity, and fewer children, in whom they invest much time, attention, and resources. There is an inverse relationship between brain size and penis size.

Europeans have been fascinated with the sexuality of "savages" since the Middle Ages, long before they actually came into contact with Africans. (The wild Irish were "lewd, lustful, and lascivious," and so were the savages of the Americas.) During the sixteenth and seventeenth centuries, several English travelers had made references to the "large Propagators" of African men, which whetted the imaginations of many Europeans. It was immediately assumed that the large propagators made African men oversexed, sensuous, and lustful, and their nudity was evidence of uninhibited and unrestrained sexual behavior. It is Rushton's conclusion that Africans thus beget a lot of children to whom they give little care.

There are some strange correlations, along with some obvious inconsistencies, in the assumptions made here. First, this amounts to a new theory of women's fertility. with the logical implication that their fertility and reproductive activities depend on the size of their mates' sex organs. But Rushton provides no evidence of a correlation between the size of men's penises and the number of children that a woman bears. This theory totally ignores variations in women's fertility as well as well-known cultural reasons for having few or many children. Moreover, the theory flounders in the light of some obviously contradictory and incontrovertible facts. *The most reproductively successful population in the world are the Chinese.* Early in the twentieth century, they had one of the highest fertility rates in the world. They got to number more than 1.5 billion people with small penises and presumably little interest in sex!

For his ethnographic information on African societies, Rushton uses one book, *Race,* published in 1974 by John R. Baker, a retired professor of biology whose specialty was the structure of the cell. Baker states in his chapters on the "Negrids" that he acquired all of his ethnographic information from seven nineteenth-century explorers whom he regards as "unprejudiced and reliable" witnesses. Worst of all, Rushton cites Freud as an authority on African children. He accepts without question the myths that they are raised more permissively than Asian and European children, and that is why they are so uninhibited and unrestrained in their sexuality. Freud held that African children are toilet-trained later and thus lack self-discipline. Although there are hundreds of anthropologists who have done ethnographic research in Africa and hundreds of historians who have published remarkable works in African history, not one was referenced in this work. It is truly ironical that the best educated immigrants now coming to the United States and England are Africans!

There is no better example of the social construction of races than Rushton's triadic scheme. What is even more extraordinary about his activities is that he sent thirty-five thousand free copies of an abridged edition of his book to scholars around the world, a level of proselytizing rarely found in the world of scholarship.

In 2004 biologist Vincent Sarich and journalist Frank Miele produced the latest of the volumes by race scientists, *Race: The Reality of Human Differences.* It is curiously a recapitulation of the Rushton book, but attempts to emphasize the theme that Africans have always been denigrated throughout human history. The authors use the same studies on IQ tests to demonstrate their belief in the inferiority of blacks and the same sources for their assertions about the existence of "race" in history. The book distorts the work of classicist Frank Snowden, who argued that there was no such thing as race or racial discrimination in the ancient world. Snowden also warned against the "tendency to read modern racial concepts into ancient documents and to see color prejudice where none existed" (Snowden 1983, 63–64). The authors also follow Rushton in referring to Bernard Lewis, the only historian of the Middle East to argue that black Africans were looked down upon by Muslim Arabs. I have shown that none of the well-known historians of the Middle East or Islam concur with Lewis on this point (see Smedley 2006). As to the presence of the idea of race in other indigenous societies, chapter 11 references some of the latest studies by modern scholars who are beginning to address this question.

Throughout the twentieth century, biological anthropologists, geneticists, human biologists, and other scientists have been making enormous progress in their studies of human heredity and variability. Their new discoveries have made it necessary and more productive to reconceptualize human physical variability without the classifications of "race." We turn to this transformation in scientific knowledge and understanding in the next chapter.

NOTES

1. So much has recently been published on intelligence tests that even a brief review would be beyond the scope of this work. Fincher 1976 has a good summary of the history, but see also Davenport 1929; Dobzhansky 1973; Fancher 1985; Kagan 1982; Lewontin 1970; Mensh and Mensh 1991; Sanday 1972; Spuhler and Lindzey 1967; and Wober 1971. This brief discussion notes only some of the high points. For a review of the many new complex psychological approaches to understanding intelligence, see Howe 1997 and Sternberg and Pretz 2005.

2. Allen Chase observes: "Few documents now available to scholars offer more devastating testimony to the fact that all so-called IQ tests yet devised are actually measurements of one's cultural experiences, and not of one's inborn or genetic mental endowment, than the different scales of the Army mental tests" (1980, 244). He gives many examples of some of the questions in the tests that clearly reflect cultural learning.

3. For a history of the eugenics movement, which continues to attract a substantial albeit diminishing group of adherents, see Haller 1963; Kevles 1985; Ludmerer 1969; and Pickens 1968.

4. German geneticists and eugenicists praised their American counterparts for providing the models that they adopted for their own laws and policies. One American eugenicist, Harry Laughlin, then director of the Eugenics Record Office at Cold Spring Harbor, was even given an honorary degree by the University of Heidelberg (see Kevles 1985, 118).

CHAPTER 13

Changing Perspectives on Human Variation in Science

During the first half of the twentieth century, certain sectors of the scientific community began to react with skepticism to the concept of race and its ideological themes. Among many scholars, race was transformed and limited in its conceptualization to biogenetic features of human groups, and new scientific definitions of *race* were introduced. Scholars made efforts to eliminate language and cultural features, that is, to remove those elements in the concept that referred to moral, intellectual, and psychological or "mental" characteristics. The success of these attempts in transmitting this perspective to other scholars and the wider public was limited. But their failure had more to do with the strength of the racial worldview in the collective consciousness and the timing of their appearance than with the scholars involved.

This history demonstrates not only the expanding influence of science but the degree to which advances in science often entail struggles between the power of popular beliefs and the researchers' need for neutrality and objectivity in acquiring and assessing new information. It was largely in the field of anthropology that accelerating advances in knowledge, changes in opinion, and the drive for objectivity in understanding and evaluating human differences were most dramatically focused. But other fields, including psychology and sociology, later reflected a similar trajectory of development.

This chapter discusses the emergence of new scientific positions on race that conflicted with older views, and the influences of a new liberal perspective in the educational establishment. Historians and social scientists began to recognize the separate social reality and functions of race. And experts in the biological sciences began to question its meaning and usefulness to science.

This does not mean that there was less interest in the subject of human biophysical variation. On the contrary, the discovery of the structure of the genetic code (DNA) has unveiled the complexity of human heredity and generated infinite new scientific queries about our diversity. A major question raised by the new data is whether the homogenization of individuals into racial categories is the best vehicle for comprehending this diversity. Some experts found the idea of race, even when used in a purely biological sense, inadequate for the task. In this chapter I explore further sources of dissatisfaction with the use of the term *race*, delineate some of the controversy over its use, and briefly outline new scientific understandings and perspectives on human variation that contradict the components of folk ideology. I then speculate on some of the implications of the trend away from the term *race* in science.

THE DECLINE OF THE IDEA OF RACE AS BIOLOGY IN SCIENCE

In the growing field of anthropology, as early as the 1890s there was some discomfort with the term *race* when used to refer to human populations. Paul Topinard exemplified this trend. The first to write a general text on anthropology, in 1876 he formulated one of the earliest and most widely used definitions of the science: "the branch of natural history which treats of man and the races of man" (Haddon [1934] 1959, 2). In 1891, however, he questioned the use of the term *race*, especially for intracontinental populations where more or less random matings of heterogeneous peoples had confused lines of descent. He also noted that "the word 'race' is hardly used by naturalists when speaking of wild animals and plants. They prefer the term 'variety,' which leaves unsettled the question of permanence, the condition sine qua non for race" (Count 1950, 175). Although he still conceded the possible usefulness of the term for large general divisions of mankind, he maintained that "race is only a subjective notion" (176). Topinard was thus early on questioning one of the central components in the meaning of race, the notion that traits are permanent and immutable, but he carried his argument no further, perhaps because of the overwhelming strength of the racial worldview. Some of Topinard's learned contemporaries deplored the various associations of the term with language or linguistic groups, as in the case of "Aryan," "Hebrew," or "Latin." They also criticized as unscientific what they saw as the stereotyping of group behavior.

Perhaps it was the imprecision of definition, the arbitrariness of classificatory schemes, or the sheer absurdity of trying to establish a scientific definition for an ideological conception of exclusiveness that did not exist empirically. In any case, some individual scientists were galvanized to dispute either the use of the term *race* or the concept itself. As early as 1900, the French anthropologist Joseph Deniker indicated objections to the use of the term among scientists because it had not been demonstrated that human groups represented subdivisions of the species in the same manner as other zoological forms.

In April 1936, an editorial appeared in *Nature* magazine under the title "The Delusion of Race." Among other things, the anonymous author criticized the definitions of race proposed by a committee of the Royal Anthropological Institute and the Institute of Sociology, which were intended to serve as guidelines for the general public. The definitions themselves contained the latest scientific information, identifying races as breeding populations, each with distinguishable genetic characteristics. However, the author went on to say:

> In so far as the races of man are concerned, these definitions, far from being generalisations from concrete realities and empirical, are no more than logical concepts, postulated for purposes of classification and investigation. In face of the actual facts of the distribution of physical characters among the population groups of the world, as they exist at the present moment, *race is a pure abstraction*. The races or types into which the anthropologist groups the varieties of Homo sapiens are ideal types built up to explain congeries of characters in individuals and groups derivative from a variety of strains, in some sort of a phylogeny. Man seems to be almost infinitely variable within a wide range, and since at least upper Palaeolithic times in the course of world-wide migration has interbred freely, with the result that the ideal types of anthropological classification, if they ever existed at all in any degree of purity, have become a matter of faith rather than of evidence. Characters on which classifications have been based are found everywhere to overlap, and both individual and population group bear witness to their inextricably mixed descent ("Delusion of Race" 1936, 636).

The author closed the editorial with the statement that the significance attached to race is a delusion.

That same year, Julian Huxley and Alfred C. Haddon published *We Europeans*, essentially a book on *race*, a term they viewed as taxonomically interchangeable with *subspecies*. Yet in it they asserted that "the existence of . . . human sub-species is purely hypothetical. Nowhere does a human group now exist which corresponds closely to a systematic sub-species in animals. . . . The essential reality of the existing situation . . . is not the hypothetical sub-species of race, but the mixed ethnic groups which can never be genetically purified into their original components" (quoted in Montagu 1969, 17). It was from this source, Ashley Montagu informs us, that he adopted the term *ethnic group*. In 1941, Montagu presented a now famous lecture, "On the Meaninglessness of the Anthropological Conception of Race" (reprinted in Montagu 1969). Since then he has consistently argued that race is a myth, "the Phlogiston of our time" (xii).

Montagu has been joined in his abnegation of the race concept in science by others who believe that it is outmoded or has lost its usefulness for describing human physical variability. They agree with Montagu that "the very notion of 'race' is antithetical to the study of population genetics, for the former traditionally deals with fixed clear-cut differences, and the latter with fluid or fluctuating differences" (Montagu 1969, 19). Frank Livingstone, in the article "On the Non-Existence of Human Races" (1969; first published in *Current Anthropology* in 1962) pointed out that there is a fundamental incompatibility between the idea of race and natural selection, which is the basic determinant of biological variation. One cannot study the causes of physical variations in the human population and still retain a belief in races, taken as fixed, permanent forms based on nonadaptive traits.

The positions taken by these scholars helped to generate a sprightly debate in the mid-twentieth century between those who would retain the use of the term and those who would eliminate it. The contemporary record showed enormous ambiguity on the matter of race and little common agreement among experts on a definition, the criteria for identifying "race," or the number of races that exist among the human species. In some circles, the debate continues (see below).

PHYSICAL ANTHROPOLOGY AND ATTEMPTS TO TRANSFORM THE MEANING OF RACE

Impetus was given to changing the meaning of race in anthropology by Franz Boas, then the most influential leader of the field in America. Boas and his colleagues began to promote the idea that *race* was (or should be) a taxonomic term referring to human groups based solely on physical and morphological characteristics. The distinctive physical traits of different races, it was argued, had not been demonstrated to be intrinsically related to a group's language, religion, customs, morals, traditions, art, laws, knowledge, or beliefs. Thus anthropologists sought to separate the physical features of diverse humankind (calling the resulting clusters "races") from language and culture, which is learned behavior. Their success would have meant a radical transformation of the meaning of race for, as shown in previous chapters, physical and cultural-behavioral elements had been cognitively and integrally fused in the term from its origin.

Boas's most significant contribution to the crystallization of this view of race stems from his anthropometric studies of children and adults. Following the then customary activities of his discipline, Boas conducted anthropometric studies on schoolchildren in Massachusetts, California, New York, New Jersey, and Puerto Rico. He studied the children of Italian and Jewish immigrants, the offspring of French Italian "mixed" marriages, Native Americans, "half-blood Indians," and mulattoes, among others. His concerns were with mental and physical growth patterns and the influences of heredity and environment on growth. What he discovered startled the scientific and intellectual communities and dislodged many of the basic assumptions of anthropometry.

Boas found that children of immigrants in a single population varied significantly from their parents in anthropometric measurements; that head form (the cephalic index) could change in one generation from round heads to long heads; and that stature, facial width, and a number of other features thought to have been fixed and unvarying due to heredity underwent sometimes drastic changes in different environments (1910–1913, 1912). These findings challenged and eventually undercut the notion of fixity and permanence of physical racial characteristics as measured by anthropometric techniques and demonstrated the plasticity of the human skeleton. Boas reintroduced the importance of environmental influences, particularly nutrition and climate, as major determinants of the final expression of many physical traits. Under the influence of Social Darwinists, "nature" or biological inheritance, as we have seen, had been promoted over "nurture" as the causative agent of human racial potential. By insisting on the notion of a rigid and unalterable nature, race thinking had hitherto precluded consideration of modifications of physical characteristics through responses to environmental forces.

Boas's findings also helped to demote the concept of "averages" as a way of describing whole populations (1940, 176), thereby undercutting much of the reified typological approach to racial identification. His works and those of his students and colleagues paved the way for the eventual recognition of the limits to the meaning and interpretation of anthropometric data as a measure of race.[1] Although not all scholars may have been fully aware of it then, such findings were also an early first step challenging certain components of the folk idea of race.

Boas was the undisputed leader of American anthropology for half a century. His students and all those influenced by the "Boasian milieu" advocated the principle of the separation of race (biology) from language and culture as one of the fundamental pillars of American anthropology. The social and historical context in which this principle proliferated helps us to comprehend the importance of this attempt to construct a new, purely biological, meaning of race.

At the time of Boas's initiation into the field of anthropology, its practitioners had begun focusing much of their attention on "primitive races" in attempts to comprehend their customs, beliefs, and practices and the workings of their minds. The racial worldview dominated virtually all scholarly attitudes toward non-Europeans, and efforts were geared to ascertaining the fundamental ("racial") nature of different groups. It was widely assumed that cognitive processes differed among the "lower" races, whose mental development was presumed to be stultified.

In the context of a society pervaded by virulent racism, Franz Boas and his students had begun their field research and publications, many of which expressed antagonism to all forms of racism. Much of Boas's own attitude was summed up in an early book, *The Mind of Primitive Man* ([1911] 1963), which laid the philosophical groundwork for the even more famous social critiques of some of his most eminent students, including Ruth Benedict, Margaret Mead, Melville Herskovits, and Otto Klineberg.

As Leslie Spier (another of Boas's students) has claimed, several of the themes of this book are now axiomatic in anthropology. He identifies them as follows: (1) There is no such phenomenon as hereditary racial purity; (2) races are not stable, immutable entities, but undergo changes due to domestication, selection, mutation, and other environmental influences; (3) "the average differences in physical traits between races is small in contrast to the great overlapping of range and duplication of types among them"; (4) there is no evidence that any race is "incapable of participating in any culture or even in creating it"; (5) "there is no identity of race, language, and culture such that physical heredity can be credited with the formulation of languages and the achievements of civilizations"; and finally, (6) some groups "are not primitive by reason of hereditary inferiority but because the circumstances of their life were more static than those of civilized men, the differences being products of their variant history and traditional equipment" (Spier 1959, 147).[2]

Major influences on Boas and his contemporaries and students were the disturbing circumstances surrounding the growth of fascism under Hitler and the horror of extreme racism manifested before and during World War II. Boas grew up in Germany at a time when European race ideas were still evolving. Although he was in America and teaching at Clark University by 1888 (he later moved to Columbia), as a Jew he was well aware of developing racial thinking in Germany and of the relationship of anti-Semitism to American race ideology and its many supporters in the United States.

When Europeans began to treat one another as subhuman in much the same manner as they had treated non-Europeans and to rationalize brutality in the name of racial purity or racial inferiority, reaction against ideas of race and racism was inevitable. Boas and his students were part of that reaction, projecting a scientific and social philosophy that opposed and refuted Nazi race ideology. Boas and his students seemed unaware of the history of race as a folk concept that had become assimilated to science. We have seen in this volume that at no time in the history of its use in referring to human beings was the term *race* reserved for groups based solely on their biophysical characteristics. From the start it was a cultural construct composed of social values and beliefs synergistically related in a comprehensive worldview and integral to the cognitive perceptions that Europeans and white Americans had of themselves and the rest of the world. The question then arises: *How does science extricate a singular component from a total folk worldview and transform it into the realm of objective, neutral science?*

The attempt in the early twentieth century to transform the meaning of race, even if only in the scientific lexicon, was bound to have limited success, perhaps in part because the premises were too radical and ahead of their time. In the wider society, the folk sense of race and race differences was far too deeply ingrained in the American psyche and culture. Despite the well-intentioned efforts of anthropologists, the fundamental folk belief in the reality of race persisted. Inevitably, there was a paradox not perceivable in academic circles at the time. To argue, as the Boasians did, that science had not proved that the races were unequal in their abilities, intellectual and otherwise, was to argue a contradiction in terms. *The central meaning of race has from its origin historically been that of inherently unequal human groups.* In terms of folk understandings and attitudes, to claim that races were equal was tantamount to transforming black into white. Since American society had done everything possible to preserve inequality between blacks and whites, it was hardly ready for such a radical transmutation.

There is another irony in the Boasians' attempts to modify the meaning of race. Houston Stewart Chamberlain and Madison Grant, among others, were engaged in the same enterprise. They wanted to separate physical characteristics from their linkage with culture and language. But they had a quite different perspective and obviously different purposes. Adhering to firmly established racial hierarchies, which had no referents in the real world, both came to believe that race was a matter of innate "inner essences" and not necessarily reflected in outward physical characteristics. Thus Grant argued that Nordics need not be tall, blond, blue-eyed, and pale. Some true Nordics are short with brown eyes and hair and olive skins, clearly a belief that later accommodated Italian fascists. But their Nordicism, and thus their racial superiority, was manifest in other forms—in their intellectual prowess, physical vigor, love of liberty, and domineering temperament (Gossett 1965). These proponents of racial superiority were operating with an understanding of race and race differences that was closer in many respects to its original late-eighteenth-century meaning than to that of the Boasians. Their concept of racial divisions made it possible for them to engage in the arbitrary assignment of race status, irrespective of biophysical realities. In this matter, they took the concept of race to its logical end, rendering it as a true political device justifying one group's domination of others.

The Boasians were combating another very powerful factor: the conservative scientific establishment that persisted in attempts to discover measurable ways of differentiating races. As we saw earlier, many scientists turned to the measuring of "intelligence" to document established beliefs about racial superiority and inferiority. Despite some anomalies that were largely ignored, IQ tests showed superior performance by whites.[3] Black inferiority thus seemed verified, and the results were widely publicized.

The entire society in the early twentieth century was permeated with such a strong sense of racial differences that Jim Crow laws, and the social customs that set the stage for them, were now nearly ubiquitous (Bennett 1964, 1975; Woodward 1974). Segregated residential areas, discriminatory institutions, and economic practices in the North matched the emergent "separate but equal" conditions of the South. Laws, customs, and social practices aimed at maintaining the separateness and exclusiveness that the term *race* conveyed. Efforts to preserve society's servile roles for blacks were largely successful in that they kept the vast majority underemployed and undereducated.

Native Americans continued to be pushed back onto reservations, where the tragic problems of tuberculosis, alcoholism, lack of education and opportunity, and especially lack of jobs intensified and exacerbated cultural idiosyncrasies. In both groups crime, alcohol, hopelessness, despair, and lassitude were often the only culturally available options. These reactions and the behavior associated with them became part of public stereotypes. It should come as no surprise that American scientists, like the rest of the population, were conditioned to a worldview that seemed to be constantly reaffirmed by the very conditions of society itself. Under the circumstances, the segregation of racial populations in national and community life was seen as natural and desirable.

POPULATION GENETICS

Between 1930 and 1950, the fundamental tenets of population genetics were established and outlined in such publications as Theodosius Dobzhansky's

Genetics and the Origin of Species ([1937] 1982). Central to these tenets was the concept of the gene pool, all the genes and allelic variations extant in a given population.[4] Populations, which were the unit of study and analysis, were defined in terms of breeding behavior. In the laboratory, plant and animal populations could be clearly delineated, because what constituted a breeding population was a consequence of artificial intervention. Although it was obvious that human breeding habits could not be so rigidly controlled, the gene pool model was still thought to be scientifically valid when applied to humans, especially where isolating mechanisms (such as geographic barriers) could be identified.

The basic features that came under examination in the study of population genetics were a variety of genetic elements found in the blood. After the discovery of the ABO blood group system, many other investigations of human blood group patterns were undertaken. This work, showing how populations could be identified by the frequencies of ABO alleles as manifest in the phenotypes, was the first suggestion that a new and more scientific way of identifying racial populations was now possible.

By the middle of the twentieth century, the structure of genetic material (DNA) in the cell nucleus had been identified, and the mode of inheritance for numerous allelic variations in certain traits had been calculated mathematically. Coincident with the new technology, the language of racial definitions in science became the quantitative theorems of population genetics (i.e., expressing population differences in terms of the proportions of genetic expressions of given traits). As a result, the morphological and typological conceptions of race were supplemented (some would say replaced) in the mid-twentieth century by a new genetic conception of race. Race differences were thus conceptualized in the scientific community as differences in the relative frequencies of hereditary traits found in all populations.

Subsequently there appeared the first attempts at worldwide or regional classifications of racial populations using the blood groups, which were seen as objective, clear-cut, measurable ways of classifying human groups. However, a number of problems beset such attempts at classification. From the standpoint of racial taxonomy, the major problem was that the blood-group patterns did not correlate with the conventional racial classifications, except in very gross and imprecise ways.[5]

After the 1950s, a more dynamic, evolutionary perspective surfaced, one of whose major tenets was that the breeding population represented the primary unit of analysis for evolutionary change (Thieme 1952). The theory was that each breeding population undergoes adaptation to a given set of environmental circumstances or constraints. The selection pressures of each environment occasion the manifestation of those traits (or allelic variations) that best promote group survival and reproduction. From the standpoint of evolutionary theory, then, races could be interpreted as products of the adaptive interaction of biogenetic systems within their particular environmental contexts. Over time, changes in the environment would introduce new selection pressures. Along with other mechanisms of change such as gene drift, mutations, and differential fertility, these would indirectly help bring about changes in the gene pool. Thus, races were seen as episodes in the evolutionary process, displaying characteristics subject to modification over long periods of time (Hulse 1962). This was a new way of looking at biophysical variation among human groups, as dynamic and changeable entities rather than as static, fixed categories.

Among the problems with the concept of races as breeding populations that biologists and physical anthropologists themselves have recognized is the question of what constitutes a breeding population.[6] What level of fertile endogamous marriage (or matings) must be maintained in order for scientists to agree to construe a group as a breeding population? Are all breeding populations races?

There were other problems having to do with the failure of the genetic model to accord with the conventional physical features used to identify races. Traits whose genetic bases are known do not manifest variations concordantly so that they cluster in a manner that makes for clear delineation of different groups (Boyd 1971, 221; Goodman n.d.; Hiernaux [1964] 1969, 43). Instead, they display one of the fundamental Mendelian laws, that of independent assortment. This means that people who are grouped together on the basis of one or two genetic traits would have to be grouped very differently on the basis of other traits. The distribution of the ABO system does not correspond on a worldwide or regional basis with the frequency distribution of MNS or the Rhesus system, and none of these correspond with the distribution of skin color or hair texture or body size. From this, we can infer that some selection of traits for relevance in the classification process would be necessary. The question then becomes, which traits are taxonomically relevant? To this date, scientists know comparatively little about the mode of inheritance of complex polymorphic traits (determined by more than a single gene or position on the DNA molecule) such as skin color, hair form, nose shape, and so forth. But these are the observable features used popularly and traditionally to identify folk races.

Most experts now feel that the older typological race concept, with each member conforming more or less to an ideal, has been totally discredited

(Bennett 1969; Birdsell 1972; Dobzhansky 1973). Some of the developments have helped to foster an orientation toward viewing human physical variations in terms of their adaptive significance or other evolutionary processes. They have also tended to deflect interest away from traditional racial studies and toward a more dynamic and eclectic comprehension of human variability, both individual and group.

Attempted genetic constructions of race have so far had little impact on contemporary social uses and beliefs about race differences in ordinary affairs. Indeed, for some experts and laypersons the genetic concept of race tends to preserve certain components of race ideology. The statistical manipulations not only continue to provide scientific legitimacy to the search for racial differences, but tend to magnify the nature of whatever differences are found.

The genetic information fails to take into consideration the fact that race is a way of looking at the world that has deep and tangled historical roots. It functioned, and continues to function, to the benefit of particular individuals and groups. The lay understanding of race, however hesitant, unarticulated, and diffuse, continues as a more accurate reflection of the sociohistorical meaning of race than that of modern science. The ideological components persist in varying strengths as part of a fixed conception of the world. What has declined in the United States since the 1960s has been the magnitude and virulence of racism—the strength with which racism's ideological components are played out. The degree of subscription to the elements of race has also been declining, as the subject matter of race waxes and wanes in the public eye. It is popular to protest against racism; it is even more common to deny its existence, primarily because we fail to understand its historical (and contemporary) meaning.

IS THERE A GENETIC BASIS FOR RACE?

Some contemporary geneticists believe that racial classifications based in geography are still useful, particularly for biomedical research (Risch et al. 2002; Foster and Sharp 2002). Using new technologies and computer programs and a huge, worldwide database, researchers have been able to discern finite numbers of clusters of DNA that accord with geographic regions (Bolnick 2008; Feldman and Lewontin 2008). These clusters, whether they are three, or five, or six, or more are perceived as geographic races, with the assumption that they have certain genetic alleles in common. Although it is not known exactly how they work, different frequencies of identified genetic alleles on different continents vary among the major populations. These continental differences have suggested to some researchers that there are at least three major racial divisions, Africans, Europeans, and Asians (some programs can show five, six, or more). The problem is that not all individuals have the genetic features (haplotypes) that correspond to their continental origins.

Most geneticists and biological anthropologists now agree with the idea that human races, in any kind of biological sense, do not really exist (Bolnick 2008; Dupre 2008). Human variation, it is argued, is extraordinarily complex, and there is much greater variation within a population than between populations. Most traits are not inherited in discrete units, but their ranges of expression are continuous and overlapping from one population to another. Virtually no traits can be scientifically utilized in an absolute way to distinguish separate populations, especially where there is any degree of propinquity (Bolnick 2008; Graves 2001). Even the frequencies of independently assorted genetic traits are discordant, and there are no genetic traits that are exclusive to one race.

Moreover, unlike other animal species that manifest geographic variation in localized populations, humankind undergoes adaptation within a cultural context. Cultural, or learned, factors not only influence the nature of the selective forces that affect the survival of certain genetic features, but also affect human mating and reproductive habits. Since the emergence at least of sapiens forms, mating customs have ceased to be random. The biological expressions of genetic transmission have been heavily imprinted by migration and social preferences and taboos. The so-called human races are thus not clear-cut, homogeneous, or uniform groupings bounded by absolute, natural lines of demarcation.

Another powerful argument against the use of the term *race* in science is that the effort to establish racial classifications and to fit all human populations into one or another category obscures and/or distorts the reality of biophysical variation, so that it is useless for the study of human evolution. For one thing, racial classifications as an end in themselves cannot provide us with explanations of how such variations originated. And the very act of attempting to compress all peoples into limited categories tends to prevent full recognition and comprehension of existing variability; that is, the ranges and gradations of specific physical features. Even in the computer-based clusters, some people appear in more than one "race." In addition, it is argued, the race concept in biology is a static one, suited to rigid typological thinking but not to modern understanding of the dynamics of genetic processes or the evolutionary significance of human diversity. Even if geneticists could agree on identifying these major clusters of peoples as genetic races, this would neither obviate nor explain the racial ideology by which we live.

THE ECOLOGICAL PERSPECTIVE: HUMAN VARIATIONS AS PRODUCTS OF ADAPTATION

One of the chief developments associated with population genetics has been the recognition of the importance of natural selection in the production of physical variation. This presupposes a dynamic process by which a population interacts with and adapts to its environment through gradual physiological changes. By the 1960s, a new mode of interpreting variations, on the basis of the adaptive significance of their expression, had come into vogue. The demonstration that many biophysical traits, once thought adaptively neutral, are quite probably the consequences of natural selection operating on existing variations produced by bisexual reproduction and mutations, was a major stimulus to research in human ecology. The basic premise is that human groups, like all other animal forms, are subject to pressures from the natural elements of their environments. In the process of adapting to such forces as climate (particularly temperature and rainfall), prevalence of diseases, food supply, and land elevation, populations experience minute changes in phenotypic and genetic makeup, some of which permit them greater reproductive, and therefore adaptive, success. The more varied the genes in the population, the greater the possibility that some individuals will survive and reproduce, passing on those variations that made them more adaptable.

For example, researchers have shown that skin color variations correspond to temperature and amount of sunlight, a fact that ancient societies well understood. Researchers have also demonstrated an association between body size and shape and habitation of certain regions of the world. Once scientists had connected the sickle-cell trait to natural selection, because in its heterozygous form it confers resistance to malaria, other adaptive linkages have been sought. Physiological adaptation to cold temperatures in the form of increased vasodilation and/or vasoconstriction, additional layers of body fat, and higher metabolic rates has been shown to be adaptively significant among Eskimos, native Australians, and Norwegians. Theoretical speculations have been offered about the adaptive significance of pygmy body size in a tropical forest environment or thin, linear body form in a hot desert environment.

Through DNA mapping techniques, researchers have plotted immunological responses that correspond to the prevalence of specific disease organisms. Speculations about the adaptive advantage of variations in hair form, nose shape, and stature have stimulated wide-ranging research on the possible adaptive aspects of other physical characteristics. Scientists today focus not so much on the clustering of traits that might distinguish racial populations as on specific genetic features and their phenotypic manifestations in given ecological settings. These scholars are finding that race (and certainly the establishing of racial taxonomies) is no longer of any relevance in these studies because the incidences of traits studied cut across population boundaries and may in fact span several of the conventional races. The variations are independent of other genetic traits but correspond to the pressures or influences of geographic, climatological, topographical, and pathological disease phenomena (Templeton 1998).

For many scholars, then, the manifestation of biophysical diversity in *Homo sapiens* is expressed most accurately in the form of clines (Brace 1964; Brues 1977; Livingstone 1969; Marks 1995). *Clines* are variations in the intensity of expressions of known hereditary traits over wide geographic regions. Skin color represents a prime example of such a cline, since its gradations are continuous and can be plotted on a map showing its correspondence to latitude and temperature variations. Human skin color variability reflects the adaptive responses of a relatively hairless primate to the forces of natural selection.

The proponents of evolutionary explanations, whose theories tend to be directional and adaptive, have detractors among some recent scholars, who propose an alternative theory. For them, much, if not most, of human biophysical variation is not so much a product of natural selection as of random mutations, accidents, and other stochastic processes not necessarily related to adaptation. They use simulated models and computer techniques to demonstrate their non-Darwinian theories. These proposed nonadaptive evolutionary processes are thought to explain much minor variability in fairly delimited populations.

What is significant is that the research of both groups can and does proceed without reference to the term *race*. "Breeding unit" or some similar concept is used to describe populations in which certain limited variations with respect to specific traits are found, such as hereditary baldness. Other traits, examined independently of social or political boundaries, can be studied in situational contexts. Race classifications neither explain nor describe the nature or significance of this variability.

From these developments and many others, it is possible to speculate that the disintegration of the components of the idea of race in American intellectual life may have already begun. The influences of liberal (and liberated) anthropological ideas have penetrated many aspects of American culture with unanticipated, and as yet uninvestigated, consequences. These great advances in science have, perhaps inadvertently, challenged the constituent components of race ideology and set in motion a possible irreversible trend in new thinking about human differences. We will take a look at some other factors, social and historical, responsible for this in chapter 14.

THE GENETIC CONCEPTION OF HUMAN VARIATION

In the 1970s, geneticists looking at a selected number of genes (parts of DNA) discovered that about 94 percent of all human variation occurs within those geographical groups that we call races (Lewontin 1972; Nei and Roychoudhury 1972, 1974). Only a minor amount of variation in genetic traits, about 7–10 percent, separates large populations (i.e., the major "racial" groups:, Africans, Asians, and Europeans), and this has proved neither constant nor significant. However, in 2001 the entire human genome was sequenced, and an even more outstanding discovery was made, that humans are genetically 99.9 percent alike. Any two humans differ from one another by about one-tenth of 1 percent of their genes. Those who are concerned with demarcating race differences focus on this one-tenth of 1 percent. This is the source of the "large" disparities they see between races.

The human genome (all of the genes in our bodies) is composed of twenty-three sets of chromosomes composed of a chemical abbreviated as DNA. Within the DNA are smaller elements comprising four nucleotides, or bases, that occur in pairs and are linked together in a twisted ladder form. Geneticists speculate that there are three billion pairs of these bases. These cluster together in various numbers and patterns along the strings of DNA, and the resulting units are what we call genes, which average about three thousand base pairs long. High-powered computers can stretch out this material so that scientists can "read" the genetic code. Scientists estimate that there are about thirty thousand genes, but most genes have alleles (different variations), so that they can be expressed in multiple ways. Changes or mutations can occur to a gene at any place on the DNA; some of the changes may be beneficial, others deleterious.

The genotype of every individual is unique, except for identical twins. People who are closely related have genotypes that are more similar to one another. People who are from geographic areas thousands of miles away tend to have greater differences among their genomes. However, differences are not found in the genes, which we all share, but in the allelic variations. No populations have alleles shared by everyone in that population exclusively. All human groups share some alleles with their neighbors, not only because of descent from common ancestors, but because humans have always mated with their neighbors.

And these allelic variations occur in peoples over a wide geographic area as clines, gradations in their expressions from one extreme to another.

The real value of genetics research has not been attempts to identify biological races, but to acquire knowledge about the relationship of genes to heritable diseases and to trace the histories and relationships of human groups over time. What little has been learned so far is that there are variations in the susceptibilities to diseases, and this is mostly a problem of individual differences. Diseases and other abnormal or deleterious conditions are not exclusive to any group, although mutations and other evolutionary changes occur within delimited populations. Once a trait or propensity becomes hereditary within a population, it can spread easily from one population to another merely by individuals who carry the trait mating and reproducing outside of the group. None of this has to do with "biological" races.

MONOGENY RECONSIDERED: THE NONPROBLEM OF RACE MIXTURE

Another transformation in scientific attitudes toward race appears even more profound and subtle and has proceeded in tandem with these developments. In an article in *Science* magazine in 1973, William Provine revealed a change in attitude among British and American scientists on the subject of race mixture. Tracing briefly some of the attitudes about interracial mating that we have already explored, Provine noted that early in the twentieth century, geneticists such as Charles Davenport and Edward East, continuing the polygenist views of the late nineteenth century, argued against race crossing. These men felt that mixture between two very different races, such as blacks and whites, produced disharmonies in hybrids of "physical, mental and temperamental qualities" and diminished the qualities of the superior race. Two other scientists, Paul Popenoe and Roswell Johnson, who wrote a widely used textbook on eugenics, "suggested that racial antipathy was a biological mechanism to protect races from miscegenation" (Provine 1973, 791). Provine observed that "published opposition from geneticists and other biologists to these arguments on race crossing was nonexistent before 1924" (792).

In the mid-1930s, Provine continued, the attitude of geneticists changed from condemnation of race mixture to a position of agnosticism, indifference, or neutrality. Yet another shift in thinking occurred during World War II. Scholarly literature following this period almost unanimously expressed the view that race mixture was harmless or possibly even beneficial to the species. This reversal in attitude, Provine notes, was accompanied by little new scientific data. He feels that the change was due to the revulsion that scientists and other educated people had against Nazi race theories and their consequences. With this transformation, the species-level (or polygenetic) sense of differences seems to have been eliminated from the concept of race in science. Logically, it should also challenge the ideological component of exclusiveness in the folk race idea.

NOTES

1. Techniques of anthropometry to obtain average or mean figures on the human body continue today, but are no longer perceived as the basis for identifying races. Measurements are used for constructing seats in airplanes, cars, buses, etc., where such configurations are useful.

2. Mark Haller 1963 (145) and Dwight Hoover 1976 (233) both underscore the fact that Boas was by no means oblivious to the racial conditioning of his time and place. He did not deny the inequality of mental traits among individuals and races and thought that the Negro's physical traits were indicative of his greater degree of primitiveness. In the late nineteenth century, Boas expressed the view that races could possibly deteriorate due to admixture, but there is no evidence that he continued with this view after the second decade of the twentieth century (see Stocking 1968). See also Baker 1998, who has explored the racial attitudes of some of the early anthropologists.

3. The most obvious anomaly was the differential in performance between white students from northern states and whites from the South, where support for education was much lower. Northern whites have been found to be more "intelligent" based on their IQ scores than southern whites on all national tests. This result should have suggested environmental determinants of test performance, but such an explanation was generally ignored. See Chase 1980, chaps. 18–22.

4. *Alleles* are defined as variations in the phenotypic expression of single gene traits.

5. For discussion of these problems see Boyd 1971, Cavalli-Sforza and Bodmer 1971, Hiernaux [1964] 1969, and Morris 1971, among others.

6. Goodman n.d., Keita 1993b, and Marks 1995 have addressed some of the problems of the continuance of "racial" thinking among biological anthropologists. See also Keita and Kittles 1997.

CHAPTER 14

Dismantling the Folk Idea of Race: Transformations of an Ideology

Racial attitudes among the American public began to fluctuate and change during the first half of the twentieth century, even though widespread racism and discrimination persisted. Popular thought was affected by two world wars involving Americans in Europe and the Pacific and by major conflicts in parts of the Third World that brought American servicemen and women into direct relationships with populations with whom they had had little or no previous experience. Americans were exposed to a wider range of physically and culturally varying peoples, who did not appear to fit very well into existing popular racial classifications.

They were also affected by the Great Depression; extensive demographic changes; the growth in education and in the experiences of the American public; the presence of new immigrants; and internal migrations, as restless Americans began to traverse the country looking for jobs and opportunities. Early in the century, millions of African Americans began to relocate from the South to urban centers in the North and West. Labor unions consolidated a working-class agenda, gained power and legitimacy during the 1940s, and slowly (albeit reluctantly) incorporated black labor. Many blacks and Native Americans served in the armed forces, returned to civilian life, and sought education and economic betterment. Others obtained employment in the growing auto, defense, and other manufacturing industries. Long-standing patterns of segregation and discrimination were still in place, but the need for workers during World War II led to the opening of many manufacturing jobs to blacks. It also led to more internal conflicts, especially after the war, as blacks began to assert their demands for equal rights and opportunities. African Americans and the newer European immigrants were now involved more than ever in the national economy and the national purpose.

During and after the war, Americans widely propagandized antiracist sentiments, and many came to believe in such sentiments themselves. Veterans of the European war returned with enhanced understanding of the need to end all forms of human hatred and conflict. This was the "war to end all wars"; the world was now safe for democracy, equality, freedom, and justice. As these veterans streamed into the universities and other centers of higher education under the G.I. Bill, many also became active in the antidiscrimination movements that sprang up around the country.

By midcentury, genetically heterogeneous and culturally distinct Spanish-speaking populations began to expand on both coasts, increasing the complexity of the melting pot. After major military conflicts in Korea and Vietnam, areas of the world once remote to the vast majority of Americans, the country soon experienced new immigration of Asian peoples and their gradual assimilation into the culture.

Black Americans and their supporters increased their pressures on the government and society to open up the franchise, especially in the South; end formal segregation and denial of civil rights; promote economic and social justice; and integrate schools and public places. New organizations emerged that were dedicated to bettering conditions for minorities and eliminating discrimination and segregation. Riots and demonstrations began to occur around the country, and by the 1960s the civil rights revolution was in full swing. Government intervention via federal legislation, beginning under the New Deal of the 1930s and including the Voting Rights Acts, Civil Rights Acts, and other legal programs, has had a major impact in compelling new forms of social behavior that broadened the freedoms of low-status races. All of these events signaled not only changes in Americans' experiences with human diversity, but also subtle transformations in the ways they looked at human variation.

Contemporary developments in science suggest that the ideology of race is slowly beginning to disintegrate. There have already been subtle changes in many Americans' perspectives on human differences, and as these changes are ongoing, an overall assessment of the trajectories must come at some future time. However, even as the power of racial ideology appears to be diminishing in some sectors of our society, certain trends manifest a powerful resistance to eliminating the idea of race as a biological reality.

THE MEANING AND LEGACY OF RACE AS IDENTITY

One of the most insidious, and tragic, aspects of the racial worldview is its substitution of a new form of identity that superseded all other traditional sources of human identity. This development is not well understood in the scholarly world today, in part because nearly everyone assumes that the concepts of *race* and *races* refer to natural phenomena and have always been a part of the human experience. As pointed out in chapter 1, wherever human physical group differences have been depicted in history, and especially where there have been conflicts, the presumption of modern race scientists is that historical societies also perceived and divided the world into "races."

In an otherwise exceptional and comprehensive work on the history of the idea of race, Thomas Gossett begins his first chapter with the mistaken assumption that ancient Egyptians, by painting people of different skin colors on their tomb walls, were representing "racial" differences. He sees race also in a few ethnocentric expressions written about the Aryan invasion of the Indus valley and "occasionally" in early Chinese thought and among the Jews, the Greeks, and other ancient societies (1965, chap. 1; see also note 1 below). Contemporary race scientists have continued this theme, opting to assume that all peoples perceive the world's populations in terms of race (Rushton 1995; Sarich and Miele 2004).

Was There Race Before the Modern World?

The elements of the ideology of race, as they have been experienced in American society and as I have identified and analyzed them in this volume, were clearly not present in any of the ancient societies of the Old World. I have emphasized this point in earlier chapters and return to the point here in large part because many scholars still insist upon a broad definition of race that incorporates all forms and incidences of conflict and negative attitudes among different ethnic groups. If one follows the analysis of this volume, it will be clear that I have attempted to refine and clarify the ideology of race as it is experienced in the United States. Racism in the United States, and certainly in South Africa, has been a qualitatively different kind of human experience from the ethnocentrism of the past, no matter how extreme. The critical element is the extreme degree to which human differences were magnified, leading to the belief, still held by many whites, that blacks are not human like themselves.

Under extreme forms of ethnocentrism, especially in times of war, differences have always been exaggerated. But race brings a qualitatively different sense of difference, one that is perceived as permanent and cannot be transcended, unlike ethnocentrism. The gulf between two groups, Europeans and Africans, was so magnified in the popular mind that it became equivalent to a species distinction. No society in the past has based social identity on biophysical features, or their presumed "essence," independent of any social factors. No society has called upon its scientists and intellectuals to constantly promote this sense of difference for public consumption.

Modern episodes of group conflict may well reflect some of the elements of race, not because these elements are indigenous to the peoples involved, but because the racial worldview has proved so useful as a rationalization for enmity that the components of this ideology have spread around the world. As I have shown, European colonial powers introduced the idea of race into numerous areas of the Third World, especially where the tactic of "divide and conquer" proved highly effective. European colonists convinced the Tutsi and Hutu of East Africa that their differences were racial, even though these peoples had lived together in relative peace, traded with one another, and intermarried before the colonial period. In Nigeria at the end of the colonial period, I heard British colonial officials discuss with Hausa peoples of northern Nigeria their racial differences from southern Nigerians, specifically Ibos and Yorubas. If indigenous populations learned that *race* was a part of their modern lexicon, it was not because it was a part of their traditions.

A brief exploration of the history of those areas of the world most connected with or relevant to the development of European societies reveals that the notion of "racial" differences never emerged in these areas. Ivan Hannaford's study of European thought, focusing on a wide range of texts from ancient times to the Reformation, provides convincing evidence of the absence of any conception of race before the seventeenth century. Race was a new way of thinking about human beings that he felt destroyed or bypassed older views of humankind and society (1996, 17).

Despite the great distances involved and the absence of modern forms of air, sea, and land travel, the peoples of the Old World predecessors of the West, Africans, Europeans, and Middle Eastern societies have always interacted. From the earliest recorded times (and we can presume even before), the peoples of the Nile Valley, the eastern Mediterranean lands, the Arabian peninsula, southern Europe, and northern and eastern Africa have visited one another, traded together, warred with one another, made alliances, and intermarried without creating social categories of race. In fact, what we know clearly from the historical record, including biblical sources, is that although great variations in skin color, body size, hair texture, and other physical features were certainly present and recognized among individuals, they were rarely commented upon. At no time were clusters of people homogenized into socially meaningful categories and ranked based on skin color or other physical features, regardless of their ethnic affiliations.

The great Greek historian Herodotus, who traveled widely in the known world of his times, described the habits, customs, religious practices, and other cultural features of various societies that he encountered. When he noted variations in skin color (and this was rare), he tells us that they were of little import. The Colchians are of Egyptian origin, he wrote, because they have black skins and wooly hair, "which amounts to but little, since several other nations are so too" (in Godolphin 1942, 130). Tacitus recognized that the German "barbarians" were physically different from the peoples of the Mediterranean, with their large frames, reddish skin, and red hair, but this was not the most significant aspect of their identity (Tacitus 1942). Most writers explained such differences as natural consequences of environmental conditions, such as the hot sun causing people to be dark skinned. No form of inequality, whether social, moral, intellectual, cultural, or otherwise, was associated with people because of their skin color or other physical features, although all "barbarians" varied in some way from the somatic norm of the Mediterranean world.

As is well known, from time to time a conquering state would expand outward and incorporate some or most of this great variety of peoples. When Alexander (the Great) of Macedon conquered peoples and lands all the way to the Indus Valley on the Indian subcontinent, he exhorted his warriors to intermarry with the peoples they conquered in order to learn their languages and cultures. Garrisons of military men were stationed all over the Roman world, from Brittany to the Danube and the Black Sea, from Gibraltar to the Tigris-Euphrates Valley and the Indian Ocean, and through the Maghreb of northwest Africa to the upper Nile Valley. They often took local women as wives. When the armies of the Moroccan king crossed the Sahara and brought down the Songhai Empire in the late sixteenth century, the soldiers stayed on in the western Sudan frontier area and intermarried with the local people.

Most of northern Africa, including Egypt's Nile delta region, has been periodically invaded and ruled by outsiders for the last three thousand years or so. Sixteen hundred years before the birth of Christ, Hyksos from western Asia invaded the kingdom of Egypt and were eventually driven out by a strengthened kingdom of Thebes on the Upper Nile. They were followed by the Hittites from what is now Turkey. Before that, Egypt had conquered Palestine, Syria, and Nubia to the south. In the first millennium BC, Libyans, Kushites, Assyrians, Persians, and then Greeks and Romans invaded and conquered this rich Nilotic civilization. In the Christian era, and after some three hundred years of Christian dominance in Egypt, Arabs from Arabia brought a new religion, Islam, and a greater variety of peoples into the Nile Valley. Various dynasties of very heterogeneous peoples ruled this land until the coming of Ottoman Turks in the sixteenth century, followed by the French at the end of the eighteenth century and finally the English. Vandals from northern Europe invaded northern Africa in the early fifth century, bringing about the demise of the Roman world and introducing their genes for blue eyes and light skins. The Byzantine navy from the eastern Mediterranean recaptured Carthage in the early sixth century, and invading Arab Muslims destroyed this great trading city at the end of the seventh century and continued to sweep across northern Africa to invade Spain in the early eighth century. In their wake they conquered or converted the Berber peoples of North Africa, as well as many peoples in West Africa and the Sahara by the twelfth century.

Neither the Roman, Greek, Muslim, nor, for that matter, the Aryan conquests in India resulted in societies stratified by race, although some of the chief ingredients, including physical differences in the populations, were clearly present. Indeed, the "biologization" (the social formation of identities based on biological features) of the world's people did not occur until the last few centuries, as we have seen (Ross 1982, 3).[1]

The differences recognized among the hundreds of populations in the Old World were ethnic differences, and ethnicity, as we have argued, is not the same as race. Ethnic groups have always existed, in the sense that clusters of people living in demarcated areas developed lifestyles (or culture traits) and linguistic features that distinguished them from others, and they perceived themselves as being separate societies with distinct names and social histories. But ethnic identity was not conceived as something ineluctably set in stone, nor was it understood as innately inherited or confused with biological features. Individuals and groups of individuals often moved to new areas or changed their identities by acquiring membership in a different group. One could learn to speak the languages of the Romans or the Greeks and participate in their cultures, even becoming a citizen of their states. Language was the avenue to new social identities, or at least to trading relationships; ethnic identity itself was fluid and malleable.

The peoples of these ancient societies seem to have understood that cultural characteristics were external and acquired forms of behavior. They exhibited ways of establishing their identities and knowing who they were that bore no relationship to their physical characteristics. Geographic location was a significant basis of identity. Different societies and localized segments of larger societies were known by the region, town, or village of their origin and by their ethnic name. That identities were fluid is indicated in the depictions of individual lives. Paul of Tarsus traveled and preached extensively throughout much of the known Mediterranean world during the early Christian era and encountered individuals of many different ethnic backgrounds. He even identified himself as a Roman on occasion when it was useful to do so (Acts 18–23).

Kinship affiliation was the most basic form of identity within local areas and sometimes beyond. With the exception of the Berbers and a few other peoples, who were matrilineal, people were known by who their fathers were, that is, by their patrilineage. The long list of "begats" in the book of Genesis in the Old Testament is an indicator of how genealogical identity in some known lineage or clan was critical to how people were perceived and how they saw themselves. Occupation was another source of identity; that Jesus was widely known as a carpenter preceded him in his travels. Scholars who have studied African history and ethnography have also been aware of the malleability of ethnic identity on that continent. New ethnic groups have emerged out of the colonial period, and individuals have been known to transform themselves according to their ethnic or religious milieus. Most Africans spoke several languages, which facilitated the molding of multiple ethnicities by providing immediate access to cultural knowledge.

Within the large states and empires of the ancient world, citizenship became an important locus of identity. The notion of citizenship, which eventually superseded even kinship, was to develop later and assume a dominant role in the context of the rise of nation-states. One's identity as a citizen was to become the premier source by which rights and responsibilities were expressed in a society.

With the appearance of the universal proselytizing religions—Christianity and later Islam—which became competitors for the souls of all people, a new focus of identity was increasingly placed on membership in a religious community. We have seen in previous chapters some of the significance of one's religious identity. This became more important as various sects broke away from the parent religious group and established themselves as rivals, for example the Protestant break with the Catholic Church and the various factions of Protestantism that emerged, and the different sects that appeared in the Muslim world (Hannaford 1996; Castro 1971). Religion was the most important aspect of one's identity in the Middle Ages and later.

All of this began to change in the eighteenth century, as a new mode of human identification was created that superseded kinship, ethnic group, village or town origin, language, religion, occupation, education, and a host of other features by which humans had commonly framed their identities in the past. Race was a form of identification that seemingly rested on the natural physical characteristics of all humans, but whose real meaning was fabricated out of social and political realities. We have seen that the creation of race imposed on the conquered and enslaved peoples gave them an identity as the lowest status groups in society. So powerful was the idea and ideology of race that it was internalized as the principal form of human identity.

We have also observed that after the American Civil War, although slavery ended, race and racial ideology remained and were strengthened by policies, laws, local customs, and practices, developed mostly in the South but found all over the country, designed to keep members of low-status races in their designated places, out of competition with the white majority.

Race as Identity

The great, often unspoken, dilemma for the low-status races in North America was, and still is, how to deal with the identities that the dominant society has imposed on them. Most minorities have had no option but to accept race as a reality and to function in American society knowing that most whites consider them intellectually and morally inferior. This is an enormous burden in an ostensibly free society, where individuals are supposedly judged on the basis of factors other than race status. As has been already noted, education, income, religious beliefs, moral and ethical standards, interests, knowledge, avocations, skills, talents, and other personal characteristics are seen by many people in the low-status races as irrelevant to the larger society. A person or group's identity as racially inferior takes precedence over any other qualities that might be present. It evokes attitudes and behavior of contempt and disrespect from the dominant white community. This situation imposes enormous stress on low-status people and is a source of much of the generalized feeling of oppression that they experience.

As they did with the African peoples, European colonists ignored the cultural and physical diversity among Native Americans and homogenized them all into a single group of more or less "savage" Indians. The wholesale decimation of the Indian population reduced their numbers, by the end of the nineteenth century, to an estimated three hundred thousand (Hoover 1976, 141). And the regimentation of many onto reservations meant that little attention was paid to their plight until recent decades. They have felt the brunt of disempowerment and oppression and of alienation from once established and viable communities.

Some activists are trying to counter the stereotype of savagery and the denigration of native cultures by harkening back to Native American lifestyles. They are endeavoring to construct a new image of Indians as a people of achievements, pride, determination, and worthiness. They were creators of beautiful art forms and democratic and egalitarian governments; they preserved the bounties of nature. Some argue for restoring the spiritual qualities of native life, imagining a gentle ethos that governed a special relationship to nature. The Indian concern and respect for nature resonates with other people, especially environmentalists, who sense that such an approach militates against the materialism and consumerism of the larger society.

The dilemma that modern-day Native Americans face is that, since conquest, they have never been able to fashion their own identities. Government policies have generally dictated who Indians were by defining the amount of "Indian blood" needed to qualify or by arbitrarily assigning memberships in tribes. This was done as part of federal and state efforts to control Indian communities and their movements and to confine those who continued to practice traditional lifestyles in delimited areas. The Dawes Act, or Indian Allotment Act, of 1887, designed ostensibly to transform Indians from members of tribal societies into citizens and landowners, required that all those persons receiving individual land allotments be of one-half or more "Indian blood" (Jaimes 1994, 49). In the twentieth century, the Bureau of Indian Affairs (BIA) has also operated with "blood quantum" criteria, stipulating that one must have at least one-fourth Indian ancestry to qualify for an Indian identity. Theoretically, those members of tribes whose "quantum" is less than one-quarter Indian ancestry are not eligible for various services of the federal government. And one must produce a certificate, issued by the BIA, that proves the needed ancestry!

This has created a morass of problems for Indian people. It has led to conflicts over, and between, various degrees of "mixed bloods" and accusations of illegitimacy; most important, it has contradicted the practices of each Indian tribe in determining for itself who are its members. Since the idea of race was not traditional in Indian societies, membership was always based on other factors, including birth and adoption. The policy of specifying degrees of Indianness by an unmeasurable "blood quantum" is indicative of the distortions that the ideology of race-as-biology has forced on the American public.

The American policy toward Indians has consisted of broken treaties, land grabs, lies, deception, violence, corruption on the part of Indian administrators, and impoverishment. In the early part of the twentieth century, some efforts were made to rectify the awful conditions in which Indians existed. In 1924 and 1925, laws were passed seeking to preserve Indian lands and prevent them from further alienation. Policymakers at both federal and state levels disagreed on whether Indians could be assimilated into the larger American society. It is a telling comment on American society that it was not until 1924 and the passage of the Indian Citizenship Act that Indians were mandated citizenship status (Jaimes 1994, 50).

THE QUEST FOR A MIXED-RACE CENSUS CATEGORY

Nothing is more indicative of the plight, and the pathology, of using race/biology as the main form of human identity than the efforts on the part of some people to establish a "mixed-race" category in the census and thus in American society.[2] As we have already seen, the race ideology that developed in the United States provided no social mechanism to recognize people whose parents were from different racial groups. In the nineteenth century, the social values of the United States made interracial sex and marriage virtually a heinous crime, if not a sin. People with part-Indian ancestry were called "mud" people, and those with black and white parentage were deemed the abnormal products of acts of unnatural mating. The social taboos against such matings continued throughout the twentieth century and still influence the majority of people.

Having been conditioned to the biological salience of *race* and to the reality of only black, white, and Indian categories, some contemporary offspring of mixed marriages have experienced psychological trauma and distress as a result of the confusion of biology and culture. Their situation and thus their arguments for a new category imply a feeling of having no identity at all because they do not exist formally as a biological, more specifically *social*, category. What compounds and complicates this tragedy is another fiction that we have seen to be one of the basic tenets of the racial worldview: the myth that biology has some intrinsic connection to culture or behavior. Some advocates of a new "mixed-race" category have argued that they need this new identity in order to recognize the "culture" of their white parent. In American ideology, a black parent presumably has "black" culture, and the white parent has "white" culture, with the unstated understanding that these are incompatible ways of life. Aside from the fact that this idea is nonsense, it continues to feed the psychic stress of a few individuals who have the feeling that they do not know who they are.

From a purely biogenetic perspective, most black Americans, and probably most Native Americans, can claim to be of "mixed" ancestry. (So can many "whites.") It has been estimated that the genetic ancestry of the average African American is about one-quarter non-African. Indeed, there is a greater range of skin colors and other physical features among black Americans than almost any other people identified as a distinct population, attesting to this mixed ancestry. We should also understand that the physical markers of "race" status are always open to interpretation by others. *Race* as social status is often in the eye of the beholder. "Mixed" people will still be treated as black or Indian if their phenotypes cause them to be so perceived by others. Insistence on being in a separate classification will not change that perception or the reaction of others to them.

As to the matter of culture, clearly the ideological myths of the racial worldview have prevented us from seeing how very much alike culturally black and white Americans are, as well as all other Americans who have been so socialized. The ancestors of African Americans have had "American" culture (indeed helped to create it) longer than the ancestors of most white Americans. Paul Bohannan and Philip D. Curtin have pointed out that half the ancestors of African Americans were already here by 1780, and I might add, instrumental in creating American culture. And, they inform us, "the similar median date for the arrival of our European ancestors was remarkably late—about the 1890s. It was not until the 1840s that more Europeans than Africans crossed the Atlantic each year" (1995, 13). Although regional, social-class, and urban-rural-suburban lifestyles may differ, all Americans have more cultural features in common than they have differences.

Unless one partner were born and raised overseas in another culture, it is most likely that both partners in a black–white mixed marriage share the same or similar lifestyles, depending on whether they were also matched by class, education, and religion. If one spouse did come from a very different cultural background, such as a recent immigrant from Asia, a child born to that family does not automatically have that culture because of the biology of the parent. Humans have to acquire cultural traits; it is learned behavior. In order for Tiger Woods, an American golfing star, to have Thai culture, his mother's background, he would have to live in Thailand and learn the language and the elements of Thai culture. But one can learn Thai culture without having a single gene from a Thai parent!

There is another consideration that too often escapes those who grapple with "ethnic" and race considerations. There is no reason why one should learn the cultures of one's ancestors merely because of some genetic or genealogical connection. For one thing, we no longer live in biblical times, wherein a list of "begats," the genealogical ties to our fathers, tell us who we are. There has already been too much "mixture" for that kind of identity to be possible. For another, none of us have the cultures of any of our ancestors of two centuries ago, or two millennia ago, because all cultures have changed, sometimes drastically, over the centuries. Cultures change all the time without corresponding changes occurring in the biological features of the culture bearers. It is the perspective of the racial worldview that mandates the belief in biologically determined cultural behavior. And this is perpetuated in American society by the popular media, daily practices, political propaganda, race scientists, and social institutions as part of folk wisdom about human differences. It is a fiction that we must work to eliminate.

BARACK OBAMA AND THE MEANING OF RACE

The election of President Barack Obama focused a great deal of attention on race. Although it may not have been obvious at the time, there is much irony and powerful symbolism in the rise of Barack Obama in terms of his person and achievements. Even before he was elected president (2008), Obama contradicted everything that Americans believe or think they know about *race*, and most of us don't yet realize this. First, Barack Obama's African ancestors, unlike most blacks in America, were not slaves in the Americas. He has a genuine African name and identity, not one that he invented for himself, as some blacks have done in recent years. Second, he was not raised in a family impacted by the legacy of slavery. He did not inherit at his grandparents' knees the legacy and the stultifying heritage of slavery and racism in America. No grandparents ever talked to him about their experiences in the bad old days of slavery and Jim Crow racism or instilled in him fear or wariness of dealing with white folks.

Most striking of all, Obama is the product of one of the oldest and strongest taboos in American society: the taboo against interracial marriage, especially the marriage of a white woman to a black man. Though most black Americans are sometimes acutely aware of their mixed ancestry, white Americans find it difficult to deal with this reality. It contradicts their conviction that one can only belong to one race, and that racial mixing is wrong or somehow unnatural (see above). What is interesting about Barack Obama is that public acknowledgment of the different "races" of his parents has been brought out into the open in most media. And the curious thing about this fact is that most media treatments have focused on questioning his "identity": Who is he "racially?" Is he really black, is he biracial, is he a hybrid (whatever that means)?

That this phenomenon should seem surprising or shocking to Americans is very strange. The first child born in North America of a mating between individuals of European and African ancestry appeared in 1620, and Americans have been giving birth to such "mixed" people continuously ever since. The problem is that historically American society never created an intermediate social status or category for "mixed" people, as did South Africa or some of the states in the Caribbean and South America.

All of this has led to numerous pundits querying his identity: Who is Barack Obama? Regardless of his name, here is a young man born into an American family with a Kansas background and clearly raised with middle American cultural values. All of his fundamental beliefs, values, and ways of behaving and thinking were transmitted to him by two generations of a middle American white Protestant family, even after they moved to Hawaii. This is his cultural identity. He is really Dorothy (the original Dorothy of *The Wizard of Oz*)! You can't get more middle American than this. The tragedy is that most Americans don't recognize this reality.

Recognized as a very bright student, he received degrees from some of the most prestigious universities in America, Columbia and Harvard, and while in law school he was elected president of the *Harvard Law Review*. He worked as a community organizer and professor of law in Chicago and was elected to the Illinois Senate and later to the U.S. Senate from Illinois. This is his real identity. Were he identified as a "white" man, this reality would be readily accepted. No one would question his basic values or suggest that he was a secret Muslim or some kind of alien. It is the power of our racial ideology that prevents most Americans from realizing the basic distinction between our cultural selves (who we really are) and our physical characteristics. The major question raised by journalists, social scientists, and pundits has to do with what Obama's election might mean for race relations in America. How much, if any, will it affect America's racial worldview and the discriminatory practices associated with it?

Political scientists and sociologists have pointed out that Obama's election reflects the strong divisions in American society about race. There is a sense of "Otherness" that many white Americans hold (Tesler and Sears 2010; Sears et al. 2000). They can neither understand nor accept a person who seems so alien, not only because he is a highly educated black man (contradicting the stereotypes that they maintain), but because of his background in Hawaii and Indonesia. Experts agree that racial hatred was a major factor in the election and continues to motivate most of his opponents (Wise 2009). The fact that Obama received 43 percent of the white vote is indicative of some positive change in American attitudes about race (Tesler and Sears 2010). But it is too early to tell the nature and direction of such change.

THE FUTURE OF THE RACIAL WORLDVIEW

It is also too early to tell whether developments in the treatment of human biophysical variation in physical anthropology textbooks represent a sustainable transformation in scientific views and understandings of human differences.

What we should understand, however, is that the sociocultural, historical, political, and economic contexts in which the folk idea of race emerged have changed drastically. Newer social, economic, ideological, and political forces, arising in the mid-twentieth century, have begun to influence the ways in which we view human differences. Also, many newer problems and issues, of an international order, occupy our attention.

From a purely anthropological perspective, however, it is certain that the idea and ideology of race will continue to change and possibly diminish in many sectors of our society. This is the nature of cultural realities; they are never static and undergo modifications due to forces over which we humans have little or no control (see White 1969, 1973). Like all evolutionary changes, most will likely not be sudden and dramatic but gradual and almost imperceptible, just as they were during much of the twentieth century. Accordingly, the racial worldview will certainly persist for a while, in various forms and intensities, and we will no doubt see episodes of racism exploding from time to time. But the circumstances and conditions that gave birth to race ideology are no longer with us, and complex new realities of the industrial-technological-information age will produce new configurations among the world's peoples. We are already seeing new political and economic alignments and the emergence of new strategies that crosscut traditional "racial" lines.

The breakup of the older colonial empires and the creation of new nation-states in Asia, Africa, and South America, responding to the propaganda of freedom, have changed the contours of international relations. Though there remains a debilitating economic dependence between the West and the Third World, the political impact, especially in the United Nations, of non-European peoples has been considerable in an age of increasing travel and immigration. Businesspeople and educators, politicians and diplomats, students and tourists from these once colonized worlds have become a part of the reality that we view frequently through television and other news media or experience directly in the major cities and especially in centers of higher learning. And the entire process of globalization has elevated the political and economic status of some peoples, such as the Japanese, the Chinese, and the peoples of India, much closer to equality with the West.

But the peoples of Africa have not benefited from the broad processes of economic and political changes, and I suspect that for racial reasons they have been left out of the capital investments and other entrepreneurial activities made available to others. Still, one must recognize that change is inevitable; we have experienced considerable modifications in the laws and practices relating to racism in the United States. Few people would have predicted the rise in political and social influence of many African Americans during the last decades of the twentieth century.

The civil rights era was a remarkable period in American history, or for that matter in the history of any country. This movement and continued political pressure from African Americans and their supporters brought into sharp relief the differences between American democratic ideology and the values and practices that so strongly contradict it. For the first time, many Americans openly confronted these contradictions—the moral duplicity and hypocrisy—to which they had been conditioned. This has led to the slow but perceptible opening of many sectors of American society and the integration of many African Americans into the middle-class mainstream. The breakdown of public barriers and the eradication of laws that called for or buttressed public segregation have had an impact on the perception of differences. The appearance of black Americans in film and frequently on television, to the degree that their portrayals depart from customary stereotypes, has had an unmonitored and therefore unknown effect on the broader public mind. We should not underestimate the power of the popular media, films, popular literature, and especially television to influence both our values and our behavior.

On this point, I speculate that media programs such as the *Oprah Winfrey Show* have probably had more of an effect on dissolving racial ideology than almost any other institution outside of the law. This is not only because of Winfrey's huge following. but because the issues that she, and others, have dealt with are generally common to all people. I suspect that a subtle connection has already been made, but is as yet unarticulated, that Americans are all very much the same in this culture. Whether dealing with gender relationships, problems of the elderly, problems of child care or child abuse, nursing mothers, the AIDS epidemic, the health concerns of different age groups, the desire to be slim to enhance our looks, or any other of the numerous human issues Winfrey's show focuses on, the similarities among people of all racial categories are thrown into sharp relief.

White Americans and Europeans have become increasingly familiar with people of color, whom they have long considered inferior. This includes especially the rise of the Japanese to full and equal competitiveness in the industrial world during the latter part of the twentieth century. But it also includes the numerous Asian and African populations and Hispanic peoples and other Caribbean and Latin American peoples who do not fit easily within conventional racial categories. Moreover, military personnel from many nations have been relocated around the world, and in the process have contributed to the genetic variability in numerous populations. Wide-ranging intermixtures of peoples have created a state of uncertainty about the racial identities of large numbers of individuals. Roger Sanjek (1994) has pointed out that increasingly larger numbers of Americans are marrying outside of their defined racial or ethnic group. This will clearly have a disquieting effect on those few who may still believe in either racial purity or the preservation of racial distinctions. However, it may also increase the existing ambiguities that surround racial identities. Uncertainties about racial identities may mean that in coming generations, race will become less obvious, and less salient, as the premier source of social identity in the United States.

A number of scenarios are possible. More than 50 percent of Asians and now Hispanics are marrying outside of their "racial" or "ethnic" groups. These marriages are primarily to whites, but there is also increasing intermarriage between blacks and whites and blacks and Asians. Marriages between blacks and other "races" have usually resulted in the children being identified with their black ancestry (unless they are sufficiently exotic-looking as to be able to voluntarily pass as white or something else). The questions must be asked, Will those Hispanics and Asians who intermarry with whites be ultimately assimilated into the "white" category? Will those marrying into the black community, with or without darker skins, continue to be identified as "black"? Are we evolving into a society in which two rather fuzzy but unequal racial tiers constitute the fundamental underlying structure?

It is of interest that American receptivity to Asian immigrants, despite some community conflicts, has generally been without much rancor. The performance of some newly immigrant Asians as intellectual leaders in high schools, colleges, and universities, particularly in science, mathematics, and high-technology fields, is bound to have a disquieting effect on those white Americans who previously accepted scores on intelligence tests as documentation of the innate superiority of Caucasians. The superior academic performance of some of these Asian students provides clear evidence of the external nature of the factors—high motivation, self-discipline, perseverance, willingness to make sacrifices, respect for knowledge—that generate excellence in all academic fields. These students also provide contrasts with many contemporary American students and the often self-indulgent, leisure-loving manner in which so many are socialized. Except for the new race scientists such as Rushton, published explanations for the success of these Asian students are notably lacking in references to "superior" genetic or hereditary qualities.

The great American experiment, involving the intermingling of people in a heterogeneous society, which sociologists used to call the "melting pot," is the best evidence for contradicting folk race ideology. Yet it is strange that few Americans have been conscious of the fact that people of all physical variations and cultural backgrounds have come to the United States and been transformed in the process of assimilation to that nebulous reality called American culture. Chinese, Russians, Africans, East Indians, Polynesians, Southeast Asians, Inuits, and peoples indigenous to the Amazon Valley have learned to walk, talk, eat, drink, and think like Americans. Too many Americans seem oblivious to this transformation in outlook and behavior and its demonstration of the extrinsic, learned nature of cultural behavior.

Yet another potential direction of development in our interpretations of human differences presented itself in the latter part of the twentieth century. In the 1970s we saw the rise of concern for *ethnicity* and *ethnic groups*. Group values, interests, and traditions of common ancestry (the "roots" phenomenon) may emerge as precepts of new forms of social relationships and interactions. The notion of *ethnic group* may well be wedded to hereditarian beliefs explicit in the concept of "breeding populations" and become a new formulation of race, containing all of the social connotations of conventional race status but applied to whatever new group permutations the public (and publicists) care to devise. Those who insist that black Americans constitute an ethnic group, or ethnic population, in the same way that the Irish, Italians, or Jews are seen as ethnic units, may be unaware that in many instances *ethnic* has become a synonym for *race* and may carry all of the ingredients of the racial worldview. Moreover, it does not release us from the racism of the past or, especially, from the idea of hereditary causes of human behavior.

THE PERSISTENCE OF RACIAL THINKING

There continues to be evidence that Americans, white, black, and otherwise, find it difficult to think logically about race or human biological variation. We are so programmed by the power of the racial worldview that we submit to the constraints of racial thinking even when it is not necessary. And we have developed and lived with so many myths about human differences, connected with the ideology of race, that they have distorted our sense of reality. In the field of medicine and health, for example, much of the research breaks down along the demographics of blacks and whites. This may be in part because of documented studies that reveal that blacks *on average* suffer higher incidences of many diseases and disabilities, such as hypertension and heart failure. Although it has been shown that there are social and environmental reasons for most of the disparities (see chapter 15), many people in the scientific and medical fields immediately leap to the conclusion that the causes are genetic.[3]

With the discovery of the complete human genome, a new vision of racial differences has become possible. Although humans are genetically 99.9 percent alike, and we all share common genes, some genes have as many as seventy different alleles (variations) that are distributed in complex ways throughout different human groups. As we have seen, some geneticists have discovered patterns in the genomes and allelic variations that correlate to large geographic divisions. These patterns seem to reflect already recognized phenotypic differences among peoples whose ancestors originated in Africa, Asia, and Europe. Finding some allelic variations within the genome that correspond to phenotypic differences among widely separated human groups is to be expected and adds nothing new to our understanding of variation. Peoples who live in proximity to one another share greater genetic similarities than peoples living at greater distances from one another, as seen in chapter 13. If scientists only sample certain selected genes of populations widely separated by geography, they can find some seemingly abrupt discontinuities. Some scientists want to interpret these resulting clusters as biological races. However, if every population in between is sampled, clinal and overlapping patterns in the genes show continuity or continuous variation.[4]

Race scientists now focus on that one-tenth of 1 percent of our genes that reflects individual differences. And they leap on any evidence that might suggest innate group differences, especially between blacks and whites (see Gottfredson 1994). But the fact is that 1) science has not yet been able to show any relationship between most of the genetic characteristics seen in the genome and phenotypic traits; 2) no genes have been found that exist in one "racial" population and not in all others; and 3) except for some inherited diseases, no genes have been found that correlate with or cause any behavioral trait, including intelligence. The result is that to this date, virtually everything stated about innate human group behavior differences (outside of known hereditary diseases) is based on inferences and speculations.

Ethnic Medicines: The Case of BiDil

One of the more recent examples of how our obsession with race causes Americans to think and behave illogically is seen in the history of the so-called ethnic medicine called BiDil. In June 2005, the U.S. Food and Drug Administration approved BiDil to treat heart failure in "self-identified" black patients. Critics of this decision point out that the significance of this drug rests in politics, legal maneuvers, and the profit motive (Kahn 2005, 2008, 2009). BiDil is a combination of two generic drugs (hydralazine and isosorbide dinitrate) that have proven effective in the past for some heart patients. BiDil did not begin as an ethnic drug; the first trials in the 1980s included both black and white patients. The research was conducted under laws that allowed research labs using federal funds to retain the intellectual property rights to their discoveries. The two researchers of BiDil, Dr. Jay Cohn and Dr. Peter Carson, established patent rights and sought arrangements with NitroMed, a pharmaceutical company, to produce it. But more studies were needed to compare this drug with ACE inhibitors. To do this research, the two doctors needed funding.

However, corporate funding was not forthcoming. The reason seems to be that the two drugs were both generic drugs that were available to everyone. The combination was not considered a new drug, and pharmaceutical companies are not willing to invest in large-scale trials of drugs that are available to all and over which they could not establish property rights (patents). When a new biotech firm showed interest in conducting some tests, BiDil was submitted to the FDA for approval. But the FDA rejected the application, apparently on the basis that it was not a new drug and would not be an economically viable product. The FDA also held that the various trials done previously did not provide sufficient statistical information for a new drug trial.

The BiDil researchers then decided to take another look at the data from earlier trials, and this led to their classifying the results by race. They then made the decision to reconceptualize BiDil as a drug for black patients with heart failure. It is known that African Americans have a high rate of heart failure, and this drug seemed to be effective for many of them.[5] This was a politically and economically astute move. As Jonathan Kahn points out, the value of the intellectual property rights rose after Dr. Carson published a paper on this aspect of the drug (2005). NitroMed then acquired the property rights, engaged public relations consultants, and "BiDil was reborn as an ethnic drug" (Kahn 2005, 112). The original patent on the drug was to expire in 2007; the new race-based patent extends to 2020, giving NitroMed a monopoly over its production for thirteen years.

No trials were conducted on nonblack "racial" groups for comparison purposes. The result is that an assumption that BiDil is only effective in blacks has become part of medical folklore; white physicians may not prescribe BiDil for whites, and white patients may well decline to take it. Yet BiDil is effective for all patients, regardless of race. The physician investigators of BiDil prescribe it for their white patients, and Dr. Cohn believes that "everybody should be using it" (in Kahn 2005, 6).

Kahn points out a disingenuous consequence of BiDil: It gains cultural capital by being characterized as a way to redress a major health disparity in a historically underserved population. The bittersweet irony is that the Association of Black Cardiologists and the Congressional Black Caucus also supported the development of BiDil; how could they not? But BiDil reifies race; it buttresses the idea of race in the law and perpetuates the notion that races are genetically discrete categories. Kahn goes on to show how NitroMed manipulated statistics, providing misleading information on mortality rates between blacks and whites, in order to promote this "ethnic" drug.

BiDil will not be the only drug advertised as an "ethnic" drug. A few years ago, the makers of Advair, an asthma drug, cautioned in their publicity that it might not work well in blacks. Some black physicians, recognizing that blacks are genetically an extremely heterogeneous population, have ignored these claims and continue to prescribe Advair. Some pharmaceutical companies believe that "ethnic" drugs are the key to future development in the drug industry. Already claims are being made for new products thought to have different rates of effectiveness in different "ethnic" groups.[6] And we shall soon see the development of new marketing strategies aimed at specific "racial" populations. Every new discovery may be scrutinized for its potential race-specific value. BiDil has opened the door for a new emphasis on race as biology.

It is likely that most Americans will see these developments as examples of dazzling progress in the medical field. It is consonant with the beliefs they already hold about significant differences among the races. It will indeed strengthen these beliefs and may help assuage some guilt feelings. By making disparities in health outcomes a matter of imputed genetic features within a population, American society can continue to ignore the real social, economic, ecological, and political causes of disparities (see chapter 15).

Race in Sports

Americans continue to accept many myths about race differences; they are part of the package of ideological ingredients that constitute the racial worldview. One of these myths relates to the contemporary dominance of blacks in certain sports, particularly basketball ("white men can't jump") and track. Few people seem to realize that the explanation for this reality lies not in the genetics of the black population, but in the opportunity structures of American society. After the Civil War, white Americans had to confront the reality of four million ex-slaves now theoretically free to participate in the economy. As we have seen, white America had long decided that blacks should remain in occupations at the bottom of the economic ladder. In time there developed only two avenues for success and advancement that allowed blacks some form of entry: entertainment and sports. Arenas of higher education were barred to the majority of blacks. As a result, young black boys grew up in a narrowly focused world. Success in that world meant, and still means, achieving stardom as an entertainer or in sports. With such a skewed view of the world and limited options, the domains of cultural experience for black youth became increasingly restricted during the twentieth century.

This has never been true for white youth. If every six foot and over black youth had the background education, broad cultural experiences, and choices and options available to young white boys, the situation in sports (and entertainment) might look very different. To underscore this point, I often point to several contemporary success stories. Richard Parsons is six feet, four inches tall, and without doubt, a lot of people anticipated that he would be a basketball player because he is black. But in the latter part of the twentieth century, career options opened wider for blacks, and today Parsons is CEO of AOL-Time Warner. Many other blacks have achieved success in business. A black woman, Ursula Burns, is now CEO of Xerox Company. Perhaps even more remarkable is the fact that a tall black man, Dr. Neil deGrasse Tyson, became an astrophysicist and is now the director of the world famous Hayden Planatarium. We need to make more black youngsters, of all heights, aware of these possibilities and opportunities in addition to sports and entertainment.

The willingness of Americans to relinquish belief in the myths subsumed in the idea of race, particularly the belief in natural inequality and group inheritance of innate behavior, will determine the degree to which race and its ideological elements can be eliminated from our worldview and vocabulary. But relinquishing a belief system that has been so critical to the American social system and our interpersonal relationships will not come easily (see Bush 2004; Wise 2010; and Kincheloe et al. 1998).

The fundamental question is, if the concept of race loses its validity, credibility, or substantive usefulness to science, does it follow that its force and meaning will be diminished in the larger society? Increasingly science and scientists are providing us with models not only of what the world is like in a mechanistic and material sense, but also of moral and ethical belief systems. We have already entered a stage in human cultural development where reliance on science for providing the basis for policy alternatives as well as new ideologies-cum-myths is a reality. This expanded role of science is a product of immense technological changes that have broadened our knowledge of the universe and co-opted for many our religious mythologies and explanations.

Many professional anthropologists are arguing for a greater role of this profession in helping to bring about the needed social changes in our racial worldview (Mukhopadhyay and Moses 1997). Anthropology specializes in researching both the biological aspects of human beings and the cultures that they have created. Theoretically, anthropologists understand the nature of culture, its external and acquired nature, its causes, its development, and its functions. Yet the enormous amount of knowledge accumulated in this field over this century, all of which contradicts the components of the racial worldview, has had noticeably little substantive impact on the society at large, its social policies, or its educational system. This attests to the power of the racial worldview over all of our minds, including those of anthropologists.

In order for anthropology to be engaged, to influence the formulation of public policy, and to educate the public, it must first transform itself. As Faye Harrison has exhorted, world anthropology must emancipate itself from the strictures of its own archaic racialized and gendered visions of the world (1991). We must ourselves fully comprehend that although our biological composition and genetic codes are essential to the development of human culture, our genes do not predispose us to have any specific culture, cultural traits, or behavior.[7] Genes do not orchestrate whether we develop an affinity for European classical music or for hard rock or jazz. Twentieth-century advances in the social sciences have fully demonstrated that different human behaviors are the product of different cultural conditioning. Because human behavior is acquired through our interaction with our social and natural environments, it is thus plastic and malleable (Goodman 2006). To a great extent, we can alter our social behavior and the conditions that give rise to it if we have the will. These are lessons sine qua non for the future decline of the racial worldview.

Developments in late-twentieth-century science reveal a growing repudiation of the idea of biologically distinct races, as biological anthropologists and molecular biologists are providing us with new ways of understanding human diversity. Given the increasing power and role of science in revealing the "objective" world and guiding our thoughts about it, this may represent the early and tentative first step toward a major social transformation, the beginning of the end of the racial worldview in America and perhaps elsewhere.

NOTES

1. I am aware that there are scholars who disagree with this position (as I have indicated in earlier discussions). Among contemporary writers, Bernard Lewis, David Brion Davis, and Paul Gordon Lauren have argued that racial prejudice has a long history. Their definitions of *race* (where given) are much broader than that given here and include intergroup relationships that most anthropologists would label *ethnic*. Space prohibits exploring this issue adequately.

2. From 1850 to 1930, a category for "mulattoes" was included in the American census, and in the 1890 census the terms *quadroon* and *octoroon* appeared briefly. The census has never been consistent in its attempts to classify races (see Prewitt 2005). What was extraordinary about the 2000 census was the inclusion of choice, whereby respondents were allowed to mark more than one racial identity. As Prewitt points out, the decision to place "mark one or more" races as a choice challenges the basic premise that "race is a bounded and exclusive trait" (11).

3. See the Institute of Medicine 2003, which sums up numerous studies on racial disparities.

4. A lot of literature increasingly indicates the clinal nature of biogenetic variation in the human species. How one sees or interprets this variation depends on the sampling strategy that one uses. See Serre and Pääbo 2004; Keita et al. 2004; and Foster and Sharp 2002.

5. As Jonathan Kahn (2005) notes, however, this applies to people under sixty-five, who constitute only 6 percent of the total deaths. After age sixty-five, the rates for blacks and whites are nearly the same, with blacks having a slightly lower rate.

6. This is a good example of the confusion of *ethnicity* and *race*. It implies that ethnicity is a characteristic of our genes!

7. This understanding of culture has an ancient history, as this volume has shown. But the explicit theoretical statement of it, best expressed in the works of Leslie White and his colleagues earlier in the twentieth century, seems to have been obfuscated in the anthropological literature of the past several decades. It is a view that needs to be resuscitated and made prominent in every anthropological text. See White 1973, and especially Sahlins 1976.

CHAPTER 15

The Health and Other Consequences of the Racial Worldview

One of the most poignant ironies of the Western racial worldview that emerged in the eighteenth century is that it has helped to create and perpetuate "racial" health inequalities. These health inequalities, in turn, reinforce the view that poorer health among people of color is the by-product of biological and genetic differences among racial groups.

The racial worldview accepts inequality as normative—that is, societies and races are inherently unequal, and people of color are "naturally" at the bottom of most social and economic indexes because of their innate inferiority. This chapter reviews evidence that racial health inequalities are the consequence of race-based structural inequities, or structural racism, rather than biological or genetic differences, and that the ways in which these inequalities are understood in U.S. public discourse continues to reinforce the racial worldview.

THE EXTENT OF RACIAL HEALTH DISPARITIES IN THE UNITED STATES

Racial and ethnic health disparities persist from the cradle to the grave. Some racial and ethnic minorities—particularly those that have faced a history of exploitation and forced displacement from their ancestral lands—experience a disproportionate burden of poor health across a host of measures, ranging from infant mortality and diabetes to cardiac disease, HIV/AIDS, and other illnesses. African Americans, American Indians, and Pacific Islanders face some of the most persistent and pervasive disparities compared to whites and some

Asian Americans.[1] For example, although the life expectancy gap between African Americans and whites has narrowed slightly,[2] African Americans still can expect to live six to ten fewer years than whites and face higher rates of illness and mortality.[3]

This gap is staggering: A recent analysis of 1991 to 2000 mortality data concluded that had mortality rates of African Americans been equivalent to those of whites in the same period, more than eight hundred eighty thousand deaths would have been averted.[4] And although some racial and ethnic groups, such as some Hispanics and Asian Americans, have better overall health status than national averages, they suffer disproportionately from diseases such as diabetes and tend to experience poorer health outcomes—particularly for measures such as cancer, infant mortality, and heart disease—the longer they and their descendants live in the United States.[5]

Similarly, the health status of subpopulations within "racial" groups varies considerably on the basis of nationality, immigration status, and other factors. For example, Vietnamese American men develop liver cancer and die from it at a rate seven times higher than that of non-Hispanic white men.[6] Vietnamese women have the highest rate of cervical cancer of any racial or ethnic group,[7] and the rate of cervical cancer among Mexican and Puerto Rican women is two to three times that of white women.[8] Native Hawaiians have the highest rate of death from breast cancer of any racial or ethnic group, and it is the leading cause of death among Filipinas.[9]

Racial and ethnic health inequality spans the life course, beginning with birth outcomes and reproductive health. Along some indicators, this inequality is growing. Between 1980 and 2000, for example, the black–white ratio of infant mortality increased 25 percent even as the overall infant mortality rate declined.[10] In addition, African American infants are two to three times more likely than white infants to have low birth weight—a key indicator of infant mortality.[11] Racial and ethnic group differences in birth outcomes persist even when socioeconomic factors are considered. For example, as figure 15.1 shows, infant mortality rates—considered one of the most sensitive indicators of population health—are higher among African Americans and American Indians/Alaska Natives than among other racial or ethnic groups, even when comparing mothers at similar levels of educational attainment. Infant mortality rates decline as mothers' education level rises for all racial and ethnic groups, but education does not erase the racial gap. Despite their high socioeconomic status, African American women with college or graduate degrees face infant mortality rates that are higher even than among white women with less than a high school education.[12]

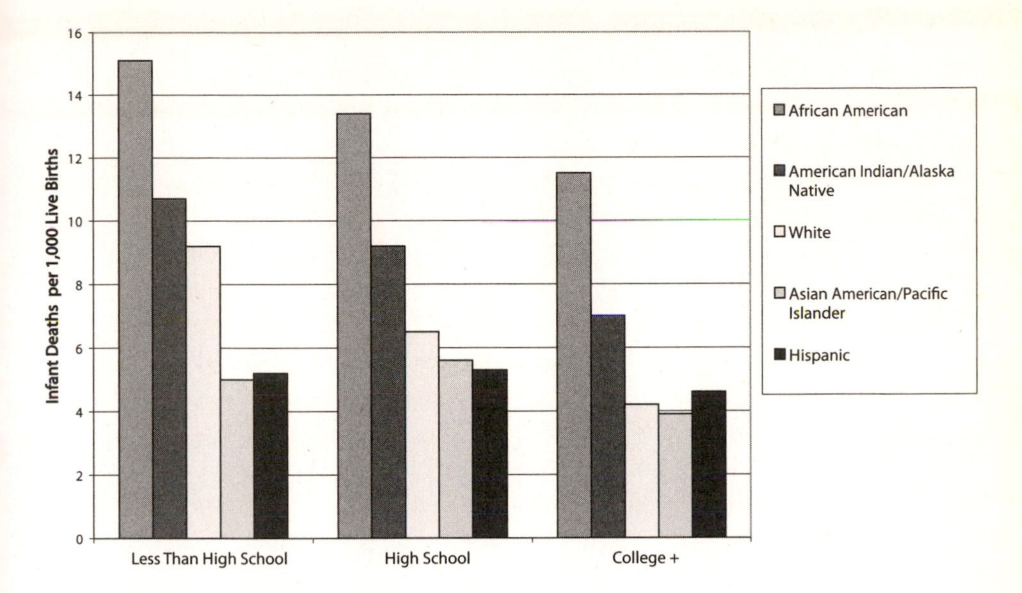

FIGURE 15.1. **Infant Mortality Rates for Mothers Age 20 and Over by Race/ Ethnicity and Education, 2001–2003**

Source: U.S. Department of Health and Human Services, National Center for Health Statistics 2007, Table 20

Women of color in the United States also fare significantly worse than white women in nearly every aspect of reproductive health. For example, African American women are nearly four times more likely to die in childbirth than white women.[13] This disparity is largely attributable to the fact that women of color, especially those who are low income, disproportionately lack access to prenatal care that is essential for healthy birth outcomes.[14] Moreover, the prevalence of many sexually transmitted infections (STIs), particularly HIV/AIDS, has reached epidemic proportions among women of color. African American women are infected with HIV/AIDS at a rate twenty-four times that of white women,[15] and African American women comprise 64 percent of women living with HIV/AIDS.[16] AIDS is also the leading cause of death for African American women aged twenty-five to thirty-four.[17] Latinas are also diagnosed with AIDS at four times the rate of white women.[18] Together, African American women and Latinas account for 82 percent of reported female AIDS cases, even though they are only 24 percent of the U.S. female population.[19] Similarly, although the number of AIDS cases declined among other racial and ethnic groups between 2001 and 2004, it doubled for Asian Pacific Islander women.[20]

THE CAUSES OF RACIAL AND ETHNIC HEALTH DISPARITIES IN THE UNITED STATES

The Western racial worldview suggests that racial health disparities are natural, based in presumed genetic or biological differences among "racial" groups. For example, until recently many in scientific and health professions assumed that the 50 percent higher rate of hypertension found among African Americans relative to white Americans is rooted in the forced migration of African slaves in the seventeenth and eighteenth centuries. This view holds that Africans who survived the Middle Passage—the often-deadly trip that newly captured slaves endured from Africa to the New World—were those who could hold more salt in their bodies. However, the "salt-slavery" hypothesis (that today's African Americans face higher rates of hypertension because they are descendants of people who could better retain sodium) has been debunked.[21] A growing body of scientific evidence points to broader social problems—not genetic or biological differences—as the key culprit in explaining heath differences between racial and ethnic groups.

The dubious value of genetic and biological explanations of racial and ethnic health status disparities is further illustrated by cross-continental epidemiologic research comparing groups that share a common ancestry. For example, Cooper and colleagues (2005) found that hypertension rates varied considerably within "racial" groups, depending on geography. Some of the highest rates of hypertension are found in European nations such as Germany, whereas some of the lowest rates were found in West Africa. Among African-descended Jamaicans, hypertension rates were double those found in West Africa, but African-descended Americans experienced rates three times higher than those found in West Africa. Figure 15.2 displays these findings.

More recent research reveals that the causes of racial and ethnic health disparities are multifactoral, that is, based in many factors. Socioeconomic differences are among the most significant factors, given the strong correlation between socioeconomic status and health. People at every ascending step in the socioeconomic gradient generally have better health than those even one step below.[22] Given the disproportionate representation of many racial and ethnic minorities in lower socioeconomic tiers, socioeconomic inequality is a major factor contributing to health inequalities. Health behaviors also certainly play a role—some racial and ethnic minorities, for example, report being less physically active than whites—but these health behaviors are often powerfully shaped by neighborhood context (discussed below). Many public health social scientists therefore believe that the fundamental structural mechanism underlying these inequalities is residential segregation, which

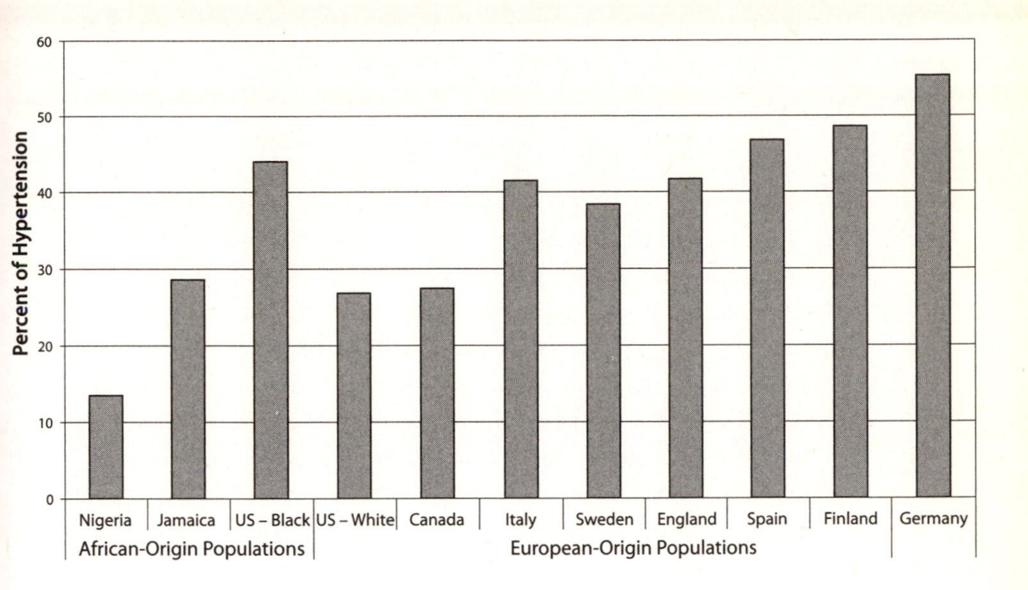

FIGURE 15.2. Hypertension Prevalence, African and European Descent Populations: Ages 35–64, Age Adjusted, Since the 1960s
Source: Cooper et al. 2005

powerfully shapes health resources, risks, and life opportunities. These forces manifest themselves in health care settings, interpersonal interactions, and institutional policies and practices. Each of these contributing factors is examined in greater detail below.

Health Care System Access and Unequal Treatment

Access to quality care is critical to the health of racial and ethnic minorities in the United States. The *National Healthcare Disparities Report* (NHDR), prepared and released annually by the U.S. Agency for Healthcare Research and Quality, is an authoritative source for the documentation of access and quality gaps. Across a range of measures of health care access, the 2006 report found that health care access and quality for people of color is overwhelmingly worse than for whites. African Americans and Latinos were found to receive poorer quality care than whites on 73 and 77 percent of measures, respectively, and Asian Americans and American Indians received poorer care on 32 and 41 percent of measures, respectively.

The most significant factor contributing to these inequities are disparities in health insurance coverage. Racial and ethnic minority and immigrant communities are disproportionately uninsured (see figure 15.3), making them especially vulnerable to health crises. For example:

- Although about 21 percent of white Americans were uninsured at any point in 2002, communities of color were more likely to be uninsured at any point (including 28 percent of African Americans, 44 percent of Hispanic Americans, 24 percent of Asian Americans and Pacific Islanders, and 33 percent of American Indians and Alaska Natives) and are more likely to be dependent upon public sources of health care.[23]
- Although Hispanic children constitute less than one-fifth of children in the United States, they represent over one-third of uninsured children.[24] Among children in fair or poor health who lack insurance (nearly five hundred seventy thousand in 2002), over two-thirds are Hispanic.[25]
- More than eleven million immigrants were uninsured in 2003, one-quarter of the U.S. uninsured.[26] Between 1998 and 2003, immigrants accounted for 86 percent of the growth in the uninsured population.[27]
- Foreign-born people are 2.5 times more likely than the native-born to lack health insurance, a gap that remains unchanged since 1993.[28]
- Women of color are more likely to be uninsured than white women. Thirty-seven percent of Latinas, 20 percent of African American women, and 36 percent of Asian Pacific Islander women are uninsured, compared to 16 percent of white women.[29]

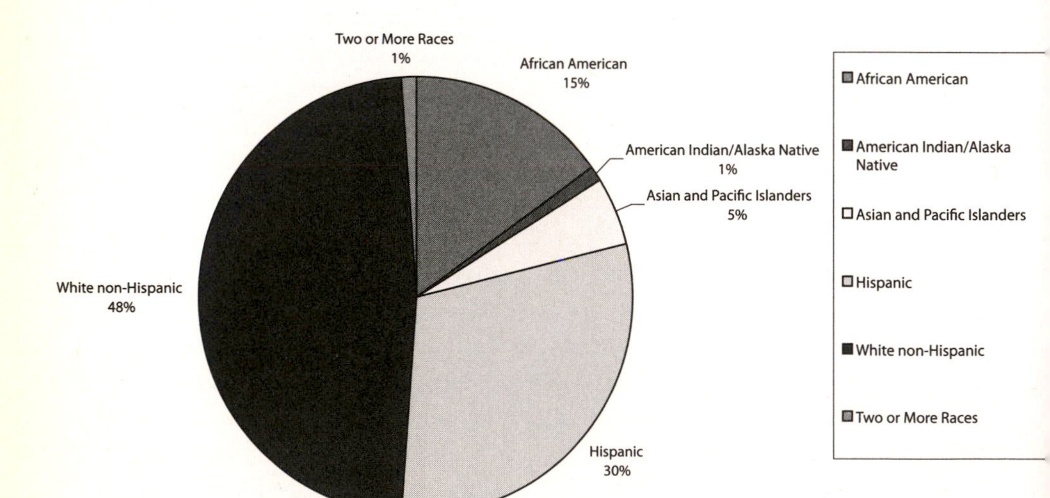

Figure 15.3. Nonelderly Uninsured by Race/Ethnicity, 2005
Source: Kaiser Family Foundation 2007

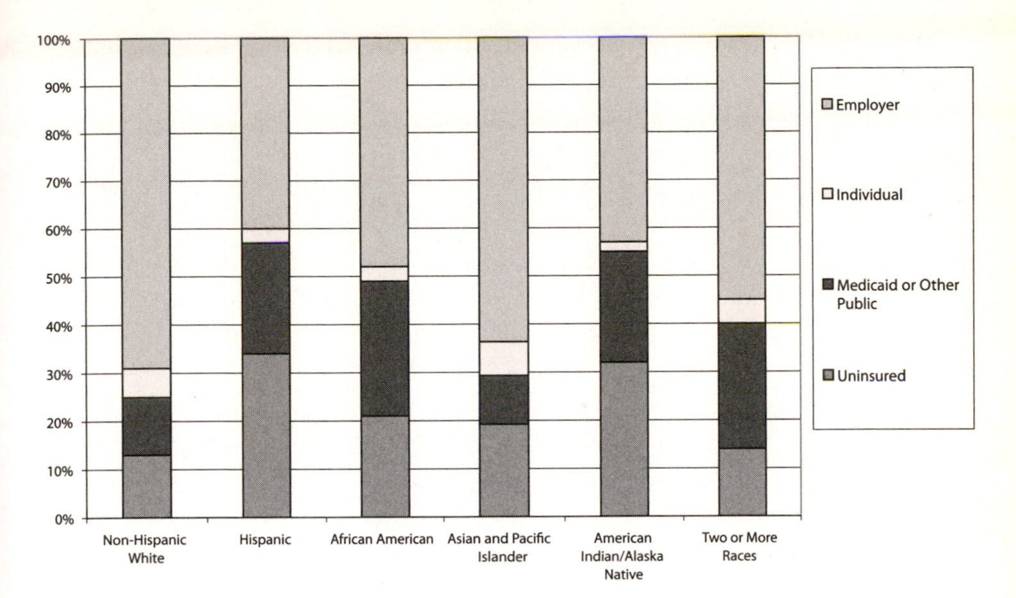

Figure 15.4. Health Insurance Coverage of the Nonelderly by Race/Ethnicity, 2005
Source: Kaiser Family Foundation 2007

The crisis of health insurance disproportionately hurts low-income families and communities of color, in no small part because health insurance in the United States remains linked to employment. Higher-paying jobs generally offer more comprehensive health benefit packages, whereas lower-paying jobs—disproportionately occupied by people of color—offer only limited health benefits, if at all, that are often accompanied by high cost-sharing arrangements with employees. Moreover, racial and ethnic minorities are disproportionately dependent on public insurance sources, such as Medicaid (see Figure 15.4). Though Medicaid has been vital for expanding access to health insurance, its limited benefit package and low reimbursement rates have a dampening effect on health care access and quality among its beneficiaries.

These economic pressures can sustain a form of "medical apartheid"—that is, separate and unequal care for low-income and minority patients.[30] For example, physicians who serve predominantly racial and ethnic minority patients are less likely to possess board certification and have greater difficulties accessing high-quality specialists, diagnostic imaging, and non-emergency admission of their patients to the hospital than physicians who serve predominantly nonminority patients.[31] A recent study of African American and white Medicare patients found the risk of admission to high-mortality hospitals was 35 percent higher for blacks than for whites in communities with high levels of residential segregation.[32] Another recent study of over three hundred thousand patients treated at 123 hospitals across the country found that minorities disproportionately receive care in lower-quality hospitals, a problem that explains the largest share of disparities.[33] The geographic maldistribution of services likely contributes to the problem. For example, a study of the availability of pain medication revealed that only one in four pharmacies located in predominantly nonwhite neighborhoods carried adequate supplies, compared to 72 percent of pharmacies in predominantly white neighborhoods.[34] Nearly one in five Latinas (18 percent) and one in ten African American women reported not seeking needed health care in the last year due to transportation problems, compared to 5 percent of white women.[35] These problems are the by-product of residential segregation and economic pressures that reward the concentration of services in outer suburbs and wealthier communities and create disincentives for practice in urban centers.[36]

Moreover, a substantial body of evidence demonstrates that racial and ethnic minorities receive a lower quality and intensity of health care than white patients, *even when they are insured at the same levels and present with the same types of health problems*.[37] Following are a few examples from the research literature:

- Insured African American patients are less likely than insured whites to receive many potentially life-saving or life-extending procedures, particularly high-tech care, such as cardiac catheterization, bypass graft surgery,[38] or kidney transplantation.[39]
- Black cancer patients fail to get the same combinations of surgical and chemotherapy treatments that white patients with the same disease presentation receive.[40]
- African American heart patients are less likely than white patients to receive diagnostic procedures, revascularization procedures, and thrombolytic therapy, even when they have similar patient characteristics.[41]
- Even routine care suffers. Black and Latino patients are less likely than whites to receive aspirin upon discharge following a heart attack, to receive appropriate care for pneumonia, and to have pain—such as the kind resulting from broken bones—appropriately treated.[42]
- Minorities are more likely to receive undesirable treatment than whites, such as limb amputation for diabetes.[43]

Several factors help explain these health care inequities.

Regular Source of Health Care. Having a regular source of health care—a local physician, clinic, or health center that patients can consider their "medical home"—is important, particularly for individuals who face or are at risk for chronic illness. When patients are able to see a health care provider consistently, they are better able to build trusting relationships, ask questions, and give and receive information. Patients who lack a regular source of health care often report miscommunication, misdiagnoses, and greater frustration about their ability to receive needed care.[44] The uninsured and underinsured, many racial and ethnic minorities, people who are not proficient in English, those who live in rural communities, and those who have low incomes are more likely to report not having a regular source of health care.[45] Yet the regular-source-of-health-care gap among racial/ethnic and income groups is growing:

- African Americans, Hispanics, and the poor and near poor (of all racial and ethnic groups) are more likely than white nonpoor groups to face barriers to having a regular source of health care. These gaps have increased since 2000. Over 42 percent of Hispanic poor and 37 percent of Hispanic nonpoor people lacked a regular source of health care in 2001 and 2002, an increase of more than 30 and 18 percent, respectively, since 1995 and 1996.[46]
- During this same period, the percentage of poor and near-poor African Americans and whites without a regular source of health care went largely unchanged. But these groups were up to 75 percent more likely than nonpoor African Americans and whites to lack a regular source of health care in 2001 and 2002.[47]
- The percentage of Hispanics from all income groups who lacked a regular source of health care increased between 1993 and 2002, despite a 15 percent decline over the same period in the ranks of white poor individuals who lacked a regular source of health care.[48]
- African American and Hispanic patients are nearly twice as likely as whites to report having a "non-mainstream" usual source of care (e.g., a hospital-based provider, rather than a private physician).[49]

Language Barriers. More than forty-six million people in the United States speak a language other than English. Of those, more than thirty-five million speak English "well" or "very well," but over ten million speak the language "not well" or "not at all."[50] Individuals with limited English proficiency are less likely than those with strong English-language skills to have a regular source of primary care or to receive preventive care. Moreover, they tend to be less satisfied with the care they receive, are more likely to report overall problems with care, and may be at increased risk of experiencing medical errors.[51] The quality of their health care therefore depends on the ability of medical professionals to effectively communicate. But many health care organizations do not provide adequate interpretation services:

- Nearly half of Latinos who are primary speakers of Spanish report having difficulty communicating with doctors or other health care providers because of language barriers.[52]
- Over one in five non-English-speaking patients avoid seeking medical help altogether because of language barriers.[53]

The Clinical Encounter. Aspects of the clinical encounter—the interaction among patients, their providers, and the health systems in which care is delivered—can play a powerful role in contributing to health care inequality. Patients and providers bring a range of expectations, preferences, and biases to the clinical encounter that can be expressed both directly and indirectly. At least part of the disparity results from biases and stereotypes that health care providers may have about racial and ethnic minorities. Experimental studies confirm that physicians can hold a host of negative beliefs about minority patients. They are presumed to be more likely to abuse drugs or alcohol and to be less educated. They aren't expected to comply with physicians' instructions, want an active lifestyle, or participate in rehabilitation if prescribed. Doctors are likely to consider white patients more "pleasant" and "rational" than black patients and to prefer white patients as "the kind of person I could see myself being friends with." These kinds of stereotypes and biases are often unconscious, the Institute of Medicine reported, but nonetheless can influence physicians' decisions regarding when and what treatments to offer.[54]

More recent research confirms that implicit biases (that is, unconscious biases that may reflect racial socialization) influence medical professionals' decision making. Green and colleagues (2007) assessed the relationship between implicit biases (as measured by a widely accepted computer-based test of the speed with which individuals make associations between people and concepts) and physicians' decisions regarding the use of thrombolysis (i.e., clot-bursting medications) among hypothetical patients in the midst of a heart attack. Although physicians reported no explicit preference for white versus black patients or differences in perceived cooperativeness, scores on implicit association tests revealed a preference for white Americans and implicit stereotypes of black Americans as less cooperative with medical procedures and less cooperative generally. More important, physicians' level of pro-white implicit bias significantly predicted their likelihood of treating white patients and not treating black patients with thrombolysis. That is, physicians who harbored the highest level of implicit racial bias were less likely to treat black heart attack patients with a potentially life-saving treatment.

Social and Community-Level Determinants of Health

Disparities in access to quality health care are not the only factors that contribute to the racial and ethnic gaps in health status. The neighborhood and community contexts in which people live powerfully shape access to health care resources and health behaviors, as well as health risks. Many people of color live in neighborhoods that are largely segregated from white Americans, and the communities in which they reside differ significantly in a number of important social, economic, and environmental conditions, in ways that can negatively influence health. People of color are also exposed to additional health risks in the form of direct or subtle racism and discrimination, which presents stressors that are exacerbated by residential segregation. These dynamics are explored below.

Neighborhood factors influence health in several ways. They exert direct effects on both physical and mental health through neighborhood conditions such as levels of crime and violence, overcrowding, and environmental exposures. Neighborhood conditions also indirectly influence health, in that the conditions of neighborhoods can either support or discourage healthy behaviors such as exercise, proper nutrition, and the development of strong social supports. The quality and availability of health care resources, as noted above, also vary by neighborhood racial, ethnic, and socioeconomic status, with low-income communities and communities of color often facing a relative paucity of such resources. Finally, neighborhood conditions structure and influence individual opportunity in ways that affect health. It is well known that population health status improves with each ascending step of the socioeconomic gradient. To the extent that neighborhoods suffer from poor schools, poor access to jobs and employment, inadequate public services such as transportation, and a lack of economic investment—all problems that disproportionately burden communities of color—the opportunity for individuals to advance economically, and therefore improve health status, is constrained.[55]

Neighborhood residential segregation is a key mechanism that perpetuates community and social determinants of racial and ethnic health disparities. Although the nation has made great progress in reducing residential segregation, the problem persists, particularly for African Americans and Hispanics. One of the most established measures of racial and ethnic residential segregation is the dissimilarity index, which can be understood as the percentage of a group's population that would have to change residence in order for the group to be evenly distributed across neighborhoods in a metropolitan area. A score of 0 is equivalent to integration representative of the total population, and a score of 100 indicates complete segregation. African Americans remain the most segregated racial/ethnic group in America, with a dissimilarity score of 64 as of 2000 (meaning 64 percent of black people would have to move if they were to be integrated into the population), though blacks are less isolated than in 1980, when they scored 73. Hispanics scored 50 in 1980 and 51 in 2000, while Asians measured as the most integrated, at 40 in 1980 and 41 in 2000.[56] Importantly, individuals do not have equal opportunities to select the communities they reside in. The practice of segregation relies on both institutional discrimination in the real estate and housing finance market and individual interpersonal discrimination based on fear and/or loathing of the racial other.[57] Whites have the strongest preference of any race for living in a neighborhood without racial outsiders, and among all races and ethnicities, blacks are the least preferred race to share a neighborhood with.[58]

Historically, the United States has been characterized by high levels of residential segregation on the basis of race, ethnicity, income, and nativity. From the late 1960s through the 1980s, poverty became increasingly concentrated in inner city neighborhoods.[59] Encouragingly, levels of racial, ethnic, and income segregation declined in many U.S. communities in the 1990s.[60] These trends are not consistent across all demographic groups, however. A 2002 study by the U.S. Census Bureau, for example, found that although levels of African American segregation declined across many dimensions between 1980 and 2000, residential segregation is still higher for African Americans than for any other group. In addition, this study found that Hispanics and Asian and Pacific Islanders also face high levels of residential segregation. On some measures of segregation, such as the degree of isolation from other groups, Hispanics and Asian and Pacific Islander Americans experienced increases in segregation over the last two decades.[61]

Residential segregation is particularly problematic when race, ethnicity, and poverty converge. An analysis of trends in the residential segregation of poor families of color, prepared for The Opportunity Agenda by the Washington, D.C.–based Poverty and Race Research Action Council (PRRAC) (2005) with researchers from the State University of New York at Albany, examined Census Bureau data on the poverty status of neighborhoods. Using data on census tracts within metropolitan areas defined in 1960, this analysis finds that the percentage of poor whites, African Americans, Hispanics, and female-headed households living in high-poverty neighborhoods (those with 30 percent or more residents living in poverty) generally declined between 1960 and 2000. But the rate of decline for poor white families was much sharper than

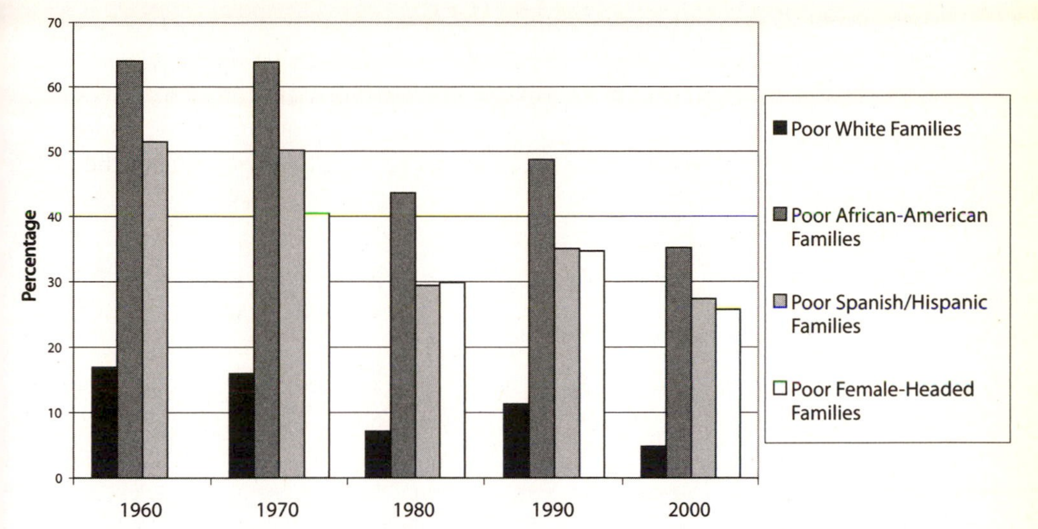

FIGURE 15.5. Percentage of Poor Families Living in High Poverty (30 Percent or More in Poverty) Neighborhoods, 1960–2000

Source: Poverty and Race Research Action Council 2005

for poor families of color. While poor African American families were 3.8 times more likely than poor white families to live in high-poverty neighborhoods in metropolitan areas in 1960, they were 7.3 times more likely than poor whites to live in high-poverty neighborhoods in 2000. Similarly, poor Hispanic families were 5.7 times more likely than poor white families to live in high-poverty neighborhoods in 2000, but were only 3.0 times as likely as poor white families to live in such communities in 1960. And while poor female-headed households were 2.5 times more likely than poor whites to live in high-poverty neighborhoods in 1970, they were 5.3 times more likely than poor whites to live in these conditions three decades later. These findings confirm other research that demonstrates that even when family income is similarly low, families of color are more likely to be relegated to high-poverty communities (see Figure 15.5).

Residential segregation harms the health of people of color in multiple ways. Segregation channels nonwhites into areas with limited financial and human resources, and such neighborhoods are home to poor public education; inadequate health care; toxic living conditions; and higher rates of disorder, crime, and incarceration. As a result, people of color often live in neighborhoods isolated from both the institutional and cultural resources needed to promote health. And though individual behaviors certainly impact health outcomes, neighborhoods not only constrain behavioral choices, they affect residents' health in ways that have nothing to do with individual behaviors.

The following examples illustrate the impact of residential segregation on public health.

Pollution and Toxic Waste. Fifty-six percent of the residents in neighborhoods with commercial hazardous waste facilities are people of color. Thus, percentages of people of color as a whole are 1.9 times greater in waste facility host neighborhoods than in nonhost areas. Poverty rates in waste facility neighborhoods are 1.5 times greater than in neighborhoods without such facilities.[62]

Poor Nutrition. Low-income neighborhoods of color often lack health-enhancing resources such as supermarkets and other sources of low-cost, nutritious food. One study showed that white Americans are five times more likely to live in census tracts with supermarkets than black Americans, and whites have three times greater access to private transportation than black Americans in similar communities.[63] So not only do whites live closer to places with the right foods, they have more resources to make nutritious choices than people of color. The availability of nutritious foods in local markets is closely tied to dietary habits and health outcomes; the more people know about nutrition and the more access they have to healthy food, the more nutritious foods they consume.[64]

Poor Quality Housing and Public Spaces. Crowding, substandard housing, elevated noise level, decreased ability to regulate temperature and humidity, and elevated exposure to noxious pollutants and allergens such as lead, smog, and dust mites are all common in poor, segregated communities. Lack of recreational facilities such as parks, gymnasiums, and swimming pools in segregated neighborhoods can discourage and impede physical exercise.[65]

Poor Public Education. Between 1995 and 2004, public school districts spent $504 billion in capital expenditures, but the money was not spent equitably. The poorest districts spent an average of $4,800 per student, whereas the richest districts spent $9,361 per student. The purpose of spending also differed by class level, as poor schools were more likely to receive funds for basic structural repairs to counteract physical decay, and wealthy schools were more likely to receive funds for educational enhancements, such as science labs.

Racial spending disparities present themselves as well, as predominantly minority districts invested the least amount per student ($5,172), and predominantly white districts invested the most ($7,102). The physical conditions of schools, such as air quality and temperature, influence property values, turnover in teacher employment, and student learning, so poor schools serving people of color present mutually reinforcing disadvantages for students, teachers, and neighborhood residents alike.[66]

Disorder, Crime, and Violence. As a result of concentrated poverty and collective inability to exert social control, segregated communities face higher rates of crime and violence,[67] which both directly affect health by increasing risk for injury and death.

The Criminal Justice System and Incarceration. African Americans, Latinos, and American Indians are disproportionately penalized and imprisoned by the criminal justice system, and impoverished urban communities with high rates of arrest and imprisonment do not develop the social bonds and networks needed to maintain order. At the national level, blacks are currently incarcerated at a rate 5.6 times that of whites, while the Hispanic rate of incarceration is 1.8 times that of whites.[68] One out of every fourteen black children has at least one parent in prison, a rate that far outpaces white children.[69] Families torn apart by incarceration have fewer human and financial resources for childrearing, and children in disadvantaged neighborhoods have fewer stewards for healthy socialization.

The Health Effects of Race-Based Discrimination, Bias, and Prejudice

In addition to structural inequality perpetuated by residential segregation, people of color face interpersonal barriers to achievement, productivity, and social integration. This notion of interpersonal racism goes beyond the structural, institutional factors that align to channel people of color toward undesirable neighborhoods and socioeconomic outcomes. *Interpersonal racism* refers to daily interactions during which people of color are denied access, humiliated, or insulted based on their race or ethnicity.

There is increasing evidence that race-based discrimination is not only emotionally hurtful, but physiologically damaging to minority Americans. A growing body of research using innovative methods is beginning to uncover the toll. For example, perceived race-based discrimination is positively associated with smoking among African Americans, and smokers find the experience of discrimination more stressful. In addition, repeated subjection to race-based discrimination is associated with higher blood pressure levels and more frequent diagnoses of hypertension.[70] In another study, black women who reported that they had been victims of racial discrimination were 31 percent more likely to develop breast cancer than those who did not.[71] Experiences of racial discrimination also are associated with poor health among Asian Americans. More than two thousand participants in a recent national survey were asked about their experiences with discrimination and their health histories. Researchers found that everyday discrimination was associated with a variety of health conditions, such as chronic cardiovascular, respiratory, and pain-related health issues. Filipinos reported the highest level of discrimination, followed by Chinese Americans and Vietnamese Americans.[72]

New models offer mechanisms to explain how racialized behavior and institutions affect health. These models "locate health disparities in the external influences of social space and the internal effects of body and brain functioning."[73] They suggest that harmful effects of discrimination are the result of chronic experiences of race-based discrimination, both actual and perceived. These processes set in motion physiological responses (e.g., elevated blood pressure and heart rate, production of biochemical reactions, hypervigilance) that deteriorate health. Importantly, these stressors can be both chronic and acute. Chronic stress associated with financial and caretaking pressures, fear of violent victimization, grief, and frustration and anger brought on as a reaction to consistent discrimination has deleterious health effects that continue even when residents from segregated neighborhoods are relocated to safer residential areas.[74] Chronic stress can lead to increased risk for coronary health disease, chronic inflammation, cognitive impairment, substance abuse, and the erosion of mental health, and has demonstrable ill health effects on other mental and physical processes.[75]

Race-related stress operates to wear down health in several ways. From a developmental perspective, the influence of negative environments associated with structural racism and residential segregation has a profound and negative effect on the health and development of young children. Childhood exposure to conditions of violence, coupled with poor education and negative social connectedness—particularly early childhood exposure to these conditions—is associated with changes in brain functioning and physiological responses. Unhealthy social spaces associated with segregation serve as the "structural lattice" for maintaining discrimination. In addition, intergenerational and life-span effects of race discrimination suggest that the health effects of racism carry forward over time in individuals and across generations. For example, low birth weight, which is more prevalent among African Americans and American Indians than other groups, is shaped by the mothers' socioeconomic conditions and affects the long-term health of the developing infant, despite generally improving opportunities and better environments for minorities.[76]

Internalized racism also negatively affects the health of people of color. *Internalized racism* refers to the acceptance by marginalized racial populations of negative societal beliefs and stereotypes about themselves; "the normative cultural characterization of the superiority of Whiteness and devaluing of Blackness, combined with the economic disadvantages of Blacks, can lead to the perception of self as worthless and powerless."[77] Internalized racism experienced by blacks who exhibit racial prejudice toward other blacks is positively associated with alcohol use and psychological stress. Studies have found a positive association between a scale capturing internalized racism and alcohol consumption. Internalized racism was also positively related to psychological distress even after adjustment for other stressors, social support, religious orientation, SES, marital status, and physical health.

In addition to institutional and internalized racism, individually mediated racism and discrimination can also contribute to health inequities as a consequence of their impact on economic opportunity, particularly in housing and employment, as illustrated below.

The Fair Housing Act of 1968 improved housing options for many racial and ethnic minorities seeking to purchase a home or obtain rental housing. But racial and ethnic discrimination in housing persists, at significant levels. Large federally sponsored audit studies—which match pairs of testers, one white and one minority, on a variety of personal characteristics and assign equivalent "background" information—find that racial and ethnic discrimination in housing markets remains significant and pervasive. A 2000 U.S. Department of Housing and Urban Development study found that whites were favored over identically qualified African Americans in 22 percent of rental housing test cases and were favored over Hispanics in 26 percent of cases. In housing sales, whites received favorable treatment over African Americans in 17 percent of tests, a decline from 1989, when whites were favored in nearly 30 percent of tests. Whites were favored over Hispanics in nearly 20 percent of housing sale tests conducted in 2000. The same study also found that Asian American testers received poorer treatment relative to white testers in 21 percent of tests of rental markets and 20 percent of housing sales markets.[78]

People of color, women, and other historically marginalized groups have made significant strides in gaining access to previously all-white and all-male jobs, particularly since passage of federal antidiscrimination laws in the 1960s and 1970s. Women currently make up over half of managers and professionals in the business sector.[79] But barriers to employment equality persist in many sectors. Audit studies of employment discrimination consistently find that job applicants of color are more likely than whites to face unfair and discriminatory treatment. A 2003 audit study of temporary employment agencies in California, for example, found that employment agencies preferred less-qualified white applicants nearly three times as often as more-qualified African American applicants.[80] And an audit study that matched African American and white college students posing as job seekers found that even white auditors who presented criminal records were more likely to receive callbacks than African Americans who did not present criminal records.[81]

CONCLUSION

Racial and ethnic health inequities are largely the result of structural racism—that is, the inequitable distribution along racial and ethnic lines of power, resources, and services that shape population health. These same forces drive much of U.S. racial socioeconomic inequality. Racism operates in many dimensions, including interpersonal, institutional, and internalized forms that disadvantage some racial and ethnic minorities and advantage the majority. Simply put, the racial worldview in the United States has harmful consequences for a disproportionate share of people of color.

NOTES

1. U.S. Department of Health and Human Services, National Center for Health Statistics 2007.
2. Harper et al. 2007.
3. U.S. Department of Health and Human Services, National Center for Health Statistics 2007.
4. Woolf et al. 2004.
5. Jasso et al. 2004.
6. McCracken et al. 2007.
7. National Asian Pacific American Women's Forum 2005, 4.
8. National Latina Institute for Reproductive Health 2006.
9. U.S. Department of Health & Human Services, Office of Minority Health 2007.
10. Centers for Disease Control 2002.
11. Centers for Disease Control 2002.
12. U.S. Department of Health and Human Services, National Center for Health Statistics 2007.
13. Centers for Disease Control 2007b, 8.
14. *AHRQ National Health Disparities Report* 2006, 160 (stating that "the proportion [of] women who initiated prenatal care in the first trimester was significantly lower" among all major ethnic groups compared with white women); Centers for Disease Control 2006, Table 26(a) (revealing that blacks and Hispanics are more than twice as likely to receive late or no prenatal care compared to white women).

15. Centers for Disease Control 2007a.
16. Centers for Disease Control 2007c.
17. Centers for Disease Control 2007c, 1; U.S. Department of Health & Human Services 2004.
18. Centers for Disease Control 2007c, 2; see also Kaiser Family Foundation 2006.
19. Centers for Disease Control 2007c, 2; see also U.S. Department of Health & Human Services 2006a.
20. Centers for Disease Control 2007c, 3.
21. Kaufman and Hall 2003.
22. Adler et al. n.d.
23. U.S. Department of Health and Human Services 2006b.
24. Robert Wood Johnson Foundation 2005.
25. The Urban Institute 2005.
26. The uninsured rate among immigrants increased dramatically in the late 1990s, following passage of the Personal Responsibility and Work Opportunity Reconciliation Act of 1996, which imposed a five-year limit on most new immigrants' ability to participate in public health insurance programs. Prior to and shortly following passage of the act (between 1994 and 1998), immigrants accounted for about one-third of the increase in the number of uninsured individuals.
27. Employee Benefit Research Institute 2005.
28. U.S. Census Bureau 2005.
29. Kaiser Family Foundation 2004; National Asian Pacific American Women's Forum 2005, 10.
30. Bronx Health Reach 2000.
31. Bach et al. 2004.
32. Sarrazin, Campbell, and Rosenthal 2009.
33. Hasnain-Wynia et al. 2007.
34. Morrison et al. 2000.
35. Kaiser Family Foundation 2002.
36. Smith 2005.
37. Institute of Medicine 2003.
38. Kaiser Family Foundation and the American College of Cardiology 2002.
39. Klassen et al. 2002.
40. Institute of Medicine 2003.
41. Kaiser Family Foundation and the American College of Cardiology 2002.
42. Institute of Medicine 2003.
43. Institute of Medicine 2003.
44. Kaiser Family Foundation 2003.
45. Kaiser Family Foundation 2003.
46. Kaiser Family Foundation 2003.
47. Kaiser Family Foundation 2003.
48. Kaiser Family Foundation 2003.
49. Lillie-Blanton, Martinez, and Salganicoff 2001.
50. U.S. Census Bureau 2003.
51. Institute of Medicine 2003.
52. Pew Hispanic Center and the Kaiser Family Foundation 2004.
53. Pew Hispanic Center and the Kaiser Family Foundation 2004.
54. Institute of Medicine 2003.

55. Joint Center Health Policy Institute and Policy Link 2004.
56. Iceland et al. 2002.
57. Massey and Denton 1993.
58. Iceland 2002.
59. Kingsley and Pettit 2003; Jargowsky 2003.
60. Jargowsky 2003.
61. U.S. Census Bureau 2002.
62. Bullard et al. 2007.
63. Morland et al. 2002.
64. Morland et al. 2002.
65. Williams and Collins 2001.
66. Filardo et al. 2006.
67. Morenoff et al. 2001.
68. Mauer and King 2007.
69. Mauer 2004.
70. Mays et al. 2007.
71. Taylor et al. 2007.
72. Gee et al. 2007.
73. Mays et al. 2007.
74. Massey et al. 2004.
75. Mays et al. 2007.
76. Mays et al. 2007.
77. Williams 2004.
78. Turner and Ross 2003.
79. "Quick Takes: Women in U.S. Management, 1950–Present" 2005; "2002 Catalyst Census of Women Corporate Officers and Top Earners in the Fortune 500" n.d.; U.S. Equal Employment Opportunity Commission 2004.
80. Bussey and Trasvina 2003.
81. Pager 2003.

REFERENCES

Adler, N. et al. n.d. *Reaching for a Healthier Life: Facts on Socioeconomic Status and Health in the United States*. John D. and Catherine T. MacArthur Foundation Research Network on Socioeconomic Status and Health. Available at http://www.macses.ucsf.edu/downloads/Reaching_for_a_Healthier_Life.pdf (accessed September 30, 2010).

AHRQ National Health Disparities Report. 2006. Rockville, MD: Agency for Healthcare Research and Quality. Available at http://www.ahrq.gov/qual/nhdr06/nhdr06.htm (accessed July 12, 2009).

Alland, Alexander, Jr. 1973. *Human Diversity*. Garden City, N.Y.: Anchor Books.

Allen, Theodore W. 1994. *The Invention of the White Race*. Vol. 1. London: Verso.

______. 1997. *The Invention of the White Race*. Vol. 2. London: Verso.

Arendt, Hannah. [1951] 1968. *Imperialism*. New York: Harcourt, Brace & World.

Bach, P. B., H. H. Pham, D. Schrag, R. C. Tate, and J. L. Hargraves. 2004. "Primary Care Physicians Who Treat Blacks and Whites." *The New England Journal of Medicine* 351, no. 6: 575–584.

Baker, John R. 1974. *Race*. Oxford: Oxford University Press.

Baker, Lee. 1998. *From Savage to Negro: Anthropology and the Construction of Race, 1896–1954*. Berkeley: University of California Press.

Banton, Michael. 1977. *The Idea of Race*. London: Tavistock.

______. 1983. *Racial and Ethnic Competition*. Cambridge: Cambridge University Press.

______. 1988. *Racial Consciousness*. London: Longman.

Barrow, R. H. 1928. *Slavery in the Roman Empire*. New York: Barnes & Noble.

Bartlett, Irving H. 1967. *The American Mind in the Mid-Nineteenth Century*. New York: Thomas Y. Crowell.

Barzun, Jacques. 1965. *Race: A Study in Superstition*. New York: Harper & Row.

Bates, Crispin. 1997. "Race, Caste, and Tribe in Central India: The Early Origins of Indian Anthropometry." In *The Concept of Race in South Asia*, edited by Peter Robb, 219–259. Delhi: Oxford University Press.

Bean, Bennett B. 1926. "Types of the Three Great Races of Man." *American Journal of Anatomy* 37: 237–270.

Bell, Alison. 2005. "White Ethnogenesis and Gradual Capitalism: Perspectives from Colonial Archaeological Sites in the Chesapeake." *American Anthropologist* 107, no. 3: 446–460.

Bell, Derrick A., Jr., ed. 1980. *Civil Rights: Leading Cases*. Boston: Little, Brown.
Benedict, Ruth. [1940] 1947. *Race: Science and Politics*. New York: Viking Press.
Bennett, K. A. 1969. "Typological vs. Evolutionary Approach in Skeletal Population Studies." *American Journal of Physical Anthropology* 30, no. 3: 407–415.
Bennett, Lerone, Jr. 1964. *Before the* Mayflower: *A History of the Negro in America, 1619–1964*. Chicago: Johnson Publishers.
______. 1975. *The Shaping of Black America*. Chicago: Johnson Publishers.
Berkhofer, Robert F., Jr. 1978. *The White Man's Indians*. New York: Alfred A. Knopf.
Berry, Mary, and J. Blassingame. 1982. *Long Memory: The Black Experience in America*. New York: Oxford University Press.
Bidney, David. 1954. "The Idea of the Savage in North American Ethnohistory." *Journal of the History of Ideas* 15, no. 2: 322–327.
Birdsell, J. B. 1972. "The Problem of the Evolution of Human Races: Classification or Clines." *Social Biology* 19, no. 1: 136–162.
Blackburn, Robin. 1997. *The Making of New World Slavery: From the Baroque to the Modern, 1492–1800*. London: Verso.
Blassingame, John W. 1979. *The Slave Community*. New York: Oxford University Press.
Bloch, Marc. 1961. *Feudal Society*. London: Routledge and Kegan Paul.
Boardman, J., J. Griffin, and O. Murray. 1986. *The Oxford History of the Classical World*. Oxford: Oxford University Press.
Boas, Franz. 1940. *Race, Language and Culture*. New York: The Free Press. Cited chapters from this volume are listed below:
______. 1910–1913. "Changes in Bodily Form of Descendants of Immigrants."
______. [1911] 1963. "The Mind of Primitive Man."
______. 1912. "Remarks on the Anthropological Study of Children."
______. 1913. "Influence of Heredity and Environment on Growth."
______. 1916. "New Evidence in Regard to the Instability of Human Types."
______. 1922. "Report on the Anthropometric Investigation of the Population of the United States."
Bober, M. M. [1927] 1965. *Karl Marx's Interpretation of History*. Reprint. New York: W. W. Norton.
Bodmer, W. F., and L. L. Cavalli-Sforza. 1976. *Genetics, Evolution and Man*. San Francisco: W. H. Freeman.
Bohannan, Paul. 1963. *Social Anthropology*. New York: Holt, Rinehart & Winston.
Bohannan, Paul, and Philip Curtin. 1995. *Africa and Africans*. 4th ed. Prospect Heights, Ill.: Waveland Press.
Bolnick, Deborah A. 2008. "Individual Ancestry Inference and the Reification of Race as a Biological Phenomenon." In *Revisiting Race in a Genomic Age*, edited by Barbara A. Koenig, Sandra Soo-Jin Lee, and Sarah S. Richardson. New Brunswick, N.J.: Rutgers University Press.
Bolt, Christine. 1971. *Victorian Attitudes to Race*. London: Routledge and Kegan Paul.
Bowser, Frederick P. 1974. *The African Slave in Colonial Peru, 1524–1650*. Stanford, Calif.: Stanford University Press.
______. 1975. "The Free Person of Color in Mexico City and Lima: Manumission and Opportunity, 1580–1650." In *Race and Slavery in the Western Hemisphere*, edited by S. L. Engerman and E. D. Genovese. Princeton, N.J.: Princeton University Press.
Boyd, W. C. 1971. "Four Achievements of the Genetic Model in Physical Anthropology." In *Human Populations: Genetic Variation and Evolution*, edited by L. N. Morris, 20–31. San Francisco: Chandler.

Brace, C. Loring. 1964. "On the Race Concept." *Current Anthropology* 5, no. 4: 313–314.

______. 1969. "A Nonracial Approach Towards the Understanding of Human Diversity." In *The Concept of Race*, edited by A. Montagu. New York: Collier Books.

Bradley, K. R. 1984. *Slaves and Masters in the Roman Empire*. Brussels: Latomus Revue D'Etudes Latines.

Breene, Thomas K., and Keith Innes. 1980. *Myne Owne Ground*. Oxford: Oxford University Press.

Brodie, Fawn. 1974. *Thomas Jefferson: An Intimate History*. New York: Bantam.

Bronx Health Reach. 2000. *Separate and Unequal: Medical Apartheid in New York City*. Available at http://www.institute2000.org/policy/medical_apartheid.pdf (accessed July 30, 2006).

Brown, Leon C. 1968. "Color in Northern Africa." In *Color and Race*, edited by J. H. Franklin. Boston: Houghton Mifflin.

Brues, Alice M. 1959. "The Spearman and the Archer." *American Anthropologist* 61, no. 3: 457–469.

______. 1977. *People and Races*. New York: Macmillan.

Buckland, W. W. 1908. *The Roman Law of Slavery*. Cambridge: Cambridge University Press.

Bullard, Robert D., with Paul Mohai, Robin Saha, and Beverly Wright. 2007. "Toxic Wastes and Race at Twenty: 1987–2007." Report Prepared for the United Church of Christ Justice and Witness Ministries. Available at www.ucc.org/assets/pdfs/toxic20.pdf (accessed July 20, 2008).

Bush, Melanie E. L. 2004. *Breaking the Code of Good Intentions: Everyday Forms of Whiteness*. Lanham, Md.: Rowman & Littlefield.

Bussey, J., and J. Trasvina. 2003. *Racial Preferences: The Treatment of White and African American Job Applicants by Temporary Employment Agencies in California*. Berkeley, Calif.: Discrimination Research Center, December. Available at www.impactfund.org (accessed August 13, 2005).

Byrd, W. Michael, and Linda A. Clayton. 2002. "Racial and Ethnic Disparities in Healthcare: A Background and History." In *Unequal Treatment: Confronting Racial and Ethnic Disparities in Healthcare*. Washington, D.C.: National Academies Press.

Campbell, Leon. 1973. "Racism Without Race." In *Racism in the Eighteenth Century*, edited by E. Pagliaro. Cleveland, Ohio: Case Western Reserve University Press.

Campbell, Mavis. 1974. "Aristotle and Black Slavery: A Study in Race Prejudice." *Race* 15, no. 3: 283–301.

Canny, Nicholas P. 1973. "The Ideology of English Colonialization: From Ireland to America." *William and Mary Quarterly* 3rd ser., 30: 575–598.

Castle, W. E. 1926. "Biological and Social Consequences of Race-Crossing." *American Journal of Physical Anthropology* 9, no. 2: 145–156.

Castro, Americo. 1971. *The Spaniards*. Berkeley: University of California Press.

Cavalli-Sforza, L. L., and W. F. Bodmer. 1971. *The Genetics of Human Populations*. San Francisco: W. H. Freeman.

Centers for Disease Control. 2002. "Infant Mortality and Low Birth Weight Among Black and White Infants—United States, 1980–2000." *MMWR Weekly* 51, no. 27 (July 12): 589–592.

______. 2006. *National Vital Statistics Reports, Births: Final Data for 2004* (September 29): Table 26(a).

______. 2007a. *Fact Sheet: HIV/AIDS among African Americans* (January): 2.

______. 2007b. *Mortality and Related Concepts* Series 3, no. 33 (February): 8.

______.2007c. *HIV/AIDS among Women* (revised June): 1. Available at http://www.cdc.gov/hiv/topics/women/resources/factsheets/pdf/women.pdf.

Chana, Subadra. 2002. "The Crafting of Human Bodies and the Racialization of Caste in India." Paper presented at the Inter-Congress of IUAES, Tokyo, September.

______. 2003. "Colonialism, Casteism, and the Myth of Race: A Historical Perspective on the Intersection of Indian Beliefs and Western Science." In *Is Race a Universal Idea?*, edited by Y. Takezawa. Kyoto: Institute for Research in Humanities.

Chase, Allen. 1980. *The Legacy of Malthus*. Urbana: University of Illinois Press.

Cohen, William. 1969. "Thomas Jefferson and the Problem of Slavery." *Journal of American History* 56, no. 3: 503–526.

Cohen, Yehudi, ed. 1974. *Man in Adaptation*. Chicago: Aldine.

Coon, Carlton S. 1962. *The Origin of Races*. New York: Alfred A. Knopf.

Cooper, R. S. et al. 2005. "An International Comparative Study of Blood Pressure in Populations of European vs. African Descent." *BMC Medicine* 3, no. 2. Available at http://www.pubmedcentral.nih.gov/articlerender.fcgi?artid=545060 (accessed July 31, 2007).

Count, E. W., ed. 1950. *This Is Race*. New York: Henry Schuman.

Covarrubias Horozco, Sebastian. [1611] 1943. *Tesoro de la Lengua Castellana o Española*. Barcelona: S. A. Horta.

Cox, Oliver C. [1948] 1959. *Caste, Class and Race*. Reprint. New York: Monthly Review Press.

Cuffel, Victoria. 1966. "The Classical Greek Concept of Slavery." *Journal of the History of Ideas* 27, no. 3: 323–342.

Curtin, Philip D. 1964. *The Image of Africa: British Ideas and Action, 1780–1850*. Madison: University of Wisconsin Press.

______. 1977. "Slavery and Empire." *Annals of the New York Academy of Sciences* 292: 3–11.

Curtis, L. P., Jr. 1968. *Anglo-Saxons and Celts*. New York: New York University Press.

______. 1972. "Anglo-Saxonism and the Irish." In *Race and Social Difference*, edited by P. Baxter and B. Sansom, 123–129. Middlesex, England: Penguin.

da Costa, Emilia Viotti. 1977. "Slave Images and Realities." *Annals of the New York Academy of Sciences* 292: 293–310.

Dalton, George, ed. 1967. *Tribal and Peasant Economies*. Garden City, N.Y.: Natural History Press.

Daniels, Roger. 1975. *The Decision to Relocate the Japanese Americans*. Philadelphia: J. B. Lippincott.

______. [1962] 1977. *The Politics of Prejudice*. Reprint. Berkeley: University of California Press.

Darnell, Regna, ed. 1974. *Readings in the History of Anthropology*. New York: Harper & Row.

Davenport, C. B. 1929. "Do Races Differ in Mental Capacity?" *Human Biology* 1, no. 1: 70–89.

Davis, Allison. 1935. "The Distribution of the Blood Groups and Its Bearing on the Concept of Race." Parts 1 and 2. *The Sociological Review* 27, no. 1: 19–34; no. 2: 182–200.

Davis, David Brion. 1966. *The Problem of Slavery in Western Culture*. Middlesex, England: Penguin.

______. 1969. "A Comparison of British American and Latin American Slavery." In *Slavery in the New World*, edited by L. Foner and E. Genovese, 69–83. Englewood Cliffs, N.J.: Prentice-Hall.

______. 1975. *The Problem of Slavery in the Age of Revolution*. Ithaca, N.Y.: Cornell University Press.

______. 1984. *Slavery and Human Progress*. New York: Oxford University Press.

Degler, Carl N. 1959–1960. "Slavery and the Genesis of American Race Prejudice." *Comparative Studies in Society and History* 2, no. 1: 49–66.

______. 1970. "Slavery in Brazil and the United States: An Essay in Comparative History." *American Historical Review* 75, no. 4: 1004–1028.

______. 1971. *Neither Black nor White*. New York: Macmillan.

Deniker, Joseph. 1900. *The Races of Man*. London: Walter Scott.

Dickason, Olive P. 1979. "Europeans and Amerindians: Some Comparative Aspects of Early Contact." In *Papers of the Canadian Historical Association*, 182–202. Ottawa: The Canadian Historical Association.

Dietz, F. C. 1932. *A Political and Social History of England*. New York: Macmillan.

Dikötter, Frank. 1992. *The Discourse of Race in Modern China*. Stanford: Stanford University Press.

______. 1997. *The Construction of Racial Identities in China and Japan*. Honolulu: University of Hawai'i Press.

Diop, Cheikh Anta. 1981. "Origins of the Ancient Egyptians." In *UNESCO General History of Africa*, vol. 2, edited by J. Ki-Zerbo. Boston: Heinemann Educational Books.

Dobzhansky, Theodosius. [1937] 1982. *Genetics and the Origin of the Species*. New York: Columbia University Press.

______. 1973. *Genetic Diversity and Human Equality*. New York: Basic Books.

Dover, Cedric. 1951. Letter to the editor, *Man*, no. 95 (April).

Drake, St. Clair. 1987. *Black Folk Here and There*. Vol. 1. Los Angeles: Center for Afro-American Studies, University of California.

Drescher, S. 1986. *Capitalism and Antislavery*. New York: Oxford University Press.

DuBois, W. E. B. 1965. *The World and Africa*. Rev. ed. New York: International Publishers.

______. [1935] 1985. *Black Reconstruction in America*. Reprint. New York: Atheneum.

Dumond, Dwight L. [1961] 1966. *Antislavery*. Reprint. New York: W. W. Norton.

Dupré, John. 2008. "What Genes Are and Why There Are No Genes for Race." In *Revising Race in a Genomic Age*, edited by Barbara A. Koenig, Sandra Soo-Jin Lee, and Sarah S. Richardson, 39–55. New Brunswick, N.J.: Rutgers University Press.

Duster, Troy. 2003. *Backdoor to Eugenics*. 2nd ed. New York: Routledge.

Ehret, Christopher. 2002. *The Civilizations of Africa: A History to 1800*. Charlottesville: University Press of Virginia.

Elkins, Stanley M. [1959] 1963. *Slavery*. New York: Grosset and Dunlap.

Employee Benefit Research Institute. 2005. "The Impact of Immigration on Health Insurance Coverage in the United States." *Employee Benefit Research Institute Notes* 26, no. 6.

Epperson, Terrence W. 1999. "Constructing Difference: The Social and Spatial Order of the Chesapeake Plantation." In *I, Too, Am America: Archaeological Studies of African-American Life*, edited by Theresa A. Singleton. Charlottesville: University Press of Virginia.

Fancher, R. E. 1985. *The Intelligence Men: Makers of the IQ Controversy*. New York: W. W. Norton.

Faust, Drew G., ed. 1981. *The Ideology of Slavery*. Baton Rouge: Louisiana State University Press.

Feldman, Marcus W., and Richard C. Lewontin. 2008. "Race, Ancestry, and Medicine." In *Revisiting Race in a Genomic Age*, edited by Barbara A. Koenig, Sandra Soo-Jin Lee, and Sarah S. Richardson, 89–101. New Brunswick, N.J.: Rutgers University Press.

Fields, Barbara. 1982. "Ideology and Race in American History." In *Region, Race and Reconstruction*, edited by J. M. Kousser and J. M. McPherson, 143–177. New York: Oxford University Press.

Filardo, Mary W., with Jeffrey M. Vincent, Ping Sung, and Travis Stein. 2006. *Growth and Disparity: A Decade of U.S. Public School Construction. Building Educational Success Together (BEST)*. Available at http://bestfacilities.org/best-home/view_SpotlightList.asp?rsview95Spotlight_PagingMove=1 (accessed February 4, 2010).

Fincher, Jack. 1976. *Human Intelligence*. New York: G. P. Putnam.

Finley, Moses I. 1968a. "Slavery." In *Encyclopedia of the Social Sciences*. New York: Macmillan and The Free Press.

______, ed. [1960] 1968b. *Slavery in Classical Antiquity*. Reprint. Cambridge, England: W. Hepper and Sons.

______. 1980. *Ancient Slavery and Modern Ideology*. New York: Viking Press.

Foner, L., and E. D. Genovese, eds. 1969. *Slavery in the New World*. Englewood Cliffs, N.J.: Prentice-Hall.

Fontaine, Pierre-Michel, ed. 1985. *Race, Class and Power in Brazil*. Los Angeles: Center for Afro-American Studies, University of California.

Foster, Morris W., and Richard R. Sharp. 2002. "Race, Ethnicity, and Genomics: Social Classification as Proxies of Biological Heterogeneity." *Genome Research* 12, no. 6: 844–850.

Fowler, H. W. [1926] 1962. *A Dictionary of Modern English Usage*. 3rd ed. Oxford: Clarendon Press.

Franklin, John Hope, ed. 1968. *Color and Race*. Boston: Houghton Mifflin.

Franklin, John Hope, and Alfred A. Moss Jr. 1988. *From Slavery to Freedom*. 6th ed. New York: Alfred A. Knopf.

Fredrickson, George M. 1971. "Toward a Social Interpretation of the Development of American Racism." In *Key Issues in the Afro-American Experience*, edited by N. I. Huggins, M. Kilson, and D. M. Fox, vol. 1, 240–254. New York: Harcourt Brace Jovanovich.

______. 1977. "White Images of Black Slaves in the Southern United States." *Annals of the New York Academy of Sciences* 292: 368–375.

______. 1981. *White Supremacy*. New York: Oxford University Press.

______. [1971] 1987. *The Black Image in the White Mind*. Middletown, Conn.: Wesleyan University Press.

______. 1988. *The Arrogance of Race*. Middletown, Conn.: Wesleyan University Press.

Fryer, Peter. 1984. *Staying Power: The History of Black People in Britain*. London: Pluto Press.

Garrett, H. E. 1945a. "Facts and Interpretations Regarding Race Differences." *Science* 101, no. 2610: 173–174.

______. 1945b. "Psychological Differences Among Races." *Science* 101, no. 2610: 16–17.

______. 1973. *I.Q. and Racial Differences*. Cape Canaveral, Fla.: Howard Allen.

Gates, R. Ruggles. 1939. "Blood Groupings and Racial Classification." *American Journal of Physical Anthropology* 24, no. 3: 385–390.

Gee, G. C., M. S. Spencer, J. Chen, and D. Takeuchi. 2007. "A Nationwide Study of Discrimination and Chronic Health Conditions among Asian Americans." *American Journal of Public Health* 97, no. 7: 1275–1282.

Genovese, Eugene. 1976. *Roll, Jordan, Roll: The World the Slaves Made*. New York: Vintage Books.

Green, A. R., D. R. Carney, D. J. Pallin, L. H. Ngo, K. L. Raymond, L. I. Iezzoni, and M. R. Banaji. 2007. "Implicit Bias among Physicians and Its Prediction of Thrombolysis Decisions for Black and White Patients." *Journal of General Internal Medicine* 22, no. 9: 1231–1238.

Genovese, Eugene, and Elizabeth Fox-Genovese. 1983. *Fruits of Merchant Capital*. New York: Oxford University Press.

Gergen, Kenneth. 1968. "The Significance of Skin Color in Human Relations." In *Color and Race*, ed. J. H. Franklin, 112–128. Boston: Houghton Mifflin.

Glasrud, Bruce A., and Alan M. Smith. 1982. *Race Relations in British North America 1607–1783*. Chicago: Nelson-Hall.

Glass, Bentley. 1953. "The Dynamics of Racial Intermixture: An Analysis Based on the American Negro." *American Journal of Human Genetics* 5, no. 1: 1–20.

Gluckman, Max. 1965. *Politics, Law and Ritual in Tribal Society*. Chicago: Aldine.

Godolphin, Francis R. B., ed. 1942. *The Greek Historians*. Vol. 1. New York: Random House.

Goldsby, R. A. 1971. *Race and Races*. New York: Macmillan.

Goldschmidt, W. 1965. "Theory and Strategy in the Study of Cultural Adaptability." *American Anthropologist* 67, no. 2: 402–434.

Goodman, Alan. 2006. "Seeing Culture in Biology." In *The Nature of Difference: Science, Society and Human Biology*, edited by George T. H. Ellison and Alan H. Goodman, 225–248. New York: Taylor and Francis.

Goodman, Alan. n.d. "The Problematics of 'Race' in Contemporary Biological Anthropology." In *Biological Anthropology: The State of the Science*, edited by N. Boaz and L. Wolfe. Forthcoming.

Goodwin, Stefan. 2009. Africa in Europe. *Vol. I: Antiquity into the Age of Global Exploration*. Lanham, Md.: Rowman & Littlefield Publishers.

Gossett, Thomas F. 1965. *Race: The History of an Idea in America*. New York: Schocken Books.

Gottfredson, Linda S. 1994. "Mainstream Science on Intelligence: An Editorial with 52 Signatories, History, and Bibliography." *The Wall Street Journal*, December 13.

Gould, Steven Jay. 1977. *Ever Since Darwin*. New York: W. W. Norton.

______. [1981] 1996. *The Mismeasure of Man*. New York: W. W. Norton.

Graham, Richard, ed. 1990. *The Idea of Race in Latin America, 1870–1940*. Austin: University of Texas Press.

Graves, Joseph L., Jr. 2001. *The Emperor's New Clothes: Biological Theories of Race at the Millennium*. New Brunswick, N.J.: Rutgers University Press.

Greene, John C. 1954. "The American Debate on the Negro's Place in Nature, 1780–1815." *Journal of the History of Ideas* 15, no. 3: 384–396.

______. 1959. *The Death of Adam: Evolution and Its Impact on Western Thought*. Ames: Iowa State University Press.

______. 1981. *Science, Ideology, and World View*. Berkeley: University of California Press.

______. 1984. *American Science in the Age of Jefferson*. Ames: Iowa State University Press.

Gregory, Steven, and Roger Sanjek. 1994. *Race*. New Brunswick, N.J.: Rutgers University Press.

Haddon, Alfred C. [1934] 1959. *History of Anthropology*. Reprint. London: Watts.

Hale, Grace Elizabeth. 1999. *Making Whiteness: The Culture of Segregation in the South, 1890–1940*. New York: Random House.

Haller, John S., Jr. 1970. "Civil War Anthropometry: The Making of a Racial Ideology." *Civil War History* 16 (December): 309–325.

______. 1971. *Outcasts from Evolution: Scientific Attitudes of Racial Inferiority, 1859–1900*. Urbana: University of Illinois Press.

Haller, Mark H. 1963. *Eugenics: Hereditarian Attitudes in American Thought*. New Brunswick, N.J.: Rutgers University Press.

Hammond, D., and A. Jablow. 1970. *The Africa That Never Was*. New York: Twayne Publishers.

Handlin, Mary, and Oscar Handlin. 1972. "The Origins of Negro Slavery." In *The Origins of American Slavery and Racism*, edited by D. L. Noel. Columbus, Ohio: Charles E. Merrill.

Handlin, Oscar. [1948] 1957. *Race and Nationality in American Life*. Reprint. Boston: Little, Brown.

Hannaford, Ivan. 1996. *Race: The History of an Idea in the West*. Washington, D.C.: Woodrow Wilson Center Press; Baltimore: Johns Hopkins University Press.

Harper, S., J. Lynch, S. Burris, and G. D. Smith. 2007. "Trends in the Black-White Life Expectancy Gap in the United States, 1983–2003." *Journal of the American Medical Association* 297, no. 11: 1224–1232.

Harris, Marvin. 1964. *Patterns of Race in the Americas*. New York: W. W. Norton.

______. 1968. *The Rise of Anthropological Theory*. New York: Thomas Y. Crowell.

______. 1995. *Cultural Anthropology*. 4th ed. New York: HarperCollins.

Harrison, Faye V. 1991. "Anthropology as an Agent of Transformation: Introductory Comments and Queries." In *Decolonizing Anthropology: Moving Further Toward an Anthropology for Liberation*, edited by F. V. Harrison. Washington, D.C.: American Anthropological Association.

Hasnain-Wynia, R., D. W. Baker, D. Nerenz, J. Feinglass, A. C. Beal, M. B. Landrum, R. Behal, and J. S. Weissman. 2007. "Disparities in Health Care Are Driven by Where Minority Patients Seek Care." *Archives of Internal Medicine* 167: 1233–1239.

Havens, George. 1955. *The Age of Ideas*. New York: The Free Press.

Herrnstein, R. J., and C. Murray. 1994. *The Bell Curve: Intelligence and Class Structure in American Life*. New York: The Free Press.

Herskovits, M. J. 1958. *The Myth of the Negro Past*. Boston: Beacon Press.

Hiernaux, J. [1964] 1969. "The Concept of Race and the Taxonomy of Mankind." In *The Concept of Race*, edited by A. Montagu, 29–45. London: Collier-Macmillan.

Hitti, Phillip. 1953. *History of the Arabs*. London: Macmillan.

Hodgen, Margaret. 1964. *Early Anthropology in the Sixteenth and Seventeenth Centuries*. Philadelphia: University of Pennsylvania Press.

Hooten, Earnest A. 1926. "Methods of Racial Analysis." *Science* 63, no. 1621: 76–81.

______. 1936. "Plain Statements About Race." *Science* 83, no. 2161: 511–512.

Hoover, Dwight. 1976. *The Red and the Black*. Chicago: Rand McNally.

Hopkins, Keith. 1978. *Conquerors and Slaves*. Sociological Studies in Roman History, vol. 1. Cambridge, England: Cambridge University Press.

Horsman, Reginald. 1976. "Origins of Racial Anglo-Saxonism in Great Britain Before 1850." *Journal of the History of Ideas* 37, no. 3: 239–262.

______. 1981. *Race and Manifest Destiny*. Cambridge, Mass.: Harvard University Press.

Hourani, Albert. 1991. *A History of the Arab Peoples*. Cambridge, Mass.: Harvard University Press.

Howe, Michael J. A. 1997. *IQ in Question: The Truth about Intelligence*. London: Sage Publications.

Hulse, F. S. 1962. "Race as an Evolutionary Episode." *American Anthropologist* 64, no. 4: 929–945.

Hunt, E. E. 1959. "Anthropometry, Genetics and Racial History." *American Anthropologist* 61, no. 1: 64–87.

Hunwick, John O. 1978. "Black Africans in the Islamic World." *Extract of Tarikh* 5: 20–40.

Huxley, J., and A. C. Haddon. 1936. *We Europeans*. New York: Harper.

Iceland, John. 2002. *Beyond Black and White: Metropolitan Residential Segregation in Multi-Ethnic America*. Washington, D.C.: U.S. Census Bureau.

Iceland, John, with Daniel H. Weinberg and Erika Steinmetz. 2002. *Racial and Ethnic Residential Segregation in the United States: 1980–2000*. Washington, D.C.: U.S. Census Bureau.

Institute of Medicine of the National Academies. 2003.*Unequal Treatment: Confronting Racial and Ethnic Disparities in Health Care*. Washington, D.C.: National Academy Press.

Jaimes, M. Annette. 1994. "American Racism: The Impact on American-Indian Identity and Survival." In *Race*, edited by S. Gregory and R. Sanjek, 41–51. New Brunswick, N.J.: Rutgers University Press.

Jargowsky, P. A. 2003. *Stunning Progress, Hidden Problems: The Dramatic Decline of Concentrated Poverty in the 1990s* (May). Available at *www.brookings.edu* (accessed October 14, 2004).

Jasso, G., D. M. Massey, M. R. Rosenzweig, and J. P. Smith. 2004. "The Health Impact of Resolving Racial Disparities: An Analysis of U.S. Mortality Data." *American Journal of Public Health*, 94(12): 2078–2081.

Jefferson, Thomas. [1787] 1955. *Notes on the State of Virginia*. Edited by W. Peden. Chapel Hill: University of North Carolina Press.

Jensen, Arthur. 1969. "How Much Can We Boost IQ and Scholastic Achievement?" *Harvard Educational Review* 39, no. 1: 1–123.

Joint Center Health Policy Institute and Policy Link. 2004. *Building Stronger Communities for Better Health*. Available at http://www.policylink.org/pdfs/JointCenter-Communities.pdf (accessed September 13, 2007).

Jones, Howard Mumford. 1942. "Origins of the Colonial Idea in England." *American Philosophical Society* 85, no. 5: 448–465.

______. 1964. *O Strange New World*. New York: Viking Press.

Jordan, Winthrop D. 1968. *White Over Black: American Attitudes Toward the Negro, 1550–1812*. Baltimore: Penguin.

Kagan, Jerome. 1982. "IQ: Fair Science for Dark Deeds." *Radcliffe Quarterly*: 3–5.

Kahn, Jonathan. 2005. "From Disparity to Difference: How Race-Specific Medicines May Undermine Policies to Address Inequalities in Health Care." *Southern California Interdisciplinary Law Journal* 15: 105–130.

______. 2008. "Patenting Race in a Genomic Age." In *Revisiting Race in a Genomic Age*, edited by Barbara A. Koenig, Sandra Soo-Jin Lee, and Sarah S. Richardson, 129–148. Piscataway, NJ: Rutgers University Press.

______. 2009. "Beyond Bidil: The Expanding Embrace of Race in Biomedical Research and Product Development." *Saint Louis University Journal of Health Law and Policy* 3: 61–92.

Kaiser Family Foundation. 2002. *Racial and Ethnic Disparities in Women's Health Coverage and Access to Care: Findings from the 2001 Kaiser Women's Health Survey*. Available at http://www.kff.org/womenshealth/20020507a-index.cfm (accessed September 25, 2004).

______. 2003. *Key Facts: Race, Ethnicity, and Health Care.* Menlo Park, Calif.: Henry J. Kaiser Family Foundation.

______. 2004. *Racial and Ethnic Disparities in Women's Health Coverage and Access to Care.* Available at http://www.kff.org/womenshealth/7018.cfm.

______. 2006. *HIV/AIDS Policy Fact Sheet: Latinos and HIV/AIDS* (December). Available at http://www.kff.org/hivaids/3029.cfm.

______. 2007. *Key Facts: Race, Ethnicity, and Medical Care.* Figure 16, 14. Available at http://www.kff.org/minorityhealth/6069.cfm (accessed July 17, 2008).

Kaiser Family Foundation and the American College of Cardiology. 2002. *Racial/Ethnic Differences in Cardiac Care: The Weight of the Evidence.* (October). Available at www.kff.org/whythedifference/6040summary.pdf.

Katayama, Kazumichi. 2002. "What Is the Race Concept for Japanese Biological Anthropologists?" Paper presented at the Inter-Congress of IUAES, Tokyo, September 23.

Kaufman, J. S., and S. A. Hall. 2003. "The Slavery Hypertension Hypothesis: Dissemination and Appeal of a Modern Race Theory." *Epidemiology* 14, no. 1: 111–118.

Keesing, R. M., and F. M. Keesing. 1971. *New Perspectives in Cultural Anthropology.* New York: Holt, Rinehart & Winston.

Keita, Shomarka O. Y. 1993a. "Black Athena: Race, Bernal and Snowden." *Arethusa* 26, no. 3: 295–334.

______. 1993b. "The Subspecies Concept in Zoology and Anthropology." *Journal of Black Studies* 23, no. 3: 416–445.

Keita, S. O. Y., and A. J. Boyce. 2001. "Race: Confusion About Zoological and Social Taxonomies, and Their Places in Science." *American Journal of Human Biology* 13: 569–575.

Keita, S. O. Y., and Rick A. Kittles. 1997. "The Persistence of Racial Thinking and the Myth of Racial Divergence." *American Anthropologist* 99, no. 3: 534–544.

Keita, S. O. Y., R. A. Kittles, C. D. M. Royal, G. E. Bonney, P. Furbert-Harris, G. M. Dunston, and C. N. Rotimi. 2004. "Conceptualizing Human Variation." *Nature Genetics Supplement* 36, no. 11 (November): 17–20.

Kevles, Daniel J. 1985. *In the Name of Eugenics: Genetics and the Uses of Human Heredity.* New York: Alfred A. Knopf.

Kincheloe, Joe L., Shirley R. Steinberg, Nelson M. Rodriguez, and Ronald E. Chennault, eds. 1998. *White Reign: Deploying Whiteness in America.* New York: St. Martin's Press.

King, James C. 1981. *The Biology of Race.* Revised ed. Berkeley: University of California Press.

Kingsley, G. T., and K. L. S. Pettit. 2003. *Concentrated Poverty: A Change in Course* (May). Available at www.urban.org (accessed November 13, 2005).

Klass, Morton. 1980. *Caste: The Emergence of a South Asian Social System.* Philadelphia: Institute for the Study of Human Issues (ISHI).

Klassen, A. C. et al. 2002. "Relationship Between Patients' Perceptions of Disadvantage and Discrimination and Listing for Kidney Transplantation." *American Journal of Public Health* 92, no. 5 (May): 811–817.

Klein, Herbert. 1971. "Anglicanism, Catholicism and the Negro Slave." In *The Debate Over Slavery,* edited by A. J. Lane. Chicago: University of Chicago Press.

Knight, F. W. 1970. *Slave Society in Cuba During the Nineteenth Century.* Madison: University of Wisconsin Press.

Kolchin, Peter. 1982. "Comparing American History." In *Reviews in American History*, 64–81. Baltimore: Johns Hopkins University Press.

Kovel, Joel. 1970. *White Racism: A Psychohistory*. New York: Pantheon.

Kuhn, Thomas. 1962. *The Structure of Scientific Revolutions*. Chicago: University of Chicago Press.

Kupperman, Karen O. 1984. *Roanoke, the Abandoned Colony*. Totowa, N.J.: Rowman and Allanheld.

Lane, Ann J., ed. 1971. *The Debate Over Slavery: Stanley Elkins and His Critics*. Chicago: University of Chicago Press.

Lane-Poole, Stanley 1990. *The Story of the Moors in Spain*. Baltimore: Black Classic Press.

Lauber, Almon W. [1913] 1970. *Indian Slavery in Colonial Times Within the Present Limits of the United States*. Williamstown, Mass.: Corner House Publishers.

Lewis, Bernard. 1971. *Race and Color in Islam*. New York: Harper & Row.

______. 1990. *Race and Slavery in the Middle East*. New York: Oxford University Press.

Lewontin, Richard C. 1970. "Race and Intelligence." *Bulletin of the Atomic Scientists* 5, no. 1: 2–8.

______. 1972. "The Apportionment of Human Diversity." *Evolutionary Biology* 6: 381–398.

Liggio, Leonard P. 1976. "English Origins of Early American Racism." *Radical History Review* 3, no. 1: 1–36.

Lillie-Blanton, M., R. M. Martinez, and A. Salganicoff. 2001. "Site of Medical Care: Do Racial and Ethnic Differences Persist?" *Yale Journal of Health Policy, Law, and Ethics* 1, no. 1: 1–17.

Littlefield, Alice, Leonard Lieberman, and Larry Reynolds. 1982. "Redefining Race: The Potential Demise of a Concept in Physical Anthropology." *Current Anthropology* 23, no. 6: 641–656.

Livingstone, Frank B. 1969. "On the Non-Existence of Human Races." In *The Concept of Race*, edited by A. Montagu. New York: The Free Press.

Lopez, Ian Haney. 1996. *White by Law*. New York: New York University Press.

Lovejoy, Arthur. 1936. *The Great Chain of Being*. Cambridge, Mass.: Harvard University Press.

Lovejoy, P. E. 1983. *Transformations in Slavery: A History of Slavery in Africa*. Cambridge, England: Cambridge University Press.

Ludmerer, Kenneth. 1969. *Genetics and American Society*. Baltimore: Johns Hopkins University Press.

Lurie, Edward. 1954. "Louis Agassiz and the Races of Man." *Isis* 45: 227–242.

Macfarlane, Alan. 1978. *The Origins of English Individualism*. Oxford: Basil Blackwell.

MacPherson, C. B. 1962. *The Political Theory of Possessive Individualism*. Oxford: Clarendon Press.

Malefijt, A. deWaal. 1974. *Images of Man: A History of Anthropological Thought*. New York: Alfred A. Knopf.

Malone, Dumas. 1962. *Jefferson and the Ordeal of Liberty*. Boston: Little, Brown.

______. 1970. *Jefferson the President: First Term, 1801–1805*. Boston: Little, Brown.

______. 1981. *The Sage of Monticello*. Boston: Little, Brown.

Mansfield, Peter. 1982. *The Arabs*. Middlesex, England: Penguin Books.

Marks, Jonathan. 1995. *Human Biodiversity: Genes, Race, and History*. New York: Aldine de Gruyter.

Massey, Douglas S., and Nancy Denton. 1993. *American Apartheid*. Chicago: University of Chicago Press.

Massey, Douglas S., with Camille Z. Charles and Gniesha Dinwiddie. 2004. "The Continuing Consequences of Segregation: Family Stress and College Performance." *Social Science Quarterly* 85, no. 5: 1353–1373.

Mathews, D. G. 1980. "Religion and Slavery: The Case of the American South." In *Antislavery, Religion and Reform: Essays in Memory of Roger Anstey*, edited by C. Bolt and S. Drescher. Folkstone, England, and Hamden, Conn.: Dawson/Archon.

Mauer, Marc. 2004. "Thinking About Prison and Its Impact on the 21st Century." Lecture Given at Ohio State University, April 14. Available at http://www.sentencingproject.org/Admin/Documents/publications/inc_osu_reckless.pdf (accessed July 27, 2007).

Mauer, Marc, and Ryan S. King. 2007. *Uneven Justice: State Rates of Incarceration by Race and Ethnicity*. The Sentencing Project. Available at http://sentencingproject.org/Admin/Documents/publications/rd_stateratesofincbyraceandethnicity.pdf (accessed July 26, 2007).

Mays, Vickie M., with Susan D. Cochran and Namdi W. Barnes. 2007. "Race, Race-Based Discrimination, and Health Outcomes Among African Americans." *Annual Review of Psychology* 58: 201–225.

McCracken, M., et al. 2007. "Cancer Incidence, Mortality, and Associated Risk Factors among Asian Americans of Chinese, Filipino, Vietnamese, Korean, and Japanese Ethnicities." *CA: A Cancer Journal for Clinicians* 57, no. 4: 190–205.

McDermott, W. C., and W. Caldwell, eds. 1951. *Readings in the History of the Ancient World*. New York: Rinehart.

Mendelsohn, Isaac. 1949. *Slavery in the Ancient Near East*. New York: Oxford University Press.

Mensh, Elaine, and Harry Mensh. 1991. *The IQ Mythology: Class, Race, Gender and Inequality*. Carbondale: Southern Illinois University Press.

Miers, Suzanne, and Igor Kopytoff, eds. 1977. *Slavery in Africa*. Madison: University of Wisconsin Press.

Miller, John Chester. 1977. *The Wolf by the Ears*. New York: The Free Press.

Miller, Loren. 1966. *The Petitioners: The Story of the Supreme Court of the United States and the Negro*. New York: Pantheon.

Mintz, Sidney W. 1961. "Review of Stanley Elkins's *Slavery*." *American Anthropologist* 63, no. 4: 579–587.

______, ed. 1974. *Slavery, Colonialism and Racism*. New York: W. W. Norton.

Montagu, Ashley. [1964] 1971. *Man's Most Dangerous Myth: The Fallacy of Race*. Reprint. New York: World Publishing.

______, ed. 1969. *The Concept of Race*. London: Collier-Macmillan.

Morenoff, Jeffrey, with Robert J. Sampson, and Stephen Raudenbush. 2001. "Neighborhood Inequality, Collective Efficacy, and the Spatial Dynamics of Urban Violence." *Criminology* 39: 517–560.

Morgan, Edmund S. 1972. "Slavery and Freedom: The American Paradox." *Journal of American History* 57, no. 1: 5–29.

______. 1975. *American Slavery, American Freedom*. New York: W. W. Norton.

Morgan, Philip D. 1998. *Slave Counterpoint: Black Culture in the 18th Century Chesapeake & Lowcountry*. Chapel Hill: University of North Carolina Press.

Morland, Kimberly, with Steve Wing and Ana Diez Roux. 2002. "The Contextual Effect of the Local Food Environment on Residents' Diets: The Atherosclerosis Risk in Communities Study." *American Journal of Public Health* 92, no. 11: 1761–1768.

Mörner, Magnus. 1967. *Race Mixture in the History of Latin America*. Boston: Little, Brown.

Mörner, M., J. F. de Vinuela, and J. D. French. 1982. "Comparative Approaches to Latin American History." *Latin American Research Review* 17, no. 3: 55–89.

Morris, Laura N., ed. 1971. *Human Populations, Genetic Variation, and Evolution*. San Francisco: Chandler.

Morrison, R. S., S. Wallenstein, D. K. Natale, R. S. Senzel, and L. Huang. 2000. "'We Don't Carry That'—Failure of Pharmacies in Predominantly Nonwhite Neighborhoods to Stock Opioid Analgesics." *The New England Journal of Medicine* 342, no. 14: 1023–1026.

Morsy, Soheir A. 1994. "Beyond the Honorary 'White' Classification of Egyptians: Societal Identity in Historical Context." In *Race*, edited by S. Gregory and R. Sanjek. New Brunswick, N.J.: Rutgers University Press.

Mukhopadhyay, Carol C., and Yolanda T. Moses. 1997. "Reestablishing 'Race' in Anthropological Discourse." *American Anthropologist* 99, no. 3: 517–533.

Myers, James P., ed. 1983. *Elizabethan Ireland*. Hamden, Conn.: Archon Books.

Nash, Gary B. 1972. "Red, White and Black: The Origins of Racism in Colonial America." In *The Origins of American Slavery and Racism*, edited by D. L. Noel. Columbus, Ohio: Charles E. Merrill.

______. 1982. *Red, White and Black: The Peoples of Early America*. Revised ed. Englewood Cliffs, N.J.: Prentice Hall.

______. 1986. *Race, Class and Politics*. Urbana: University of Illinois Press.

______. 1992. *Red, White and Black: The Peoples of Early America*. 3rd ed. Englewood Cliffs, N.J.: Prentice Hall.

Nash, G., and R. Weiss, eds. 1970. *The Great Fear: Race in the Mind of America*. New York: Holt, Rinehart & Winston.

National Asian Pacific American Women's Forum. 2005. *Reclaiming Choice, Broadening the Movement: Sexual and Reproductive Justice and Asian Pacific American Women—A National Agenda for Action*. Available at http://www.napawf.org/ (accessed November 2, 2008).

National Latina Institute for Reproductive Health. 2006. *Reproductive Health of Latinas in the U.S.* Available at http://www.latinainstitute.org/pdf/ReproHealth.pdf (accessed October 30, 2009).

Nei, M., and A. K. Roychoudhury. 1972. "Gene Differences Between Caucasian, Negro and Japanese Populations." *Science* 177, no. 4047: 434–435.

______. 1974. "Genetic Variations Within and Between the Three Major Races of Man, Caucasoids, Negroids and Mongoloids." *American Journal of Human Genetics* 26: 421–443.

Noel, Donald L. 1972. "Slavery and the Rise of Racism." In *The Origins of American Slavery and Racism*, edited by D. L. Noel. Columbus, Ohio: Charles E. Merrill.

Nott, Josiah, and George R. Gliddon. 1854. *Types of Mankind*. Philadelphia: Lippincott, Grambo.

Oakes, James. 1990. *Slavery and Freedom: An Interpretation of the Old South*. New York: Alfred A. Knopf.

O'Farrell, Patrick. 1971. *Ireland's English Question*. New York: Schocken Books.

Olson, Steve. 2002. *Mapping Human History: Discovering the Past Through Our Genes.* Boston: Houghton Mifflin.

Opportunity Agenda. 2006. *The State of Opportunity in America*, Figure 6–3, p. 119. Available at http://opportunityagenda.org/state_opportunity_report (accessed September 23, 2008).

Outram, Simon M., and George T. H. Ellison. 2006. "The Truth Will Out: Scientific Pragmatism and the Geneticization of Race and Ethnicity." In *The Nature of Difference: Science, Society and Human Biology*, edited by George T. H. Ellison and Alan H. Goodman, 157–179. London and New York: Taylor & Francis.

Oxford English Dictionary of Historical Principles. 1933. Oxford: Oxford University Press.

Pager, D. 2003. "The Mark of a Criminal Record." *American Journal of Sociology* 108, no. 5: 937–975.

Palmer, Colin. 1976. *Slaves of the White God*. Cambridge, Mass.: Harvard University Press.

Parent, Anthony S., Jr. 2003. *Foul Means: The Formation of Slave Society in Virginia, 1660–1740*. Chapel Hill: University of North Carolina Press.

Patterson, Orlando. 1982. *Slavery and Social Death*. Cambridge, Mass.: Harvard University Press.

Pearce, Roy H. 1953. *The Savages of America*. Baltimore: Johns Hopkins University Press.

Penrose, Boies. 1955. *Travel and Discovery in the Renaissance, 1420–1620*. Cambridge, Mass: Harvard University Press.

Perdue, Theda. 2003. *Mixed Blood Indians: Racial Construction in the Early South*. Athens: University of Georgia Press.

Pessen, Edward. 1985. *Jacksonian America*. Revised ed. Urbana: University of Illinois Press.

Pestana, Carla G. 2003. "A West Indian Colonial Governor's Advice; Henry Ashton's 1646 Letter to the Earl of Carlisle." *William & Mary Quarterly* LX, no. 2.

Peterson, Merrill. 1962. *The Jefferson Image in the American Mind*. New York: Oxford University Press.

______. 1970. *Thomas Jefferson and the New Nation*. New York: Oxford University Press.

Pew Hispanic Center and the Kaiser Family Foundation. 2004. *Survey Brief About the 2002 National Survey of Latinos* (March). Available at www.kff.org (accessed January 23, 2006).

Pickens, Donald. 1968. *Eugenics and the Progressives*. Nashville, Tenn.: Vanderbilt University Press.

Pierson, Donald. 1942. *Negroes in Brazil*. Chicago: University of Chicago Press.

Pieterse, Jan N. 1992. *White on Black: Images of Africa and Blacks in Western Popular Culture*. New Haven: Yale University Press.

Pirenne, Henri. [1925] 1952. *Medieval Cities*. Reprint. Princeton, N.J.: Princeton University Press.

Poliakov, Leon. 1982. "Racism from the Enlightenment to the Age of Imperialism." In *Racism and Colonialism*, edited by R. Ross. The Hague: Martinus Nijhoff.

Poverty and Race Research Action Council. 2005. Analysis of U.S. Census Bureau data, with the assistance of Nancy A. Denton and Bridget J. Anderson.

Prewitt, Kenneth. 2005. "Racial Classifications in America: Where Do We Go from Here?" *Daedalus* (Winter).

Provine, William. 1973. "Geneticists and the Biology of Race Crossing." *Science* 182, no. 4114: 790–796.

Puzzo, Dante. 1964. "Racism and the Western Tradition." *Journal of the History of Ideas* 25, no. 4: 579–586.

"Quick Takes: Women in U.S. Management, 1950–Present." 2005. *Catalyst* (July). Available at www.catalyst.org (accessed September 24, 2005).

Quinn, David B. 1958. "Ireland and Sixteenth Century European Expansion." *Historical Studies*. New York: Hilary House.

______. 1966. *Elizabethans and the Irish*. Ithaca, N.Y.: Cornell University Press.

Real Academia Española. [1726–1739] 1737. *Diccionario de la Lengua Castellana*. Madrid: Francisco del Hierro.

Reed, T. E. 1969. "Caucasian Genes in American Negroes." *Science* 165, no. 3895: 762–768.

Risch, Neil, Esteban Burchard, Elad Ziv, and Hua Tang. 2002. "Categorization of Humans in Biomedical Research: Genes, Race and Disease." *Genome Biology* 3, no. 7: 1–12.

Robert Wood Johnson Foundation. 2005. *Going Without: America's Uninsured Children*. Available at www.rwjf.org.

Robinson, R., J. Gallagher, and A. Denny. 1968. *Africa and the Victorians*. Garden City, N.Y.: Anchor Books.

Ross, Robert, ed. 1982. *Racism and Colonialism*. The Hague: Martinus Nijhoff.

Rotberg, Robert. 1965. *A Political History of Tropical Africa*. New York: Harcourt, Brace & World.

Roth, Cecil. 1964. *The Spanish Inquisition*. New York: W. W. Norton.

Rout, Leslie B., Jr. 1976. *The African Experience in Latin America*. Cambridge, England: Cambridge University Press.

Rowe, John Howeland. 1974. "The Renaissance Foundations of Anthropology." In *Readings in the History of Anthropology*, edited by R. Darnell. New York: Harper & Row.

Royal, Charmaine D. M., and Georgia M. Dunston. 2004. "Changing the Paradigm from 'Race' to Human Genome Variation." *Nature Genetics Supplement* 36, no. 11 (November): s5–s7.

Rubin, V., and A. Tuden. 1977. "Comparative Perspectives on Slavery in New World Plantation Societies." *Annals of the New York Academy of Sciences* 292.

Ruchames, Louis. 1969. *Racial Thought in America*. Amherst: University of Massachusetts Press.

Rushton, J. Philippe. 1995. *Race, Evolution and Behavior*. New Brunswick, N.J.: Transaction Publishers.

Sahlins, Marshall. 1976. *The Use and Abuse of Biology*. Ann Arbor: University of Michigan Press.

Sakamoto, Hiroko. 2002. "Historical View of the Chinese Concept of Race." Paper Presented at the Inter-Congress of IUAES, Tokyo, September 23.

Sanday, Peggy R. 1972. "On the Causes of IQ Differences Between Groups and Implications for Social Policy." *Human Organization* 31, no. 4: 411–424.

Sanders, Edith R. 1969. "The Hamitic Hypothesis: Its Origin and Functions in Time Perspective." *Journal of African History* 10, no. 4: 521–532.

Sanders, Ronald. 1978. *Lost Tribes and Promised Lands: The Origins of American Racism*. Boston: Little, Brown.

Sanjek, Roger. 1994. "Intermarriage and the Future of Races in the United States." In *Race*, edited by S. Gregory and R. Sanjek, 103–130. New Brunswick, N.J.: Rutgers University Press.

Sarich, Vincent, and Frank Miele. 2004. *Race: The Reality of Human Differences*. Boulder: Westview Press.

Sarrazin, M. V., M. Campbell, and G. E. Rosenthal. 2009. "Racial Differences in Hospital Use after Acute Myocardial Infarction: Does Residential Segregation Play a Role?" *Health Affairs* 28, no. 2: w368–w378.

Sauer, Carl O. 1971. *Sixteenth Century North America*. Berkeley: University of California Press.

Scheidt, Walter. 1950. "The Concept of Race in Anthropology and the Divisions into Human Races, from Linnaeus to Deniker." In *This Is Race*, edited by E. Count. New York: Henry Schuman.

Sears, David O., John J. Hetts, Jim Sidanius, and Lawrence Bobo. 2000. "Race in American Politics: Framing the Debates." In *Racialized Politics: The Debate About Racism in America*. Chicago: University of Chicago

Serre, David, and Svante Pääbo. 2004. "Evidence for Gradients of Human Genetic Diversity Within and Among Continents." *Genome Research* 14: 1679–1685.

Shils, Edward. 1968. "Color, the University Intellectual Community and the Afro-Asian Intellectual." In *Color and Race*, edited by J. H. Franklin. Boston: Houghton Mifflin.

Shirer, William L. [1959] 1988. *The Rise and Fall of the Third Reich*. New York: Simon & Schuster.

Shuey, Audrey. [1958] 1966. *The Testing of Negro Intelligence*. New York: Social Science Press.

Sio, Arnold A. 1964–1965. "Interpretations of Slavery: The Slave Status in the Americas." *Comparative Studies in Society and History* 7: 289–308.

Skidmore, Thomas E. 1972. "Toward a Comparative Analysis of Race Relations Since Abolition in Brazil and the United States." *Journal of Latin American Studies* 14, no. 1: 1–28.

Skinner, Elliot P. 1964. "West African Economic Systems." In *Economic Transition in Africa*, edited by M. J. Herskovits and M. Harwitz, 77–97. Evanston, Ill.: Northwestern University Press.

Slotkin, J. S., ed. 1965. *Readings in Early Anthropology*. London: Methuen.

Smedley, Audrey. 1996. "Review of *The Bell Curve*, by Richard Herrnstein and Charles Murray." *Current Anthropology* 37 (February): supplement.

______. 1998. "'Race' and the Construction of Human Identity." *American Anthropologist* 100, no. 3: 690–702.

______. 2006. "Race: The Reality of Human Differences: Vincent Sarich and Frank Miele's Use of History." *Transforming Anthropology* 14, no. 1: 57–63.

Smith, D. B. 2005. *Eliminating Disparities in Treatment and the Struggle to End Segregation*. New York: The Commonwealth Fund.

Smith, Page. 1976. *Jefferson: A Revealing Biography*. New York: American Heritage Publishing.

Snowden, F. M., Jr. 1970. *Blacks in Antiquity: Ethiopians in the Greco-Roman Experience*. Cambridge, Mass.: Harvard University Press.

______. [1970] 1983. *Before Color Prejudice*. Revised ed. Cambridge, Mass.: Harvard University Press.

Snyder, Louis L. 1962. *The Idea of Racialism: Its Meaning and History*. Princeton, N.J.: D. Van Nostrand.

Soderlund, Jean R. 1985. *Quakers and Slavery: A Divided Spirit*. Princeton, N.J.: Princeton University Press.

Spencer, Frank. 1982. *A History of American Physical Anthropology*. New York: Academic Press.

Spier, Leslie. 1959. "Some Central Elements in the Legacy." *American Anthropological Association Memoirs* 61, no. 89.

Spitzer, Leo. 1948. *Essays in Historical Semantics.* New York: S. F. Vanni.

Spuhler, J. N., and G. Lindzey. 1967. "Racial Differences in Behavior." In *Behavior-Genetic Analysis,* edited by J. Hirsch. Bobs-Merrill Reprint. New York: McGraw-Hill.

Stanton, William. 1960. *The Leopard's Spots: Scientific Attitudes Toward Race in America, 1815–1859.* Chicago: University of Chicago Press.

Steinberg, Stephen. 1989. *The Ethnic Myth.* Revised ed. Boston: Beacon Press.

Stepan, Nancy. 1982. *The Idea of Race in Science: Great Britain 1800–1960.* London: Macmillan.

Sternberg, Robert J., and Jean E. Pretz, eds. 2005. *Cognition and Intelligence: Identifying the Mechanisms of the Mind.* Cambridge: Cambridge University Press.

Stocking, George. 1968. *Race, Culture, and Evolution.* New York: The Free Press.

Sutch, Richard. 1975. "The Breeding of Slaves for Sale and the Westward Expansion of Slavery, 1850–1860." In *Race and Slavery in the Western Hemisphere,* edited by S. Engerman and E. Genovese. Princeton, N.J.: Princeton University Press.

Swartz, M., and D. K. Jordan. 1976. *Anthropology.* New York: John Wiley & Sons.

Sweet, Louise. 1965. "Camel Raiding of North Arabian Bedouin: A Mechanism of Ecological Adaptation." *American Anthropologist* 67, no. 4: 1132–1150.

Tacitus. 1942. *The Complete Works of Tacitus.* Translated by A. J. Church and W. J. Brodribb.

Takaki, Ronald, ed. 1987. *From Different Shores: Perspectives on Race and Ethnicity in America.* New York: Oxford University Press.

______. 1989. *Strangers from a Different Shore: A History of Asian-Americans.* New York: Random House.

Takezawa, Yasuko. 2003a. "Comments." In *Is Race a Universal Idea?,* edited by Y. Takezawa. Kyoto: Institute for Research in Humanities.

______. 2003b. "Race and Racism in Imperial Japan." In *Is Race a Universal Idea?,* edited by Y. Takezawa. Kyoto: Institute for Research in Humanities.

Tannenbaum, Frank. 1947. *Slave and Citizen: The Negro in the Americas.* New York: Oxford University Press.

Taylor, Teletia R., with Carla D. Williams, Kepher H. Makambi, Charles Mouton, Jules P. Harrell, Yvette Cozier, Julie R. Palmer, Lynn Rosenberg, and Lucille L. Adams-Campbell. 2007. "Racial Discrimination and Breast Cancer Incidence in Black Women." *American Journal of Epidemiology* 166, no. 1.

Templeton, Alan R. 1998, September. "Human Races: A Genetic and Evolutionary Perspective." *American Anthropologist* 100, no. 3: 632–650.

tenBroek, J. 1969. *Equal Under the Law.* 2nd ed. London: Collier Books.

Tesler, Michael, and David O. Sears. 2010. *Obama's Race: The 2008 Election and the Dream of a Post-Racial America.* Chicago: University of Chicago Press.

Thieme, F. 1952. "The Population as a Unit of Study." *American Anthropologist* 54, no. 4: 504–509.

Thomas, G. E. 1975. "Puritans, Indians and the Concept of Race." *The New England Quarterly* 48, no. 1 (March): 3–27.

Tindall, George B. 1988. *America: A Narrative History.* 2nd ed. New York: W. W. Norton.

Tise, Larry E. 1987. *Proslavery: A History of the Defense of Slavery in America.* Athens: University of Georgia Press.

Tobias, Phillip V. 1972. "The Meaning of Race." In *Race and Social Difference*, edited by P. Baxter and B. Sansom, 19–43. Middlesex, England: Penguin.

Toqueville, Alexis de. [1831] 1945. *Democracy in America*. Vol. 2. Reprint. New York: Vintage.

______. *The European Revolution and Correspondence with Gobineau*. Translated by John Lukacs. Westport, Conn.: Greenwood Press.

Tomiyama, Ichiro. 2002. "The Diffusion of the Idea of Race and Its Application in Japan." Paper Presented at the Inter-Congress of IUAES, Tokyo, September 23.

Trevor, J. C. 1951. Letter to the editor, *Man*, no. 96 (April).

Turner, M., and S. Ross. 2003. *Discrimination in Metropolitan Housing Markets: Phase 2—Asians and Pacific Islanders*. Washington, D.C.: U.S. Department of Housing and Urban Development.

"2002 Catalyst Census of Women Corporate Officers and Top Earners in the Fortune 500." n.d. *Catalyst*. Available at www.catalyst.org (accessed September 25, 2005).

Tylor, E. B. [1881] 1946. *Anthropology*. Reprint. London: Watts.

______. [1871] 1958. *Primitive Culture*. New York: Harper & Row.

The Urban Institute. 2005. *Fast Facts on Welfare Policy*. Available at www.urban.org.

U.S. Census Bureau. 2002. *Racial and Ethnic Residential Segregation in the United States: 1980–2000*. Washington, D.C.: U.S. Department of Commerce, August.

______. 2003. *Ability to Speak English by Language Spoken at Home*. Available at http://www.census.gov/population/cen2000/phc-t37/tab01a.pdf (accessed March 19, 2007).

______. 2005. *Income, Poverty, and Health Insurance Coverage in the United States, 2004*. Washington, D.C.: U.S. Government Printing Office.

U.S. Department of Health & Human Services. 2004. *AIDS and Women* (December). Available at http://www.hab.hrsa.gov.

______. 2006a. *African-Americans and HIV/AIDS in the United States* (June). Available at http://www.hab.hrsa.gov.

______. 2006b. *The National Healthcare Disparities Report* (January). Available at http://www.ahrq.gov/qual/nhdr05/nhdr05.htm.

U.S. Department of Health and Human Services, National Center for Health Statistics. 2007. *Health, United States, 2006*. Washington, D.C.: U.S. Department of Health and Human Services.

U.S. Department of Health & Human Services, Office of Minority Health. 2007. *Health Status of Asian American and Pacific Islander Women*. Available at http://www.omhrc.gov/templates/content.aspx?ID=3721 (last modified April 20, 2007).

U.S. Equal Employment Opportunity Commission. 2004. *Glass Ceilings: The Status of Women as Officials and Managers* (March). Available at www.eeoc.gov (accessed October 14, 2005).

Van den Berghe, Pierre L. 1967. *Race and Racism*. New York: John Wiley & Sons.

Vander Zanden, J. W. 1959. "The Ideology of White Supremacy." *Journal of the History of Ideas* 20, no. 3: 385–400.

Van Evrie, John H. [1861] 1969. *White Supremacy and Negro Subordination*. New York: Negro Universities Press.

Vaughan, Alden T. 1965. *New England Frontier: Puritans and Indians, 1620–1675*. Boston: Little, Brown.

Wagatsuma, H. 1968. "The Social Perception of Skin Color in Japan." In *Color and Race*, edited by J. H. Franklin. Boston: Houghton Mifflin.

Walvin, James. 1980. "The Rise of British Popular Sentiment for Abolition, 1787–1832." In *Antislavery, Religion and Reform: Essays in Memory of Roger Anstey*, edited by C. Bolt and S. Drescher. Folkstone, England, and Hamden, Conn.: Dawson/Archon.

Watson, Alan. 1987. *Roman Slave Law*. Baltimore: Johns Hopkins University Press.

Watson, James L., ed. 1980. *Asian and African Systems of Slavery*. Berkeley: University of California Press.

Weaver, P. R. C. 1972. *Familia Caesaris: A Social Study of the Emperor's Freedmen and Slaves*. Cambridge, England: Cambridge University Press.

Webster, Yehudi O. 1992. *The Racialization of America*. New York: St. Martin's Press.

Westermann, W. L. 1955. *The Slave Systems of Greek and Roman Antiquity*. Philadelphia: American Philosophical Society.

White, A. D. [1896] 1965. *The History of the Warfare of Science with Theology in Christendom*. New York: The Free Press.

White, Leslie. 1969. *The Science of Culture: A Study of Man and Civilization*. 2nd ed. New York: Farrar, Straus and Giroux.

White, Leslie, with Beth Dillingham. 1973. *The Concept of Culture*. Minneapolis: Burgess Publishing.

Wiedemann, Thomas. 1987. *Greek and Roman Slavery*. Oxford: Clarendon Press.

Williams, D. R. 2004. "Racism and Health." In *Closing the Gap: Improving the Health of Minority Elders in the New Millennium*, edited by K. E. Whitfield. Washington, D.C.: Gerontological Society of America.

Williams, David R., and Chiquita Collins. 2001. "Racial Residential Segregation: A Fundamental Cause of Racial Disparities in Health." *Public Health Reports* 116, no. 5: 405–416.

Williams, Eric. [1944] 1966. *Capitalism and Slavery*. New York: Capricorn.

Williamson, Joel. 1984. *The Crucible of Race*. New York: Oxford University Press.

Wise, Tim. 2008. *White Like Me: Reflections on Race from a Privileged Son*. Revised ed. Berkeley, Calif.: Soft Skull Press.

______. 2009. *Between Barack and a Hard Place: Racism and White Denial in the Age of Obama*. San Francisco: City Lights Books.

______. 2010. *Colorblind: The Rise of Post-Racial Politics and the Retreat from Racial Equity*. San Francisco: City Lights Books.

Wober, Mallory. 1971. "Race and Intelligence." *Transition* 40 (December): 17–26.

Woodward, C. Vann. 1974. *The Strange Career of Jim Crow*. 3rd ed. New York: Oxford University Press.

Woolf, S. H., R. E. Johnson, G. E. Fryer, G. Rust, and D. Satcher. 2004. "The Health Impact of Resolving Racial Disparities: An Analysis of U.S. Mortality Data." *American Journal of Public Health* 94, no. 12: 2078–2081.

Wright, Louis B. 1965. *Religion and Empire*. New York: Octagon.

Wyatt-Brown, Bertram. 2002. *The Shaping of Southern Culture*. Chapel Hill: University of North Carolina Press.

INDEX